The King's Passengers

to
Maryland and
Virginia

Peter Wilson Coldham

HERITAGE BOOKS
2006

HERITAGE BOOKS
AN IMPRINT OF HERITAGE BOOKS, INC.

Books, CDs, and more—Worldwide

For our listing of thousands of titles see our website
at
www.HeritageBooks.com

Published 2006 by
HERITAGE BOOKS, INC.
Publishing Division
65 East Main Street
Westminster, Maryland 21157-5026

Other books by the author:

*American Loyalist Claims, Volume 1: Abstracted from the Public Record Office,
Audit Office Series 13, Bundles 1-35 and 37*

Lord Mayor's Court of London Depositions Relating to Americans, 1641-1736

International Standard Book Number: 978-1-58549-582-4

INTRODUCTION

An important anniversary occurring in the year this book is published - but one unlikely to be widely celebrated - is the fourth centenary of an Act of Queen Elizabeth I providing for the "Punyshment of Rogues, Vagabonds and Sturdy Beggars" by transporting them overseas to expiate their offences by hard labour. The explorer Richard Hakluyt is usually credited with fathering this idea, and in 1584 recommended that "the multitude of idle and mutinous persons within the realm . . . whereby all the prisons are stuffed full . . . might be employed . . . in western parts sawing and felling of timber and in planting of sugar canes." It is difficult to resist the conclusion that this now forgotten Act largely determined the demography of the British colonies in southern America, the West Indies and even Australia.

Virginia was recommended in 1606 as a most suitable place to send idle vagrants, an idea supported by Governor Dale of Virginia five years later. By 1615 the practice of commuting to a term of transportation the death sentences imposed on those found guilty of the less heinous capital offences found legal expression in an edict of the Privy Council. After referring slavishly to the King's singular clemency and mercy, the edict provided that those so pardoned should be "constrayned to toyle in such heavey and painefull workes as such a servitude shalbe a greater terror to them than death it selfe."

Until more formal schemes were devised for the pardoning and transportation of felons, the process has every appearance of having been vague and haphazard. The King's favourites who had interests overseas were sometimes allowed to impress a quota of condemned prisoners and the young Virginia Company in 1620 was even encouraged to round up 100 children from the streets of London to "redeem their souls from misery and ruin" by packing them off to Virginia. Those children who proved disobedient or obstinate were to be imprisoned and punished. It was left to the reforming zeal of the victorious Parliamentary forces to introduce a regular and systematic method of emptying English gaols. It began with an order to transport 900 Scottish "rebels" to Virginia in 1650 and 300 the following year to New England. By the middle of that decade the Parliament was able to congratulate itself that beggars and wandering rogues were no longer to be seen in those parts which they had formerly infested. From now on the Patent Rolls (PRO: C66) regularly included lists of felons in London, Middlesex, the six Assize Circuits and three Palatinates of Chester, Durham and Lancashire, who were to be formally pardoned on condition of their accepting a period of "voluntary" transportation to the West Indian or American plantations. An Act cynically titled "For the Better Relief of the

i

Poor" in 1662 made it lawful for Justices of the Peace to transport any rogue, vagabond or sturdy beggar adjudged to be incorrigible.

The system of transportation, such as it was, began to fall to pieces by the end of the seventeenth century: the colonies had learned to refuse the importation of convict labour and few merchants could now be found to take on the financial risk of shipping and selling them. By the end of 1697 the City of London was so overrun by disorderly prisoners that the Government was finally forced into accepting the need to subsidise the transportation trade. Before any new arrangements could come into effect, however, a continental war overtook the country, almost immediately followed by the first Scottish rebellion of 1715. Traditional methods were employed to dispose of the Scots prisoners who, fortuitously, provided a blueprint for the future conduct under State auspices of a burgeoning trade in transported convicts.

Early in 1718 the Act "for the Further Preventing Robbery, Burglary and other Felonies, and for the More Effectual Transportation of Felons" passed into the statute book. Its provisions remained essentially unchanged until the American Revolution of 1775 rendered the Act redundant, though the experience gained during the six decades in which it was applied can be clearly detected in the subsequent transportation schemes to Australia. After 1718 all but the most heinous or most trivial crimes could attract a sentence of transportation for seven or fourteen years, though the King still retained the prerogative of pardoning those sentenced to death for their crimes on condition of their serving in the colonies. For the first time, also, the Privy Purse was to be used to defray the cost of shipping felons from London, Middlesex, the Home Counties (Essex, Hertfordshire, Kent, Surrey and Sussex) and Buckinghamshire which together accounted for some two-thirds of the country's criminal population. It is largely due to the direct financial interest of the State that there survives in English archives such a superb and virtually complete collection of transportation records for this period. The more recent identification within Maryland archives of documentary evidences for the landings there of English felons has now prompted this attempt to provide a survey of convict passenger lists for those embarked for Maryland and Virginia between 1718 and 1776.

It has been frequently remarked that English convicts form by far the largest class of identifiable emigrants to the Americas - well over 50,000 and rising as additional records are traced - yet relatively little attention has been paid so far to researching and publishing the relevant historical and genealogical data which is accessible on both sides of the Atlantic. For example, very few of the surviving County Quarter Sessions records in England, almost all containing unique references to transported felons, have been decently calendared, let alone transcribed or indexed. Regrettably also, much of what has been published on the subject has suffered from poor research, scholarship and presentation. Though it would be grossly arrogant to claim that the records now presented are either comprehensive (indeed they are far from it) or free from error, every attempt has been made to compare one set of documents with another and to refer back to the original court documents where discrepancies have been noticed.

Contemporary Records

The preamble to the 1718 Act referred specifically to the failure of previous transportation schemes to deter "wicked and evil-disposed persons . . . [who] have often neglected to perform the conditions [of transportation] and returned to their former wickedness" and to "the great want of servants who might be the means of improving and making the Colonies and Plantations more useful." After serving their full term, those transported were to be regarded as having been pardoned, though any who returned to England before the expiry of their term of transportation were to be executed. To ensure that the requirements both of the law and of fiscal accountability were safeguarded, the merchants who shipped condemned convicts overseas were required to give financial security for their safe delivery and the ships' captains to procure from the port of entry in America a certificate of their landing. Furthermore the colony of Maryland, where one in every ten white adult males was reckoned by 1755 to be a British convict, had, from the inception of the Transportation Act, required proof of each felon's conviction to be registered in a local court. Together these stipulations ensured the recording and survival of a great mass of documentary evidence regarding the names and movements of this category of involuntary emigrants. For Virginia, most of whose records before 1776 were destroyed at the burning of Richmond in 1865, the surviving English records are unique.

Of the more than 300 convict ships identified as having crossed the Atlantic from the ports of London, Bristol, Liverpool and Bideford between 1716 and 1776, only a dozen or so were destined for the West Indies or the Carolinas, and then only before 1730. Thereafter Maryland or Virginia were the invariable destinations. A pattern quickly developed whereby the principal English prisons were cleared on a regular basis two or three times a year at times to suit maritime requirements and the demands of tobacco exporters in the colonies. From 1718 to 1742 a prominent London merchant named Jonathan Forward held the appointment of "Contractor for the Transports" and was initially paid £3 a head for each transported felon, soon rising to £5. Forward was succeeded by an unsavoury character named Andrew Reid who was, in turn, replaced in 1762 by John Stewart. In 1772, after the death of Stewart, the Treasury decided to abrogate the system of appointing and paying contractors, having discovered that there were merchants ready to clear the gaols at their own expense and rely on the profits from the sale of felons to cover their costs. A pioneer in this area was Duncan Campbell who reported to a House of Commons committee in 1779 that he had sold common male convicts for an average of £10 each, females at £8 to £9, and tradesmen for £15 to £25. He had transported 473 felons a year taking between 100 and 200 persons in one ship.

The western counties of England, which contributed handsomely to populating Maryland with their surplus criminal fraternities, had no State subsidy to fall back on and therefore had to rely on local transportation contractors based in the ports of Exeter, Bridport, Barnstaple and finally Bristol. The impact of American independence upon the penal systems in these areas was as devastating as it was slow to dawn. Well into 1784 the County Courts were continuing to make out transportation orders requiring convicts to be transported to America while the local gaols bulged at the seams with waiting prisoners. Efforts by County Clerks to arrange shipping to America were universally met with rebuffs and excuses such as "Not one of [the vessels] will take convicts, having all of them hourly applications to take passengers which they cannot accommodate." (Dorset Quarter Sessions MSS). At last central government had to come to the rescue by accepting large numbers of county prisoners for work in the hulks moored along the Thames in London.

How desperate the situation had become may be gauged from the frantic - and ultimately disreputable - attempts made by the English government to continue dumping its convicted prisoners in the American plantations. The last gasp came with the despatch of the *George*, under the assumed name of the *Swift*, ostensibly to Nova Scotia but in fact to Baltimore, under the command of Capt. Thomas Pamp. There on 24 December 1783 he successfully landed a cargo of felons but triggered off American resolve never again to allow the importation of felons. An attempt by the London government in 1784 to repeat the achievement of the previous year was an unmitigated failure. A final effort was made in 1787 when 131 convicts were shipped from Dublin by the *Chance* and 73 of them landed on a desert island called Haneago. From there they were taken to New Providence Island and, in July 1788, 14 men and 8 women were put on board the

Prince William Henry, Capt. William Thompson, to be shipped to Baltimore only to be refused entry. The Government of Maryland was urged "to take suit as may be necessary for the safety of citizens and the integrity of Government which we think most grossly insulted." (MSA: MSS S1005-16525).

Duncan Campbell, the last officially appointed "Contractor for the Transports," provides an almost seamless continuity between the system of convict transportation as it was envisaged in 1718 and the more developed schemes devised to populate the early Australian settlements. As a chief adviser to the Government on penal reorganisation during and after the American debacle of 1782, he would have agreed with the Parliamentary Committee of 1785 that transportation "answered every good purpose that could be expected of it" by "reclaiming prisoners and turning them into good citizens" and was "not attended with very much expense to the public." After serving as Superintendent of the Thames Hulks, Duncan Campbell became one of the principal architects of the schemes which launched the First and Second Fleets to Australia. His family and business papers are, indeed, preserved in an Australian archive (the Mitchell Library in Sydney) and provide an invaluable insight into the transportation trade as it was conducted during the latter years of the eighteenth century.

Where to Look for further information

With the exception of some convicts sentenced in the Midland Circuit, the name, place of residence and offence of each convict listed in this volume should be found on a Bill of Indictment enrolled amongst the records of each session of the Assize or Quarter Session Court. Indexes to original documents within these classes are virtually non-existent but an alphabetical list of felons known to have been sentenced to transportation between 1614 and 1775 has been compiled as *The Complete Book of Emigrants in Bondage* (Genealogical Publishing Co. Inc., Baltimore, 1988).

a) Court Records

The Assize (or Gaol Delivery) Courts were responsible for trying the gravest crimes. The Old Bailey jurisdiction, which covered all criminal cases arising within the City of London and the County of Middlesex, held separate Sessions eight times a year, each resulting in a roll of documents recording the proceedings. The records covering London are at the Corporation of London Records Office, and those for Middlesex at the London Metropolitan Archives.

Outside the metropolis, England was divided into Circuits presided over by travelling judges who visited each county in turn, usually twice a year, and the records of each Session in each county were similarly enrolled and are preserved in the Public Record Office, Kew, Richmond, Surrey TW9 4DU, within the following classes:

Home Circuit (Essex, Hertfordshire, Kent, Surrey, Sussex).
Gaol Delivery Rolls ASSI 35

Western Circuit (Cornwall, Devon, Dorset, Hampshire, Somerset, Wiltshire).
Gaol Delivery Books ASSI 23
Order Books ASSI 24
Crown Minute Books ASSI 21

Oxford Circuit (Berkshire, Gloucestershire, Herefordshire, Monmouthshire, Oxfordshire, Shropshire, Staffordshire, Worcestershire).
Gaol Delivery Rolls ASSI 5
Crown Minute Books ASSI 2

Norfolk Circuit (Bedfordshire, Buckinghamshire, Cambridgeshire, Huntingdonshire, Norfolk, Suffolk).
Gaol Delivery Rolls ASSI 16
Gaol Books ASSI 33/1, 34/17, 33/2-5
(one volume in this series held by Gray's Inn Library as Ms 45).
Indictment Rolls ASSI 35

Northern Circuit (Cumberland, Northumberland, Westmorland, Yorkshire).
Crown Minute Books ASSI 41
Gaol Books ASSI 42
Indictment Rolls ASSI 44

Midland Circuit (Derbyshire, Leicestershire, Lincolnshire, Northampton-shire, Nottinghamshire, Rutland, Warwickshire).
The records of this Circuit prior to 1800 were destroyed.

Chester & Flint Palatinate
Rough Minute Books CHES 35/24
Crown Minute Books CHES 21/7
Session Rolls CHES 24

Durham Palatinate
  Crown Minute Books DUR 15/1, 16/1
  Assize Rolls DUR 17
  Assize Proceedings DUR 19/3

Lancaster Palatinate
  Minute Books & Pardons PL 28/1-3
  Assize Rolls PL25
  Indictments PL 26

b) State records

After 1655 and before the Transportation Act of 1718, deserving prisoners in each Circuit were selected to be reprieved from the gallows on condition of their accepting a term of transportation. Each formal pardon, signed by the King, was enrolled in the great series of Patent Rolls preserved in the Public Record Office as Class C 66. The voluminous correspondence maintained between the judges, Assize clerks, prison administrators and the central bureaucracy in London, including appeals and reports, has also been faithfully preserved amongst Class SP (State Papers), principally SP 44 (Appeals, Petitions and Reprieves) and SP 36/141-159 (Petitions and Law Officers' Reports).

The British Treasury which became responsible after 1718 for payments to contractors in respect of the transportation of felons from the London, Middlesex, Home Circuit and Buckinghamshire prisons, maintained meticulous records of the numbers and names of those so disposed of and, very often, of the ships involved. Ledgers in PRO Class T 53 (Warrants for Money) contain the names of transported felons from 1718 to 1744 and documents in Class T 1 (Treasury Board Papers) from 1750 to 1772, with occasional gaps.

c) County Records

The records of Quarter Session and Borough Courts which exercised the power in every county (though less frequently and for less serious cases) to transport convicted offenders, are all preserved in the London and some 50 County or Borough Record Offices. In addition, almost every Record Office holds some non-juridical records relating to convict transportation ranging from bonds with contractors and ship captains to detailed correspondence. In addition to such resources, the Corporation of London Record Office holds copies of Landing Certificates in respect of most convicts delivered from London, Middlesex and the Home counties to American ports between 1718 and 1736.

d) Printed resources

The best known Who's Who of the criminal classes of the 18th century is the series of *Old Bailey Sessions Papers* which record the trials and sentences of almost every felon that passed through the Old Bailey during that period. The *Gentleman's Magazine* also reported the trials though less consistently or extensively, and often gave details of the sailings of transport ships.

THE ARRANGEMENT OF THIS BOOK

The first section is devoted to a chronological listing of all the convict passenger lists so far discovered in the repositories and categories described above. Within each listing, those transported - known throughout the English -speaking world as "The King's Seven-Year Passengers" - have been arranged by their county of origin and then in alphabetical order of surname. Further information about each person listed will usually be available, first by reference to the printed sources already mentioned, then by research in the relevant London or county Sessions records. It should, however, be emphasized that many more transported felons than are listed in this work will be found in the *Complete Book of Emigrants in Bondage* previously referred to.

The second section consists of an alphabetical listing of transported felons advertised as "runaways" in Maryland, Virginia and Pennsylvania newspapers of the eighteenth century. Where individual runaways may safely be identified with those listed in the first section, this has been indicated. The original newspaper references have been obtained from transcriptions made by Richard Cox from the *Maryland Gazette* for the *National Genealogical Society Quarterly* Vols. 68-69, *seriatim*; and those listed in Karen Mauer Green's *The Maryland Gazette 1727-1761* (Frontier Press, Galveston, 1989); in Robert K. Headley Jr.'s *18th-Century Virginia Newspapers* (Genealogical Publishing Co., Inc., Baltimore, 1987); and in Farley Grubb's *Runaway Servants, Convicts and Apprentices Advertised in the Pennsylvania Gazette, 1728-1798* (Genealogical Publishing Co., 1992). I am particularly indebted to Ed Wright and Bob Barnes who expended much time and effort in identifying and abstracting these sources.

A third, and briefer, section, contributed by Bob Barnes and based principally on his researches, is devoted to case histories of some English felons who made their mark in the land of their exile and whose descendants are entitled to remember them with some pride.

In his book *Bound for America: the Transportation of British Convicts to the Colonies, 1718-1775* (Oxford: Clarendon Press, 1987), Roger Ekirch drew attention to the large number of convicts who were purchased to work in the ironworks of Maryland. He attempted to trace the origins of 145 felons in Kent Co, records but was able to identify only five with certainty (pp.144-145; a further 395 male convicts imported into Kent and Queen Anne's Cos. were also made the subject of investigation but here only eight could be positively identified (pp. 180-181). The proportion of identifiable felons amongst the population of colonial Maryland and Virginia has grown appreciably with the comparative studies reflected in this book but the ease and frequency with which convicts and "runaways" changed their names coupled with the vagaries of contemporary spelling will always present a problem to conscientious genealogists and historians.

Researches made independently by Bob Barnes have shown that several early inhabitants of Baltimore Co. started life in Maryland as detainees "at His Majesty's pleasure," some going on to acquire land by patent, purchase or lease, in order to settle down and raise families. Of the twenty case studies outlined here, all were married, fourteen are known to have had children, and some are known to have descendents living today.

SOURCES AND ABBREVIATIONS

The sources for each ship passenger list are shown against individual headings. From 1718 until the end of 1746 there are reasonably consistent lists of transported convicts from London, Middlesex and the Home Counties included in Treasury Money Order Books (T53). Thereafter and until 1750 (and even later where gaps exist) some of the passenger lists have been compiled from surviving Bonds and Sessions Records. From 1750 to July 1772 extensive use has been made of surviving passenger lists in Treasury Board Papers (T1). Between July 1772 and 1776 Bonds and Sessions Records have again been invoked. All known Maryland record sources have been examined and combined with data from English archival repositories. Lastly those County Quarter Sessions records which are accessible have been examined and relevant material added to the shipping lists.

The following abbreviations have been adopted:

1783 AL: Assessment List of 1783. Transcribed by Robert Barnes and Bettie S. Carothers and published as *1783 Tax List of Baltimore County, Maryland*. Lutherville: Carothers, 1978.
1790 CE: Heads of Families...First Census, 1790, Maryland.
AA Co: Anne Arundel Co., Maryland.
AL Co: Albemarle Co., Virginia.
BA Co: Baltimore Co., Maryland.
BAAB: Baltimore Co. Administration Bonds.
BAAD: Baltimore Co. Administration Accounts, Libers 6-10, MSA.
BAAM: *Baltimore American*.
BACT: Baltimore Co. Chattel Records; Libers 1 and 2 at MSA. Liber 3 at MHS. Liber 4 at MSA.
BADB: Baltimore Co. Debt Book.
BAJA: *St. James' Parish Register, 1787-1815*. Compiled by Bill and Martha Reamy. FLP.
BALR: Baltimore Co. Land Records.
BAMI: Baltimore Co. Court Minutes.
BAOR: *Baltimore County Overseers of Roads, 1693-1793*. By Henry C. Peden, Jr. FLP.
BAPA: Records of St. Paul's Parish. By Bill and Martha Reamy. 2 vols. FLP, 1989.
BARP: *Revolutionary Patriots of Baltimore Town and Baltimore County*. By Henry C. Peden, Jr. Westminster: Family Line Publications.
BATHa: *St. Thomas Parish Marriages, 1738-1995*. FLP.
BATHb: *St. Thomas Parish Baptisms, 1732-1995*. FLP.
BATL 1783: See 1783 AL.
BCF: *Baltimore County Families, 1659-1759*. By Robert W. Barnes. Baltimore: Genealogical Publishing Co., Inc., 1989.
BFG: *Baltimore Federal Gazette*.
BO Co: Botetourt Co., Virginia.
CAL Co: Calvert Co., Maryland.
CAR Co: Caroline Co., Maryland.
CBEB: *Complete Book of Emigrants in Bondage*. By Peter Wilson Coldham. Baltimore: Genealogical Publishing Co., Inc.
CE Co: Cecil Co., Maryland.
CHA Co: Charles Co., Maryland.
CHE Co: Chesterfield Co., Virginia.
CLRO: Corporation of London Record Office, Guildhall, London EC2P 2EJ.
CMSP: *Calendar of Maryland State Papers*. (various series).
GSV: *The Green Spring Valley: Its History and Heritage*. 2 volumes. *Volume One: A History and Historic Houses*. By Dawn F. Thomas. *Volume Two: Family Genealogies*. By Robert Barnes. Baltimore: The Maryland Historical Society, 1975.
CU Co: Culpeper Co., Virginia.
DO Co: Dorchester Co., Maryland.
FA Co: Fairfax Co., Virginia.
FR Co: Frederick Co., Maryland.
FRV Co: Frederick Co., Virginia
HAGE: *St. George's Parish Registers, 1689-1793*, by Bill and Martha Reamy (Westminster: Family Line Publications, 1988).
HAL Co: Halifax Co., Virginia.
HAR Co: Harford Co., Maryland.

HARP: *Revolutionary Patriots of Harford County*. By Henry C. Peden. Bel Air: Bel Air Copy Center, 1985.

HAWB: Harford County Will Book.

IBCP: *Inhabitants of Baltimore County, 1763-1774*. By Henry Peden. Westminster: Family Line Publications.

IBCW: *Inhabitants of Baltimore County, 1692-1763*. By F. Edward Wright.FLP.

KE Co: Kent Co., Maryland.

KG Co: King George Co., Virginia.

KW Co: King William Co., Virginia.

LA Co: Lancaster Co., Virginia.

LC: Landing Certificate.

LMA London Metropolitan Archives, 40 Northampton Road, London EC1R 0HB.

LO Co: London Co., Virginia.

MCHR: Maryland Chancery Records, including *Abstracts of Chancery Court Records of Maryland, 1669-1782*. By Debbie Hooper. FLP.

MDAD: Maryland Administration Accounts.

MDTP: Maryland Testamentary Proceedings.

MG: *Maryland Gazette*

MGSB: *Maryland Genealogical Society Bulletin*.

MINV: Maryland Inventories Liber.

MJ: *Maryland Journal*

MJBA: *Maryland Journal and Baltimore Advertiser*.

MPL: Maryland Patent Liber.

MSA: Maryland State Archives, Annapolis, Maryland.

NGSQ: *National Genealogical Society Quarterly*.

NO Co: Northumberland Co., Virginia.

OR Co: Orange Co., Virginia.

PAG: *Pennsylvania Gazette*

PE Co: Prince Edward Co., Virginia.

PG Co: Prince George's Co., Maryland.

PPGC: Pardon Papers 1777-1836,
   Abstracts by F. Edward Wright in *Maryland Genealogical Society Bulletin*, Vol. 32 No. 4.

PRO: Public Record Office, Kew, Richmond, Surrey TW9 4DU.

QA Co: Queen Anne's Co., Maryland.

QS: Quarter Sessions.

RI Co: Richmond Co., Virginia.

RO Co: Rockingham Co., Virginia.

SCBC: *Sketches of Citizens of Baltimore City and Baltimore County*. By Sallie Mallick. FLP.

SJSG: St. John's and St. George;s Parish Registers, 1696-1851, by Henry C. Peden. FLP.

SM Co: St. Mary's Co., Maryland.

SO Co: Somerset Co., Maryland.

ST Co: Stafford Co., Virginia.

TA Co: Talbot Co., Maryland.

VG: *Virginia Gazette*.

VGNI: *Virginia Gazette* or *Northern Intelligencer*.

VGP: *Virginia Gazette* (pub John Pinkney).

VGPu: *Virginia Gazette* (pub Alexander Purdie).

VGR: *Virginia Gazette & Richmond Chronicle*.

WA Co: Washington Co., Maryland.

WE Co: Westmoreland Co., Virginia.

WO Co: Worcester Co., Maryland.

Peter Wilson Coldham
Purley, Surrey, England

Easter 1997
AMDG

Felons convicted in the Summer Assizes of 1718, transported from Bideford by the *Sophia*, Capt. John Law, and registered in Queen Anne's Co., Maryland in March 1719. (MSA: CR 49,080-IK A, ff. 208-212). Also listed in Kent Co. records (CR 42,840-8533 f. 54).

Cornwall

Bennet, Samuel
Brenton, John
Crapp, Mary
Gale, Richard
Grantlett, John
Jacob, Thomas
Leane, Robert
Obryan, William
Patty, Charles
Vivian, William

Devon

Bennett, George
Brook, William
Clarke, James
Clements, Jonas
Collins, Walter
Farren, William - 14 yrs
Gayer, Andrew
Gregory, Anthony
Judd, David
Mewdon, William
Newton, Daniel
Quick, Thomas
Rall, John
Ruslake, John
Scarborough, Joseph

Shute, Henry
Spettigue, Burchett
Stevens, William
Taylor, William
Thomas, John alias Baker, Lewis
- 14 yrs
Underhill, Robert Jr.
Underhill, William
Westlake, Joseph
Wood, John

Dorset

Grigg, James
Legg, William - 14 yrs
Seaward, Joseph
Stacy, Thomas
Throttle, Robert

Somerset

Abbott, John
Arney, John
Freestone, Walter
Orney, John
Pippen, John
Rossiter, John
Sellwood, Sarah
Stone, Thomas
Tippett, Thomas

Felons shipped from London to Maryland by the *Worcester* frigate, Capt. Edwyn Tomkins, in February 1719 and registered at Annapolis in June 1719. (PRO: T53/27/220; CLRO Mss 57.7.3; MSA: TP4).

Middlesex

Allen, John
Barton, William
Bignall, Sarah
Bishop alias Cane, Mary
Boulton, Richard
Bowge alias Bowse, Mary.
Brown, Catherine
Brown, James - 14 yrs -
   died on passage
Brown, Jane - 14 yrs
Burton, Elizabeth, alias Black Bess
Bush, Nathaniel - died on passage

Butler, William
Casson, Thomas
Chapbelll, Charles - 14 yrs
Cole, John, alias Crawford, William
   - 14 yrs
Conner, William
Cordell, Sarah
Cox, Charles.
Crookshanks, William
Cross, John
Davies, Elizabeth
Davis, Martha
Davison, Jane
Day, Elizabeth

1

Dickinson, Mary
Dickson, William
Dodd, Joseph - 14 yrs
Edwards, Robert
Edwards, Thomas*
Egan, Bernard
Fenwick alias Peers, Frances
Flood, Francis - 14 yrs
Foster, Mary
Furness, Amy
George, Elizabeth
Gibson, Thomas
Goddin, William
Goodram, Thomas
Greenwood, William - 14 yrs
Harding, Mary
Harper, Sara
Hawkins alias Dighton, Dorothy
Hawley, Martha
Hewson, Mary alias Tomkyns, Martha
Hill, John - 14 yrs
Holliday, Joseph
Howard, Ann
Hudson, Charles*
Jarvis, Simon
Joy, Mary
Keefe, Henry
Laban, Catherine
Lloyd, Ann
Mansfield, Sarah
Mash, Phillis
May, Henry - 14 yrs
McDonald, Elizabeth.
McDonald, John
Milbourne, Catherine
Mills, Frances
Oldfield, John
Perry alias Floyd, Henry

Phillips, William
Poole alias Robinson, George
Porter, Elizabeth
Quitty, Daniel
Read alias Morris alias Dalton,
Mary - 14 yrs
Reynolds, Edward
Robinson, Edward - 14 yrs
Rogers, John
Saul, Thomas.
Shaw, John
Smith, Elizabeth
Smith, Francis
Smith, Margaret - 14 yrs
Smith, Sarah
Steps, Peter
Stevens, Thomas
Stoneham, James
Tanner, Tobias
Thomas alias Adams, Alice
Thompson, Henry
Thompson, Robert. - 14 yrs -
died on passage
Turner, John
Turpin, Elizabeth
Twelves, George
Wally, Mary
Watkins, Jane
White, Richard
Whitten, Mathew - 14 yrs
Wiggins, Thomas - 14 yrs
Wilkey, John
Wilson, James
Wisdale, Roger
Wiseman, Henry
Withey, Daniel
Wonnell, James
Young, John

*Not found on LC.

Felons transported from London by the *Margaret*, Capt. William Greenwood, in May 1719 and registered in Maryland records. (PRO: T53/27/266; CLRO Mss 289.6.4; MSA PL 5 f. 18).

Essex

Braechan (Branchin), Thomas: sold to William Orrick
Cassy, Mary: sold to Mr. Rosenquist
Dobson, John: sold to Benjamin Williams
Eagleston, Richard: John Gaskin
Gibbons, John: sold to Patrick Sympson & William Black

Martin, James: sold to John Richardson
Poole, Thomas: sold to Patrick Sympson & William Black

Hertfordshire

Dickerson, Nathaniel: sold to William Black
Everett, John - died on passage
Hinckley, Francis: sold to William Black
Ingram, Richard - died on passage
Miller, James: sold to William Martin
Robinson (Robertson), William: sold to Mordecai Price
Stanley, William: sold to Patrick Sympson

Kent

Alexander, Joseph: sold to Patrick Sympson & William Black
Baker, John: sold to Patrick Sympson & William Black
Brown alias Smith, John - died on passage
Garrett, Thomas*
Mincher, John: sold to Patrick Sympson & William Black
Pledge, William: sold to Patrick Sympson & William Black
Smith, Michael: sold to Peter Galloway
Tudor, Richard: sold to Patrick Sympson & William Black

Lincolnshire

Jenkins, William: sold to John Nelson
Trix, Robert*

London

Abthorpe (Althorpe), Thomas: sold to Peter Pinchton
Barker, Martha: sold to Daniel Carter
Batt, Thomas: sold to Patrick Sympson & William Black
Bayley, Thomas - died on passage
Chamberlain, Richard: sold to John Straw
Crawford, John: sold to Mr. Polea of Annapolis
Cringin alias Scringin, James: sold to Patrick Sympson & William Black
Dawson, John - died on passage
Dobbs, Elizabeth: sold to Joseph Pettibone
Evans, James: sold to William Jones
Filstar?, Lewis: sold to Jonathan Pridale
Foster, Ann: sold to Patrick Sympson & William Black
Gardener, Rachel: sold to William Hawkins
Haynes, Winifred: sold to John Welch
Holloway alias Scott, Jane: sold to Patrick Sympson & William Black
Johnson, Peter: sold to Matthew Ashley
Jones, James: sold to Edward Hearpe
Jones, Rebecca: sold to Edward Mallux
Lewis, Katherine: sold to William Rowles
Martin, Sarah: sold to John Gaskin
McDonald, Matthew: sold to Samuel Chaney

Molineux, Edward (Edmond) - died on passage
Nead, Susan: sold to Patrick Sympson & William Black
Nelson, John: sold to Richard Snowden
Owen, Elizabeth: sold to Edward Smith
Page, Joseph: sold to John Buckingham
Patience, John: sold to Patrick Sympson & William Black
Patience, William: sold to Richard Snowden
Pearce, Anne: sold to Patrick Sympson & William Black
Perkins, Mary: sold to Patrick Sympson & William Black
Reade, Francis: sold to Henry Wright
Reynolds, Arnold: sold to Ambrose Nealson Sr.
Richardson alias Capstick, Daniel: sold to Henry Wright
Rogers, Grace: sold to James Smith
Smart, Joseph: sold to William Martin
Smith, Margaret - 14 yrs
Spurgeon, William: sold to Richard Snowden
Stiffe, Elizabeth*
Sutton, Mary*
Thirby alias Kirby, Mary: sold to Patrick Sympson & William Black
Tooley alias Hewitt, Elizabeth: sold to Peter Hyat
Watson, Joseph: sold to Richard Snowden
Williams, Thomas: sold to John Welch
Wilson, Gilbert: sold to John Payburn
Wilson, Mary: sold to Patrick Sympson & William Black
Woodman, Thomas: sold to William Black
Woodward, John: sold to Timothy Sullivan

Surrey

Barker, John: sold to Richard Snowden
Bendley, Jonathan: sold to Patrick Sympson & William Black
Binks, Jacob: sold to William Pinkstone
Bray, William: sold to Thomas Rouls
Brindley Jonathan: sold to Patrick Sympson
Bursfield, Thomas: sold to Caesar Ghiselin
Butler, Thomas: sold to Andrew David
Daryel (Derayley) alias Reily, Jaques - 14 yrs: sold to Thomas Joneson
Dickenson, Arthur: sold to Andrew Bell
Dumbrell, Edward: sold to Stephen West
Dunton, John - 14 yrs: sold to John Amslow
Elby, Thomazin - 14 yrs: sold to Dr. Charles Carroll
Eley, Elizabeth*
Ellmore, Thomas - 14 yrs: sold to Ambrose Nealson
Ford, John of Clapham: sold to Timothy Sullivan
Green alias Harvey, Abigall: sold to Mrs. Bransome
Haley, Richard: sold to Patrick Sympson
Hambleton, William: sold to Peter Hyat
Hamstead, James: sold to John Young
Harker, John: sold to David Bele
Harman, Thomas: sold to John Cornelius
Harris alias Withers, William: sold to Philip Jones
Hays, Robert: sold to Patrick Cragin

Heather, Elizabeth: sold to Samuel White
Holmstead, James*
Hughes, John - 14 yrs: sold to John Summerland
Jones, Richard*
Lucas, Thomas: sold to Peter Galloway
Milcham, William: sold to Widow Newman
Naggs, Sarah: sold to Peter Galloway
Nest, John: sold to John Baldwin
Noble, Susannah: sold to Jonathan Prasher
Parrimore, William: sold to John Gaskin
Peirson, Richard: sold to George Harman
Plummer, Isaac: sold to William Davies
Randall, Thomas: sold to Philemon Lloyd Esq.
Roades, Benjamin: sold to Mr. Polea of Annapolis
Robinson (Robertson), Richard: sold to William Anderson
Seagar, Richard: sold to William Black
Snagg, Thomas (Sarah): sold to Peter Galloway
Thomas, James: sold to Richard Chaney
Toleard, Ursula: sold to Jonathan Prather
West, John: sold to John Baldwin
Williams, George: sold to Patrick Sympson
Wood, William*
Yeo, William: sold to Richard Hampton

Sussex

Drowning, Thomas*
Milton, John: sold to Nathaniel Stincham
Rennolds, Thomas: sold to Richard Nelson
Rose, Richard: sold to Patrick Sympson & William Black
Sturt, Robert: sold to John Welch
Symonds, Elizabeth: sold to Gustavus Hesseltine

Unidentified

Spurgeon, Ann: sold to Rosanna Lees

*Not found on LC.

Felons transported from London to Maryland by the *Susannah & Sarah*, Capt. Peter Wills, in October 1719 and registered in Annapolis in April 1720. (PRO: T53/27/415; CLRO Mss 57.7.5).

London

Atsey (Adsley), John
Beele, Mary - 14 yrs
Birch, John
Blackwell alias Ridgway, Sarah - 14 yrs
Blanchflour, Elizabeth - died
Bourne, Henry - died
Bridges, Elinor - 14 yrs
Bridges, John
Bromfield, Robert
Brudenell, Charlot - 14 yrs
Bryan, Darby
Cane, Thomas
Capp, George - 14 yrs - died
Chapman, Margaret - 14 yrs
Clarke, Susanna

5

Clerke, Stephen
Cooke, Susanna
Cooper, Elizabeth
Curree, Elizabeth
Davis, Henry*
Dawson, Elizabeth
Deane, Elizabeth
Dennis, Margaret
Dowlas, Mary
Drake, Joshua (Joseph) - died
Evans, Patrick
Evans, William
Eylmore, Symon - 14 yrs
Filewood (Philwood), John - 14 yrs
Fletcher alias Weeden, Jane - 14 yrs
Foster, Charles
Frances, Mary
Frost, John
Gambell, William - 14 yrs
Godfrey, Robert
Gossage, William
Gray, Martha, alias Dow, Mary
Green, John
Gregory, William
Henly, Dorothy
Hillison, Robert - 14 yrs
Hutchins, John
Hutchins, Mary
Jakes, Elizabeth
Jervis, Richard
Jones, Thomas - 14 yrs
Kettle, James - died
Kingsbury, Sarah - 14 yrs
Knight, Rose
Lamb, Kennitt
Larkin, Benjamin
Lewis (Luing), Susanna - died
Lisence, Richard (Ruth)
Lowe (Law), John
Marvell, William*
Miller, John
Mills (Miles), Thomas
Minns, Mary
Morgan, Richard
Morgan, Robert

Nelson, Robert
Newland (Newton), John- died
Newman, Thomas
Northam, Jervis
Perry, William
Ragg, Isaac
Rance, Noble - died
Randall, John - died
Roberts, Thomas
Rowland alias Newland, John - died
Soden, John
Steele, John
Stewart, Sarah
Tadlock (Dudlock), Dorothy
Taylor, John
Tyler, Hannah
Ward, Sarah
Weedon alias Fletcher, Jane
Whippy, Edward
Williams, Margaret
Willison (Wilson), William
Wood, Mary (2)
Wright, Thomas - 14 yrs
Wyer, John
Yeo, Samuel

Unidentified

Berry, Henry - died
Bibby, Edward
Blunt, Sarah - died
Dixon, John
Dudlock, Dorothy
Gilstone, Mary
Higgison, Joseph
Howell (Hawel), John
Killosop, Robert
Simonds, John
Woods, Martha
Woolford, Henry

Northumberland

Nelson, Thomas

*Not found on LC.

Felons transported from London by the Honor**, Capt. Robert Russell, in May 1720 and registered in Port York, Virginia, in January 1721 (PRO: T53/28/157; CLRO Mss 57.7.7).

London

Andrews, Jasper
Best, Jane
Bond, William - escaped in Vigo
Braxton (Blackstone), John
Brett, Anne
Brown alias Cassell, Thomas
Bryan, Joseph*
Busby, Edward - escaped in Vigo
Chapman, Anne
Clay, Samuel - escaped in Vigo
Cook, Pendell, alias Smith, Richard
Dalton, James - escaped in Vigo
Deely alias Dealing (Dowling), Samuel
Fann, Elizabeth*
Finley, Ralph
Goddard, Anthony - escaped in Vigo
Godwin, Hannah*
Goodchild, Elizabeth (Hester)
Grey, Martin - escaped in Vigo
Griffiths, John - escaped in Vigo
Harwood, Thomas - escaped in Vigo
Heathcote, Edward
Heathcote, James - died on passage
Helston, Mary
Hinchman, Charles
Holliday, James
Huntridge (Hawtree), Isabel
Hutchins, Elizabeth - died on passage
Ireland alias Nichols, Anne
Isaacs (Isaacson), William - escaped in Vigo
Jones, Elizabeth*
Jones, Mary
Kidgell, Jane
Kingham, Thomas - escaped in Vigo
Layfield, John
Lloyd (Floyd), Susanna

Martin, Zephaniah
May, Sarah
Mercy alias Massey, James - escaped in Vigo
Miller, Dorothy
North, Mary
Pindar, John*
Price, Benjamin
Price, Thomas
Rigby, Elizabeth
Robinson, William*
Rose, Joseph*
Selby, Mary
Smalman, Martha
Smith, Elizabeth
Smith, Susannah
Smith, William
Weedon, Isaac
Wells, Anne*
Wetherall, William - escaped in Vigo
White, John
Wilson, David
Wilson, James - escaped in Vigo
Wilson, Margaret
Winterbottom, Joseph
Wrenn, Sarah*
Wynne, William

Unidentified

Downes, Abel
Gibbons, Mary
Guthrey, Margaret
Knap, Thomas
Pendell, John
Raine, Sarah
Sallway, Mary
Winch, Richard - died at sea

*Not found in LC.

**Twenty convicts overcame the crew after the ship's departure from London and forced the original Captain, Richard Langley, to put into Vigo where they escaped. All the papers relating to the conviction of those on board were destroyed.

Felons transported from London consigned by Jonathan Forward to Thomas Cockey in Maryland by the *Owner's Goodwill*, Capt. John Lux, in August 1720 and registered in Annapolis in November 1720. (PRO: T53/28/332; MSA: PL 5 f. 262).

Kent

Amison, Jonathan
Baker, Richard
Barnes, Mary
Dugannon, Peter
Ellis, John
Hewitt, Robert
Maynard, Thomas alias Ransford,
   Jonathan
Meting, Matthew

Myers, Edward
Salter alias Browne, Thomas
Simpson, William
Soutter, William
Stanford, Margaret
Thompson alias Yates, Charles
Wild, Henry
Wilmore, Joseph

Felons transported from London by the *Gilbert*, Capt. Darby Lux, in October 1720 and registered in Annapolis in May 1721. (PRO: T53/28/331; CLRO: Mss 57.7.8).

Essex

Bull, Mathew - died on passage
Clement, Robert - died on passage
Coe, John - died on passage
Germyn, Robert*
Goose, Robert
Gorden, Jane, aged 50, brown hair
Griggs, George*
Hazlewood als Earsly, Philip*
Hewson, Thomas*
Howard, John, weaver aged 29, dark
Morse, John - died on passage
Prichard alias Jones, Thomas -
   died on passage
Way alias Green, George*
Younge, Mary - died on passage

Hertfordshire

Alcock, Ann aged 16, fair
Archer, John - died on passage
Blackwell, Henry - died on passage
Brown, Robert*

London

Andrews, Jasper
Bennet, Samuel, husbandman aged   57,
black complexion
Birch, Joseph*
Bostwick alias Bostock, Thomas -
   died on passage

Burras, Joshua, clog maker aged 21,
   dark
Cawthorne, Charles*
Edmonds, John, aged 31,
   husbandman, dark
Emery, Henry - 14 yrs*
Florey, Thomas, aged 19, dark
Gilbert, Elizabeth, aged 24, dark
Grant, Thomas*
Higday (Heden), Thomas, butcher
   aged 22, dark
Higgins, Mary, aged 40, dark
Hughes, Mary, aged 32, black hair
Johnson, Joseph, aged 24, dark
Lowe, Elizabeth, aged 19, fair - 14 yrs
Mason, Ann, aged 26, brown hair
Poor, Abraham*
Smith, Ann, aged 27, dark
Thompson, Alice, aged 21, dark
Townley, Margaret, aged 21, dark
Vine, Michael*
Walter (Walton), Samuel, aged 27,
   dark, husbandman
Willford, David, aged 26, dark
Williams, William, aged 16, fair
Wright, Edward, aged 19, fair,
   watchmaker
Wright, Mary - 14 yrs - died on passage

Middlesex

Allen, James, aged 21 dark
Andrews, Anne, aged 27, black hair

Barham (Batrim), Thomas - for life -
  died on passage
Beard, Gilbert aged 37, dark
Blacksby, Edward*
Boswell, John, butcher aged 25, fair
Boswell, William - died on passage
Bowring [Bowen], Mary*
Branscombe [Brandsom], George,
  aged 17, dark
Brewington, John, aged 18, fair
Burrill, Anne, aged 18, fair
Butler alias Clarke alias Smith alias
Bull,
  Thomas, aged 35, dark, husbandman
Chew, Hannah aged 31, fair
Clare, John, weaver aged 21, fair
Cooper, Grace, aged 28, dark
Cornelius, Peter, weaver aged 20, dark
Crumpton, Katherine, aged 40, dark
Cullum, Elizabeth, aged 16, dark
Davis, Sara*
Doleman, Rebecca, aged 35, dark
Dye, Penelope, aged 23, black hair
Eales, Mary*
Frith [Firth], Elizabeth, aged 19, fair
Fuller, John*
Giles, William, aged 23, black hair
Glasford (Glascow), Richard, carver
  aged 18, dark
Gray, John, barber aged 29, fair
Hall, Elizabeth, aged 23, dark
Harris, Mary, aged 34, fair
Haylin [Hellin], Dorothy [Mary] -
  died on passage
Higgins, Edward*
Holstock, Hannah, aged 21, fair
Hughes, Mary, aged 32, black hair
Husseller, Edward*
Hutchinson, Henry, aged 18, fair
Jones alias Simpson, Mary*
Kelley, Hugh, aged 22, fair
Long, Hannah, aged 40, black hair
Martin, Susanna, aged 20, fair
Mathews, Christopher*
Mayo (Mayam), Robert, aged 21,
  dark, weaver
Miller alias Meller, Sarah, aged 15,
  brown hair
Moore, Charles*
Nelson, Henry, poulterer, aged 22, dark
Parish, Alexander, aged 57, black
  hair, tallow chandler

Payne, Thomas, aged 33, dark
Pettiford, Elizabeth*
Powell, Anne, aged 27, dark
Preston, Edward, aged 20, dark,
  periwig maker
Raven, Anne, aged 34, dark
Raven, Henry, aged 37, black hair,
  locksmith
Richards, Richard, aged 26, dark
Riddlesden, William, attorney at law,
  black hair, aged about 40
Robinson, William, aged 21, ruddy,
  fisherman
Sadler, Anne, aged 19, brown hair
Sidwell, William - 14 yrs*
Smith, John, aged 53, carpenter
Smith (Smithson), Mary, aged 26,
  brown hair
Spearman, Mary, aged 17, fair
Speed, Benjamin*
Stafford, Matthew, aged 27, brown hair
Story, Catherine, aged 35, dark
Wade, William, aged 35, barber
Wells, Sarah - 14 yrs*
Wilson, Peter, aged 21, dark

Surrey

Aldridge, John alias Anthony*
Barnwell, Mary Falicia, aged 21, fair
Benson alias Fudges, John, aged 37,
  black hair
Carlile, Richard, aged 48, dark
Dobson, George, barber aged 24,
  black hair
Edmonds, John, husbandman
  aged 31, dark
Fudges alias Benson, John, aged 37,
  black hair
Harris, Sarah*
Henshaw, Nicholas*
Horner, Barthena (Parthena), aged 28,
  dark
Miller, Ann, aged 27, brown hair
Price, Margaret (Katherine), aged 30,
  dark
Spratlye, James, aged 17, dark
Tayler, Martin*
Turner, Richard*
Twelves alias Green, Elizabeth,
  aged 22, black hair
Williams alias Coose, John*

Worthing, Thomas*

Sussex

Hood alias Pilling, William, aged 30,
    black hair
Oxley, James*
Peacock, William*

Unidentified

Alcock, Thomas, aged 25, dark
Ashby, John - died on passage
Bates, Edward, aged 20, dark
Bayley, Francism aged 25, dark
Blackwell, Henry - died on passage
Brown, Mary - died on passage
Burton, Elizabeth, aged 22, black hair
Charman, Isabel - died on passage
Close, Richard, aged 24, dark
Coleson, William - died on passage
Coulson, John, miller aged 21, ruddy
Cross, Charles, aged 24, dark
Dickinson, Robert, husbandman,
    aged 33, black hair
Fielding, John - died on passage
Haines, Sarah, aged 25, dark

Hair, Robert, aged 21, dark
Hanshaw, Nicholas, aged 25, fair
Ingram, Mary, aged 53, brown hair
Johnson, Peter, aged 21, dark
Knight, Ann, aged 23, brown hair
Late, Honor, aged 28, dark
Laxon, Edmond, aged 22, dark
Matthews, Katherine - died on passage
Miller, John - died on passage
Painsworth, John. husbandman aged 22,
    black hair
Parke, Elizabeth, aged 30, red hair
Penniston, Henry, weaver aged 20, dark
Pinock, William - died on passage
Power, Edward, shoemaker
    aged 16, fair
Rawlings, William, tailor aged 24, dark
Richcraft, Thomas, aged 25, dark
Roe, John, aged 22, dark
Sands, Elizabeth, aged 40, black hair
Smith, Deborah - died on passage
Steans, Thomas, carpenter
    aged 28, dark
Story, John - died on passage
Strickland, Robert, husbandman,
    aged 39, dark
Yates, Mary, aged 24, dark

*Not found on LC.

Felons transported from London to Virginia by the *Prince Royal*, Capt. Thomas Boyd, in August 1721 and registered at Port Rappahannock in April 1723. ((PRO: T53/29/146; CLRO: Mss 57.7.13).

Kent

Hougham (Huffam), Solomon Jr. (QS)

London

Ambler, Martha
Annable, Samuel
Anthony, John - died
Benfield, Thomas
Bennett alias Burdett, Hester
Blake, Frederick
Browne, Richard
Butlas alias Neale, Rebecca - 14 yrs
Collier, Zachary
Cranfield, Henry
Deplosh, Peter
Dunn, Thomas

Edwards, John
Festrope, Anne - 14 yrs
Gersey, Philip
Green, Sarah - 14 yrs
Harding, Alice
Hurst, Christian
James, George
Jones, Elizabeth
Jones, Humphrey - died
Jones alias Harding, Ruth*
Langton, Elizabeth
Newton, Stephen
Nun alias Powell, James
Pierce, Thomas
Pitts, John
Rippon, William
Rose, John
Shanks, Elizabeth - 14 yrs

Shaw, William - died
Smith, John
Smithurst, William - 14 yrs
Soaper, Robert
Taylor, Daniel
Wells, Elizabeth
Wetherill, William
White, John - died
White, John
White, Rebecca
Williams, Randolph
Wood, John
Yeomans alias Booth, Margaret
  - 14 yrs

Middlesex

Armstrong, Thomas
Atkins, Mary
Baily, Henry
Beaule alias Handy, John
Boyce, Samuel - died
Bridgman, William
Browning, James
Burroughs, William - 14 yrs
Butcher, Thomas
Camell, Anne
Cane, William
Clerk, Samuel
Clowds, Millicent
Cotterell, Edward
Cox, Thomas
Cremer, Susanna
Dalton, John
Davies, Vincent*
Donington, Robert - died
Downes alias Robinson, Susanna
Durham, George
Ellett, Lewis
Elmes, Thomas - 14 yrs
Fleming, Elinor
Fletcher, Mary alias Joyce
Fluellin, William
Foster, David
Gibson, Sarah
Giles, William, alias Saunders, Charles
Gilman, Susanna
Gordon, John

Grant, John*
Hawkes, Henry - 14 yrs
Hubbard, John*
Johnson, Mary
Johnson, Robert - 14 yrs
Johnson, Sarah - 14 yrs
Jones, Daniel
Jones, John
Jones, Richard - died
Lacey, James
Lindsey, Richard
Lloyd, Lewis alias Ellis
Meakins, John
Molloy, Mary - 14 yrs
Oates, Mary
Page, Grace
Payne, William*
Price, Mary
Quin, Richard
Ralphs, Richard
Rawson, Elizabeth
Rhodes, Robert
Rouse, William - died
Showell, John
Simpson, Anne
Smith alias Richardson, Elizabeth
Smith, Elizabeth
Smith, Martha
Smith, Thomas
Stiles, Elizabeth
Stockdale, Elianor
Tarborne alias Sherborne alias Starkey,
  Sarah
Thompson, William - died
Unwin, John
Verum alias Green, Charles
Walden, Lawrence - died
Walker, Thomas - died
Wharton, Cuthbert
Wilcox, John
Wilson, Margaret
Withers, Rebecca

Unidentified

Grant, John
Marret, Arthur - died
Ryan, William

*Not found in LC

11

Felons transported from London by the *Mary*, Capt. John Friend, and landed in Port York, Virginia in June 1721. (CLRO Mss 57.7.9).

Unidentified

Butcher, Charles
Crisp, William
Miller, John
Milliner, Thomas
Perkins, Henry

Potter, Lawrence
Sassier, Ann
Sinfield, William
Stades, John

Felons transported from London to Maryland by the *Owners Goodwill*, Capt. John Lux, in August 1721 and registered at Port Annapolis in July 1722. (PRO: T53/29/147; CLRO: Mss 57.7.11).

Berkshire

Banks, William - 14 yrs
Knight, William
Mead alias Hoare, Thomas - 14 yrs
Perry, Robert - 14 yrs
Williams, John - 14 yrs

Cambridgeshire

Fryer, John
Ragg, Susanna
Thompson, Richard

Essex

Bell, John
Berry, Matthew
Fox alias Alderidge alias Folkes, John
Haper, Peter
Heading, Nower alias Hadon, Noal
Hewson, Edward
Jarrold, Abraham
May, John
Offery, Mathias
Pierce, David
Price, Edward
Rich, Jonathan
Right, Samuel
Saville, Edward
Smith, Roger
Turner, William

Leicestershire

Goodwin, Thomas
Scott, Elizabeth

London

Harris, Ann
Short, Jane

Middlesex

Clerke, Margaret
Delafontain, Mary Ann
Fares alias Smith, Catherine
Hubbard, Elizabeth
Payne, Elizabeth
Richardson, Anne
Sheppeard, Mary
Smitham, Stacey

Surrey

Bullen, Joseph
Gambell, John
Jones, William
Quale, Edward

Unidentified

Allcock, Margaret
Hopman, Margaret
Lyons, Hugh
Macy, Judith

Felons transported from London to Maryland by the *William & John*, Capt. John Thompson, in October 1721. (PRO: T53/29/453).

Hertfordshire

Alman, Samuel
Ward, Robert
Windmill alias Francklin, John

Kent

Banks, Thomas
Bassock, Thomas
Burgesse, Jonas
Hadden, William
Harman, Mary
Henshaw, John
Hopkins, Thomas
King, John
Mallard, Peter
Mickleburgh, Daniel
North, Elizabeth

Primus, Thomas
Rolfe, Thomas
Rose, Sarah
Savage, John
Simpson, Thomas
Smith alias Knight, John
Turner, William
Walker, Mary

Surrey

Alexander, John
Baker, George
Doe, John
Gore, Christopher
Grew, Charles
Phillips, Stephen
Wells, Mary

Felons transported from London by the *Gilbert*, Capt. Darby Lux, in January 1722 and registered in Annapolis in July 1722. (PRO: T53/29/451; CLRO: 57.7.10).

London

Andrews, Jasper
Beaton, John
Brimley, Jonathan
Clapper, Mary
Corder, Edward
Drummer, Alexander
Farthing, Richard - 14 yrs - died
Gardiner, James
Gilbert, Bond*
Gilbert, William*
Graystock, Charles
Hart, John
Harvey alias Coates, Mary
Jones, John
Langley, William
Laws, Samuel
Mason, John
Mobbs, Elizabeth
Moor, Rebecca
Murry, Henry
Parker, Elizabeth
Pearce, Jane
Sweetman, Ann
Sympson, Thomas

Warminger, James
Warminger, John
Williams, Henry
Wilson, Margaret
Winfield, William

Middlesex

Alcock, John
Anderson, Richard
Angel, John
Atkinson, Elizabeth
Baily alias Dozzington, Elizabeth
Barker, Frances
Bickerton, John - 14 yrs
Brown alias Wright, Elizabeth
Calfe, James
Conner alias Canner, Joseph
Cropper, William
Cryer, William - 14 yrs
Ellen, Margaret
Gibb, James
Goulstone, Mary - 14 yrs
Graham alias Grimes, Hannah - 14 yrs
Green, John
Hargrove, Elizabeth

13

Headley, John
Herbert, Sarah
Hogg, James - 14 yrs
Holmes, Robert
James, Thomas
Johnson alias Jordan, Mary
Katherines, Edward
Kingham, Thomas
Lee alias Lees, John
Lewis, John
Mason, Edward
Merritt alias Walden, Anne
Mills, Nathaniel - died
Mitchell alias Michener, John*
Moor, John
Mountaine, Mary
Nash, John
Page, John
Perkins, Hannah
Phenix, Alice
Royton, John
Seaton, John
Serjeant alias Higgins, John
Shelton, Walter
Skill alias Thompson, John
Slaughter, Rebecca
Smith, Mary
Spencer, William - died

Stephens, Mary
Storey, John
Thomas, Edward
Twiddy, Mary
Vaughan, John
Veale, Daniel
Walker alias Bouchier
    alias Hitchman alias Smith, Mary
Walton, Robert - 14 yrs
Williams, William
Wynn, Francis

Surrey

Berry, Mathew*

Unidentified*

Atkins, Elizabeth
Berry, Harry
Caydor, Edward
Greeves, John
Hardacker, William
Hatcher, Thomas
Lewis, Samuel
Peaten, John
Price, Thomas
Wicker, John

*Not listed in bond.

Felons transported from Exeter by the *Reformation*, Capt. Philip Weare, in September 1721 and registered in Baltimore Co. records in August 1722. (MSA: BALR IS G 34)

Devon

Berriman, William - 14 yrs
Brisk, John
Camp, Thomas - 14 yrs
Camp, William - 14 yrs
Commins, Nicholas
Geaton (Gaten), William - 14 yrs

Griffith (alias Glanfield), Sarah
Hill, Thomas
James, John
Lux, John - 14 yrs
Quick, Elizabeth
Wyatt (Whyett), Martha

Felons transported from London by the *Forward*, Capt. Daniel Russell, in October 1722 and recorded in Annapolis in June 1723. (PRO: T53/30/118; CLRO: Mss 57.8.41).

Berkshire

Behoe, Moses
Irwing, John

Thomas, John
Wright, Giles

Essex*

14

Brewer, Mary
Hayes, Samuel
Hayward, Anne
Mully, John
Quin, Richard
Smith, John
Usher, Sarah
Williams, Phila

Hertfordshire*

Pagitt, Elizabeth
Parker, Stephen
Stoakes, John

Kent

Eades, Richard
Francis, George
Uffleman Peter (Oferman, Anthony)
Wamsley, John
Weller (Willert), William

Lincolnshire

Dyer alias Dyen, Mary

London

Allstone, John
Baker, Elizabeth
Bowle, William
Davies alias Dawson, Mary
Dyer, Susannah
Fisher, Thomas
Fortee, Jacob
Fox, Barbara*
Gilbert, William
Green, Walker - 14 yrs
Hullman, Isaac
Johnson, Robert
Jones, Griffith
Myers, Samuel
Nicholls, John
Peck, Jane*
Pomroy, John
Poole, Susannah
Rice, Thomas
Smith, Thomas
Sutton, Robert
Swan, Anne*
Tinsley, Thomas

Wake, Susanna*
Wakelin, Thomas - 14 yrs
Walker (Wayland), Elizabeth
Ward, Katherine*
Wedgwood, John*
Williams, Elizabeth*
Williams, Thomas.

Middlesex

Anderson alias Blacklock, Martha
Baxter, Anne
Berry, Joseph
Boat, John.*
Booth, Joseph
Bristow, William
Bullman, John
Burden (Burton), Elizabeth
Burkin, Jane
Churchill, Sarah
Croft, Robert
Deroffe (Deloas), Elizabeth
Etheridge, Thomas
Fisher, John
Fisher, Margaret
Ford, Margaret
Freeman, Elizabeth
Gascy, John
Glanister, Thomas
Glover, John
Greenland, John
Harlow, Mary
Hill, Thomas
Low, Anne
Mattison, Hugh
Murphy, John - 14 yrs
Owen, Mary
Perry alias Newman, John
Peters, William
Phesant, James
Reed, Richard
Ridman (Redman), Thomas
Robinson, William
Smith, Joseph
Starkey alias Newman alias Smart, Henry
Thorne, George
Ward, William*
Wheeler, Susanna
Wilshire, Thomas
Wyld, Abel (Abraham)

Rutland

Presgrave, Jeremiah
Vine, Rowland

Surrey

Block, Jane
Cane, Anne
Green, John
Hopkins alias Hughes, Thomas
Horseman, Henry
Porter, Daniel
Ricks, James*
Sarcott (Surcoat), Francis
Timpson, Thomas
Weldon (Weedon), John
Woodfield, John

Sussex

Dyer, John*
Elmes, John*
Emery, John
Fowler (Fewtle), Ward
Perry, Edward
Phillips, Paul
Ripping, Robert
Vincent, John*

Unidentified

Avery, James
Bolton, John
Brompton, Richard
Davies, Emanuel
Hutchings, Thomas
Priest, Catherine
Rowland, Elizabeth
Russell, Elizabeth
Timson, Moan

Felons transported from London by the *Jonathan*, Capt. Darby Lux, in February 1723 and registered in Maryland in July 1724. (PRO: T53/30/341; CLRO Mss 57.7.17).

London

Anderson, James, aged 16, fair
Bell, James, tailor aged 20, dark
Cole, Samuel, aged 27, dark
Dixon, John, aged 17, fair
Dyer, John, hatmaker aged 21, dark
Finlow [Phenlo], Lydia, aged 19,
   brown hair
Fisher, Berthia, aged 46, dark
Lynch, Charles - died on passage
Pollett [Pawlett], Edward, aged 20, fair
Pritchard [Pritchet], David, shoemaker,
   aged 24, dark
Walker, Elizabeth, aged 21, fair
Walker, Stephen, aged 35, fair
Wanklin or Vauchlin, Francis, 16, dark
Watkins, John, aged 21, carpenter,
   brown hair

Middlesex

Beesly, Thomas, brickmaker
   aged 21, fair
Burroughs, Mary, aged 22, black hair
Crady, John, aged 22, fair

Edwards, William, aged 19, dark
Ennis, Richard, wheelwright aged 20,
   dark
Flint, John, weaver aged 23, brown hair
Fullerton, Arthur, aged 19, dark
Gates, Jeremy als Peter, weaver
   aged 41, dark
Hargrave, Solomon, aged 21, fair
Harris, John, baker aged 25, dark
Hayes, Margaret (Mary), aged 30, dark
Knight, Elizabeth - died on passage
Martin, William, aged 20, dark
Moulton [Morton], Samuel, painter,
   aged 21, fair
Nicholls, Thomas, aged 22, weaver, fair
Nutt, Sarah, aged 22, brown hair,
   - 14 yrs
Richmond, Jane, aged 17, fair
Roberts, Jonathan, aged 28, fair
Rose, William, aged 31, husbandman,
   dark
Russell, Jonathan, aged 21,
   glass grinder, dark
Watson, Arthur, aged 69, dark
Williams, Thomas, aged 21, fair - 14 yrs

16

Northamptonshire

Brewin, Benjamin, aged 25, dark

Unidentified

Fitchgarrald, Margaret, aged 22, dark
Forster, Humphrey, aged 17, wigmaker,
  dark
Johnston, Charles, aged 20, fair
Linnett, Francis, aged 30, weaver, dark
Lynn, Elizabeth, aged 27, brown hair

Mortimer, Edward, aged 20, brown hair
Rix, James, aged 28, fair
Silver, Thomas, aged 23, husbandman,
  dark
Thomas, Joan, aged 25, fair
Thomas, William, aged 28, brown hair
Ward, Richard, aged 22,
  husbandman, fair
Watts, Thomas, aged 25,
  wig maker, fair
Williams, John, aged 57, grazier, dark

Felons transported from London by the *Alexander*, Capt. John King, in July 1723 and recorded at Annapolis in September 1723. (PRO: T53/30/340; LC).

Buckinghamshire

Busby, Joseph - died on passage
Davis, Samuel
Foulkes, James
Hewson, John
Morgan, Eliner
Pales, Edward
Snow, John
Tomlin, Thomas
Tomlin, William - 14 yrs

Essex

Clarkin alias Larkin, John
Green, Henry
Jackson alias Johnson, John - died
Lees, John
Page, Sarah - died

Hertfordshire

Allen, Nathaniel
Cope, John
Gearish, Thomas
Newton alias Duncombe, Richard
Shepard, William
Brick (Brisk), William
Bullen, Joseph
Cassell, Mary
Chandler, Mary - 14 yrs
Evans, Richard
Garraway, Jeremiah
Glassbrook, Samuel

Godson, Mary
Hackabout, Francis
Hobbs, Ann
Hurst, Philips
Jones, Humphrey
Lewis, Edward
Michaell, John
Noller, Elizabeth
Owen, Henry
Robinson, Elizabeth
Robinson, John
Slye, Thomas
Stewart, James
Thornton, Jane, alias Black Jenny
Washfield (Washford), James
Watts alias Watson, Thomas
Wells, Sarah - 14 yrs

Middlesex

Allen alias Totty, Frances
Allen alias Biggs, Joseph
Barlow, Ralph
Barlow, Solomon
Beckett, Robert
Bennett, Samuel - died on passage
Bissett, Mary
Bowes, Margaret
Bowman, Elizabeth
Burk alias Wellum, Jane
Chapman, John
Come, Richard
Drew, Isaac - died on passage
Dunn, Arthur (Henry)
Eastlick, Samuel

Gay, Anne
Grant, Sarah
Heath, James
Hicks, James
Howard, Martha
Humphryes, Thomas
Inon, Henry*
Jackson alias Waller, Mary
Jones, Humphrey
Jones, John
Jones, Winifred
Key, William
Lyon alias Lawrence, Benjamin
Mapp, John
Meredy, Mary
Minskipp, Thomas
Motherby, Charles
Parsons, William
Paul, Mary
Plant, Elizabeth
Porter, Martin
Salmon, Samuel
Smith, Elizabeth
Stephens, Roger
Steward, Elizabeth
Summerfield, William - 14 yrs
Swinburn, Richard*
Upson (Hopson), John
Usk alias Ulk, Samuel
Walker, Mary
Whetcomb, Sarah
White alias Blood, Catherine
Whitehall, John
Wilburn, Sarah

Sussex

Darby, John - died on passage
Dashwood, Richard - died on passage
Wickham, Thomas
Wise, Stephen

Surrey

Cramford, Mary
Dayly, Nathaniel
Dennis, Joseph
Douglass, William
Drumond, Robert
Dunce, John
Gerrard, Isaac
Jordan, George
Pewter, Samuel
Ricketts, John
Sparks, Alice
Sutton, Joseph
Symonds, William (John)
Templeman, Henry

Unidentified

Bennet, Samuel - died on passage
Breffit, Mary - died on passage
King, Mary
Newman, Elizabeth
Parker, John - died on passage
Porter, Martha
Smith, Thomas - died on passage
Swansby, Richard
Whiteborn, John
Whitley, Joseph - died on passage

*Not on LC

Felons transported from London to Virginia by the _Forward_, Capt. Daniel Russell, in October 1723. (PRO: T53/30/453).

Essex

Beechy alias Petchy, Elizabeth
Cooper, John
Fogg alias Trigg, John
Harper, Thomas
Hucks, Fouck
Towers, Jane
White, John

Hertfordshire

Carter, William - but pardoned
Digby, George
Mascall, John
Sawyer, Henry

Kent

Brown, Jane

Butler, Ann
Goodman alias Gudburne, Mark
Groves, Jane
Russell, Thomas
Trapnall, Simon
White alias Fearn, Mary
White, William
Winch, John

London

Collyer, Mary
Doyle, Elizabeth
Foot, Margaret
Frazier alias Revett, Jane
Freeman, John
Graham, Thomas
Ingram, Barbara
Myer, Samuel
Newport, Susanna
Piman, William
Simpson, John
Stretham, William
Trueman, Sarah
Swan, Thomas

Middlesex

Allen, Thomas
Aliastone, Mary
Anger, Elizabeth
Baker, Anne
Barraile, John
Bibby, Elizabeth
Bowen, William
Buckle, Elizabeth
Come, Richard
Cooley, John
Curtis, Katherine
Dearing, Hester
Devon, Martha
Drummer, Elizabeth
Gibson, William
Golding, Margaret
Golding, Thomas
Hall, Anne
Hickman, Elizabeth
Justice, Hugh
Lane, William
Leech, Anne
McDaniel, Mary
McGuinis, William

Pearse, William
Perry, Catherine
Pritchard, Edward
Serjeant, Susanna
Smith, William
Whalebone, John
Wright, John

Surrey

Beeby, Richard
Brown, Thomas
Carpenter, Susanna
Collett, John
Covill, John
Hancock, Richard
Hooker, John
Mills, Eleanor
Potter, William
Shakerly, Sampson
Sutcliffe, William - 14 yrs
Wall, John

Yorkshire

Askew, Anna
Austin, John
Barber, John
Best, Thomas
Britton, John - 14 yrs
Brown, Robert alias Glenton, John
Cook, Thomas
Cox, John - 14 yrs
Ellerthorpe, Richard
Ellis, Robert
Elsworth, Sarah
Foster, William
Gill, William
Hancock, Benjamin
Harrison, John
Hunt, Elizabeth
Illingworth, Israel
Ingham, Anne - 14 yrs
Laycock, Matthew
Mayes, Robert
Middlemore, William
Moor, John
Overen alias Overend, Stephen
Parker, John
Pickles, John
Robinson, George
Simpson, Henry

19

Sissons, John
Skelton, John - 14 yrs
Swan alias Richmond, William
Taite, William
Waddilove, Mary
Walker, William
Wallis, William alias Husband
Waterhouse, Thomas

Watson, Robert
Watson, William
Webster, Jonathan - 14 yrs
Weighill, James
Wetherell, George (James)
White, Richard
Wilson, John

Felons transported from London by the *Robert*, Capt. John Vickers, in July 1724 and registered at Annapolis in June 1725. (PRO: T53/31/255; CLRO 57.7.19).

Berkshire

Grout, Charles
Hughs, Andrew
Ricks, Sarah wife of William

Buckinghamshire

Baker, Thomas
Hawtrey, William* - 14 yrs
Holden, Ann - 14 yrs
Ingram, William - 14 yrs
Morgan, Edward
Priest, Abraham*
Priest, Daniel*
Randall, Nicholas

Essex

Biggs, Sarah
Burridge, John*
Hinchman, John
King alias Kingston, Charles
Paine, John alias Thomas
Pratt, William
Same, George*

Kent

Blanch alias Branch, John*
Bootts, Richard*
Gouldsmith, John
Hutton, Benjamin
Leath, John*
Medhurst, William
Page, Jonathan
Rogers, John
Williams, John

Leicestershire

Beaseley, Isaac

Northamptonshire

Tutin, Daniel
Wilson, Samuel

Nottinghamshire

Siddall, John

Shropshire

Wright, Joseph, alias Broadway, Robert

Staffordshire

Forrester, Elizabeth
Jones, Henry

Surrey

Applethorpe or Abthorpe, John
Bland, Sarah
Brady, Mary
Brimington, Mary
Dobson, Thomas*
Evans, Job
Franks, Elizabeth
Green, Elizabeth
Hincks, William
Holmes, Robert
Hudson, Jonathan
Hudson, Lewis
Hutton, Henry
Ingram, William*
Longford (Langford), Robert
Maynard, Anne

Roberts, Francis
Robinson (Robertson), Robert
Salter, Henry
Snell, Richard
Wallis, William
Warren, Peter
Wright, Mary

Sussex

Barnes, James

Worcestershire*

Jones, Thomas

Unidentified*

Aires, Gerrard
Blower, Martha
Mercer, Joseph
Page, John
Pearce, Daniel
Rakestraw, John
Scott, Burrade
Smith, James
Wilkinson, John

*Not on LC.

Felons transported from London by the *Forward*, Capt. Daniel Russell, in October 1724 and registered in Annapolis in June 1725. (PRO: T53/30/453; CLRO: Mss 57.7.20).

Bedfordshire

Franklin, Robert

Berkshire

Ricks, William - 14 yrs
Turner, Richard Jr.

Cambridgeshire

Laster, Benjamin

Derbyshire

Harper, Edward
Gibbins, Thomas
Maugham, Mary

Hertfordshire

Chapman, John
Jones, Edward
Wharton, Benjamin

Kent

Thomas, Edward
Updale, Elizabeth*
Ward, John

London

Beech, Sarah
Betty, Robert
Burnstone, Samuel
Busby, Christian
Hambleton, Robert
Hare, Thomas*
Jackson, Margaret
Jacobs, Simon*
Ketcher, Samuel
Leadbeater, Ann
Mead, John
Montear (Mountain), Martha
Morris, Elizabeth*
Smith, Abraham
Smith alias Ashburn, Joseph
Southernwood, Anne
Sympson, Mary
Thorpe, Henry
Vantear, John

Middlesex

Aldesea, Stephen*
Allison alias Cotsworth, Miles
Armitage (Hermitage), Mary
Badcock, John
Ball, John*
Bellam, Elizabeth
Bishop, Thomas

21

Bradshaw (Brensher), William
Brown, John
Browne, Martha
Bunn, Diana (Durance)
Burk (Buck), Leonard
Candy alias Powell, Elizabeth
Chapman, Thomas
Clark, Mary
Clay, Anne*
Clinton, Valentine
Collins, Faith
Collyer, Mary
Coulson, Chester
Cowley alias Curtis, Mary*
Crafts, Ralph
Doeman (Doleman), Thomas
Dowler, Anne
Drake, Elizabeth
Duffey, Alice
Duty, Matthew
Eaton alias Layton, Paul
Eeles, Mary*
Francis, Elizabeth
Garrett, Mary
Hall, Norris
Hall, William
Harris, Mary
Hawkins, Thomas
Henly, Hannah
Hill alias Hilliard, Mary
Hudson (Hodson) alias Thickhead,
    William
Hutchins, Robert
Jackson, James
Jeffryes, Christian
Johnson, Samuel
Jones, Hannah
Lacks alias Locks, Mary
Lamb, Anthony
Lee, Susanna
Lees alias Hippworth, Mary*
Lock, William alias John
Man, Henry
Mobbs, Thomas
Montross, Francis (John)
Morgan, William
Mould (Moales), William
Newborne (Newbold), James
Pain (Pen), Hannah
Pew, Anne
Poinctain, John
Probert, Alice

Rainsbury, Mary
Reeves, Thomas
Rumsey, John
Russell, Susanna
Sharlow, Elizabeth
Shepherd, Thomas
Shettle, Mahaleel
Sparkes, John
Spicer, Robert
Stewart, James, alias Emerson, Francis
Todd, Thomas
Vicary, Mary
Wakeling, Elizabeth
Watkins, Griffith
Wetherell, Francis
Wilkins, Joseph
Williams, Elizabeth
Wilson, Anne
Wilson, John
Winter (Winton), Thomas
Wynne, Bacon

Oxfordshire

Davenport, Thomas - 14 yrs
Lipscombe, Stephen*
Metham, Margaret
Pickett (Pigitt), William - 14 yrs
Wicks, Edward - 14 yrs

Surrey

Butcher, James
Davies alias Hope, Elizabeth
Dudbridge, Richard*
Edwards, William
Hirst, Jonathan
How, James
Murgatroyd, Elizabeth

Unidentified

Connaway, Solomon
Durham, Stephen
Farquhar, Alexander
Firbuck, John
Gorsuch, John
Griffin, John
Harris, Oughton
Hodges, Richard
Johnson, John
Lardner, Thomas

Latham, Priscilla
Martin, John
Ringrose, Moses

Roberts, Ann
Salter, John
Strawbridge, Richard

*Not on LC.

Felons transported from Lyme Regis by the *Martha*, Capt. William Read, and registered in Potomack, Virginia, in December 1724. (Certificate in Dorset Records Office & Western Circuit Calendars).

Devon

Butcher, John
Middleton, John
Middleton, Richard

Devon

Butcher, John
Middleton, John
Middleton, Richard

Dorset

Cass, Thomas
Ellis, Walter
Crandon, Abraham

Odford, Thomas

Somerset

Brown, John
Ellis, Roger
Pool, Robert
Trott, John

Wiltshire

Carter, Henry
Gale, John
Martin, John
Petty, Thomas
Pinchen, Francis
Silcox, Susan

Felons transported from London by the *Rappahannock Merchant***, Capt. John Jones, in December 1724 and registered* in Rappahannock, Virginia, in April 1725. (PRO: T53/31/376; CLRO: Mss 57.7.18).

London

Atkinson, John
Baker, Benjamin
Barnett, Robert, alias Lawrence, John
Branch, Ann
Breedon, Elizabeth - 14 yrs
Brittain, John
Bucknell, William
Burroughs, Amy
Cheesman, Robert
Crofts, Alice
Draper, Robert
Dyer, Stephen
Ealing, John
East, Samuel - 14 yrs
Edmonds, Jeremiah
Edwards, Edward(2)
Ellicks, John

Fielding, Willoughby
Fowles, Stephen - 14 yrs
Francis, William
Grove, William - 14 yrs
Hardey, Elizabeth
Hawks, Mary
Hughes, Sarah
Hutchinson, Daniel
Jackson, Eleanor
Jones, William
Killmister, Mary
Martin, Jane - 14 yrs
McDonald, Sarah
Newport, John
Nocks, Catherine - 14 yrs
Noon, Mary
Owsman, Moses - 14 yrs
Page, William
Ramsey, Hannah

Ryder, John
Smith, Luke
Smith, William
Starling, Sarah
Stephens, Elizabeth
Thompson, Dorothy
Ure, John
Vanderhurst, John
Vaughan, James
Watson, Isaac
Whitebourn, John - 14 yrs
Williams, John (2)
Windram, John - 14 yrs
Yeo, John
Zeanell, Phillip

Lincolnshire

Bradley, Thomas - died
Burret, Thomas - died
Read, Ely
Shaplin, William - died

Middlesex

Allison, Mary wife of Miles
Blewitt, William - 14 yrs
Bonner, John - 14 yrs

Brown, William
Bruffe alias Browse, Thomas - 14 yrs
Burgess, Peter
Clerk, Isaac
Colethorpe, Robert
Collins, James
Dawson, Sarah
Doyley, Timothy
Gibbons, Samuel - 14 yrs
Harvey, William
Hide, Joseph - 14 yrs
Hutchings, Susanna - 14 yrs
Jacques, Frances
Jones, Mary
Kenear, David
Lazenby, Thomas
Martin alias Lewen, John
Montgomery, Ester
Moreby, Richard
Sands, Frances - 14 yrs
Slate, Frances
Smith, Elizabeth (2)
Taylor, John
Watson, Joseph
Wild, John - 14 yrs
Wilkinson, Richard
Wynne, Richard - 14 yrs

*but stating only that 94 convicts were aboard of whom 84 were landed.
**Capt. Jones died of smallpox when his ship reached Falmouth: 38 convicts died
on passage. (PRO: C11/1223/28).

**Felons transported from London in April 1725 by the *Sukey*, Capt Atkins Coultis
(but formerly John Ellis who died on passage), and registered at Annapolis in July
1725.** (PRO: T53/32/93; CLRO Mss 57.7.21)

Berkshire

Armstrong, Solomon
Church, Henry - died on passage
Robinson, Joseph - 14 yrs
Turner, Edward - 14 yrs - died
Watkins, John

Buckinghamshire

Chilcott, John - 14 yrs
Cottoway, Thomas
Peirce, William

Cambridgeshire

Gilson, Jeremiah - 14 yrs
Holdsworth, John - 14 yrs

Essex

Andrews, Aaron - died on passage
Field, John - died on passage
Moses, Thomas - died on passage
Ralph, John - died on passage
Seward, Samuel
Lenox alias Smith, Mary
Searle, George

Huntingdonshire

Warden, Thomas - 14 yrs - died

Kent

Brewer, John
Cartwright, Elizabeth
Leeds, Ann
Lombart, John - died on passage
Lovegrove, John
Mann, William
Mason, Robert
Pepper, Thomas
Tomlin, William

Middlesex

Allington, Anne - died on passage
Allis alias Hall, Margaret
Bacon, Mary
Baker, Susanna
Bowler, John
Brooks, Samuel
Burge, Thomas
Burroughs alias Burrus, Sarah
Burton, Abraham
Butler, Thomas
Butler, William
Charleton, Thomas
Cole, Robert
Dixey, Richard
Drake, Daniel
Dumount, Anthony
Dunt, Mary
Dyson alias Dickson, Edward
Edwards alias Casey, Elizabeth
Fann, Susanna wife of John
Fitzhitt, Margaret
Fleetwood alias Piper, Jane
Fox, George
Gascoine, Sarah
Glynn, Henry
Gold alias Beadle, John
Golding, Richard
Gordon, Charles
Hanns, Thomas
Harper, Philip
Harvey, Mary wife of Thomas
Herring, Michael
Hilliard, Mary
Holford, Thomas

Jenks, Mary - died on passage
Johnson, Joseph
Johnson, Thomas
Jones, Anne
Kenly, Arthur
Lewis, John
Lewis, William
Linneke, Anne Mary
Martin, Elizabeth
McGey, Thomas
Miers, Sarah
Morris, Bartholomew
Nicholls, William
Palmer, Thomas
Parsons, Elizabeth
Pearce, Jane
Pearce, Robert
Phillips, James - died on passage
Phillips, William
Pickton, John
Pope, John
Powell, Elizabeth
Purchase, George
Quinn, Edward
Randall, John
Roberts, Margaret
Sadd, William
Saunders, John
Scott, Edward
Scott alias Holden, Elizabeth
Scurrier, Richard
Seymour, William
Shaw, Samuel
Shepherd, Thomas
Stephens, Mary wife of John
Stillita, Jane
Symonds, Hannah
Thomas, Richard
Tibbs, John
Troale, Anne
Turner, Thomas
Vaughan, John
Walker, Hugh
Watts, Jane
White, Elizabeth
Winston, Thomas
Wood, Elizabeth

Monmouthshire

Barnes alias Price alias Carne, William

Surrey

Abbis, Edward
Cliff (Clifts), Mathew
Davis, Thomas
Elisha (Elliston), Joseph
Foy, Margaret
Mason, Henry
Roberts, John
Siddale (Sidwell), Richard
Slates, William
Tayler, Richard
Wood, Grace
Woodward, John

Sussex

Bradley, Thomas
Goldham, Mary
Jones, John
Leggett, John - died on passage
Parker, Thomas - died on passage
Richardson, Thomas - died

Unidentified

Aaron, Moses - died on passage
Basse, John
Bawn, Mary
Burges, William
Cattoway, Thomas
Cole, John - died on passage
Daniell alias Disnell, John
Ferrill, Ann
Hillaton, Jane
Lambeth, John - died on passage
Mair, William
Nicholson, John - died on passage
Paxton, Daniel
Peach, William - died on passage
Purie, William
Radish, Alse - died on passage
Rich, Henry
Shaw, William - died on psaage
Sulch, John - died on passage
Taylor, Thomas - died on passage
Walterton, James

Felons transported from London by the *Forward*, Capt. Daniel Russell, in September 1725 and registered at Annapolis in June 1726. (PRO: T53/32/219; CLRO Mss 57.7.22).

Cumberland

Harrison, William

Derbyshire

Harper, Edward
Maugham, Mary

London

Armitage (Hermitage), Thomas
Badger, Charles
Bagford, John
Barrance, James
Belcher, George
Bennet, Catherine
Best, John
Blake, Penelope*
Blake, Jane
Broadstreet, John
Cartwright, Peter
Childs, Elizabeth
Claxton, John*

Cole, William
Davis, Edward
Dickenson, David*
Elliot, Edward
English, George
Gandy, Elizabeth
Green, John*
Halfpenny, Robert
Harney, Edward (Harley, Edmond)
Harwood alias Churchman, Ann
Henley, Hannah
Hobbs, John
Hull, Samuel
Hullman (Hollaway), Isaac
Hussey, Ann
James, Harris
Knight, Sarah
Lane, Benjamin
Large, Philip
Larkin, John
Lemon, John
Macclesfield (Manfield), Thomas
Madren, Mary
Miller, Mary

Moor, Elizabeth
Moulson, Robert
Paul, Rawson
Rayner (Reighner), Sarah
Savage alias Bailey, Mary
Short, John
Southall (Southern), Solomon
Springthorp, Ruth
Stainbank, William
Stevens, John
Tongue, John
Wade, Henry
Warner, Elizabeth
Webster, Thomas
Wells or Weales, Mariah
White, Elizabeth - 14 yrs
Williams, Thomas

Middlesex

Aberdeen, Nicholas
Allen, Hanna wife of John
Barlow alias Murphy, Elizabeth
Beacham (Beachman), John
Beales, William
Belchier alias Kempster alias Fowell,
    Susanna - 14 yrs *
Bennett alias Tipping, Mary
Beule, Thomas
Bevan, Philip*
Blackman, Robert*
Brace, Mary wife of John
Brathwait, Martha*
Burton, James
Champaigne, Nicholas
Clancey alias Clarke, William
Clarke, James
Collins, Samuel
Covington, Peter
Daniel alias Acres, Hannah wife of
    John Acres
Dickson, Edward
Dixon, Anne
Dorrell, Catherine*
England, John
Fullifull (Followfield), John
Gainer, Magdalene
Gill, George
Glover, Elizabeth
Goodwin, William
Hall, Thomas

Hancock, John
Harrison, Joseph
Harrison, Thomas*
Heath, Robert
Heaton alias Hall, Elizabeth
Henley, Rebecca
Herring, James
Hetherington, Walter
Jacobs, Simon alias Guest, Joseph
Johnson alias Thompson, James*
Jones, Edward (QS)
Kelley, Richard
Le Count, David
Lee, Joseph
Marshall, Edward
Martin, Robert
Mathews, Mary*
Mead, Martha
Miles, John
Morgan, Elizabeth
Mullicken, Robert
Norton, Hannah
Ogden, Joanna*
Paris, Jane
Partridge, Sarah*
Pearce, Mary
Pimble, Sarah*
Powell, Elizabeth*
Price alias Wright, Anne
Rawlins, Thomas
Richardson, Mary
Roberts, Margaret
Silkwood, Margaret - 14 yrs
Smith, Jophenix*
Spurrier alias Hall, Elizabeth
Stevens, William
Stewart, James alias Emerson, Francis*
Temple, Mary wife of John
Thetford, Edward
Walker, Anne
Walker, Elizabeth
Wall, Mary
White, John*
Wilks alias Peisley, Thomas
Wood, Jane
Wright, Elizabeth

Nottinghamshire

Booth, George

Unidentified

Burrage, Richard
Griffin, Richard
Howard, William

Hustus, Morris
Jeavon, William
Manning, Samuel
Ray, William
Rosomond, John

*Not included in LC but possibly amongst the ten (unnamed) who died on passage.

Felons transported from London to Virginia by the *Rappahannock Merchant*, Capt. Charles Whale, in November 1725 and registered in Port Rappahannock in August 1726. (PRO: T53/32/220; CLRO Mss 57.8.24 & 25).

Essex

Hackett, Charles
Sharp alias Sharper, William.

Hertfordshire

Holden, Robert - died on passage
How, Joseph - died on passage
Orton, John - died on passage

Kent

Cannabe, Robert - died on passage
Elms, Edward*
Hawkins, William
Horn, Mary
Jarrett, Robert - died on passage
McKley alias McKny, William
 - died on passage
Smith, Thomas*
Smith, William
Symonds, John - died on passage

Leicestershire

White, William

Lincolnshire

Barrett, Thomas
Bradley, Thomas
Chapman, Thomas
Drury, Robert
Hill, Luke
Howard, Stephen
Lilley, Samuel
Pendal, John
Steward, Stephen Jr. - died
Taylor, William

Woodhouse, John - died on passage

London

Adams, Richard
Day, John
Fergusson, James
Gearing, Thomas
Gibbons, William
Gray, Sarah
Gray, William - 14 yrs
Green, George - died on passage
Hicks, Thomas
Hughes alias Giller, Ann
Isaacson , Susan
Longmire, William - 14 yrs
Mann, John
Page, Robert
Plant (Platt), John - 14 yrs
Revell, John
Russell alias Brown, Elizabeth - 14 yrs
Steel , John - 14 yrs
Webb, Nicholas - died on passage

Middlesex

Cooe, Rachael - died on passage
Cotton, Margaret
Cuzee alias McKecky, Joseph
Doyle, Elizabeth
Evans, Winifred - died on passage
Hand, Philip
Hanshaw alias Fanshaw, Sibilla
 - died on passage
Harvey, Thomas*
Herbert, Thomas
Hide, Joseph
Holmes, James
Hughes, John
James alias Bainton, Esther - died

Jefferson, Henry
Johnson, Lawrence - died
Kiffe, Robert
Lloyd, John - 14 yrs
Martin, William - 14 yrs - died
Moor, William - died on passage
Pain, Anne
Pattison, Jane - died on passage
Sculthorpe, John
Serjeant, Robert - died on passage
Sharpe, Elias
Stevens, Mary
Swainson, Rowland - 14 yrs - died
Tongison (Tonkinson), Mary
Turner, Joseph*
Warren, Alexander
Wilks, Edward - died on passage
Williams, Isabella* - 14 yrs

Northamptonshire

Burnam, Samuel - died on passage
Haynes, Richard - died on passage

Suffolk

Norman, John - died on passage

Surrey

Andrews, Thomas
Boram, Mary - died on passage
Dunce, John

Dunkin, Joseph - died on passage
Edwards, William
Gray alias Walter, Mary
Hargrave, Isaac
Holt, Sarah
Kempstock, John
McDowgall, John. - died on passage
Randall, John
Salter, Mary
Smith, Hannah
Smith, Thomas - died on passage
Stringer, Mary

Unidentified

Adams, Edward
Bush, James - died on passage
Church, Robert - died on passage
Finch, Samuel - died on passage
Fisher, John
Fisher, William - died on passage
Franklin, Thomas
Mills, William
Parker, John - died on passage
Rainbow, Robert - died on passage
Riddle, Richard (Robert) - 14 yrs
Shand, Philip
Shaplin, William - died on passage
Stavey, William
Walker, Andrew - died on passage
Wilkinson, Joseph - died on passage
Williams, Elizabeth

*Not found on LC.

Felons transported from London by the *Supply*, Capt. John Rendell, in February 1726 and registered at Annapolis in May 1726. (PRO: T53/32/383; CLRO Mss 57.8.23).

Kent

Elsom, Robert
Leake, James
Smith, William

London

Axford, Elizabeth
Bennett, Mary
Bennet, William
Bowers, Ann

Brooks, William
Dent, Hainsworth
Dunstar, Katherine
Elliott, Christopher
Fielder, John
Gordon, John
Harrison, Thomas
Harrop, Thomas
Howard, John
Love, Thomas
Loveringham, Richard
Marshall, Robert

Marshall, Thomas
Miles, John
Moore, William - 14 yrs
Oddy, Francis
Pert, Ann
Pew, Margaret
Pinn, William
Shales als Bayley, John
Shepherd, Margaret
Ward, William

Middlesex

Apton, Samuel alias Slim John
Astell, Mary
Baron, Anne
Boswell alias Ward, Mary
Brown, Thomas
Butler, Jane
Carter, John
Chandler, Elizabeth
Collins, Robert
Coston, Hannah wife of John
Darby, John, alias MacDiamod, Owen*
Dearing, Redmond
Elwood, John
Felles, John
Fielder, Sarah*
Foden, Richard
Fowell, Martha
Freeman, Daniel
Gilbert, Samuel
Gladwin, Moses - 14 yrs
Goulding, Elizabeth - 14 yrs
Grace, Edward
Hall, Anne - 14 yrs
Hall, Isabella
Heachstone, William
Henderson, Elizabeth
Holman, John
Horne, Thomas
Hudson, Elizabeth, alias Combot,
   wife of John
Jones, Henry

Jones, William
Leigh, Edward
Leighton, Agnes
Leighton, Richard
Lestrange, Thomas
Lewis, Anne
Matthews, Mary
Moses, Benjamin
Noble, Phyllis
Oney alias Honey, John
Peirson, Rachel
Plowman, Mary
Randall, Thomas
Richards, Mary
Rogers, William
Shoebridge, John
Smith, John
Stringer, John
Sturges, William.*
Taylor, Joseph
Williams, Richard
Wright, John

Yorkshire

Aaron alias Claron, Thomas
Ashburn, Mary
Ashford, Elizabeth
Atkinson, John (QS)
Baker, John (QS)
Birkenshaw, Joyce wife of Nicholas
   (QS)
Blakey, William
Burrough, Anthony
Easterby, Elizabeth (QS)
Gunson alias Harrison, Mary
Harwood, John
Hogan, Thomas
Illingworth, Jonathan (QS)
Jagger, Benjamin (QS)
Jenkins, William (QS)
Mortimer alias Morteman, Edward (QS)
Williamson, Thomas (QS)

*Not on LC

30

Felons transported from London by the *Loyal Margaret*, Capt. John Wheaton, in June 1726 and registered at Annapolis in December 1726. (PRO: T53/32/386; CLRO Mss 57.8.26).

Derbyshire

Williamson, James

Kent

Carrington, Alice
Colebrooke, Samuel - died
Flood, William
Harrison, Henry - died on passage
Powell, Thomas
Terrett, Catherine

Middlesex

Ambrose, Ann
Anderson, Thomas
Atkins, Charles
Atkinson, Thomas
Ayres, Jeremy*
Bignall, Rebecca
Bledall, William*
Boswell (Bowell), John
Butler, Ann, alias Jones, Margaret
Campbell alias Toms, Christiana
Carpenter, John
Cartwright, Thomas*
Charlton, Josiah
Clark, Thomas
Cluff, Hannah
Coxhead, Mary
Dobson, Francis
Ellwood alias Bable, Ann* - 14 yrs
Farrall, Bridget
Farrell, John - died on passage
Fleetwood, Thomas
Fletcher, Elizabeth
Fox, Sarah
Grimes (Gaines), John
Hall, Mary - died on passage
Harris, Isabella
Hastings, Katherine
Hatton, John
Hopkins, James
Howard, Ann*
Hutchings (Hutchingson), Sarah
Keeble, William
Kennedy, John

Keys, Miriam
Lawrence, William
Loveday, Mary
McGee, John
McLane, Ann*
Mills, John
Molineaux, Jonathan
Moreton, William
Munn, William - died on passage
O'Conner, Philip Charles - died
Orchard, John
Phillips alias Brown, Mary,
  alias Dennis, Catherine
Plowright, Mary
Powell alias Tutcher, Thomas
Read, Rebecca
Roberts, James
Robinson (Robertson), John
Rositor, John
Shepherd, Elizabeth, alias Penny,
  Hannah, alias Edgware Bess.
Simkins, Edward
Slider, Mary
Smith alias Clark, William*
Stanley, Temperance
Stewart, James
Swetman, John - died on passage
Thompson, Judith*
Thompson, William*
Trigger, Mary - 14 yrs - died
Trueboy, Richard*
Tyler, Mary
Walker, Joseph
Walker, Priscilla
Watson, William
White, George
Williams, Tudor
Young, Nathaniel

Staffordshire

Gosling, John - 14 yrs - died
Load, John - 14 yrs - died
Robinson, Mary (QS) - died
Ward, Esther (QS)

31

Unidentified

Blake, William
Brock, Samuel - died on passage
Cartwright, James - died on passage
Clark, William
Coal, Mary - died on psaage
Cooke, Judith
Earos, Jeremiah
Floyd, William

Hoskins, Catherine
Howard, Christian
Hughes, Christopher
Jenkins, Edward
McClain, Jane
Miles, John
Newman, John - died on passage
Penny, Hannah - died on passage
Thomas, William
Zachery, Ann

*Not on LC

Felons transported from London to Virginia by the *Forward*, Capt. Daniel Russell, in October 1726. (PRO: T53/33/294).

Buckinghamshire

Billingsley, Francis
Gibbs, Richard
Paine, Thomas
Smith, William
Tabellier, Lewis
Towers, Richard

Essex

Boyce, John
Brown, Thomas
Daniel, William
Dickinson, James
Doe, John
Howard, James
Knight, William
Peates, William
Radley, George
Rusted, Robert
Serjeant, William
Smith, John
Steward, Charles
Wilks, Emanuel
Wilks, Henry

Hertfordshire

Amis, Richard
Barker, Henry
Copps, James
Godman, Edward
Hicks, Henry
Rook, William

Kent

Brinton, Benjamin
Hughes, John
McGregor, Robert
Nicholls, Henry
Stanton, John

London

Arnold, Christian
Ayres, Elizabeth
Bird, Francis
Bird, Thomas
Bishop, Elizabeth
Blewett alias Bowler alias Dixon, Mary
Brewer, Henry
Buckingham, Ann
Burrows, John
Cater, Mary
Davis, Ann
Edginton alias Edgerton, John
Gudgeon, Abraham
Harrison, John
Higginbottom, Richard
Hobbs, Sara
Holmes, John
Hughes, Isabella
Jackson, John
Jeffs, Mary
Kates alias States, Francis
Lawson alias Turner, Sara
Legg, James
Newmarsh, Jonathan
Palley, John
Phoenix, Walter

32

Plowman, William
Price, Edward
Raven, George
Scuffam, Mary - 14 yrs
Spurling, Mary
Temple, John
Todd, Disney - 14 yrs
Treen, Joseph - 14 yrs
Turner, George - 14 yrs
Turner, Stephen
Vye, Henry - 14 yrs
Williams, Mary
Wilson, Joseph

Middlesex

Akres alias Aires, Thomas
Anderson, John
Arnold alias Onyon, Catherine
Boswell, Edward
Brittain alias Bradshaw, Ann
Chambers, Stephen
Clarke, Elizabeth
Coker alias Cowen, Jane
Cotes, Mary wife of George
Darban, Sarah
Deal alias Dean, John
Dun, John
Flower, William
Heppard, William
Hill, Robert
Hopkins, James
Hudson, Sarah
Hutchins, John - 14 yrs
Ives, Joanna
Johnson alias Cabbige, Samuel
Kind, Thomas
Lane, Hannah wife of Edward
Lewen, Abraham
Luckey, Isabella
Lyndsey, Jane
Mackdonnale, Patrick

Marvel, Mary
Morgan, Robert
Neves, Thomas
Piner, Thomas
Quesnell, Magdalen
Rivers, Elizabeth
Robinson, Margaret
Rymes, William
Simonds, Margaret
Still, William - 14 yrs
Tool, Christian
Turner, Elizabeth
Vanderancker, Elizabeth
Venham, Philip
West, Thomas - 14 yrs
Williams, Mary
Wright, John

Surrey

Bryan, Elizabeth
Byham, Ann
Dean, John
Edward, Robert
Griffith, Mary
Harris, John
Hodgkins, Edward
Marshall, Richard
McQueen, Sarah
Moody, Charles
Price alias Cock-Her-Plump, Sarah
Steere, Daniel
Todd, William
Wainman alias Swainman, Lawrence

Sussex

Bates, John
Bayly, Thomas
Jones, John
Osburn, John

Felons transported from London to Maryland by the *Rappahannock Merchant*, Capt. Charles Whale, in March 1727. (PRO: T53/33/296).

London

Arter, Jane
Ashcomb, John
Best, Andrew
Bond, Phillip

Broom alias Brown, John
Cook, Farmer
Cope, Robert
Crisp, Edward
Dawson, William
Field, Elizabeth - 14 yrs

Forbes, James
Gold, Mary
Green alias Rowling, Ann - 14 yrs
Hambleton, Arthur
Hastings, John
Hewood, Joseph
Hill, Thomas
Huggins alias Votier, Elizabeth - 14 yrs
Hussey, Mary
Joseph, Isaac
Loyd, John
May, Samuel
Mayhew, John
Moses alias Fotherby, Susan
Plumbly, Matthew
Roberts, Sarah
Rose, John
Rushfield, Joseph
Salmon, Rowland
Shaw, George
Taylor alias Harwood, Margaret
Vernham, Albert
Whitaker, Thomas
Williams, Martha

Middlesex

Anderson, Michael.
Arnold, Richard.
Ashmore, Elizabeth
Barton, Elizabeth
Bayes, William
Bracley, Mary
Brewell, Susan
Bryant, Richard
Carteen, Charles
Castle, Sarah

Clark, Mary
Condron, James
Coram, William
Dennis, Jane
Douglas, John
Drew, Martha
Edwards, Thomas
Eyres, Joseph
Flaningham, Judith
Folks, John
Gane, John
Hill, John
Hopkins, Elizabeth
Huntley, Ann
Johnson, Elizabeth
Jolly, Mary
Jones, Sarah
Joshua, Levi
Lane, Ann
Linny alias Groves, Sarah.
Marwood, Jonas
Mason, Patrick
Mathews, Ann
Mutes, Mary
Oliver, Mary
Pennard, Sarah
Phipps, John - 14 yrs
Pinfold alias Perkins, George
Roberts, William
Rose, George
Spawford, Mary
Tate, George
Travers, Elizabeth
Wall, Luke
West, John
West, William
Williams, James

Felons transported from London to Virginia by the *Susanna*, Capt. John Vickers, in July 1727. (PRO : T53/33/364).

Buckinghamshire

Burroughs, Thomas
Eyre, Thomas
Holdsworth, Robert
Martin, Joseph
Monford, Thomas
Swaine, Richard
Turpin, Thomas
Wilson, Stephen

Essex

Clifford, John
Dines, Isaac
Noble, Mark
Yates, John

Hertfordshire

Hungate, Charles
Randall, Thomas

Kent

Bell, Mary
Brooker, John
Harper, Katherine
Holbrooke, Francis
Loyd, Jane
Simpson, Jane
Smith, John
Wakefield, Thomas
Wells, Joseph

London

Ball alias Brawden alias Swift,
Elizabeth.
Billcox, Thomas.
Boucher, John - 14 yrs
Brooks, Elizabeth
Broom alias Brown, John
Combe, John
Evans, John
Ford, Bowyer
Harris, John
Perrin, Thomas
Ransford, John
Read, William
Sherlock, Simon
Spawfoot, William
Wilson alias Smith, John
Wise, Susanna

Middlesex

Allen, Elizabeth
Ashton alias Hamilton, John
Baccus, Thomas
Beddo, William
Blakes alias Colhoun, John
Bosley, William
Bradshaw alias Bradyer, Rose
Britchford, John
Browne, Mary
Caper, William
Clark alias Forton, Mary
Crafter, William
Crouch, Sarah
Eades, Jane
Fretts, Mary
Gane, John
Gardner, Henry
Godfrey, John

Green, Crispin
Green, Robert
Herbert, Elizabeth
Hewitt, Rachell
Hicks, Thomas
Holland alias Priest, Mary
Hudson, Thomas
Hughes, Mary
Jenkins, Thomas
Jordan, Ann
Kennett, George
King, Margaret
King, James
Laughland, Joseph
Layton, Paul
Luck, Catherine
Luck, Mary
Manning, Margaret
McMillen, William
Mead, Margaret
Modesty, Thomas
Norwood, Richard
Parry, Ann
Platt, Elizabeth
Prickle, Richard
Rashfield, Jacob
Rawlins, Charles
Rook alias Palmer, Ann
Rose, Richard
Ryder, Robert
Ryley, George
Smith, George
Somes, Thomas
Spires, Deborah
Starkey, George
Strong, James
Stubbings, John
Tattershell, James
Vines, Mary
Ward, John
White, Sarah

Surrey

Carrell, William
Cock, Ann
Esling, Samuel
Gollidge alias Shute, Mary
Kirk alias Oakley, Sarah
Knowler, Shelwin
Randall, Thomas

Stafford alias Page alias Terry,
  Elizabeth
Stevens, Robert
Threed, William

Sussex

Adams, Thomas
Cornwell alias Cockham, Mary
Vager, George

Felons transported from London by the *Forward*, Capt. William Loney, in October 1727 and registered in Rappahannock River, Virginia, in May 1728. (London & Middlesex Bonds; CLRO Mss 57.8.28).

London

Barrett, Ann
Beaton, Robert
Berry, Thomas
Cromey, Jane - 14 yrs
Eades, Roger
Fordham, Edward
Hoskins, Thomas
Joseph, Jacob
Lewis, Anne*
Marjoram, William - 14 yrs
Martin, Richard
Morgan, John - 14 yrs
Satterfield, Sarah (Elizabeth) - 14 yrs
Steward, James*
Wade alias Boucher, Elizabeth - 14 yrs
Wagstaff, William
Welch, James - 14 yrs

Middlesex

Atkinson, Joseph - 14 yrs
Brooks, Robert
Carballo, Jacob
Carr, Abraham
Cross, Arthur
Davis, Thomas
Gilbert, Elizabeth - 14 yrs
Green, Lawrence
Hardy, Matthew
Hawkins, Mary
Haybarn, Isaac
Herbert, Richard
Jones, Alexander
Jones, Mary
Lloyd, Elizabeth
Lucas, Elizabeth wife of Abraham
May, Thomas
Morris, Thomas - 14 yrs
Nalfing, Philip
Norton, Richard

Nugent, Edward
Pearsey, Henry
Pratt, John - 14 yrs
Read, Benjamin
Reynolds, Mary
Richardson, Mary
Rowland, Edward - 14 yrs
Senior, Jane - 14 yrs
Sherlock, Silvia - 14 yrs
Smith, Jeremiah
Smith alias Randall, Mary - 14 yrs
Stokes (Stocks), Margaret
  wife of Richard
Swiselman, Ernest - 14 yrs
Whittingham, Samuel
Wight, Samuel
Williams alias Newell, Sarah - 14 yrs

Northamptonshire

Driver, John

Nottinghamshire

Ingman (Ingram), Grace
Norman, William - 14 yrs

Surrey

Meedy, Joseph*
Milliner, Anne*
Worrall, Thomas

Sussex

Bates, John

Unidentified

Birch alias Appleby alias Minsall,
  Anne*
Blunt, John

Castell, William
Connell, William
Coop(er), Arthur
Coxon, Edward
Crosby, Mary
Dodd, John
Fletcher, Charles
Freeman, John

Griffen, Joseph
Jenkins, Anne
Lee, William*
Lewis, Jane
Luff, John
Merser, Robert
Ratifie, William

*Not found on LC; twenty-seven felons died on passage.

Felons transported from London to America [by the *Oak*?], Capt. William Williams, in December 1727. (London & Middlesex Bonds).

London

Adamson, Walter
Bayne, James
Brooks, Jane
Davis, William
Evans, Elizabeth
Fry. Patience
Haddon, Thomas
Hatton, Matthew
Hutson, Daniel
Jerman, Hugh
Mew, Rachel
Moss, Christopher
Salkeld, Thomas
Whitington, Edmund
Wise, Susanna

Middlesex

Ansees alias Ansells, Hugh
Avis, James alias Mitchell, John
Baker, John
Banion, William
Barrett, Anne
Bourn, James
Browne, Grace - 14 yrs

Bruce, Rosamond
Coix, Susannah
Dove, Mary
Drawood, Robert
Durley, William
Fry, William
Glover, Sarah
Hague, Mary
Howard, William
Jenkins, Joseph
Mitchell, James
Percivall alias Howse, Joseph
Redman, Letitia
Reynolds, John
Richards, Elizabeth
Robinson, Margery
Rudd, John
Shard, Emanuel
Smith, Mary
Smith, Thomas
Stanton, Anne
Symonds, Peter
Thomas, Diana
Turner, Anne
Wakefield, Mary
Walley alias Wainscott, Richard
Wilson, John

Felons transported from London by the *Elizabeth*, Capt. William Whitethorne, in June 1728 and registered in Port South Potomack, Virginia, in August 1729. (PRO: T53/34/154; CLRO Mss 57.8.30).

Berkshire

Card, Charles
Colman, William
Dereham, William
Matthews, John - 14 yrs

Millind, John
Newington alias Bowen alias Reed,
  Sarah
Ward, William

Buckinghamshire

Langston, Henry

Essex

Dawson, Nicholas
Flower, Joseph
Maine, John*
Thimbleby, Samuel*

Hertfordshire

Folkner, Richard
Hawkins, William
Sibthorpe, John

Kent

Rodan, Martha
Walbrook, Thomas*

London

Adcock, Thomas
Amos, Josiah
Atkins, William
Bannister, William
Barrett, William
Beadle, Anthony - 14 yrs
Bloxham, Joseph
Broster, Susan
Bryan (Bryant), Catharine
Burton, Sarah
Buxton (Boyton), Elizabeth
Currant alias Chadwick, Elizabeth
Dawson, Mary
Deane, Mary
Drew, Jonathan
Field, Elizabeth
Fletcher, Ambrose - 14 yrs
Ford, Thomas
Fowler, Mary
Fuller, William
Harris, John
Howard, Thomas
Jackson, Samuel
Jenkins, Mary
Johnson, Joseph
Lawrence, Philip
Lewis, Mary
Lucas, Peter

Lucas, William
Mason, Thomas*
Mountague, Margaret
Ord, Dorothy - 14 yrs
Pidgeon, John
Pitcher, Edward
Price, John
Ramsay, Robert
Salter, John*
Saunders, George
Shann, William - 14 yrs
Stewart, John
Watkins, Elizabeth
Wilson, William
Winnick, Elizabeth
Wood, Jane
Yellop, Thomas

Leicestershire

Serjeant, Hugh

Middlesex

Anderson, David
Applebey, Robert
Bailey, William
Barnes, James
Bartlett, Thomas, alias Wheatley, Henry
Beale, John
Boardrey, Paul
Boston, Joseph
Bray, Judith
Burditt, John
Burk, John
Butler, John
Cartwrite, Hannah
Collins, Mary*
Conolley, Margaret
Davis, John
Davis, Thomas
Deane, Joseph
English, Rebecca
Evans, Richard
Garrell, William
Gerrard, Jane
Halfhide (Hafferside), Frances
Harper, Alexander
Hasard, William
Hoar (Haws), Ann (Catherine)
Hughes, Ann*
Hughes, John

Hutchson, Sarah
Hutton, John
Johnson, Benjamin*
Jones, Ann
Jones, Sarah
Keys alias Kemp, Thomas
Klinsmith, Lawrence
Lambert, Jane
Lewent (Lavant) alias Archer, Mary
Lewis, Elizabeth wife of Thomas
Mansfield, David
Mathews, George
McCoy, Mary
McGuire, Daniel
McKool, Elizabeth
Moor, Timothy
Morgan, Joseph
Morrell, Elizabeth
Oxford, John
Parker, John
Parsons, William
Perkins, Joseph - 14 yrs
Pickett, James
Poole, Sarah
Potter, John
Prince, Joseph
Raine, Simon
Richardson, John*
Rowell, Edward
Smith, Robert
Spurgeon, John - 14 yrs
Stewart, Duncan
Stiles, Mary
Vaughan, Edward
Vine, Susanna
Walton, Edward
Webb, Mary

Wheatley alias Allison, Hester

Northamptonshire

Cole, George
Davis, David
Odell, John
Wattar, John

Surrey

Addison, Thomas
Cobbey, Walter
Cobitch, William
Cormack, Benjamin
Deckron, John
Heath, Bartholomew alias James
Hilliard, Elizabeth
Jones, John
Pickering, John*
Richards, Elizabeth
Trevitt, Robert
Williams, John
Windy, John
Wing, John

Sussex

Cook, William
Limbrish, Thomas
Todman, John*

Unidentified

Rickson, John
Simpson, John
Tomlinson, John

*Not on LC

Felons transported from London by the *Forward*, Capt. William Loney, in November 1728 and registered in Rappahannock, Virginia, in June 1729. (PRO: T53/34/303; CLRO Mss 57..8.29).

Buckinghamshire*

Ens, Thomas
Everin, Richard
Tayler, Ann
Warner, Edward

Essex*

Bush, Thomas

Hertfordshire*

Cole, Rebecca
Crippen, Mary

Harte, Henry
Rutter, John
Savile, Richard

London

Appleyard, Elizabeth
Baker, Edward - died on passage
Bentley, Martha
Boddoe, John
Bradey, Benjamin
Bridges, John
Bristow, Margaret
Butteris, Thomas
Carter, Timothy - died on passage
Churchill, William
Collyer, Thomas
Core, Mary
Darvall alias Neeves, Sarah
Dorney, Philip
Gascoyne, Richard - died on passage
Golding, Frances
Green, Ann
Higgins, Mary
Kent, Edward
Markham, Margaret
Matthews alias Paine, Sarah
McMillion, Philip
Pagett alias Curtis, Martha
Pierce, Thomas
Powell, Thomas - died on passage
Price, Mary - died on passage
Pruett, William
Rymer, Martha
Simpson, James
Warner, Daniel
Yates, William - died on passage
Yure, William

Middlesex

Barkley, Anne - died on passage
Bates, John
Baugh, Jonathan
Boulton alias Gatley, Mary
Briggs, Jane
Brooks, James - died on passage
Burt, William
Caner, Jane
Cook, William
Critchett, Mary
Dunbarr, Elizabeth

Flaxton, Elizabeth
Giles, George
Glover, James
Goldsby, Edward
Gregory, Richard
Hall, Joyce wife of Hector - died
Hilliard, Philip
Laws Elizabeth
Lovejoy, William
Marscey (Massey), Nathaniel
Miller, Margaret
Nickson (Nicholson), John - 14 yrs
Oakley, Alice
Page, Margaret
Paine, Joshua
Parrott, Thomas - died on passage
Robinson, John*
Romane, Elizabeth
Start, John
Stephens, William - died on passage
Sutcliffe, James
Taulton, John
Thompson, Mary - died on passage
Tilbury, Anne - died on passage
Tillard, Elizabeth - died on passage
Tudor, Woodward
Wagstaff, Thomas
Ward, Mathew
Ward, William
Warwick, Edward
Whittaker, Thomas
Wiechard, Anne
Williams, Anne
Williams, Edward
Willshire, Mary
Young, Susanna

Surrey*

Brampton, John
Collyer, Catherine
Deane, Peter
Frost, Joseph
Meedy, Joseph
Milliner, Anne
Taylor, Jane

Sussex*

Bennett, John

Unidentified   Pallatt, Elizabeth

*Not on LC

Felons transported from London by the *Patapsco Merchant*, Capt. Darby Lux, in March 1729 and registered at Annapolis in October 1729. (PRO: T53/34/418; CLRO LC).

Essex

Hardman, John

Hertfordshire Cole, Rebecca
Crippen, Mary
Harte, Henry
Hutchin, Thomas
Rutter, John
Savile, Richard
Stanton, William

Oney, Samuel

Kent

Mitchell, John
Walker, Richard

London

Avis, James, alias Mitchell, John
Ayres, John.
Bevan, Rice - died on passage
Bird, Joseph
Blair, Margaret
Bostick, Henry
Cade, Rebecca
Cheney, Charles
Cole, Elizabeth
Cummings, John
Dew alias Holloway, Mary
Fenn, Martha
Filter (Felter), John
Gibson, Ann Jr.
Gowen, James
Gray, George
Holford, Elizabeth
Holloway, Judith - 14 yrs - died
Holmes, William
Jones, Evan
Kemp, Mary

Kinnett, Benjamin
Marsh, Thomas
Masters, James
Milford, David
Nuttall, Robert - died
Owen, Thomas
Parks, Edward
Taverner, Sarah
Varnum, Oliver
Wicks (Weekes), Mary
Wilkinson, Margaret
Wood, Eady

Middlesex

Adams, Samuel - died on passage
Allen, Mary
Allen, Thomas
Andrewsby (Andersby), Jane
Atkins, Edward
Baker, Ann wife of James
Burgess, Jane - died on passage
Butsell, William
Butterfield, John
Clendon (Clinton), Susan - died
Clutterbuck, Joseph
Connelly, Michael
Constable, Robert
Crawford, Daniel
Crawley, John
Curtis, John
Darke, John
Dawkins, Richard
Dimsdale, Mary
Dunn, John
Durham, Robert - died on passage
Everett (Everard), John
Fox alias Bond, Hannah
Gray, Samuel
Green, Richard
Hanner alias Hanmer, Elizabeth
Hanser, Mathew
Harvey, Mary

41

Ives alias James, William
Jarvis, Anne
Johnson, Edward
Johnson, Thomas
Jones, Thomas
Jones, William
Lee, Mary
Lewis, Samuel - 14 yrs
Messenger, John
Moor alias Holland, John
Mote, Elizabeth
Mumford alias Waters, Margaret
Newman, Robert
Nichols, Ann
Pedder, John
Roberts, Edward - 14 yrs
Scott, Richard
Smith, James
Smith, Joseph

Snell, Richard
Stevens, John
Stoakes, Anne
Thornton, Jane wife of Joseph
Tilley, William - 14 yrs - died
Tipler, Ann wife of John
Turner, Thomas
Twitt, Katherine wife of Robert
Walker, Mary
Watson, Jane - died on passage
Weal, John
Westell, Patience
Wood, William
Wyman (Weyman), Michael

Unidentified

Foggett (Faggot), Mary
Williams, Edward

*Not on LC

Felons transported from London by the *Forward*, Capt. William Loney, in November 1729 and registered in Virginia in June 1730 (PRO: T53/35/43; CLRO Mss 57.8.33).

Buckinghamshire*

Collett, William
Cooke, Thomas
Craydon, Richard
Griffen, Tobias
Haywood, Robert
Viner alias Vincent, Richard

Essex*

Allen, Jeremiah
Davis, John
Eades, Henry
Garrett, Joseph
Judd, William
Sanders, William
Searle, John
Surridge, Richard
Symonds, John
Thorne, John
Vale, Robert
Wayman, Samuel
Wells, John

Hertfordshire*

Gawdery, Thomas
Horsefall, Luke
Rickard, Lawrence

Kent*

Clarke, Richard
Goode, John
Standfast, Richard
Tuffield, William
Webb, Richard

London

Batt, Esther
Budd, Mary
Cowell, Mary
Cox, Grace - died on passage
Dent, Ann
Evatt, Henry - died on passage
Foster, James
Green, Margaret - died on passage
Haley, Alice
Hall, Robert

Hargest, William - died on passage
Hawes, Benjamin
Howard, John
Hughes, John
Johnson, Elizabeth
Johnson, Mary
Lilley, Jeremiah
Manning, Charles
Marks alias Middleton, William
Neale, Laurence
Palmer, Mary
Patten alias Pottinger, Jane - died
Pendrill, Elianor - died on passage
Price, Joseph
Ralph, James
Salter, Thomas
Sampson, Thomas
Smith, Judith
Stewart, Mary
Tate, James
Taylor alias Burleigh, William
Wallexelson, Thomas

Leicestershire

Miles, William - 14 yrs

Middlesex

Arwood, Mary - died on passage
Bankes, Arthur - died on passage
Barrow, John - died on passage
Bennett, Elizabeth - died on passage
Bernard, Henry
Berry, Anne - died on passage
Bradey, Thomas - died on passage
Brooken, Joseph - died on passage
Brookes, Josiah
Browne, Jane
Browne, Katherine
Browne alias Jones, Margaret - died
Butler, James
Carpenter, Elizabeth
Coleman, George
Collings, Isabella
Conyers, Grace
Cowsell, William
Crouch, Absalom
Dance, Rebecca
Dawes, George
Dixon, John
Downing, John

Drinkwater, William - died
Durdin, Jane - died on passage
Eglin, John
Field, William
Forgeom, Mary
Foster, Elizabeth - died on passage
Fry, Jane
Girling, Elizabeth*
Godfrey, Joseph
Gootree, John - died on passage
Hawkins, John
Herbert, Anne
Hewitt (Havitt), Lewis
Hoskins, Sarah
Hughes, Mary - died on passage
Hurst, Anne*
Johnson, William - died on passage
Jones, Samuel
Kempe, Amey
Kilburne, Richard
King, John - died on passage
Kingsberry, Thomas - died
Lane, Jane
Little, William - died on passage
Lovey, John
Morray, Roger
Newcombe, John
Newcombe, Robert - died
Oakeley, Thomas
Owen, John - died on passage
Page, William - died on passage
Pemberton alias Pendry alias
    Pendrick alias Pendroon, Jane
Phillips, Charles
Powell, George
Rand, Benjamin
Raven, Margaret
Rawlins, Elizabeth
Salmon, Samuel
Satcher, Thomas
Saunders, Thomas
Saunderson, Joseph
Shale, Sarah
Shepherd, Elizabeth
Simkin, Thomas
Smith alias Bryan, Anne
Smith, John
Starling, Elizabeth - died on passage
Stockwell, James
Tanner, Mary
Thompson, Anthony - swam away
    at Gravesend

43

Thompson, John
Ward, Michael
Woollam alias Woolard, John - died

Surrey*

Boone, Samuel
Buskin, Thomas
Chester, Christopher
Dibble, John
Huggitt, Charles
Hughes, Richard

Ling, Maurice
McEther, Timothy
Parker, Mary
Pegden, William
Rich, Elizabeth
Thinwood alias Phillips, John
Thompson, Robert (2)
Williams, Thomas

Unidentified

Robinson, Timothy - died

*Not on LC

Felons transported from London by the *Patapsco Merchant*, Capt. Darby Lux, in March 1730 and registered at Annapolis in September 1730. (PRO: T53/35/174; CLRO Mss 57.8.34).

London

Alexander, Margaret, alias Brown, Elizabeth
Arnold, Henry Mitchell - 14 yrs
Bailey, Walter
Beavers alias Hopkins, Bridget
Birch, Richard
Bolton, Martha
Boscowe, James
Budd, Henry
Carlisle, William
Colthurst, Mary
Coverley, Thomas
Cox alias Shears, Mary
Crowney, Paul
Earle, James
Emerson, Mary
Fairley, Ann
Fancia, Obadiah
Fountain, Francis
Fox, Thomas
Francis, John
Frazier, Susan - 14 yrs
Hartley alias Hatley, Hannah - 14 yrs
Ingleton, Christopher
Jones, William
Jones, Mary
Lacy, Edward
Liddall, Mary
Martin, Frances
Martin, Mary
Mills, Elizabeth - 14 yrs

Oakley, Thomas
Oliver, John
Peacock, Richard - died on passage
Prosser, Charles - 14 yrs
Robinson, Leonard
Scott, Andrew
Simmons, John
Smith, Elizabeth
Smith, George
Smith, Richard
Speed, Francis - died on passage
Stephens, Richard
Tanner, Martin Peter
Thomas, Hugh
Ware, William
Wharton, Katherine
Whitehead, Charles
Wright, Francis

Middlesex

Addes, Thomas
Allen, Henry
Arnold, James
Beard, Daniel
Beavor, Sarah
Bellass (Bellows), Anne
Bennet, William - died on passage
Bibby, Thomas.
Bingham, Benjamin
Browne, Joseph - died on passage
Bull (Budd), James.
Burgess, John

44

Burrard alias Johnson, Samuel.
Burridge, Hannah
Carr, Robert
Downes, Anne
Elias, Leien
Ferris, James - 14 yrs
Freeman, Charles
Griffin, Francis
Hart, Robert
Harwood alias Badger alias Radford,
   Mary - 14 yrs
Herringshaw, Ruth
Hiser, John
Hudson, Peter
Hughes, Anne
Hughs, William
Jerbin, Jasper - died on passage
Lawrence, Margaret - 14 yrs
Manley, James
Manning, Rebecca
McDaniel, John
Milton, Anne
Moseley, Thomas
Oldfield, Eleanor - 14 yrs
Pantree, John - 14 yrs
Pomfrey, James - died on passage

Powell, Hester - died on passage
Pugh, Philip
Rhodes, Jervis - 14 yrs
Rich, John
Rogers, Richard - 14 yrs
Rogers, Thomas - 14 yrs
Roper, Richard
Rumsey, John - died on passage
Ryan, Jeremiah
Shepherd, Samuel
Siggins alias Perkins, Mary
Smith, John
Spencer, William
Spicer, Francis
Taverner, Joseph - died on passage
Walters, Philip
Wilkins, Nicholas - died on passage
Williams alias Foster, Mary
Williams, Christian
Witham, Henry
Wright, Joseph

Unidentified

Higgins, Elizabeth - died on passage

Felons transported from London to Virginia by the *Smith*, Capt. William Loney, in September 1730. (PRO: T53/35/179).

Essex

Bayley, Walter
Beinton, Thomas
Chauncer, Henry
Dolline, John
Evans, Henry
Gold, John
Gouldson, William
Griffith, William
Heath, John
Meakings, John
Moulson, William
Osborne, John
Pownall, John
Smith, Andrew
Tyler, John

Hertfordshire

Bradley, Edward
Featherstone, Mary

Groves, Henry
Hide, Henry
Stanley, Nathaniel
Stayner, Richard
Walker, George
Williams, Peter

Kent

Ansell, Henry
Curd, Sarah
Decruze, John
Dorman, Edward
Hammond, Thomas
Pate, John
Roberts, Philip
Spariner, Richard

Surrey

Allen, Thomas
Atherton, Robert

Axeley, James
Booley, Thomas
Chivers, Thomas
Cole, Thomas
Copeg, Henry
Count, William
Dixon, John
Evans, Francis
Farding alias Ferne, James
Fitzgerald, Mary
Freeman, Alice
Gurry, William
Helmes, Henry
Hill, John
Hudson, John
Jones, William
Kidman, John
King, Joseph
Lee alias Twyford, Downs
London, Elener
Maderson, Rachel
Marsh, Susan

Mitchell, James
Partridge, Mary
Peirey, John
Pond, Elizabeth
Powell, William
Pye, John
Ray, John
Roberts, Mary
Taylor, Thomas
Utber, John
Wood, William
Yates, Willdy.
Young, John

Sussex

Jeffery, John
Short, Aron
Smith, James
Thresher, Richard
Tydey, Thomas

Felons transported from London by the *Forward*, Capt. George Buckeridge, in October 1730 and registered in Port South Potomack, Virginia, in January 1731. (PRO: T53/35/380; CLRO Mss 57.8.35).

London

Bates, Margaret
Branbery, Ann - 14 yrs
Brennan, James
Brooks, Matthew
Broomhall, Sarah
Brown, Charles
Burnham, John
Buskley, John
Butler, John.
Clark, Benjamin
Coffee, Peter - 14 yrs
Cooper, Thomas
Cormick, Dennis
Cornwell, Mary
Davies, Elianor
Davies, John
Disherman, Gabriel
Douby alias Turby, John
Eaton, Margaret, alias Irish Pegg
Fenton, Robert (John)
Fletcher, John
Fox, Elizabeth
Garle, Christopher

Gates, Peter
Gray, John
Hanson, Richard - 14 yrs
Hassey, Ann
Jackson, Elizabeth
Jackson, Sarah
Jewques, William
Johnson, Robert
Joyce, Christopher
Kidd, Ann
Leather, John
Levy, Abraham
Lewen, John
Lewer alias Owen, Catherine
McColley, Andrew
Miller, Susannah
Morris, William
Moulton, James
Nicholson, Bartholomew
Perkyns, John
Piner, Ann
Pritchard, Samuel
Procter, Martha
Reed, Ann
Roach, Elizabeth

Sandford, Benjamin
Seabrook, William
Shaw, Robert
Short, Thomas
Smith, Ann alias Elizabeth wife of John
Taylor, John
Thompson, Mary
Wilcox, Thomas

Middlesex

Anderson, Jane
Anderson, John
Ayres, Deborah wife of Robert
Bagley alias Bagerley, Anthony
Baker, William
Barker, William
Bennett, Nicholas
Bew, Thomas
Binstead, Thomas
Bishop, Gamaliel
Blanchett, James
Bone, Elizabeth*
Box, Mary wife of Edward
Brown, George
Browne, Margaret
Brown, Mary
Burton, Leonard
Bushby, John*
Cannon, Catherine
Carter, John
Clarke, Mary
Collins, John
Collins, Mary
Collins, Susanna wife of John
Cooper, Mary
Cornish, Charles
Cross, Mary
Daloon alias McGuy, Jane
Dalton, Andrew
Deane, Francis
Deane, Lidia
Dickson, Margaret (Mary)
Dixon, David
Downing, Georg - 14 yrs
Durham, Thomas - died on passage
Edwards, Mary - died on passage
Everett, Robert
Ford, Sarah
Fox, John
Franceys, Richard
Golstone, Robert

Gray, Margaret
Griffis alias Butler, Thomas - 14 yrs
Guy, William
Gwinn, James
Hacker, William
Harris, John
Head, John - 14 yrs
Hemings, Susanna
Hickman, Elizabeth
Hobson, Margaret
Jenkins, Jane
Jones alias Jenkins, Jane
Jones, John
Jones, Richard
Lane, Jane
Lawrence, Sarah wife of Thomas
Leader, Alice
Lewis, Richard
Long, Mary Jane
Mallard, Stephen
McConnell, Mary
Milkins, William
Montgomery, Hannah wife of Andrew
Naylor, Ann, alias Mary
  wife of John Vesper
Perry, Strongfaith
Reeves, George
Reynolds alias Bush, James
Richardson alias Bundy, Elizabeth
Ridgeley, Richard
Robinson, Ann
Robinson, Joseph - 14 yrs
Roffe, John
Rusher alias Hays alias Dennis,
  Mary
Scott, Elizabeth, alias wife of
  Robert Bridgewater
Shaftoe, Edward
Shewswood, John - 14 yrs
Shrimpton, William - 14 yrs
Skagg, Elizabeth wife of Richard - died
Smith, Frances wife of Richard
Smith, Mary (2)
Spaul, Thomas
Stader, Robert
Stader, Thomas - 14 yrs
Storey, Ann
Taverner, George
Thompson, Thomas
Thorne, Sarah
Tisdall, Charles
Tizard, John - 14 yrs

Wagg, Thomas
Walker alias Walters, Margaret
Waters alias Robinson, Catherine
Watson, Mary
Watts, Mary - died on passage
Wheeler, Robert
Wilkinson, William
Williams, Thomas - 14 yrs
Williamson, James

Willson, James
Winwood, Mary

Unidentified

Dinham, Thomas
Scagg, Elizabeth
Turley, John

*Not on LC

Felons transported from London by the *Patapsco Merchant*, Capt. Darby Lux, in March 1731 and registered in Port Annapolis in 1731. (PRO: T53/35/496; CLRO: Mss 57.8.36).

London

Allright, John
Bellmassett, Humphrey
Bevis, George
Billings, Christopher
Boston alias Wilmot, Thomas
Brooks, John
Bucknall alias Foot, Magdalen
Corneck alias Cormack, Charles
Day, Alice
Ellis, John
Fleming, Elizabeth
Goodwin, William*
Hall, Joseph
Hilton, John
Hudson, Eleanor
Hudson, Thomas
Kent, John - died
Ladmore, Thomas*
Lancaster, William
Lee, Lewis
McCarty, Mary
O'Neal, Margaret
Perry, Barnaby
Porter, Richard
Rogers, James
Taylor, Jane
Welsh, Edward
Westmore, Elizabeth
Wilson, Ann

Middlesex

Appleton, Mary
Askew alias King, Mary

Beale, George
Bowdon, Robert
Buckle, Constance - 14 yrs
Burchinough, Sarah wife of John
 - 14 yrs
Butcher, John
Carrill, John
Cheshire, John
Connor, Jane wife of John
Cross alias Civility, Sarah
Davis, Honor wife of John - 14 yrs
Davis, William
Deacon, Elizabeth wife of Colbert
Eaton, Charles - died
Evans, Alice
Farrell, William
Fieldhouse, Joseph - died
French, Thomas
Gage, John
Gawthorne, Samuel
Gilbert, Charles
Goodwin, Edward Sr.*
Goodwin, Matthew
Gosseloe, Hannah
Hall, Thomas
Harris, Ann
Hawes, Mary
Highton, William
Hillary, John - died
Hilliard, Sarah
Howell, Elizabeth wife of Henry
Husband, Christopher
Isaacson, William
Johnson, Mary
Knight, John
Lambeth, Elizabeth

Lewis, Francis
Lewis, Margaret wife of John
Mansell, William - 14 yrs
Marshall, Isaiah
Marshall, Nehemiah
Meacham, Edward
Melshaw, Mary
Moore, Arthur
Nevill, Thomas
Nodder, John
Oxley alias Williams, Margaret
Page, Sarah
Parsons, John
Parsons, Mary
Peck, James
Pipping, Nathaniel
Price, Philip
Purtle, Thomas
Ray, Charles - not transported

Ryland, William - died
Smith, Mary - 14 yrs
Smith, William
Sowray, Malachy
Strange, Katherine wife of Elias
Thompson, Ann
Tillbry, Sarah
Watson, Mary - 14 yrs
Wheeler, Edward - died
White, William
Whitton, John
Wilson, Thomas - died
Winsale, Margaret
Winyard, William
Wood, Daniel
Woodhouse, Mary
Wyatt, John
Wynne, William
Young, Thomas

*Not on LC

Felons transported from London to Virginia by the *Bennett*, Capt. James Reed, in April 1731. (PRO: T53/35/498).

Essex

Dennis, Richard.
Pace alias Gould, Richard.
Revell, John
Sheffield, John

Hertfordshire

Bennett, Richard.
Perry, Cavalier.
Smith, William.

Kent

Allen, Jonathan
Gasson, Edmund.
Goodman, Thomas.
Jones, John.

Sussex

Keep, Andrew.

Surrey

Blackbourne alias Young, Margaret
Brookman, James
Corey, Richard
Faithfull, Jonathan

Felons transported from London by the *Smith*, Capt. William Loney, in September 1731 and registered in Virginia in 1732. (PRO: T53/36/138; CLRO Mss 57.8.37).

Buckinghamshire*

Hickes, Richard
Tackett, Edward
Thresher, James

London

Allen, Ann
Armstrong, Elizabeth, alias Little Bess
Atkins, Mary
Bean, Thomas
Bennett, Richard - died on passage
Bentley, John - 14 yrs

Booth, William Edmund
Bradborne, Thomas
Broughton, Eunice
Cornwell, James
Davis, Eleanor
Dowle, John
Downing alias Doney, Mary
Fagen, Nicholas
Fielding, Thomas
George, Robert - died on passage
Gigg (Grigg), Thomas
Goodson, Joseph
Johnson, George
Jones, Thomas
Kaghill, John
Key, Anthony
Meers, John - died on passage
Redman, Martha - died on passage
Reynolds, Hannah - died on passage
Roberts, Elizabeth
Roberts, William
Rogers, John
Ryon, John
Seaver, Valentine
Smith, Mary
Tickner, William
Todd alias Lax, Ann
Ventland alias Vinckland, Elizabeth
Watkins, Thurstus alias Eustace
Wood, Richard

Middlesex

Aldridge, John
Amos, Ann
Baker, Mary wife of Benjamin
Banks, John
Barton, Leonard - died on passage
Beaton, James
Bellamy, William
Betts, Thomas
Brenan, Martha
Browne, John
Bryan, Eleanor wife of Thomas - died
Bye, Sarah
Cambell, Hugh
Camfield alias Campbell, Elizabeth - died
Cane alias Dixon, John
Clitheroe, John
Cockett, John
Cole, Elizabeth

Costin, Mary
Cross, John
Dancer, John
Davis, Christopher
Davis, Robert
.Day, William
Emley, George
Emley, John
Farrell, Edward
Gill, Elizabeth - died on passage
Griffin, Thomas
Griffiths, Mary
Hart, Peter
Haynes, John
Hobbs, James
Hudson, Mary
Jack, Jane
Johnson, Mary - died on passage
Jones, John
Jones, Thomas
Jones, Roland
Little, John
Mates, Cornelius
Martin, Edward
McDonald, Robert
McDonnell, John
Nanny, Martin
Payne, John
Pettit, Thomas
Powell, Luke
Pulla, Dominique
Quail, Richard
Ray, Daniel
Roberts, John - died on passage
Ross, Penelope wife of Peter
Rowe, Mary, alias wife of John Cane alias Dixon
Savage, Ann
Serjeant, William
Sharp, Robert - died on passage
Shaw, Alice, alias Lewis, Mary - died
Sollis, Elizabeth
Strongarm, William
Sweetman, William
Tarrant, Henry
Taylor, Thomas
Vernon, Ann wife of Thomas
Watson alias Johnson, Esther
Watson, Thomas
Waybank, Elizabeth wife of William
Wells, Ann
West, William

Willmott, Thomas
Woodward, Elizabeth alias Franklin
 - died on passage
Wools, Richard*

Wiltshire

Sympson, William - 14 yrs

*Not on LC

Felons transported from London to Virginia by the *Forward* , Capt. George Buckeridge, in December 1731. (PRO: T53/36/212).

Essex

Butcher, John
Lillyman, Robert

Kent

Elphy, Joseph
Heweston, Anne
Ingram, William
Ingram, Augustus
Taylor, Richard

London

Askew, Charles
Bremer, Christopher
Brookes, Mary
Coventry, Thomas
Crabb, Mary
Dawgs, Amy
Everett, John
Hawkins, Elizabeth
Kelly, Margaret
Mathews, George, alias Kiddy George
Perkins, Charles
Rouse alias Drouse, John
Sheen, Mary
Stockwell, John
Templeman, Edward
Thomas, Margaret
Thomas, Smalman
Walter, John
Williams, John
Young, Richard
Young, Timothy

Middlesex

Abraham, Mary wife of James
Ballard, John
Browne, Eleanor

Butterfield, George
Connaway, Terrence
Cornelius, Joseph
Cox, Alice
Darvan, Joseph
Diplow, Henry
Dorigny, Francis
Ellwood, Hester
Fothergill, William
Garrett, William
Harris, Jane
Hickman, Sarah wife of Benjamin
Hyde, Richard
Jackson alias Jaquet, William
James, John
Jones, Timothy
Maiden, Ann
Mayhew, Nathaniel
Mayo, Rosamund
McLin, Ann
Miles, Charles
Oggers, James
Orchard, James
Peterson alias Paternoster, Joseph
Priestman, James
Richmond, Francis
Salsbury, Mary
Shelton, Henry
Shepherd, Elizabeth wife of Philip
Smaldy, John
Smith, Elizabeth wife of John
Smith, Robert
Spawl, John
Thomas, George
Thorovit alias Thorowitz, Louisa
Ward, Thomas
Webb, John
Williams, William

Surrey

Anderson, Ann

Bishop alias Castle, Martha
Bradrilk, James
Cheney, John
Eager, Florence
Emerson, Thomas
Grace, Susan
Merrit, Richard
Murrell, Muriel

Newland, John
Pritchard, William
Scott, James
Stringer, George
Stringer, Michael
Ward, John
Whittles, Austin

Felons transported from London by the *Patapsco Merchant*, Capt. Darby Lux, in April 1732 and registered in Annapolis in October 1732. (PRO: T53/36/305; CLRO Mss 57.8.38).

Essex*

Chandler, Joseph
Ewens, John
Gewen, Thomas
Little, Elizabeth
Marshall, Thomas
Ratcliffe, James
Saffell, Samuel
Scott, John
Slaughter, Mary

Hertfordshire*

Bentley, William
Smith, George
Stokes, Edward
Wheatley, William

Kent*

Brady, Terence
Burton, Abraham
Floyd alias Harris, Diana
Ingram, Robert
Maidman, James
Pegden, John
Steele, Thomas
White, Richard

London

Curry, Rose
French, Katherine - 14 yrs
Giles alias Curry, Elizabeth
Lyth, Robert
McCoy, John
Middleton, Thomas
Moss, William

Owen, James - 14 yrs
Sharpe, John
Stewart, Charles
Taylor, Henry
Turner, John
Waite, John
Willcox, Margaret

Middlesex

Baker, Elizabeth wife of Thomas
Barnes, Jane
Coniers, Lewis
Cooper, Mary
Cunnycut, Nicholas
Dale alias Dell, Edward - 14 yrs
Davis, Uriah
Evans, Edward
Foy, Margaret
Grant, Catherine
Hodges, Sarah - died on passage
Hutton, Anne
Knight, Deborah
Newell, William - 14 yrs
Palmer alias Hincks, Ann - 14 yrs
Peaverley, John - 14 yrs
Platt, John
Russell, Alexander
Salmon, Mary
Shepherd, Sara
Snailes alias Snailhouse, Hannah
Taylor, Christopher
Thacker alias Spaw, Esther
Turner, Elizabeth
Wright, James

Surrey*

Baker, James

Barratt, Joseph
Cowper, John
Cross, Robert
Davis, Elizabeth
Harvey, Sofia
Hawkins, Elizabeth
Higgs, James
Johnson, Thomas
Mobbs, Philip
Seddon, Isaac
Seddon, Nathan

Thorn, Robert
Tooth, Mary
Wale, Ann
Willoughby, John

Sussex*

Beechin, Richard
Friend, Simon
Robinson, William
Stevens, Thomas

*Not on LC

Felons transported by George Buck of Bideford, Devon, by the *Falcon*, Capt. Matthias Marsh, to Maryland in October 1732 and registered in Kent Co. records on 3 March 1733 (MSA: CR 40,516-8535 ff. 64-69).

Cornwall

Alcock, George
Arnold, Mary
Pearce, John.
Pearce, William

Devon

Atkey, William
Berry, John
Blake, Henry
Clarke, Joseph
Frost, William, weaver
Goodyear, John
Hill, Elizabeth - 14 yrs
Hingston, William
Lane, Humphrey
Legg, Grace - 14 yrs
Mixon, William
Muggeridge, Joseph
Newman, Willmott wife of William
  (QS)
Rodd, Robert Sr.
Saul, Sarah
Sparke, John (QS)
Tarr, Joane (QS)

Tucker, Peter
Woons, John

Dorset

Adams, John
Batt, George - 14 yrs
Bennett, William alias Dodd, Ezekiel
  (QS)
Carter, George - 14 yrs
Case, James (QS)
Churchill, Jane wife of William
Garrett, Valentine
Pearce alias Newport, Richard - 14 yrs

Somerset

Arland, Thomas (QS)
Duke, Henry
Farthing, Anne (QS)
Frost, William. (QS)
Hosegood, George
Jeffery, Richard (QS)
Leach, John (QS)
Marshall, Thomas
Pengelly, Alexander
Smith, John

Felons transported from London to Virginia by the *Caesar*, Capt. William Loney, in October 1732. (PRO: T53/36/423).

Essex

Simpson, Andrew

Smith, Elizabeth

Hertfordshire

Andrews, Joseph
Church, James
Laman, William

Kent

Deering, William
Groves, Richard
Harris alias Homer, John
Hill, Thomas
Lowe, Robert

London

Bennet, Catherine
Betts, Abraham
Bluck, Mary
Borthwick, James - 14 yrs
Cane, John
Chalkley, John
Collier, Ann
Crotch alias Yarmouth, John
Emerton, Frances
Eves, Joseph
Fellows, Margaret
Fossett, Dorothy - 14 yrs
Fuller, John
Gigle, William
Gillett alias Mouth, John - 14 yrs
Hampton, Mary
Palmer, John
Pardoe, Elizabeth - 14 yrs
Plew, John
Rankey, Margaret
Scott, George
Sheldrick, Elizabeth
Sherrard, Francis
Sherrington, William
Smith, Henry
Tomlin, Mary
Watson, Rachael
Wheeler, Robert
Wright, Martha

Middlesex

Atwood, Hannah
Bailey, John
Ball, John
Barrett, Henry - 14 yrs
Bates, Richard
Beake (Bean), William - died

Bowen, John
Bradey, Farrell
Bradley, Mary
Briggs, Sarah
Buckingham, Mary
Burch, James
Canterell, John
Cheney, Elizabeth
Chorley, Joseph - 14 yrs
Clarke, Ann
Crawley, Edward
Cray, Paul
Dangerfield, Richard - 14 yrs
Davis, Henry
De Pree, Bartholomew Marrier
Defoe, Henry
Devie, Lewis - 14 yrs
Erle, Richard
Fossett, William
Fryer, William
Gibbs, John
Gladman, John - 14 yrs
Goodman, John
Goodwin, Sarah
Grew alias Le Grew, Jane
Guy, Stephen
Hammersly, Ann wife of Thomas
Harris, Grace
Harris, Judith
Harrold, Martha wife of Edward
Harvey, William
Hazard, Richard
Head, Robert
Heath, Henry
Hobbs, Elizabeth
Holmes, Matthew
Hosier, Ann
Hughes, John
Ireland, Mary
Ireman alias Bennett, James
James, Elizabeth wife of William
Jones, Martin
Ketcher, Mary
Lamley, Francis
Layston, Elizabeth
Lefoe, Daniel
Leicester, John
Lightfoot, Daniel
Lilly, William
Markes, Frances
Marman, Margaret
Newbole, Henry

Nowden, Ann
Owen, John
Page, Elizabeth
Paviour, John
Peake, Elizabeth
Phillips, James
Powell, Sarah
Rayner, Elizabeth
Reynolds, George
Rippon, Richard
Robins, John - 14 yrs
Robins, Valentine - 14 yrs
Robinson, Joseph
Sampson, Sarah
Sharp alias Alston, Mary
Stevens, Philip
Sullivan alias Johnson, Mary
Sutton, Edward
Taylor alias Wild, Elizabeth
Thaxton, Susannah
Vartry, Mary
Wallis alias Palmer, Hannah
Watson, Richard

Welch, Mary
Wentland, Ann - 14 yrs
Wiggmore, Richard
Young, Catherine

Surrey

Addison, Joseph
Batchelor, Richard
Chick, John
Gurney, Benjamin
Harvey, John
Jones, Ann
Lee, Thomas
Salter, Hannah
Wilkinson, William
Wood, Ann

Sussex

Styles, John A.
Woods, Anthony

Felons transported from London to Virginia by the *Smith*, Capt. George Buckeridge, in February 1733. (PRO: T53/37/10).

London

Adams, Jane
Ashley, Daniel
Austin alias Furmentine, Elizabeth
Chamberlaine, Elizabeth
Danslow, James
Flack, John
Friend, Rowland
Friend alias Rowland, Susannah
Jones, Mary
Nethercliffe, John
Norcott, John
Powell, Eleanor
Roberts, William - 14 yrs
Sanders, Catherine - 14 yrs
Sealy, Hannah
Slow, Edward
Stanton, Elizabeth
Swanson, Thomas
Wharton, Susannah
White, Joseph

Middlesex

Baker alias Beezley, John.
Barrett, Sarah
Booker, John - 14 yrs
Boscantine, Charles
Browne, Phillis
Chalmer, Alexander
Churchill, Mary
Cornelius alias Useley, Barbara
Drew, John
Dunn, Margaret
Evershett, Thomas
Gale, Jane wife of Thomas
Godfrey, Benjamin
Good, Mary
Harper, Edward
Hawkins, John
Hawkins, William
Holloway, Mary
Hunter, Thomas
James, Mary
Jenkings, John - 14 yrs
Laverstick, Alice alias Sarah
Moge, Joseph

Moulder, John
Pointer, Thomas
Poole alias Powell, John
Ravenscroft, Frances
Reeves, Elizabeth wife of George
Rigsby, Jane
Sharpe, Frances
South, Mary
Stapleton, Charles
Stapleton, Sarah
Taylor, Anne
Thomas alias Murry, Mary

Tomlinson, Jame
Trevillian, Mary wife of Simon
Urton, John
Walker, Eleanor
Walmsley alias Lucas alias Johnson,
 Sarah
Warren, Catherine wife of John
Warren, Susanna
Watson, Richard
Williams, Sarah
Williams, Susanna

Felons transported from Bideford to Maryland by George Buck in the *Falcon*, Capt. Matthias Marsh, in 1733 and registered in Kent Co. records in April 1734. (MSA: CR 40,516-8535 ff. 105-111).

Cornwall

Corham, Thomas (QS)
Stephens alias Pearce, Thomas
 - 14 yrs

Devon

Hayne, Thomas - 14 yrs
Johns, Robert
Lean, Richard - 14 yrs
May, Catherine (wife of John) - 14 yrs
Mullins, Jane wife of Richard (QS)
Pearce, Elizabeth
Taylor, Thomas - 14 yrs
York, William (QS)

Dorset

Fountaine, John
Webber, Thomas

Somerset

Addicott, John (QS)
Addicott, William (QS)
Allen, Robert (QS)
French, George (QS)
Knowles, John (QS)
Mead, Methuselah
Palmer, William
Patridge, Love (QS)
Sevier, Elizabeth

Felons transported from London by the *Patapsco Merchant*, Capt. Darby Lux, in April 1733 and registered in Port Annapolis in November 1733. (PRO: T53/37/11; CLRO Mss 57.7.39).

Berkshire

Clarke, John
Crawford, Thomas
Williams, Francis

Buckinghamshire

Bland, Francis - 14 yrs
Collins, Thomas
Peake, James
Thonge, Richard

Essex

Carter, Samuel
Hafen, Joseph
Myalls, William*

Hertfordshire

Arnold, Timothy*
Haynes, Francis
Rolfe, Thomas*

Kent

Chadwick, Hannah
Hooper, John*
Mercer, Richard
Paris, Richard*
Squire, Robert*
West, Benjamin*

London

Atkinson, Christopher
Bellamy, Elizabeth*
Burdett, Benjamin
Cassey, Mary (Elizabeth)
Cobb, Daniel
Cook, Thomas
Crone, William - 14 yrs
Franklin, Mary
French, George
Garnett, Margaret
Hastings, James
Herbert, Anne (Hannah)
Hitchings, Joseph
Jones, Thomas
Kingstone, Thomas
Lovett, William
Norwidge, Robert
Poulton alias Lowcross, Martha
Randall alias Mackdonall, Sarah
Taylor, John
Tredwell (Threadwell), Richard
Vert, Catherine
Wharton, John
White, John
Whitehead, Timothy
Wilkinson, Samuel

Middlesex

Abrams, William
Albrighton, William
Allam, Michael*
Atterbury, William
Bates, William
Black (Blake), Barbara
Boyle, Christopher
Brooker, Robert*
Coney, Elizabeth
Conyers, Eleanor
Delavan, Catherine*
Dennis, Joseph

Dixon, Martha
Dowland (Doland), William*
Durham alias Hunt, Elizabeth
Earle, Elizabeth*
Earley, Mary
Evans, Elizabeth
Felton, George
Fuller, Bartholomew
Gregory, Alice
Hanah, Mary
Handcock, Henry
Hargrove, Nathaniel
Howard, Hannah
Howard, Thomas
Hutchins, Anne
Hutchins (Hutchinson), Charles
Jones, William
Judson, Jane wife of William*
Lefever, Mary
Lloyd, Robert
Lynch, Charles
Makepeace, Anne
Moore, Richard
More, Guy
Ogilby, Catherine
Passmore, Mary
Powell alias Fisherman, John
Powell, John
Raven, William*
Roberts, Anne
Sharpcliff (Sharplift), Thomas
Sikkard, Mary*
Silk, Mary
Thompson, William
Tracey, Catherine
Wadsworth, Thomas
Watson, Mary
White, Edward
White, William

Surrey

Anderson, William
Collyer, Richard
Eddens, John
Gorbe, William*
Lewin, Mary
Perry, Elizabeth*
Welch, William

Sussex

Overington, Thomas
Turner, Matthew

Wiltshire

Harding, John
Hiscock (Hitchcock), Roger
King, Thomas
Lydeat, James
Minson (Munson), Richard - 14 yrs
Salsbury, William
Simper alias Crop, Sarah
Smith, Isaac

Unidentified

Arle, Elizabeth
Balis, Elizabeth
Ballam, Mary
Barry, Elizabeth
Baylis, John
Bivon, Joseph
Brewer, George
Dowland, William
Duneford, Catherine
Edwards, William
Ellam, Michael
Hinkson, Richard
Holmes, Richard
Jackson, Jane
King, Charles - runaway
Lidget, James
Seamour, Thomas
Thomas, William

*Not on LC.

Felons transported from London to Virginia by the *Caesar*, Capt. William Loney, in January 1734. (PRO: T53/118 & 212; CLRO: Mss 57.8.41).

Buckinghamshire*

Hollis alias Hammond, Mary
Hurndale, Ann
Parrot, Thomas
Rainbow, Robert
Stenting, Edward
Wheeler, John

Essex

Dolphin, Joseph
Dunton, Thomas
Lee, Philip
Palmer, William
Parsons, Elizabeth
Spooner, Peter
Theed, Thomas
Whitlock, William - died on passage

Kent

Burdett, Thomas
Bromley, John - 14 yrs
Cammell, William.
Cave, George.
Chickley, William.
Crank, William

Dawson, George
Dodd, Henry
Dominicus, John
Dore, Edward
Fish, William
Goodall, Rebecca
Harper, William
Hopkins, Ann
Jackson, James
Jones, John
Kempson, John
Knight, Mary
March, John
Moore, Anthony - died on passage
Moore, William
Pember, Catherine
Rann, Elizabeth - 14 yrs - died
Read, Robert
Robinson, Elinor
Rogers, William
Sanders, Sarah
Walker, Ann
Wilbert, William
Wylie, John

Middlesex

Abraham, Thomas

Allen alias Jones, Eleanor
Annitts, Mary - died on passage
Baker, Elizabeth
Baker, Susanna
Bamber, Robert
Bannister alias Jones, Isabella
Bates, William
Batt, Jonathan
Beeding, Bridget
Bennett, Thomas
Binnell, Alice
Black, Robert
Bray, Hester
Burden, Thomas*
Butler, Mary
Carter, Dorothy
Cockett (Crockett), Francis
Cole, Richard
Connell, Thomas*
Cook, John
Cook, Richard
Cook, Sarah
Cox, John - died on passage
Crab alias Masterman, John
Dew, Elizabeth
Emery, Isaac
Ferminer, Hannah
Flax, Samuel
Forward, Mary
Freelove, John
George, Daniel, alias Little John
Gibson, Abram
Giddins, John
Gordon, Mary
Hermond (Harman), William
Hopkins, Elizabeth
Hudman, John
Hunt, William
Jackson, William
Johnson, Isabel
Jonas, Thomas
Jones, Nehemiah
King, Mary wife of Thomas
Lawes, Elizabeth wife of William
Lawrence, John
Lucas, William - died on passage
Marshall alias Olave, John
Maxey, John
Mills, John, alias Mollying Jack
Moore, John

Moses, Susan
Muntford, Ann
Oliphant, James
Orrick, Mary wife of John
Pearce, Abram
Peters, Otto*
Ramshaw, Mary
Reynolds, Thomas
Rogers, Benjamin
Rowland alias Rowlat, Thomas
Royley, Mary
Shanks, John
Sickwell alias Aldis, William
Stephens, Richard
Tate alias Taylor, Mary
Taylor, Edward
Thomas, Philip
Tremain, Martha wife of Peter
Trimlett, Ann
Vaughan, George
Walker alias Hatter, John
Webb, Margaret wife of John
White, Susanna
Whiteing, Mary
Wilson, Thomas
Wright, John
Wright, Mary

Surrey*

Carpender, Thomas
Hunt, Joseph
Parker, John
Purcell, Henry
Steavens, James
Storey, John
Wilson, Robert

Unidentified

Austin alias Thompson, Eleanor
Boddenham, Edward
Harnett, Bartholomew
Hart, Henry
Keightley, Christopher
Moreton, Rose
Pixley, Robert
Powers, Edward
Sauce, John
Stones, Elizabeth wife of Robert

*Not on LC

Felons transported from Bideford to Maryland by George Buck in the *Unity*, Capt. Thomas Rowe. in April 1733 and registered in Kent Co. records in November 1733. (MSA:CR 40,516-8535 ff. 89-91).

Cornwall

Chubb, John
Walters, Richard

Devon

Ellett, Robert
Evans, Edward

Headdon, William
Hubbert, Henry
Jones, Anne wife of Thomas
Jones, Thomas
Leathern, James
Stanbury, William
Williams, Roger
Wills, Joseph

Felons transported from London to Maryland by the *Patapsco Merchant*, Capt. Darby Lux, in April 1734. (PRO: T53/37/304).

Essex

Manning, Samuel
Snow, John

Hertfordshire

Rolfe, Thomas

Kent

Hartley, Francis
Paris, Richard

London

Bugden, Tobias
Carter, Rebecca
Cox, Elizabeth
Davis, William
Durrant, John
Dutton, Joseph - 14 yrs
Grubb, Arabella
Jenkins, Henry
Marshall, Thomas
Mason, John
Nash, Elizabeth
Nicholls, James
Shaw, Dorothy
Smith, Mary
Walters, James
White, Mary
Whitesides, Henry
Yates, Thomas

Middlesex

Arrowsmith, John
Baugham, John
Bennett, Sarah
Berry, Margaret
Brown, Elizabeth
Brown, Susanna
Buck, Peter
Bullock, William
Butler, Elizabeth
Clever, James
Cotterell alias Baines, George
Davies alias Pritchard, William
Dolphin, Elizabeth
Gilbert, Susan wife of John
Goat alias Fatty, Mary
Harrington alias Arrington, Mary
Hinch, Joseph
Humphries, John
Huster, Thomas
Johnson, Barbara
King, Bernard Lipscomb
Long, Grace
Longsworth, Peter
Mackel, Isabel wife of John
Martin alias Andrews, Mary
Price, Richard
Rawlinson, William
Smith, Ann
Sparkes, Margaret
Taylor, Thomas
Thomas, Robert
Tilson, Henry
Tisden, Mary

Traviss, John, alias Moco Jack
Williams, Barbara
Wilson, Richard
Worrill, Henry

Surrey

Gorbe, William
Grindall, Margaret
Paterson, Susanna
Peyton, Ann
Pilker, Francis
Porter, Mary

Felons transported from Bideford to Maryland by George Buck in the _Falcon_, Capt. Matthias Marsh, in September 1734 and registered in Kent Co. records in March 1735. (MSA: CR 40,516-8535 ff. 149-162).

Cornwall

Arthur, John (QS)
Chelew, Nicholas
Conner, Temperance - 14 yrs
Crocker, Elizabeth (QS)
Marks, Nicholas (QS)
May, William (QS)
Meisey, William (QS)
Webb, Thomas (QS)

Devon

Bonneval, John
Collins, John (QS)
Coomb, William
Davy, Honor
German, Mary
Goff alias Newberry, Thomas
Jolly, John - 14 yrs
Jones, Mary
Lang, James - 14 yrs
Mallett, Joseph - 14 yrs
Moore, John

Morgan, Job
Seller, Agnes (QS)
Skinner, Anthony
Sparkes, Mary - 14 yrs
Thomson, Elizabeth
Toole, Christopher
Tucker, Thomas
Williams, Jane
Wills, Mary - 14 yrs
Witheridge, Joan
Wollacott, John

Dorset

Lane, Robert - 14 yrs
Williams alias Munday, Thomas

Hampshire

Cock, Richard - 14 yrs
Dew, John - 14 yrs
Gauntlett, William
Luke, William
Palmer, Robert - 14 yrs
Rutt, John - 14 yrs

Felons transported by George Buck of Bideford, Devon, in the _Hawk_, Capt. William Hopkins, to Maryland in September 1734 and registered in Kent Co. records on 2 April 1735 (MSA: CR 40,516-8535 f. 164)

Devon

Farthing, Samuel - 14 yrs

Somerset

Ashman, Isaac - 14 yrs
Brewer, Edward
Emmott, Nathaniel (QS)
Herman, Robert

Kerril late Bennett, Mary
Knight, Jonathan
Moore, William (QS)
Norris, Thomas - 14 yrs
Palmer, John
Pavior, John (QS)
Slee, Thomas
Somers alias Somerhays, John
Thomas, John - 14 yrs
Warren, Robert

Webb, Richard   Wills, Hugh - 14 yrs

Felons transported from London to Virginia by the *Caesar*, Capt. William Loney, in January 1735. (PRO: T53/37/446; CLRO Mss 57.8.41).

Buckinghamshire*

Burroughs, Mary
Evans, Robert
Garbitt, William
Haycroft, John.

Essex*

Church, Thomas
Farrin, John.
Gormwood, Samuel, alias Deeves, John
Hale, Ann (Joseph) - died
Haylock, Abraham.
Read, Sarah.
Rushbrooke, Benjamin
Stevenson alias Davy, Solomon.
White, Orlando.
Molieure, John

Kent*

Hatcher, George.
Moss, Thomas
Williams, Thomas

London

Abrahams, Mordecai
Anthorp, Corbet
Bailey, John
Baldwyn, Nicholas - 14 yrs
Ballance, Edward
Banks, William
Bingham, Joseph - died on passage
Bostock, Nathaniel.
Budd, Robert
Bullen, Elizabeth
Chambers, Thomas*
Cole, Ann
Collins, Mary
Cook, Elizabeth - died on passage
Dobson, Francis
Dunn, John
Dunn, Joseph
Glynn, Mary

Hodges, Frances
Hook alias Cofield, Elizabeth
Howard alias Crafts, Hester
Jervice, Aron
Jones, John
Keeble, Eleanor
Langford, Edward
Letherington, Elizabeth
Matthews, Mary
May, Jane - died on passage
Owen, John - died on passage
Pimm, Emanuel
Roberts, William
Robinson (Robertson), Jane
Smith, George
Snape, Nathaniel
Sturt, John
Taylor, Mary
Tracey, Mary
Walker, Samuel - 14 yrs
Wattson, Ann
Williams, George - died on passage
Willmott, Derry - died on passage
Wright, Elizabeth

Middlesex

Armson, Thomas
Baker, Margaret wife of Robert
Barber, Robert
Bean, William - died on passage
Bolton, John - died on passage
Boucher, Elizabeth
Bromley, Catherine - died
Brown, John
Brown, Mary wife of Sexton
Coe, Catherine*
Coombes, Catherine
Cooper, Elizabeth - died on passage
Cotterell, Barbara
Cross, Richard
Crowther, Percival
Cupit, Judith - died on passage
Damaree, Edmund - died on passage
Day, Mary
Dutton, Francis

Elwood alias Cook, Ann
Esbury alias Eddows alias Eddoways,
    Thomas - died
Ewer, Thomas
Fletcher, William - for life
Gill, Mary.
Green, John
Griffin (Griffith), Sarah
Griffith alias Shovel alias Shuffle,
    William
Hacker, Jane
Hall, Ann - died on passage
Hart, Joseph - died on passage
Herring, John
Hornby, Mercy (Mary)
Hunt, Jane
Hunt, Mary wife of John
Jarvis, James*
Jellard, William
Kelley, Eleanor
Knight, Ann
Lamporne, Edward
Lindsey, Thomas
Lively, Matthew
Lloyd, Richard
Lucas, Catherine* (QS)
Marling, Mary
Matkins, Elizabeth
Meachum, Mary alias Martha - died
Morgan, Sarah - died on passage
Newell alias Blackhead, William
Perkins, Ann
Perry, Isabella wife of Peter
Phillips, William
Pridmore, Thomas
Richardson alias Pect
    alias Taylor, Elizabeth
Robinson, Richard

Roof, Sarah - died on passage
Rush, Mary
Saunders, Martha
Scole, Jane
Shepherd, Richard
Shepherd alias Drew, Martha - died
Simmonds, Ann
Smith, Ann
Smith, Charlotte wife of Samuel
Smith, Mary
Smith, Mary - died on passage
Smith, Sarah
Stubbs, John
Swan, Mary
Taylor, Ann wife of John
Taylor, Elizabeth - died on passage
Taylor alias Roberts, Jane
Teno, Elizabeth wife of Thomas
Thompson, Charles
Thursby, Sarah
Turner, Jane
Upton, Thomas
Wheatley, John.
Wheeler, Mary
Williams, Elizabeth
Williams, Elizabeth wife of Henry
Williams, Mary - died on passage
Williamson, James
Wilson, Richard
Wood, Elizabeth wife of Francis

Surrey*

Cornoe, John
Fitzgerald, Martin
Humphry, George
Sears, Giles

*Not on LC

Felons transported from London by the *Patapsco Merchant*, Capt. Darby Lux, in April 1735 and registered in Annapolis in October 1735. (PRO: T53/38/80; CLRO Mss 57.7.42).

Essex*

Chaple, Henry
Dowset, Joseph
Furness, John
Holt, Ormond
Jump, Mary

Justice, William
Pearcey, Ann
Preston, John

Hertfordshire*

Hunt, James

63

Jones, Charles - 14 yrs
Pratt, Francis
Smith, William

Kent*

Beard, John
Bishop, William
Jones alias Walker, Elizabeth
Knight, James
Lucas, Joseph
Smyther alias Guyver, Sarah
Sutron, William
Tasker, David
Waters, Holden

London

Anslow, Jane
Bear, William
Brocas, Thomas
Collins alias Tilly alias Burroughs, Mary
Cummins, William
Deasley alias Deardsley, Howard
Dowle, Jacob
Foster, Fortune
Gilpin, Thomas
Harford, Hannah
Jennings, Henry
Jones, Ralph
Owen alias Gardner, Margaret - 14 yrs
Roach, Robert
Rogers, Joseph
Stevens, Joseph
Tomlin, Elizabeth
Votiere, Peter
Williams, Robert

Middlesex

Bateman, Thomas - 14 yrs
Beamont, Thomas
Bentley, William
Berkshire, John
Bradley, John
Bryan, George
Byrne, Anthony
Clarke, John - 14 yrs
Conner alias Doyle, Margaret
Frame, Matthias
Hughes, Peter

James, Sarah
Jenkins, Thomas
Kelly, John
Lindsey, Anthony
Luelling, Samuel
Matthews, Mary wife of John - 14 yrs
Mills, Margaret
Mitchell, James
Morgan, Mary
Oliver, John
Pearce, Thomas*
Powell, Sarah
Rawlins, James
Rogers, William
Scott, John
Sharpells, Henry
Short, Nicholas
Smith, Elizabeth
Smith, William
Spenceley, John
Stiffney, John
Stiles, John
Storey, Henry
Street, Rebecca wife of John
Thurman, Charles
Vanstechelen, Ann
Viner, Jane
Ward, Ann
Wardlow, William
Webb, Sarah
Whitmore, William
Willicomb (Williams), William

Shropshire

Powell, Thomas

Surrey*

Bulney, John - 14 yrs
Lackey, John
Page, Edward
Picton, Margaret
Rack, John
Taylor, Edward - 14 yrs
Walton, Mary
Waterer alias Waters, John Jr.

Sussex*

Martin alias Marchant, Thomas - 14 yrs
Saires, Edward - 14 yrs

Saunders, John

Unidentified

Butler, Mary
Denton, William

Jackson, William
Jenkinson, William*
Penn, Mary*
Perrin, Mary
Shurman, Charles*

*Not on LC

Felons transported from Liverpool by the *Squire* in May 1734 and registered in Maryland in August 1735. (Derbyshire Mss).

Derbyshire

Basnett, John
Beardsley, John
Clay, Joseph.

Foulson, Henry
Newton, Thomas

Felons shipped by George Buck of Bideford by the *Amity* of Bideford, Capt. Robert Maine, by agreement of 16 September 1735 and registered in Queen Anne's Co. on 3 March 1735/6. (MSA: MdHR 9015 - RT C f.160)

Somerset

Burridge, Thomas
Cutler, Francis (QS)
Draper, William (QS)
Furber, John (QS)
Handy, John (QS)
Irish, Richard (QS)

Lee, Mary (QS)
Long, Joseph
Ploughman, Mary
Pugsly, John (QS)
Rossiter, Nicholas (QS)
Simmons, John - 14 yrs
Thorne, Thomas (QS)

Felons transported from London by the *John*, Capt. John Griffin, in December 1735 and registered at Annapolis in September 1736. (PRO: T53/38/255; LRO Mss 57.8.44).

London

Browne, William*
Caseley, Samuel
Deakin alias Peacock, Mary
Green, Richard
Hargrove, Hester
Nice, Charles
Quint, Crisse
Rider, Frances
Rogers, John
Stringer, Elizabeth
Winfield, Richard

Middlesex

Anderson, George

Ash, Richard - shown as landed
     from *Dorsetshire* in 1736
Barthelemi, James*
Bayes, John
Bell, Catherine
Blackerby, Ann - when sentenced
     she cursed the court
Bramsby alias Bramsey, Thomas
Calkin, Timothy
Christie alias Ware, Agnes
Craft, Ann
Dalby, Susan
Davis, Margaret*
Forward, Ambrose
Funnell, John
Gee alias Geeze, Ann*
Hague, James

Highfield, Jane
Hughes alias Dennison, Catherine
Hunton (Hunter), Mary
Johnson alias Rose alias Brasie, Mary
Jones, Elizabeth
Jones, William
Malcolm alias Price, Lidia
  wife of James
Monke, Elizabeth
Neal, Mary
Parker, John
Parrott, John
Payne, Constabella

Rice, William
Richardson, Sarah
Robinson, Ann
Roche, Mary
Salter, Jemima
Smith, John, a boy
Smith, Mary
Smith, Susan
Taylor, Elizabeth
Walker, Mabell
West, Jarvis
Woodward, Catherine

*Not on LC

Felons transported from London by the *Dorsetshire*, Capt. William Loney, in February 1736 and registered in Virginia in September 1736. (PRO: T53/38/256; CLRO Mss 57.8.43).

Buckinghamshire*

Chandler, Mary
Pratt, Randolph

Essex*

Rootham, John
Sexton, Thomas

Hertfordshire*

Lee, Paul
Long, William

Huntingdonshire

Smith, Sarah - died on passage

Kent*

Beverley, John
Fenn, James
Russell alias Rochester, Stephen
Scales, Richard
Slate, George
Venner alias Paine, John

London

Ballard, John
Barber alias Lane, Thomas

Barlow, Margaret
Berkley, Elizabeth
Breadcott, Hannah - died
Butcher, William - died
Deane, Joshua - for life - runaway
Drury, Ann - died
Dunwell, Katherine
Dwyer, John
Edmonds, Ann
George, John
Grant, Charles
Green, Elizabeth
Greenwood, Sarah - died
Grindley,Elizabeth
Hamilton, George
Hawkins, Ann
Hayman, Thomas
Hobby, John
Holdsworth, James
Holmes, Mary
Hubbard, Samuel (James)
Hughs, Christopher
Johnson alias Maritime
  alias Smith, Mary
Johnson, William
Jones, Hugh
Jones, Mary
Knight, John
Marshall, Thomas - 14 yrs - died
McCartney, Arthur
Mount, Thomas - died
Peacod, Richard

66

Peale, Charles - for life
Poole, Lewis
Robinson, Hester - died
Rohick, Barnaby
Sears, Robert
Simmons, Thomas - 14 yrs
Smith, Elizabeth wife of Thomas - died
Snaesby, Samuel
Stanning, John
Stevens, Elizabeth - died
Stockman alias MacGwin, Daniel
  - 14 yrs
Tea, Elizabeth - 14 yrs
Thompson, Ann
Tracey, Robert
Wilson alias Wilkinson, Robert
Wootton, Mary - 14 yrs
Wright, John

Middlesex

Allen, George
Ash, Richard
Ashby alias Ashley, Mary
Bailey alias Satchwell, Sarah
Beesley, William
Belmorshed, Humphrey
Bendyfield, Sarah
Bride, Ann
Byrom alias Byron, William
Clarke, Arabella
Claymore alias Clymer, Margaret
Daniel alias MacDonagh, Charles
Doughton, Ann
Dumontier, Hester*
Easton (Eason), Thomas
Elliott, Sarah wife of Thomas*
Forster, William
Fort, Francis*
Franceys, John
Gardner, Francis
Garland, Elizabeth wife of Edward
Gilbert, Frances wife of Thomas
Goff, Ann
Griffith, Mary
Haines, Ann wife of Samuel
Hall, Ann - died
Hall, Philip - died
Hartley, Sarah
Hewett, Edward
Hodgson, George
Horne, Charles*

Hutchins, Anne
Jenkins, John
Jones, Charles*
Jones, Elizabeth - died
Joyner, John
Kibble, John
King, Susan
Legg, Jane
Leman, Henry
Lloyd, Mary
Matthews alias Wright, Mary
McMulling, Mary wife of James
Mead, Nightingale
Morris, Elizabeth wife of John
Plunkett, Ann
Purdon, Meriel - died
Richardson, John
Scarcity, William
Shepherd, John
Sibballs, Robert
Simmonds, Charles, a little boy
Smith, Elizabeth
Sutton, George
Swift, Gabriel - died
Taylor, Ishmael
Taylor, John
Tippett, Matthew
Tooley alias Goodbury, Elizabeth,
  alias wife of Cuthbert Walton
Topping, William
Tyers alias Beard, Ann
White, Richard
Winnington, Nathan
Wright, Ann - died

Sussex*

Ewen, William
Gasson, Henry
Moore, Mary
Wells, Thomas
Wiltshire, John

Surrey*

Alders, Anthony
Banes, John
Buckley, Butler
Deboe, John
Ford, James (Francis)
Gailks, Mary
Goodrod, Mary

Hamond, Thomas
Harrison, John
McQuin, John
Mills, John
Morgan, Edward
Richeson, Thomas
Salmon, Mary
Welman, Matthew

Unidentified

Barrett, Hester
Beshaw, Josiah - died
Clark alias Bush, Mary
Cutting, Edward
Ditchburn, Elizabeth
Dunn, Richard

Frankus, Charles - died
Gag, Margaret - died
Hasledine, Nathaniel
Holloway, George
Jackson, Edward
Jordan, Mary - died
Manley, Sarah
Matts, Sarah
Newby, James
Newman alias Worth, Michael
Ormsbey, Edward
Precious, Elizabeth
Robertson alias Roberts, William
Scott, Isabel wife of John
Southerland, Barnard - died
Wheatherhead, Joseph

*Not on LC

Felons transported from Liverpool by the *Squire*, registered in Maryland in April 1736. (Derbyshire MSS).

Derbyshire

Bowden, Edward
Foulson, Henry

Hibbard, Samuel

Felons shipped by George Buck of Bideford by the *Amity* of Bideford, Capt. Robert Maine, by agreement of September 1736 and registered in Queen Anne's Co. in May 1737 (MSA: CR49,082-RT B ff. 15-17).

Dorset

Farr, George
Fancy, Abel - 14 yrs
Forrest, Robert (QS)
Mullett, William - 14 yrs
Pyke, Thomas - 14 yrs
Willett, Jonas

Hampshire

Arlot, Francis
Fish, Thomas - 14 yrs
Green, John
Haskett, Joseph - 14 yrs
Hooker, William
Hooker, Thomas
Penford, Daniel

Felons transported from London to Maryland by the *Patapsco Merchant*, Capt. Francis Lux, in May 1736. (PRO: T53/38/337).

Buckinghamshire

Bacon, Martin
Bull, John
Preest, James
Yeoman, Samuel - 14 yrs

Essex

Baskett, Richard
Boatman, George - 14 yrs
Crean alias Crane, Nathan
Miles, Thomas
Mullens, John - 14 yrs

Southen, Thomas

Hertfordshire

Cadman, Joshua
Hunt, Edward
Norman, Mary
Smith, Ann

Kent

Babbs, James
Banks, John
Davis, John
Hickman, William
Lamb, James- 14 yrs
Pickering, John Christopher
Wood, Richard

London

Barnes, Mary - runaway
Bean, Susannah
Berry, Catherine
Brewer, Ann
Brown, Ann
Davis, Elizabeth
Dean, John
Goodman, Mary
Goodwin, William
Jones, Martha
Justice, Henry
Lemon, Elizabeth
Middleton, Frances
Murphy, Sarah
Perkins, John
Price, Samuel
Rutliss, Wharton
Sanger, Stephen
Sheppard, Hannah
Travillion, Simon
Turbutt, Isaac
Turner, Stephen alias John
Visage, George
White, Mary
Williams, Grace
Wood, Mary
Wright, Martin

Middlesex

Alder, John

Bird, George
Brannan, Elizabeth
Busk, John
Carter, Timothy
Coombs, Elizabeth
Denny, Mary
Douglas alias Redhead, Elizabeth
Draper, John
Eagle, John
Evans, Ann
Fiander, John
Field, Mary
Fitzgerald, Jane.
Foster, Elizabeth
Foulks, William
Foxley, William
Garnett, Mary wife of John.
George, Thomas
Hadley alias Wilkins, Martha
Hart, Abigail
Haydon, Samuel
Hinds, Peter
Hopkins, Ann
Hords, Martha wife of John
Hutchinson, Simon
Ineon, Richard
Johnson alias Roch, Matthias
Keeble alias Tibley, Robert
King, Robert
Lawrence, Ann wife of Thomas
Lawrence, Hannah
Lefevre, Louis.
Matthews, Elizabeth
McKenny, William
Netherwood, William
North, Catherine
North, Elizabeth
Parker, Ruth
Pennylow, John
Pool, Mary wife of John
Pope, Francis
Richardson alias Delany, Sarah
Russett, James
Ryan, Thomas
Scarenbone, John Peter
Seavell, Ann.
Shaw, William
Small, Mary
Smith, Elizabeth
Stanland, John
Stringer, Ralph
Thomas, Isaac

Thompson, John
Toney, Anthony
Vaughan, George
Venus, Elizabeth
Welsh, George
Whale, William
White, James.
Whitehead, Elizabeth
Wilford, Eleanor
Williams, Frances
Wreathcocke, William
Wynn, Mary
Yardley, Mary

Surrey

Bradshaw, Joseph
Hand, James
Jones, Thomas
Sadler, Philip
Warren, John
Webb, William

Unidentified

Hughes, Grace
Hughes, Mary

Felons transported from London to Virginia by the *Dorsetshire*, Capt. William Loney, in January 1737. (PRO: T53/36/256).

Buckinghamshire

Chaplin, Thomas

Essex

Edwick, Elizabeth
Hardy, Nathaniel
Hughes, Henry
Jones, John
Kelly, Jane
McQuire, Bernard
Parker alias Knight, Thomas
Simpron, Robert
Sutton, John
Thredgall, John
Vere, Sarah
Woodbourne, William

Hertfordshire

Clapham, William
Hicks, William.

Kent

Johnson, John
Mainy, Lawrence
Morse, Richard

London

Anteel, Susanna
Bolt, Robert

Brown, Thomas
Charleton, Elizabeth
Chidley, John
Churchman, Edward
Cramp, Stephen
Croft, Robert
Cross, Hannah
Dixon, Joseph
Fielding, Joshua
Francis, William Caddy
Greenwood, Sarah - died on passage
Hart, Elizabeth
Hogg, Sarah
Jackson, William
Matthews, Richard
Morris, Thomas
Pew alias Edwards, Sarah
Powis, Thomas
Ripley, William
Saunders, William
Whitley, Ann
Wright, Lydia

Middlesex

Adams, George
Anderson, Mary
Ashman, Ann wife of Samuel
Bailey, John
Barnwell, Elizabeth
Barrow, Mary
Blackbourn, James
Branikan, Terence
Broughton, Samuel

Buckley, Mary
Bullivant, Joseph
Burgess, Frances wife of Thomas
Buzell, Ann
Careless, Thomas
Cary, Eleanor wife of Joseph
   alias McCarey
Caseing alias Cason, Ann
Cisty, John
Clarke, Margaret
Clarke, William, "a little boy"
Cole, Sarah
Connelly, Margaret
Cousen, Eleanor - 14 yrs
Crewdson, John
Crowder, Eleanor
Cryer, William
Davis, Elizabeth wife of Thomas
Davis, Francis
Dayley, Richard
Dimsdell, Zachary Ogden
Dobson, William
Doleman, Thomas
Dumontier, Hester
Dyer, Ezekiel
Dyer, Mary
Eades, Isaac
Edwin, Dorothy
Elsey, Thomas
Evans, Simon
Farmworth, John
Field alias Taylor alias Pritchard, Ann
Fitzpatrick, Daniel
Folgee, Robert
Fox, Humphrey
Gardner, Elizabeth wife of Thomas
Grasshoof, Deborah
Green, William
Griffiths, Owen
Halcomb, Martha
Hannah, Jacob
Harbert, Henry
Hargrove, John
Hewitt, Ann
Hibbins, Nicholas
Higginson, Eleanor,
   alias wife of C. White
Hill, Benjamin
Hughes, Mary
Hutchinson alias Hudson,
   Ann wife of John
Inch alias Hinch, Thomas

Jackson, William
James alias Jones, Mary
Johnson, Samuel
Johnston, William
Jones, George
Jones, Thomas
Lawrence, Philip
Long alias Frost alias Fleabite, Richard
Lowder, John
Macleroy, James
Mallabar, John
Martin, Thomas
Matthews, James
Moody, Andrew
Nash, Edward
Netherwood, William
Noble, Joshua alias Civil Joe
Nurse, John
Olive, Frances
Orchard, Abigail wife of Charles
Pell, Gerard
Pollard, Robert
Potter, Zachariah
Powell, Elizabeth
Powell, John
Priddle, Thomas
Puddiford, John
Rash, Joseph
Read, James
Read, William
Richards, Elizabeth
Santon, Richard
Savage, Richard
Shropshire, Mary
Singleton, Sarah
Smith alias Busco, Mary
Smith, William
Stanley, John
Stevens, Susanna wife of Thomas
Stevens, Thomas
Street, Diana wife of Henry
Studder, Elizabeth
Surry, Ruth
Swan, Mary - died on passage
Sykes, Francis
Taylor, Jeffery
Taylor, Mary wife of William
Turbett, Hannah
Twinney, Thomas
Watts, Joan
Watts, Samuel
Weaver, Stephen

Williams, Elizabeth

Surrey

Bennett alias Bennell, Ann
Cockran, Francis
Edwards, Thomas
Ford, James (Francis)
Graham alias Grimes, Robert
Grainger, James
Hills, Elizabeth
Jollop, Samuel

Jones, Mary
Jones, Samuel
Porter, Martha
Travers, Phillis
Welch, Edmund

Unidentified

Bateman, Edward
Mitchell, Samuel
Pool alias Botley, Pelyna

Felons shipped by George Buck of Bideford by the *Amity* of Bideford, Capt. Robert Maine, by agreement of September 1737 and registered in Queen Anne's Co. in April 1738 (MSA: CR 49,082-RT B ff. 131-137).

Cornwall

Charlock (Chelew), Nicholas (QS)
Eales, Richard

Devon

Ingram, Stephen (QS)
Martyn, John
Peirse, William
Richards, John
Stone, George
Thorn, John

Dorset

Alner, John (QS)
Atkins, John
Blandford, John (QS)
Pitman alias Bealing, John (QS)
Still, Moses (QS)

Hampshire

Blackmore, James - 14 yrs
Dallimore, Benjamin
Marlow, James - 14 yrs
Mathews, Thomas
Plumsey, William alias Warwick,
    Joseph

Felons transported from London to Virginia by the *Forward*, Capt. John Magier, in May 1737. (PRO: T57/39/123).

Buckinghamshire

Rigby, Elizabeth
Sheriff, Matthew
Smith, Jonas

Essex

Austin, John
Brian, William
Butcher, Sarah
Cropwell, John
Drain, John
Fuller, William

Grainger, William
Hart, George
Harwood, William
Hudson, Jonathan
Lawrence, William
Middleton, Mary
Reynolds, John
Richardson, Henry

Hertfordshire

Basten, John
Johnson, Henry
Staines, Thomas

Kent

Allen, John
Barrows, Richard
Daniel, Thomas
Eager, James
English, James
Firle, Thomas
Hermes, John
Huggins, William
Perry, William
Peters, John
Potter, William
Shields, Robert

Sussex

Catt, John
Elliott, William
Greenaway, William
Keefe, David
Pigott, Thomas
Reeder, John
Stedman, Christopher
Stedman, John Sr
Stedman, John Jr
Walter, Elizabeth
Wells, Thomas
Wood, William

Surrey

Bourne, William
Bull, Henry
Carless, John
Casey, Richard
Coleman, John
Jordan, William
Keeble, Richard - runaway
King, James
Laws, Sarah
Mathews, James
Mathews, Richard
Pell, Richard
Penny, William
Price, Nathaniel
Sheppard, Mary
Southerton, Richard
Thompson, Edward
Tidmarsh, Grace
Vernon, Elizabeth
Wall, Thomas
Winckworth, John
Withers, John
Yates, Elizabeth
Yates, Richard
Yates, William

Felons transported from London to Maryland by the *Pretty Patsy*, Capt. Francis Lux, in September 1737. (PRO: T53/39/121).

London

Baker, Nicholas
Barrett, John
Bradford, Elizabeth
Brewer, George
Browne, Mary - 14 yrs
Carnes, Thomas
Collard, Stephen - 14 yrs
Cooper, John
Darlington, William
Dunnick, John
Edwards, Thomas
Egleston, Joseph
Farmer, Elizabeth
Felton, Dorothy - 14 yrs
Gladwin, Moses - 14 yrs
Hargrove, Thomas
Hinson, Samuel

Hubbard, William
Jones, Evan
Jones, Thomas
Jones, William
Macconey, James
Moreton, Samuel - 14 yrs
Newman, Ann - 14 yrs
Norris, John
Oliver, Robert
Palmer, Catherine
Phratter (Fratter), Phillis - 14 yrs
Presgrove, George
Ricketts, Thomas - 14 yrs
Seers, Constant
Skinner, William
Smith alias Sims, John - 14 yrs
Steel, John
Stevenson, Francis
Thompson, James

Thornhill, Samuel
Turner, Simon
Waters, William
Williams, Robert
Wood, Robert

Middlesex

Abbott, James
Ady, Jonathan. - 14 yrs
Aldridge, Mary
Anderson, Ann
Arrowsmith, Martha
Atkins, Joseph
Bailey, Isaac
Baker, Mary wife of James
Barnes, Storme
Bayliss, James
Benion, Peter
Blunt, Richard
Bone, William - runaway
Bourne alias Bone alias Byre, John
Boyle, Elizabeth wife of Dennis
Brammer, George
Bulbrooke, William
Burne, Charles
Butler, James
Clapton, John
Clapton, Joseph
Clemson, William
Coleman, Eleanor
Cook, Richard
Crockett alias Rockett, John
Cundell, Robert
Dace, Daniel
Davis, Thomas (2)
Debell, Richard
Dixon, John
Dowgard, Daniel
Fitzgerald, Gerard - 14 yrs
Farmer, Elizabeth
Fox, Margaret - 14 yrs
Furnis, James
Gew, George
Gough alias Goff, William
Gray, James
Grimstone, Samuel
Gulliforth, Ann
Hall, Henry
Haperjohn, Alice
Hardware, Ann

Hatton alias Hatter, William
Higgins, Susanna
Hornbrook, Thomas - 14 yrs
Hutchinson, John
Inglebird, William
Ingram, James
James, Robert
Johnson, Henry
Kempton, Mary - 14 yrs
Kilcup, Thomas
Middleton, Mary
Mobbs, Elizabeth
Montague, Elizabeth
Moreton, Charles
Morris, John
Morris, Thomas - 14 yrs
Moulding, James
Newby, Bever
Nicholls, Joanna
Oram, Samuel
Peircemore, Rebecca
Phillips, John
Place alias Jones alias Emanell, John
Pollard, Catherine - 14 yrs
Pritchett, John - 14 yrs
Pye, Mary
Pyke, John
Robinson, Martha
Saunders, Robert
Savell, James
Sherwood, Benjamin
Silley, Sarah
Smith, Eleanor
Smith, Mary wife of Robert
Sowton, Mary
Stanley, James
Starr, William
Strangbridge, Christopher
Steel, John
Stubbs, John
Sturgeon, Obediah
Sutton, Abraham
Underwood, Anthony
Vizard, Nathaniel
Walker, John
White, Mary
Wilmott, Stephen
Wilson, Ann
Wilson, James
Woolley, Richard

Felons transported by agreements of April 1737 with George & John Buck of Bideford by the *Hawk*, Capt. William Hopkins, from Bideford, and registered in Kent Co. records 25 November 1737 (MSA: CR42,840-8536 ff. 109-118).

Cornwall

Berriball, Pasche
Bodys alias Bodway, William
Carwithy, Thomas (QS)
Curtis, Mark
Hobbs, John Jr. (QS)
Maine, Abraham (QS)
May, William
Meager, William (QS)
Rundle, Richard
Vincent, Richard

Devon

Chapple, Joseph
Cole, Ulalia
Hatch, William - 14 yrs
Lovell, Robert
Patty, David
Tambin?, Edward
Thorn, William
Treasy, Mary
Wilkinson, Richard

Hampshire

Coles, Elizabeth
Light, William
Spratt, Sarah

Felons transported by agreement of 24 October 1737 with George Buck of Bideford by the *Raven*, Capt. Thomas Kenney, from Bideford, and registered in Kent Co. records 30 November 1737 (MSA: CR 42,840-8536 f. 121).

Somerset

Baker, Roger (QS)
Collipriest, John - 14 yrs
Eglon, Robert
Francis, Thomas
Hart, John
Hickman, John
Ingram, Richard
Knight, Isaac - 14 yrs
Lashington (Lackington), James - 14 yrs
Perry, Ralph

Pickford, Mark
Purse, Bernard
Smith, John - 14 yrs
Sorrell, Daniel
Townsend, Mary - 14 yrs
Tush, John
Vanstone, Jonas - 14 yrs
Wheeler alias Ayres, William (QS)
Wilkins, Samuel - 14 yrs
Williams, John

Felons transported from London to Virginia by the *Dorsetshire*, Capt. John Whiting, in January 1738. (PRO: T53/39/182).

Buckinghamshire

Burt, Aaron
Griffith, Christopher
Pakes, William
Pitts, Francis

Essex

Amiss, Robert
Bulling, Richard
Davis, John

Kemp, Benjamin
Phillips, John
Ploser alias Plaser, Christopher
Williams, John

Kent

Boyce, William
Denley, James
Grimes, Thomas
Hoardley, Thomas
Merryfield, Samuel

75

Page, Thomas
Paine, Matthew
Plummer, Daniel
Reader, Benjamin

London

Broad, Mary
Call, Robert
Cook, John
Eastoby, William
Eyres, Robert
Fisher, Joseph
Gilham, Joseph
Grinley, John
Hill, Richard
Hitchcock, Thomas
Jones, Thomas
Lloyd, John
Parker, Joseph
Pomeroy, John
Revell, Hannah
Rolls, John
Sharp, William
Shaw, Ann
Smith, Ann
Sturt, John
Symonds, Peter
Walker, John
Waters, James
Williams, Abel
Wynd, John

Middlesex

Adams, Eleanor
Adams, George
Archer, Elizabeth wife of William
Aris, Edward
Avery, Thomas
Beesly, Ann
Bevan, Thomas
Cade, Elizabeth
Campbell, Elizabeth wife of William
Chapp, Thomas
Clarke, Eleanor wife of William
Clark alias West, Sarah
Clark, William
Cox, Ann
Crawley, Christopher
Currer, Nicholas - 14 yrs
Davis, John

Davis, Thomas
Dillon, James
Donnoly, Hannah
Drew, William
Drummond, Joseph
Eusden, Mary wife of William
Fitzgerald, James
Fossett, Alice
Furnell, William
Goodall, John
Hacker, Jane wife of Thomas
Hamilton, John
Hart, John
Hindmarsh, James
Howard, William
Jefferson, James
Jessop, Robert
Jones, John
King, Ann
Kitchinman, William
Landress, Sarah
Lane, Thomas
Lavender, William
Low, Elizabeth
Marlborough, Francis
Margetson, Eleanor
McDermont, William
McDonald, James
Mollett, Edward
Monk, George
Murray, Richard
Norwood, Elizabeth wife of John
Nugent, Elizabeth
Overs, Sarah
Parker, Ann
Parrott, Charles
Pink, John
Pooley, William
Purney, Mary Sr
Read, Ann
Rice, Ann wife of John
Saunders, William
Sherlock, John
Shufflebottom, Elizabeth
Smith, Mary
Stevens, William
Taylor, John
Taylor, Samuel
Turner, Susan wife of John
Wackett, Arthur
Ward, Mary
Whalebone, Duke

Woodcock, Thomas

Surrey

Dunn, Dennis
Dymsdale, Sarah
Holmes, John
James alias Seeker, Mary
Mann, Richard
Sear, Richard
Smith, Charlotte
Storr, Thomas
Street, Henry

Strudwick, William
Symonds, Ann
Threadwell, Joseph
Warren, Anthony
White, John
Wilmot, James
Wood, Knightly

Unidentified

Shaw, John
Watson, Elizabeth

Felons shipped by George Buck of Bideford by the *Amity*, Capt. Robert Maine, by agreement of October 1738 and registered in Queen Anne's Co. in March 1739 (MSA: CR 49,082-RT B f. 214).

Cornwall

Basely, William
Cloore, Agnes, spinster (QS)

Odgers, John

Felons shipped by John Buck of Bideford by the *Leopard* of Bideford, Capt. Mathias Marsh, by agreement of January 1738 and registered in Queen Anne's Co. in May 1738 (MSA: CR 49,082-RT B f. 143).

Devon

Craig, Matthew
Conibeer, Anthony
Govier, Anthony
Homes, Jonas

Ireland, William
Sheers, John
Taylor, William (QS)
  - pardoned before transportation

Felons transported from London to Virginia by the *Forward*, Capt. John Magier, in June 1738. (PRO: T53/39/248).

Essex

Graydon, Christopher - 14 yrs
Hewitt, Christopher
Hills, Sarah
Rowden, Thomas - 14 yrs
Sewell, John
Stevens, Robert
Waterman, John (QS)

Hertfordshire

Skyrrell, Richard

London

Ayres, Leonard
Benson, James
Bristow, Susannah
Bugdon, John alias Samuel - 14 yrs
Burnett, James
Cann, John
Cooke, Mary
Cope, James - 14 yrs
Darby alias Darley, James
Davenport, Abraham - 14 yrs
Franklyn, Richard - 14 yrs
Hall, John
Hewitt, Joseph

Isaacs, Mary
James, Thomas
Jones, James
Jones, William - 14 yrs
Leng, Catherine - 14 yrs
Maddy, William
Mandevill, Mary
Maunder, Mary
McEnny, Andrew
Miller, William
Moses, William
Pannery, Honor
Scales, Richard
Simmonds, William
Small, Dorrell - 14 yrs
Smith, Elizabeth
Smithson alias Smith, Joseph
Stevens, John
Webb, Jane
Welsh, John
Wharton, Sarah
Williams, Mary

Middlesex

Abbott, John
Bailey, John
Baldwin, Richard
Beard, Sarah
Bishop, John
Blackwell, John
Bricken, Robert
Bromley, Margaret wife of Edward
Brown, John
Brown, Philip
Chest, John
Clark, Mary
Clark, William - died
Cockran, Nathaniel
Coggin, John
Cundell, Edward
Currance, William
Daniell, Richard
Davis, Sarah
Deane, Richard
Douglass, Mary,
  - alias wife of Roger Allen
Dunn, Ann
Ellsmore, Edward
Flurry, Edward
George, Thomas
Gibbs, Charles

Giles alias Rook, Henrietta Maria
Gradley, John
Graham, James
Griffiths alias Parrott, Ann
Haws, Richard
Herbert, Elizabeth
Hickman, John - 14 yrs
Holloway, Thomas
Hunter, Adam
Jenkins, Thomas - 14 yrs
Jones, Mary wife of Thomas
Kelly, Valentine
Kirk, Grafton - 14 yrs
Kniveton alias Kniviston, John
Lamb, John
Lashbrook, William
Lee, Edmond
Liberty, Samuel
Lovett, John
Mann, David
Mann, Francis
Mayham, Thomas
McCue, John
McKenzie, Mary
McLean, William - 14 yrs
Monro, Jane
Moreland, William
Morris, John
Osborn, Anna Maria
Owen, George
Page, John
Page, Mark
Parks, James
Phillis, Joseph
Powell, James
Reeves, Abraham
Rutter, Ann wife of Samuel - 14 yrs
Saunders, Richard
Savill, Thomas
Schovell, Philip
Seneca, Mary
Shaw, Elizabeth
Shores, William
Simmonds, William
Smith, Jonathan
Sparkes, William
Stephens alias Naylor, Esther
Thomas, John
Travis, Joseph
Walker, Samuel
Walkey, Benjamin
Waters, Thomas

Watson, Francis
West, Mary
West, Thomas
Whittingham, Joseph
Wignall, Thomas
Wilson, Mary
Wockley, Margaret
Wood, Martha
Wright, Martin - 14 yrs

Surrey

Aronson, John
Buckley, Edward
Ealing, Samuel, a youth - for life
  - runaway
Hammond, John, a youth - for life
Headford, John
Hollowood, John

Lister, Mary
Miles, Thomas
Morey alias More, Joseph - 14 yrs
Syms, Isabella
Wells, Joseph

Sussex

Bird, John
Cheeseman, William - 14 yrs
Grayling, John
Grisbrook, Henry
Harman, William
Holman, Thomas
Pope, Isaac
Robertson, James
Ross, Henry
Taught, John
Williamson, William - 14 yrs

Felons transported by agreements of September 1738 with George & John Buck of Bideford by the *Hawk*, Capt. William Hopkins, from Bideford, and registered in Kent Co. records 4 April 1739 (MSA: CR 42,840-8536 ff. 189-194).

Devon

Croscombe, Ann of Barnstaple (QS)
Webber, Humphrey of Pilton (QS)

Hampshire

Appleton, Thomas
Frost, William
Pottinger, William

Uffell, Roger
Ward, Job
Woodason, Richard

Wiltshire

Eyre alias Wheeler, James - 14 yrs
Hindy, James
Pointer alias Foreman, Richard (QS)
Wilkins, Phillis

Felons transported from London to Maryland by the *Genoa*, Capt. Darby Lux, in October 1738. (PRO: T53/39/409).

Buckinghamshire

Bond, Uriah
Groom, Edward Jr.
Hart, John
Kemp, Henry
Norraway, Thomas
Scott, John - for life
Tomlinson, Thomas

Essex

Bullock, James
Chamneys, John - 14 yrs

Sands, Thomas
Watson alias Williams, John.
White, John.
Wicks, Thomas - 14 yrs

Hertfordshire

Brett, William.
Brooks, Edward.
Clark, Edward.
Hunt, William.
Whiting, Thomas - 14 yrs

Kent

Ayres, John.
Baker, James.
Burgess, John.
Clarke, John.
Dunn, Dennis.
Holloway, John.
Luck, George.
Martin, Elizabeth - 14 yrs
McGea, Andrew.
Sawyer, William.
Standitch, Mary.
Tracey, George - 14 yrs
Tripp, William
Williams, Francis.

Sussex

Emery, Elizabeth
Marsh, Richard
Parker, Edward - 14 yrs

Surrey

Berry, Timothy
Bray, John - 14 yrs
Cole, Richard - 14 yrs
Dixon, John - 14 yrs
Fitzhugh, Robert
Gill, Mary
Green, George - 14 yrs
Kelly, William.
Morris, William - 14 yrs
O'Bryan, Walter
Washford, Mary - 14 yrs
Wilson, Robert

Felons shipped by Ethelred Davy of Exeter, merchant, to Maryland by agreements of November & December 1738 and registered in Queen Anne's Co. on 6 June 1739 (MSA: CR 49,082-RT B ff. 227-232).

Devon

Binney, James - 14 yrs
Crabb, Joseph - 14 yrs
Dare, Richard
Gent, George
Lanman, Philippa (QS)
Pengilly, John (QS)
Perkins, Richard - 14 yrs
Pulsevir, Catherine (QS)
Radford, George (QS)
Stewart, Joseph - 14 yrs
Summers, Sarah (QS)
Webb, Richard - 14 yrs
Williams, John (QS)
Woodward, John

Somerset

Commons, Thomas - 14 yrs
Harris, William (QS)
Jones, Robert
Lollard, Barnard (QS)
Manning, William (QS)
Palmer, John (QS)
Quick, John (QS)
Skelton, Richard
Slape, Thomas
Slocombe, George
Stokes, Richard
Sutton alias Andrews, John (QS)

Felons transported from London to Virginia by the *Dorsetshire*, Capt. John Whiting, in January 1739. (PRO: T53/39/408).

London

Acre alias Acrey, Sarah
Benbrook, Abraham
Birch, William
Bull, John
Casey, Patrick
Collins, John

Conner, Gamble
Crompton, Thomas
Curtis, Thomas
Duncombe, Samuel
Fawkes, John
Fenn, Hugh
Fletcher, John

Gaffney alias Jenkins, Ann
    wife of Henry
Green, John - 14 yrs
Guise, Mary
Hammond, Lambert
Harbin, Robert
Hill, Henry
Hollis, Jane
Hutton, Thomas
Jackson, John
Jarmain, John
Kelly, Daniel
Lacey, John
Markson, Sharlotte
McClow, Daniel
Miles, John
Mobbs, Martha
Moore, William
Nicholson, Jane
Pain alias Page, James
Randall, Richard
Roberts alias Davis, John
Robertson, Isabella
Rustin alias Harris, Elizabeth
Ryley, John
Satcher, Thomas
Stiles, Jane
Turner, Francis
Webster, Sarah
White, Henry
White, William
Wilson, Owen
Winstanley, James

Middlesex

Aris, Edward
Beesly, Ann
Bevan, Thomas
Billingsly alias Low, Jane
Bradley, Joseph
Bradstreet, Francis
Bright, Stephen
Burgis, John
Busco, Elizabeth
Carter, Thomas
Chamberlain, George
Clarke, Samuel
Cobridge, John
Cockran, William
Collyer, Elizabeth
Cox, Thomas

Davis, Elizabeth
Elliott, Samuel
Fletcher, Elizabeth
Floyd, Thomas
Foulkes alias Fox, George
Fox, James
Ghost, Joseph
Glass, John
Gorman, Eleanor
Gough alias Goff, Mary
Growden, Ann
Gush, James
Hall, Joseph
Hall, Mary
Hammond, Elizabeth
Hatcher, George
Hatton, Edward
Hatton, William
Hawkins, Joseph
Hazard, Walter
Hicks alias Burford, Ann
Hipwell, William
Hodges, Elizabeth
Hooper, Henry
How, Samuel
Howard, John
Jenkins, John
Jones alias Browne, Thomas - 14 yrs
King, Elizabeth
Lawless, James
Ledman alias Powell
    alias Hudson, Mary
Lemocks, Elizabeth
Letts, Elizabeth
Longmore, Ann
Lyford, William
Matthews, John - runaway
Moody alias Moodon,
    Elizabeth wife of Thomas
Mumford alias Mountfield, Robert
Murray, Judith - 14 yrs
Nash, William
Nock, George
Packer, James
Parker, William
Parsons, Mary
Peirse, Abraham
Phillipson, John
Pomroy, Samuel
Rigby, John - 14 yrs
Robinson, William
Salmon, Michael

Seagoe alias Wilson, Margaret
Seymour, Mary wife of Thomas
Simpson, Catherine wife of Charles
Smith, Middlemore
Smith, Richard
Stanford, William
Stuart, Elizabeth
Thomas, Ann

Vibault, Lancelot
Ward alias Butler, Elizabeth
Wells, Edward
Wells alias King, John
Welsh, Eleanor
White, Elizabeth
Wilkinson, John
Woodcock, Sarah - 14 yrs

Felons transported from London to Virginia by the *Forward*, Capt. Benjamin Richardson, in April 1739. (PRO: T53/39/448).

Buckinghamshire

Cooper, Mary, spinster
Cubbidge, John
Hagget, John
Turnham, Thomas

Essex

Green, James - 14 yrs
Grey, John
Lightbourn, Joseph - 14 yrs
Pitchfield, Thomas
Potter, William
Sadler, Daniel
Warren, John
Yates, Samewell

Hertfordshire

Noar, William
Sturgeon, John - 14 yrs

Kent

Davis, William
Fisher alias Gallway, Thomas
Howard, Richard
Lamb, James
Newell, Luke
Pearkey, Mary
Pearse, Ann

London

Cock, Thomas
Compton, Thomas
Hughes, John
Hungerford, John
Legate alias Legget, John

Rogers, Jonathan
Strait, George
Taylor, Thomas

Middlesex

Allen, Ann
Berry, Mathias
Booth, Elizabeth
Bosworth, John
Connelly, William
Crockett, John
Davis, Henry
Deane, Samuel,
   alias Edwards, Thomas
Duncalfe, William
Evans, Mary
Fossitt, Richard
Gordon, Ann
Grimson alias Grimshaw, James
Harrington, John
Keeble, Richard
Lowder, Elizabeth
O'Neal, Ferdinando
Postlewaite, Hugh
White, Sophia wife of John

Surrey

Cannon, John
Cole, Henry
Cole, Mary
Cotterell, George
Crochifer, Robert
Dixon, Richard
Lee, William
Miller, Richard
Parfett, Christopher
Parsons, James
Selby, William

82

Wells, Samuel

Sussex

Gurr, Thomas

Felons transported from London to Maryland by the *Sea Nymph*, Capt. Adam Muir, in July 1739. (PRO: T53/39/453).

London

Cross, Charles
Darby, Owen
Davey, Robert
Davis, Thomas - 14 yrs
England, John
Foster, Thomas
Greenaway, William
London, Martha - 14 yrs
Norman, Peter
Owen als Freeman, Thomas
Pattison, William
Pyke, Eilzsha als Letitia alias Alicia
Reynolds, Elizabeth - 14 yrs
Seymour, Charles Stewart
Smith, Thomas
Williamson, John

Middlesex

Alexander, William
Batson, Mordecai
Bell, Margaret
Berry, Michael
Birch, Mary
Bird, Bertram alias Bartholomew
  - runaway
Bird, George
Blayman, Hannah wife of John
  alias Blindman, Anne
Bolingbrooke, Mary
  alias wife of James Deal
Boulin, Honor
Bull, William
Campbell, Edward
Carey, Henry
Coleman, Joseph
Coleman, Thomas
Cope, Eleanor
Cope, John
Cunningham, Hugh
Darlington, James
Davis, Elizabeth
Dunn, Paul

Evett, Elizabeth
Fife, John
Fisher, Thomas
Francis, Mathias
Garnet, Richard
George, Little
Giles, Mary wife of James
Glass, Anthony
Gray alias Jones, William
Hays, Ann
Higginson, Charles
Hitchins, Joseph
Hume, Joseph
Hunt, Edward
James, John - dead
Jenkinson, Edward
Jones, John
Knafton, Francis
Laycock, Martha wife of Richard
Mayhan, James
McCollough, William
Melishaw, Sarah wife of Thomas
Mitchell, John
Morris, Mary
Murtogh, Bryan
Nash alias Nass, Abraham
Neves, Daniel
Partridge, Joseph
Rassell (sic), Thomas
Rider, John
Rithock, Sarah
Sanderson, alias Saunders
  alias Alexander, Thomas
Savage, Thomas
Sayward, Mary
Sedgwicke, Richard
Smith, Jane
Smith, Thomas
Stanton, Adam
Stephens, John
Talbott, John
Tipping, John
Turner, James
Wells, Daniel
Whitehouse, Jeremiah

Williams, John   Wright, John

Felons transported from London to Virginia by the *Duke of Cumberland*, Capt. William Harding, in October 1739. (PRO: T53/40/45).

Buckinghamshire

Hulls, Richard
Mills, Vincent
Rogers, James
Smith, John

Essex

David, William - for life
Langstaff, Thomas - 14 yrs
Savaree, Elizabeth
Stokes, John - 14 yrs

Hertfordshire

Bridges, John
Dockerill, James
Field, Rowland

Kent

Devan, James
Hawes, Jane
Lefebure, Joshua
Powell, Hannah
Walpole, John
Wyborn, John

London

Bignall, James
Butteriss, Robert
Curry, Ann
Davis, William
Dennis, Thomas
Dickenson, William
Gooder, Catherine
Guy, William
Johnson, Anthony
Jones, William, alias Wright, John
Neale, William
Oakley, Christopher
Price, Marina
Richardson, Joseph
Turner, Elizabeth
Wood, Elizabeth

Middlesex

Britt, John
Butler, Thomas
Cartwright, Elizabeth
Cawkin, Alice
Coates, John - 14 yrs
Coffley, William
Cummins, Patrick
Curtis, Mary wife of Thomas
Davis, Sarah wife of Thomas
Deane, William
Devon, Elizabeth wife of Michael
Edwards, John
Eels, William
Fowley, Thomas
Fry, William
Gainsley, Jane
Goldsmith, Elizabeth
    wife of Thomas
Hanna, Daniel
Hayney, Nicholas
Jones, Mary
Lloyd, William
Neale, Richard
Proby, Thomas
Rookes, Elizabeth
Smith, Martha wife of Thomas
Studder, Henry
Thompson, Anne
Waters, John

Surrey

Allcock, Lawrence -14 yrs
Brookes, Samuel
Bullock, Mary - 14 yrs
Durham, John - 14 yrs
Exelby, John - 14 yrs
Ledger, Newberry - 14 yrs
Marsh, Mary, widow
Peirce, Isaac
Sellers, Thomas
Smith, Nathaniel - 14 yrs
Thomas, John - 14 yrs

Sussex

Cooper, John

Hollands, Robert - 14 yrs
Ward, Thomas

Felons transported from London by the *York*, Capt. Anthony Bacon, in February 1740 and registered in Maryland in June 1740. (PRO: T53/40/45; *Maryland Historical Magazine* Vol. 43 pp. 55-59).

London

Anderson, John
Bartley, James
Brown, John
Cardell, William - 14 yrs
Cooke, John
Deane, Thomas
Dunkersly, Benjamin
Eakins, James
Edmunds, Jacob
Evans, James
Franklin, Caesar
Hare, Jarvis - 14 yrs
Henning, Thomas
Hubbard, Ephraim
Hughes, Lucy
Irving, John
Jackson, Elizabeth
Johnson, Mary
    alias wife of John Chapman
Jones, William
Kingman, Sarah - 14 yrs
Lord alias Laud, Richard
Mackloud, Richard
Maxwell, William
Meredith, James
Merring, Richard
Myers, John
Peartree, Samuel
Plummer, John
Price, Ann alias Hannah alias Johannah
Samuel, Myers
Smith, Michael
Stanley, Sarah
Stuart, James
Sullivan, Daniel
Turner, William
Underwood, Richard
Ward, Elizabeth
Ward, Thomas
Warren, John
Watson, Thomas
Went, James

Wood, James
Wood, Mary.

Middlesex

Abbott, Martha
Anderson, James
Beezely, Moses
Bellgrove, Benjamin - died in Newgate
Berry, William
Betts, Margaret
Bignoll, Marmaduke
Birch alias Birchman alias Burchmore,
    William
Blackett, Joshua
Blake, John
Bolton, Elianor, widow
Brockwell, James
Brooks alias Smith, Francis
Brown, William
Castle, Mary
Chapman, Henry
Claxton, John
Cole, Diana
Davis, Thomas
Deacon, John
Delane, John
Downes alias Vaughan, George - 14 yrs
Downes, James
Duggen, John
Elliott, Mary
Ellis, Margaret
Flack, Francis
Ford, Richard
Gaytes, Isaac
Graves, William
Green, Elizabeth
Green, William
Groom, Ann wife of Jacob
Groom, Charles
Groves, Edward
Hardcastle, Mary wife of John
Hastings, John alias Lord Hastings

Heckman, Mary
Holmes, Elizabeth
    alias wife of John Fowles.
Jones alias Faulkner, Alice
Jones, Sarah
Kipps, William
Liddiard, Sarah
Matthews, John
Mitchell, John
Morgan, John
Patterson, John (2)
Peake, Rebecca, widow
Peake, William
Potter, John
Powell, Samuel
Price alias Davis, Elizabeth
Reynolds, Arnold
Seale, William

Shaw, William
Smith, Elizabeth
Smith, John
Snowd, William - 14 yrs
Stewart, William
Stiles, James
Street, Thomas
Stringer, Ann
Sumners, Sarah
Thompson, Hannah
Tizzard, John
Wells, Ann alias wife of Thomas Wilson
Wells, Joseph - 14 yrs
Wicks, John
Williams, Ann
Winter, Thomas
Withers, Sarah

Felons transported from London to Virginia by the *Essex*, Capt. Ambrose Cocks, in June 1740. (PRO: T53/40/204)

Buckinghamshire

Fryer, Henry
Howse, William
Leadbeater, Edward
Reading, Robert
Smith, Thomas

Essex

Cheslin, Samuel
Cocker, Thomas
Cooper, John
Fincham, John
Fincham, Robert
Gordon, John
Hall, Ann
Huntur, James
Johnson, Joseph
Lewen, Joseph
McDonald, Mary
Monk, George
Newman, Daniel
Salmon, John
Trotter, John
Wakelyn, Daniel (QS)
Wharley, John
Wood, Daniel

Hertfordshire

Boswell, Charles Sr.
Boswell, Charles Jr.
Boswell, Hannah
Boswell, Letitia
Boswell, Ruth
Burden, John
Fuller, George
Harris, Thomas
Kemp, Jonathan
Prestidge, John
Trip, John

Kent

Brailsford, John
Cammell, Daniel
Geary, Elizabeth
Hadlow, Mallian
Hopday, Stephen
Hussey, Michael
Jones, John
Spain, Augustin
Swan, Elizabeth
White, John
White, Matthias

London

Bowling, Rachel
Domingus, Mary
Hales, Elizabeth - 14 yrs
Harding, Martha
Humphreys, Frances - 14 yrs
Hunt, Ann
Impey, Thomas
Isgrigg, William
Jarvis, Elizabeth - 14 yrs
Perkins, Mary
Stanton, Peter
Stockdale, Daniel
Thompson, Robert
Toppin alias Hackery, Mary
Wilcox, Elizabeth

Middlesex

Ash, Ann
Bennett, John
Bolton, Joseph
Buckley, Cornelius
Candy, Mary
Cane, John
Disney, William
Elsey, John
Foster, Mary
Gilbert alias Steel, John
Gleed, William
Hart, John
Harvey, Ann
Heape, Samuel
Hetherington, John
Hill, Samuel - 14 yrs
Langham, John
Manning, Dorothy
Mudgett, Elizabeth wife of Thomas
North, Mary wife of John
Parsons, Samuel
Pettey, Ann, spinster
Poole, Rachel
Rane, Ralph
Ranson alias Bickley
  alias Chickley, Sarah;
    alias Sarah the Cork Cutter
Ravenhill, John
Sharpless alias Sweet, John
Smith alias Drogheda, Mary
Tilgon alias Tilgo, John
Watson, Elizabeth
Webb, John
White, Jane
Whitney alias Dribray, Elizabeth
Wiggins, Robert
Woodford, Robert

Surrey

Addison, William
Ashfield, Thomas
Ashwell, John
Blackbourne, John
Bray, William
Cooper, Joseph
Dove, Nicholas
Durham, Elizabeth
Flack, John
Gill, Thomas
Hall, Richard
Hollis, John
Hudson, William
Ives, Edward
Kerr, James
Lawlore, John
Matthews, James
Owen, Jane
Poultney, Thomas
Seawell, Mary
Sedgwick, Martha
Sparkes, William
Thompson, John
White, Elizabeth
Wiggins, Thomas

Sussex

Hardy, Mary
Hodges, William
Savage, James

Felons transported from London to Maryland by the *Vernon*, Capt. Henry Lee, in January 1741. (PRO : T53/40/289, 291).

Buckinghamshire

Weatherley, John

Essex

Ashley, James
Denny, Abraham
Fish, John
Gibbs, Sarah
Johnson, Joseph
Mallard, George
Neal, Thomas
Richardson, Mary
Robins, Richard
Wallis, Francis

Hertfordshire

Whepson, William

Kent

Busan, Philip
Busan, William
Dubrocq, Alexander
Dubrocq, Petre
Hills, Samuel
Hills, William
Langley, Gilbert
Norris, Robert
Priddon, Thomas

London

Andrews, William
Armstrong alias Armistead, Ann
Blackborn, Herbert
Cape, Ann
Cawdell, John
Davis, John
Foster, Richard
Gilliford, John Glew
Grice, Katherine
Hallam, James
Harrison, Michael
Isaacs alias Jacobs, Rachael - 14 yrs
Jackson alias Martin, Elizabeth
Laxton, Sarah - 14 yrs

Legg, John
Matthews, Elizabeth
Mayne alias May, John
Mickey, Elizabeth - 14 yrs
Newberry, James
Phillips, William
Procter, Christopher
Steward, James
Twaites, William
Walker, Atty alias Hetty alias Hester
Wilson, William

Middlesex

Anderson, Joseph
Atkins, Lydia , widow
Bethell alias Bethwin
    alias Barwin, Arthur - 14 yrs
Brammah, Susanna
Brewer, Sarah wife of John
Bull, Mary wife of John
Burt, Jonathan
Clayton alias Hughes, Sarah
Crow, Thomas
Dobbs, James
Dunstan, Ann, spinster
Fox, John - runaway
Hall, Hannah, spinster
Hancock, Abraham
Hicks, Ann,widow
Hudson, Sarah
Jones, Richard
Long, Patrick
Martin, Elizabeth
McCartney, James
Newlove, Sarah, spinster
Newman, Richar
Peacham alias Perry, Mary, spinster
Prince, Hannah wife of Robert
Rice alias Bully, George
Selby, Frances, widow
Smith, Ann
Symmons, Frances, spinster
Tasker, George
Turner, Arthur
Welch, William
White, George - 14 yrs
Youins, Rachael, spinster

Surrey

Ashwell, John
Lawlore, John
Sedgwick, Martha
Thompson, George
Wiggins, Thomas

Sussex

Norris, Thomas
Penticost, Richard
Quinnell, Ann, spinster
Redford, Richard
Whatman, William
Wood, Hannah
Woodman, William

Felons transported from London to Virginia by the *Harpooner*, Capt. John Wilson, in January 1741. (PRO: T53/290).

London

Bailey, Robert
Baker alias Frohen, Johanna
Brown, Sarah
Buckley, James
Burchett, Mary
Cane, Thomas
Clarke, John
Connell, Collumb
Davis, Elizabeth
Davis, Henry
Dennett, Thomas
Duckett, Rachael
Griffin, Robert
Horabin, John
Ingersole alias Waskett, Ann
Innes, Solomon
Isaacs, Solomon
Lynley, Henry
Miles, Charles
Nicholls, Richard
Paine, Edward
Price, Mary
Randall, John
Watkins, Christian
Watmore, James
Wilson, Robert
Yeates, Mary

Middlesex

Anderson, Ann
Anderson alias Strong, Mary
Ayloffe alias Ayliffe, Thomas
Baldock, Richard
Barber, Charles
Barns, Henry

Beale, John
Bennett, Elizabeth wife of Mark
Bristow, John
Brown, Mary
Bullock, Edward
Cable, John
Coates, George
Connolly alias O'Hara, Ann
Damarin alias Dammearon, William
Depenn, Mary spinster
Devinois alias Devenis, Susannah
Evans, Mary, spinster
Evans, Richard
Fisher, Elizabeth
Fuller, Mary
Greenaway, Hannah.
Greeves alias Hollett, Mary
Griffin, Martha wife of Edward
Hall, Ann
Harwood, Mary
Higgs, George
Holding, Rebecca wife of George
Hudson, Ann
Hughes, Joseph
Hunt, Mary
Hutchins, Thomas
Kendall, George
Keys, Thomas
Lunn, Ann
Mahone alias Bignell, Rose, widow
Mason, Elizabeth
McCarty, Mary
Miller, Anna Maria
Mills, Mary wife of Thomas
Moore alias Floud, Jane, widow
Mounslow alias Barnett, John
Murphy, John
Neale, Ann

Newcomb, Mary, widow
Peterson, Richard
Plater, Maria
Pomfrett, Thomas
Powell, John
Purvis, James
Robinson, John
Ruskin, Thomas
Sargery, John
Saunders, Stephen
Savage, Cane
Smith, William
Stephens, John
Steward alias Hastings, Mary
Stewart, Hannah,
  alias Yorkshire Hannah
Thrift, Hester

Wallford, Mary
Wallgrove, Roger
Warren, Jasper
Warrin, Catherine
Weblin, William
Webster, William
Weller, John
Welling, Elizabeth wife of John
Williams, John
Williams, Samuel
Wilson, Sarah wife of Thomas
Wilson, William
Winter, William
Wood, Brittania, alias
  wife of Charles Woolstonecraft
Woolstoncraft, Charles
Yeates, Robert

Felons transported from London to Maryland by the *Speedwell*, Capt. William Camplin, and *Mediterranean*, Capt. George Harriot, in April 1741. (PRO: T53/40/337).

Buckinghamshire

Busby, John
Cater, Thomas
Chambers,Thomas
Clever, William
Crater, Thomas
De Frayne, James
Sharp, Thomas
Smith, Thomas
Wingrove, Thomas

Essex

Boxteed, Thomas
Bragg, John
Brown, John
Burton, William
Cantrell, James
Cooper, John
Curtis, Mary
Doe, Daniel
Gooderham, William
Gurling, Robert
Houching, Susan
Lasker, Susan
Madwell, James
Paice, John
Poulter, Owen
Reeve, Robert

Renalls, Thomas
Scott, William
Solme, Jacob

Hertfordshire

Burling, William
Crain, Jasper. 14 yrs
Eoy, Thomas
Gilbert, Sarah
Horwood, Edward
Hyam, George. 14 yrs
Olloway, Isaiah
Skegg, George
Skegg, William
Stanes, Ezekiel

London

Clay alias Johnson, Elizabeth
Coleman, Penelope
Davis, Elizabeth - 14 yrs
Miller, Hester
Provost, Mary
Shute, Ann

Middlesex

Addleton, John
Archdeacon, William - runaway

Barron, Mary
Beale, Bridget wife of John
Beale, John
Blenheim, Francis
Bosman, Edward
Browne, Edward
Brown, Sarah
Budd, Richard
Burdus, John
Buswell, Thomas
Chamberlain, Ann
Cole, William
Collins, John
Copeland, Mary
Cornish, Samuel
Courtney alias Oliver, Hannah
Draper, John
Duckett, Thomas
Duell, William
Eccles, Ann
Elton, William
Evans, Mary wife of Richard
Extell, Emanuel
Farnham, Robert
Greenhalgh alias Galleof, Ann - 14 yrs
Griffiths, Morgan
Groom, Mary
Hogin alias Eagan, Nicholas
Hooper, John
Howard, Ann
Jackson, Mary wife of William
Jennings, Jane
Jewers, Ann
Johnson, John
Jones, Ann
Jones, John
Kingsland, Thomas
Lane, Edward
Lawler alias Butler, Margaret
Letherland, George
Madder, Edward
Mason, Peter
Moring, Thomas
Mullins, Margaret
Murrell, Sarah
Nash als Goulding, Mary - 14 yrs
Newell, Margaret - 14 yrs
Osbaldston, Robert
Painter, George
Palson, Sarah wife of William

Pennington, John
Perry, William
Pratt, James
Rance alias Godfrey, Elizabeth
Robinson, Ann
Robinson, Hannah - 14 yrs
Smith, Ann wife of Charles
Stone, William
Sturt, Elizabeth
Tanner, Thomas
Tate, Mary
Taylor, Edward
Turner, Richard
Wayland als Hickson, Ann
White, James
Wild, Thomas
Wilkinson, John
Williams, Elizabeth
Wills, Joseph
Wilmore, Elizabeth
Woodford, Charles
Woodward, Mary

Surrey

Carr, John
Channell, Edmund
Clark, Thomas
Dunn, William
Etherington, William
Flood, John. 14 yrs
Foster, Thomas
Glover, George
Green, Charles. 14 yrs
Hogg, Richard
Linguard, Isaac
Medcalf, George
Nicholson, William
Porter, William
Salmon, Mary
Smith, Catherine
Webster, Martha
Wilson, John

Sussex

Penfold, William
Read, William
Rolfe, Mary - 14 yrs
Trump, Richard - 14 yrs

Felons transported from London to Maryland by the *Speedwell*, Capt. William Camplin, in April 1741. (PRO: T53/40/337).

London

Abraham, Ann
Arm, Elizabeth
Billingham, Mary - 14 yrs
Chilcott, John - 14 yrs
Conway, John
Crawford, Thomas
Day, Robert - 14 yrs
Elwin alias Jones, Ann - 14 yrs
Handfield, Thomas - runaway
Hubbard, James - 14 yrs

James, Ann - 14 yrs
King, Ann
Laycock, Richard - 14 yrs
Linsay alias Millar, Lucretia - 14 yrs
Marriott, Richard - 14 yrs
McIntosh, Daniel - 14 yrs
Norgate, Nathaniel - 14 yrs
Rugby, Andrew
Watkins, John - 14 yrs
Wheatley, William - 14 yrs

Felons transported from London to Maryland by the *Milner*, Capt. John Dixon, in May 1741. (PRO: T60/17/291).

Kent

Collis, Abraham
Dumbrain, Daniel
Kingsland, John
Matthews, Samuel
Nicholls, Richard

Pearless, Samuel
Polson, William
Spreadbarrow, John
Watts alias Mead, Thomas

Felons transported from London to Maryland by the *Catherine & Elizabeth*, Capt. William Chapman, in May 1741. (PRO: T53/40/338).

London

Barton, Thomas
Burn, Timothy
Coale, Joseph
Ramsbury, John
Shooter, Charles - 14 yrs

Middlesex

Bird, Charles
Bowers, William
Dennison, Mathias - 14 yrs
Ellard, Samuel

Hale, William
Hayes, Thomas
Kirby, Benjamin
Lesborough, Richard
Leveritt, John
Lowin, Thomas
McKenny, Daniel
Oxley, Thomas
Reeves, George
Storer, John
Taylor, Thomas
Toms, John
Wallis, John, alias Black Jack

Felons transported from London to Maryland by the *Sally*, Mr. William Napier, in September 1741. (PRO: T53/40/415).

Surrey

Hill, Thomas
Lemon, William

Lewis, John
Rogers, William

Stratford, John   Ward, Ann
Twells, Alice

Felons shipped by Ethelred Davy of Exeter, merchant, [probably by the *Philleroy*], Capt. Peter Symons, by agreement of September 1741 and registered in Queen Anne's Co. in April 1742 (CR 49,082-RT B ff. 448-416).

Bristol

Clark, John
Crow, Sarah
Davis, Velvider
Howell, Sarah
Jefferis, Hester
Jefferis, Margaret
Lewis, Mary
Lovell, Mary
Morris, William
Thomas, Mary
Trapp, Thomas
Wheeler, Jonas

Cornwall

Bennett, John
Grey, Samuel
Harris, Francis
Long, Elizabeth
Perkins, Anne wife of John (QS)
Perkins, John (QS)
Roskrogue, Anne

Devon

Beavis, William
Blackmore, Thomas (QS)
Clogg, Robert Jr. - 14 yrs
Clogg, William
Crocker, Elizabeth, spinster
French, Richard
Morey, Stephen
Poe, George
Warren, Margaret
Welsh, Joseph
Williams, James

Herefordshire

Aspy, Thomas
Cooper, Francis
Davis, Thomas
Eliman, Thomas
Howells, Anthony
Jaunsey, John
Morgan, Richard - 14 yrs
Parsons, John (QS) - runaway
Pritchard, Ann - 14 yrs
Pritchard, Ezekiel - 14 yrs
Pritchard, Thomas
Sant, William
Stokes, Joseph
Stokes, Charles
Tippens, Edward
Williams, Mary

Monmouthshire*

Jenkins, William
Rosser, John
Spencer, Edward

Wiltshire

Amor, John - 14 yrs
Bowden, Samuel (QS)
Burchall, Earle
Chappel, Grace (QS)
Haines, Jane (QS)
Pearse, Richard
Say, Richard (QS)
Spicer, John (QS)

*All to serve Peter Symons in Maryland.

Felons transported from London to Maryland by the *Kitty*, Capt. Robert Anderson, in October 1741. (PRO: T60/17/360).

Kent

Cox, George   Dugmore, Edward

Felons transported from London to Virginia by the *Sea Horse*, Capt. John Rendell, in November 1741. (PRO: T53/40/414 & 416).

Buckinghamshire

Hams, Bethia
Hows, John - 14 yrs
Putland, Elizabeth

Essex

Brown, Rose
Coates, John
Cobbs, Richard
Eaton, Francis
Jackson, Robert
Mayhew, Philip
Parker, Andrew
Pluckrose, John
Stephens, John
Stock, John
Taylor, John
Wash, James

Hertfordshire

Broadway, John
Grigg, Ann
Grover, John
Smith, John

Kent

Earle, Enoch
Holstock, John
Hoysted, Robert
Kitching, John
McIntosh, John
Paterson, Robert
Wakefield, Samuel
Wooden, Elizabeth

London

Bazil alias Basil, Susannah

Bennett, James
Blackwell, Charles
Brooks, Matthew
Bunce, Margery - 14 yrs
Collins alias Collyer, Martin
Crump, East
Dunn, Godfrey
Evans, Anne
Gibbs, Elizabeth - 14 yrs
Gillard, Salisbury
Haynes, Elizabeth
Hoskins, Ann
Jacobs, Sarah
Knash, Richard
Marshall, Sarah
Miller, Joseph
Randall, George
Roe, John. L.
Scott, William
Thompson, Stephen
Twist, Benjamin
Weeden, Edward
Wright, John

Middlesex

Alder, George
Allen, William
Anderson, Procter
Ashley alias Ashby, Elizabeth
Bozeley, Mary
Brown, James
Cart, Mary wife of James
Castle, Ann
Clarke, Mary wife of Jonas
Conner, William
Cottell, Thomas
Cox, William
Cummins, Edward
Deacon, John
Earl, Isaac
Eccles, Elizabeth

94

Eccles alias Pugh, Mary
Eliot, Joseph
Evans, Mary
Ford, Elizabeth
Foreshoe, Margaret
Francklin, Rachael
Freeman, James
Girl, Joseph
Grey alias Grace, Mary
Grey, William -14 yrs
Gummery, Mary
Harris, Edward
Heater, James
Herbert, Elizabeth
Hickman alias Brogden, Ann
Hilliard, Sarah
Holland, Samuel
Inglesby, Mary
Jacobs, John
Johnson, Thomas
Jones alias Carnaby, Elizabeth
Jones, John
Lee, William
Loton, Sophia
Marsinder, Ann
Martin, Sarah
Mason, Mary
Mathews, Rebeccah
McDonnell, James
Meeke, Thomas
Neal, Thomas
Nicholson, Edward
Norman, Elizabeth
Norris, Mary - 14 yrs
Ovis, William
Poole, Josiah
Pregnall, Joshua

Pritchard, Richard
Pyechly alias Piper, James
Raymond, Rebecca
Rutherford, Mary
Rutherford, Richard
Saunders, Charles
Saunders alias Cooke, Susanna
Smith, John
Smith, Mary
Smith alias Rouse, Mary
Smith, Robert
Steadman, Catherine
Stevens, Robert
Swift, Ann
Sykes, William
Thompson, Nicholas
Thornton alias Portobello, Elizabeth
Walton, Susannah wife of Aaron
White, Frances
White, John
Wildicke, Joseph
Wills, Thomas
Wilson alias Johnson, Hannah,
    alias Scutt, Mary
Wood, Benjamin

Sussex

Burgess, William
Giles, Sarah - but stopped
    & transported Jun 1742
Jarret, William
Martin, William
Pulton, John
Wells, Jeremiah - runaway
Wood, Margaret

Felons transported from London to Maryland by the *Industry*, Capt. Charles Barnard, in February 1742. (PRO: T53/40/484).

Kent

Sharpe, Elizabeth

London

Barrett, James
Bentley, Mathew
Cooper, Thomas
Darling, Ann
Farrow alias Jackson, Elizabeth - 14 yrs

Fry, Patience
Gibbs, John
Halford, William
Hewitt, Thomas
Hinds, John
Homine, John
Jackson alias Holmes, Elizabeth
Johnson, George
Lilleston, John, alias Jones, Robert
Linsey, Mary
Middleton, Charles

Noon, William
Ottey, Abell
Phillips, Samuel
Pilgrim, Richard
Sadler, Isabella
Scott alias Walker, Mary
Sneed, Robert
Steadman, Ann
Telley, William
Tipton, Elizabeth
Vincent, John
Wells, William
Whitehead, Richard
Williams alias Morrice, Ann
Wincks, Joseph

Middlesex

Albert, Henry
Atterbury, Henry
Baker, Richard
Bennett, Elizabeth - for life
Benny, Susan - 14 yrs
Brown, William
Burgess, Richard - 14 yrs
Bursey, Richard
Cate?, James
Chambers, Ann
Cullam, Thomas
Cullimore, James
Davis, Moses
Davis, Catherine
Day, Ann
Doggett alias Lyons, Elizabeth - 14 yrs
Fleet, Elizabeth wife of Joseph

Freeman, John
Friend, Thomas
Goast, Mary wife of William - 14 yrs
Green, John
Hardy, Elizabeth - 14 yrs
Harris, Mary wife of Thomas
Henshaw, Charles
Hepworth, John
Holdsworth, Joseph
Jenkins, John
Johnson, James
Johnson, William
Jones, Sarah
Laban, George
Lander, George
Lloyd, David
Low, Benjamin
Low, John
Mansfield, Thomas
Morgan, Eleanor
Oldbury, Samuel
Overton, Thomas
Perry, Mary
Price, Elizabeth
Quartermaster (Quarterman), John
Redrup, Daniel
Rice, Mary
Rossiter, Hannah
Ruby, Thomas - 14 yrs
Scott, John - 14 yrs
Shamble alias Wells, Elizabeth Mary
Simonds, Mary
Simpson, Mathew
Stackpool, George

Felons transported by unknown ship [? the *Lyme*] from Lyme Regis in April 1742 by Robert Fowler Coade and registered in Prince George's Co., Maryland. (PRO: Western Circuit Order Books; MSA: Land Records of PG Co Liber Y, ff. 553-560).

Cornwall

Fawcett, Edward - 14 yrs
Ferand, William (QS) - 14 yrs
Hoare, Robert
Honey, Joseph
Johns, Elias
Johns, John
Johns, Stephen
Key, Richard - 14 yrs
Lane, John
Nicholls, Ann

Nicholls, Mark - 14 yrs
Pearse, John - 14 yrs
Polkinghorne, Grace (QS)
Smallacombe, Thomasin - 14 yrs
Trenarry, Richard
Tucker, Grace - 14 yrs
Veale, Jane
Weene, Elizabeth wife of John

Devon

Berry, Samuel (QS)

Roberts, Richard Jr. (QS)

Dorset

Aglen (Anglin), William
Allen, Thomas
Basely, John (QS)
Bridle (alias Froome), Henry (QS)
Daw, Samuel
Ewing, Samuel - 14 yrs
Gillham, Michael (QS)
Old, John - 14 yrs
Piceford, Robert - 14 yrs
Shean, Joseph
Strawbridge, Robert

Wiltshire

Allen, James

Bettesworth, Thomas
Boyce, James (QS)
Harding, Moses (QS)
Lorrell, Matthew
Lumbard, Sarah
Monk, Rinaldo - 14 yrs
Moore, Edward
Scammell, Edward - 14 yrs
Stone alias Clefts, Philip (QS)

Worcestershire

Armstrong, John
Catstre, Vincent
Handy, John
Marlborn alias Maulbourn, Enoch
Molland, Thomas
Taylor, Samuel

Felons transported from London to Maryland by the *Bond*, Capt. John Gardiner, in April 1742. (PRO: T53/40/485).

Buckinghamshire

Bradley, William
Butler, Richard - 14 yrs
Grommett, Francis - 14 yrs
Mayes, George
Waring, Ann

Essex

Bishop, William
Edwards, Mary
Fuller, Turpin
Hitch, John
Lark, James
Scott, John
Southwell, John
Spencer, Laurence
Upwin, John
White, Thomas
Williams, Francis

Hertfordshire

Barford, Elizabeth
Bawcock, John
Clarke, James
Davis, Thomas - 14 yrs
Hannah, James - 14 yrs

How, Samuel
Scott, James

Kent

Abbott, Thomas
Benfield, William
Bourand, Francis
Clark, Thomas - 14 yrs
Dutton alias Holmes, Elizabeth
Dutton, Martha
Harris, Richard
Hoarnden, James
Kingsland, David
Love, John
May, Elizabeth
Morfield, William - 14 yrs
Perce, Edmund
Quynn, John - 14 yrs
Read, John
Rives, James
Wells, James - 14 yrs

London*

Biggs, Mary
Bird, Thomas
Cunningham, James
Nicholls, Nathaniel

Nicholls, Robert
Preston, Dorothy
Russet, James
Twist, Thomas

Middlesex*

Baker, John
Brooks, John
Cameron, Duncan
Carter, Thomas
Cheek, George
Coopey, Joseph
Cox, Samuel
Devall, Margaret wife of Joseph
Edridge, Elizabeth
Floyd, William
Fryer, John
Gibbons, Elizabeth*
Mason, Robert
Nelson, Ann
Palmer, James
Porter, Edward

Rackett, Alice
Shambler, John
Stevens, Ann

Surrey

Balcombe, Edward
Balcombe, Elizabeth
Ball, Philip
Fox, John - 14 yrs
Hardy, Elizabeth
Johnson, William
Lancaster, Nathaniel
Lewis, Peter
More, Richard
Moseley, Richard
Norris, William
Prew, William
Salmon, John
Stevens, Thomas
Upham, John
Walsham, Robert - 14 yrs

*All recorded in Prince George Co., Maryland, Land Records, Liber Y, f. 562

Felons transported from London to Maryland by the *Bladon*, Capt. Samuel Laurence, in June 1742. (PRO: T53/41/129).

London

Atkinson, John
Briers, William
Bunch, Robert
Burk, Sarah
Chad, William
Cross, Thomas
Emes, John
Harris, James
Lee, Ferdinando
McEnnis, Frederick
Moon, George
Roper, Richard
Salmon, John
Steadman, James
Triquett, Peter
Wilks, Thomas - runaway
Wilson, Cecilia
Wiltshear, George

Middlesex

Adley, Hannah wife of George,
  alias Hannah Lane
Barber, Elizabeth
Barrett alias Massey, Margaret
Berritt, Ann
Bride alias Bine, Mary
Catlin, Thomas
Charlton, John
Donegan alias Dongan, Patrick
Earle, Elizabeth
Fairfax, William
Glover, Thomas - 14 yrs
Glynn, John
Godfrey, Ann
Grant, William
Green alias Lile, Jane
Hale alias Dickenson, Mary
Henry, George
Kilburn, Reuben
Lyons, Elizabeth
McDonald, Ann

Miller, Mary
Penny, Martha
Pinner, Elizabeth
Pope, George
Pratt, James
Price, Stephen
Read, John
Scriven, George
Sutton, Elizabeth
Terry, Martha
Watson, Elizabeth

Sussex

Camell alias Scamell
  alias Fielder, Sarah
Giles, Sarah but stopped & transported
  in Jun 1742
Guillane, John
Higgs, Mary
Martow, Jacob
Rolf, John
Stowman, William

Felons transported from London to Maryland by the *Forward*, Capt. John Sargent*, in September 1742. (PRO: T53/41/130).

Buckinghamshire

Brookes, Thomas
Cock, Thomas

Essex

Franks, Richard
King, William
Larkin, Benjamin - 14 yrs
Moss, Robert - 14 yrs
Page, Joshua - 14 yrs
Sallows, Robert - 14 yrs
Sexton, Nathaniel
Ward, Patrick

Hertfordshire

Chambers, Thomas
Head, Edward - 14 yrs
Rimes, William
Smith, John - 14 yrs
Wrigglesworth, Joseph

Kent

Barber, John
Davis, Hugh
Dixson, John
Ford, William
Hatfield, William
Oliver, Nicholas
Randoll, Sarah
Reynolds, Ann
Steddall, Elizabeth
Tipper, John 14 yrs

Tolhurst, John
Turner, Richard alias John - 14 yrs
Watson, William - 14 yrs
Wilson, Thomas

London

Brannon, Thomas
Broomhall, Mary
Clayton, William
Donahoo alias Davison, Margaret
Flemmar alias Flemming, William,
  alias Silver Heels
Head, Susanna
Higginson, John
Jackson alias South, William
Marlow, Mary
Page, Mary
Vowells, Mary

Middlesex

Bloxam, John
Bunn, Thomas
Burnham, Esther
Cratsman, Jane
Davis, Catherine
Davis, Margaret
Elmes, Elizabeth
Emms, Susanna
Glover, William
Holland alias Lee, Ann - 14 yrs
Hutchins, Margaret
Hyatt, Sarah
Johnson, Martha
Lambert, John

Lumley, Margaret
McCoy, James
Miller, Jane
Neale, Anna Maria
Newland, James
Parsons, Elizabeth
Pigg, Joseph - 14 yrs
Robinson alias Bisse, Mary
Shields, Elizabeth
Staples, Mary
Walker, Caleb
White alias Shays, Mary
Wood, Dorothy
Wood, Samuel - runaway

Surrey

Burrows, Charles - 14 yrs
Johnson, Mary
Stent, Thomas
Webster, Margaret

Sussex

Mepham, Richard
Merchant, Thomas
Piggot, William

* Of the original 74 felons embarked in London 58 died on passage. Sargent was prosecuted in 1744 for cruelty to his passengers but acquitted. The ship was taken prize by a Spanish privateer on her homeward voyage.

Felons shipped by George Buck of Bideford by the *Kent*, Capt. John Bissick, by agreements of November & December 1742 and registered in Queen Anne's Co. in June 1743 (MSA: CR 49,082-RT B ff. 539-540).

Devon

Baily, Simon - 14 yrs
Cockram, George - 14 yrs
Croot, Bartholomew - 14 yrs
Dewdney, William (QS)
Dodd, Anne - 14 yrs
Drown, William - 14 yrs
Gale, John - 14 yrs
Harding, Amos - 14 yrs
Hellier, Richard - 14 yrs

Hooper, Richard - 14 yrs
Jeffery, Susanna
Kerslake, William - 14 yrs
Merry, Mary wife of Samuel of Exeter, dyer (QS)
Southwood, John - 14 yrs
Spurway, Daniel - 14 yrs
Staddon alias Stanton, John - 14 yrs
Taylor, Stephen - 14 yrs
Wheeler, Lawrence - 14 yrs

Felons transported from London to Virginia by the *Justitia*, Capt. Barnet Bond*, in April 1743. (PRO: T53/41/227).

Buckinghamshire

Dormer, John
Calcott, William
Hawthorn, Richard

Essex

Brooker, Penelope
Coping, Thomas - 14 yrs - died
Fenny, William
Gallant, Ambrose (QS)
Griffith, Henry - 14 yrs
Masterman, John

Sasser, John - 14 yrs - died

Hertfordshire

Long, Mary
Piggott, Ralph - 14 yrs
Sherston, John - 14 yrs
Strickett, Arthur

Kent

Bailey, John
Brown, James
Catt, Nicholas - died on passage

Kinardy, Frances
Lee, Anne
Stewart, John - died on passage
Thomas, Jane
Trueman, Thomas
Wann, Richard
Young, Elizabeth

London

Barber, Jane
Barrow, Honour
Birk, Richard
Brighton, Daniel
Budd, Robert - 14 yrs
Clements, Margaret
Coars, Isaac
Cooley, Richard - 14 yrs
Creech, Sarah
Cromley, Henry
Dawson, John
Dutton, Thomas
Goody alias Goodwin, John
Haney alias Heaney, John
Hayes, Philip
Huddle, Thomas
Isaacs, Tobias
Masham, Ann
Newton, Charles - 14 yrs
Peterson, Christopher
Raven, Hannah
Roberts, Dorothy
Robinson, Margaret
Ross, Thomas
Rowland, Catherine
Staples, Daniel
Waters, William
Watson, Daniel
Welsh, Mary

Middlesex

Baker, Margaret
Belott, Daniel
Bennett, John
Bird, William - for life
Bluck, John
Booker, Samuel
Braxton, Thomas
Brockley, Catherine
Brown, George
Brown, Edward

Brown, Isabella - 14 yrs
Broxton, Thomas
Campbell, Alexander
Campbell, George
Cartwright, Dicken
Crank, Sarah wife of John
Creighton, John
Cumberford, John
Danby, Catherine
Delany, Robert
Dixon, William - 14 yrs
Edwards, William - 14 yrs
Elford, Mary
Eves, Jane
Farrell, Francis
Forrester, Patience - 14 yrs
Graham, Jane
Gray, Elizabeth
Gray, William
Harper, Bartholomew
Harps, Susanna
Harril, Thomas
Harrison, Rowland
Hartley, Harry
Heber, John
Hobson, Hannah
Hopson, Richard
Hudson, Thomas - 14 yrs
Hughes, Charles
Hyth, John
Larrett, Edmund - 14 yrs
Lawn, Dorothy wife of Charles
Logan, Robert
Low, John
Low, Mary
Ludford, Francis
Massey, Sarah
McCullock, John
Mecan, William
Miller, William
Morgan, Mary wife of George
Mullener, John
Poland, Christian
Powell, Elizabeth
Riley, Mary
Russell, Jane
Salter, Elizabeth wife of Mathew
Spurham, George
Squires, Robert
Stone alias Booth alias Moley, Ann
Tanner, Charles
Thackham, William

White, Hannah
Wood, Jane - 14 yrs
Woodcock, William

Surrey

Bradford, Thomas
Briggs, John
Coombs, Thomas
Dealey, Mary
Hale, William
Lawrence, John

Reed, Mary
Rowe, John
Standfad, Mary
Tongue, Charles
Tongue, Mary
White, Henry

Sussex

Durham, John - died on passage
Howell, Henry - died on passage
Simmonds, Thomas - died

*Bond was prosecuted with Capt. John Sargent of the *Forward* for maltreatment of his passengers on this voyage but was found not guilty.

Felon transported from London to Maryland by the *Bond*, Capt.Matthew Johnson, in April 1743. (CLRO: London Bond).

London

Hassell, Richard - 14 yrs

Felons transported from London to Maryland by the *Indian Queen*, Capt. Edward Maxwell, sailing in May 1743. (PRO: T53/41/326).

London

Burk, Alice
Butcher, Ann
Crab, James
Markham, Joseph
McGrew, James
Musket, James
Read, John
Smith, William

Middlesex

Ayers, Mary Lhuillier
Birch, Joseph
Broom, James
Burridge, Thomas
Cavenagh, Honor - for life
Chappell, Mary

Cooke, John
Cooms, William
Gillam, John
Guttery, James
Harris, Elizabeth
Haven, Thomas
Haynes, Francis
Kelly, Catherine
McKay, John
Robinson, John
Slate, Ann
Stanfield, Elizabeth
Taylor, Cordelia - 14 yrs
Taylor alias Brown, Sarah
Wickett, Daniel - 14 yrs
Wilford, Rachel
Wilson, Ann
Wynn, Alice

Felons transported from London to Maryland by the *Essex*, Capt. John Hunter, in May 1743. (CLRO: London Bond).

London

Burk, Alice

Butcher, Ann

Crab, James
Markham, Joseph
McGrew, James

Musket, James
Read, John
Smith, William

Felons transported by agreements of August 1743 with John Buck of Bideford and Capt. William Bissick [by the latter's ship *Raven* from Bideford], and registered in Kent Co. records 20 February 1744. (MSA: CR 42,840-8537 ff. 62-67).

Bristol

Anderson, Hester
Ashmore, William
Carter, Sarah
Galloway, John
Gilbert, Henry
Harman, Elizabeth
Jones, Anne
Jones, Welthian
Knowles, James
Lane, Thomas
Legg, Henry
Mayo, Mary

Parry, Mary
Smith, Anne
Thomas, Elizabeth
Wall, Hugh

Monmouthshire

Jenkins, William
Morris, William

Worcestershire

Farranton, Jasper

Felons transported by agreements of September & October 1743 with John Buck of Bideford [by the *Globe*?], Capt. John Bissick, and registered in Kent Co. records 10 March 1744 (MSA: CR 42,840-8537 ff. 71-77).

Devon

Arscott, Richard Jr. - 14 yrs
Bragg, William
Brockington, Philip (QS)
Dyer, Benjamin
Griffin, Edward (QS) - runaway
Hawkins, Jane
Hele, Robert (QS)

Jarvis, Michael - 14 yrs
Jewell, William (QS)
Mitchell, Richard - 14 yrs
Osmond, Ann (QS)
Pearce, John - 14 yrs
Remmet, Sarah (QS)

Felons transported to from London to Virginia by the *George William*, Capt. Jack Campbell, in November 1743. (PRO: T53/41/327)

Buckinghamshire

Cloathier, William - 14 yrs
Jackson, John
Ricketts, William

Essex

Clark, John
Mallery, Mathew
Pierce, Thomas
Pont, John

Savil, William
Smith, John

Hertfordshire

Rixon, Jacob
Shoreton, Mathew
Tatton, Joseph, alias Priest, James
Taylor, William

Kent

Day, Andrew
Heroe alias Harrow, Rebecca
Hollingberry, Richard
Leven, Edward
Reeve, Joseph
Smith, Richard

London

Bartlet, Sarah
Brown, John
Cannon, Susannah
Collin (Collier), Samuel
Cordwell, James
Ewers, Martha
Harris, Elizabeth
Harris, Henry
Hendrick, John
Henley, Sarah
Hoden alias Haydon, Mary
Holder, Elizabeth
Jefferys, John
King, James
Knight, James
Mackan alias Mackaron, John
Muckleston, Elizabeth alias Irish Nell
Mulbury, James
Pennyfather, Michael
Purser, Joseph
Pybee, Alexander
Richardson, John
Rutt, James
Stevens, John
Taylor, Sarah
Treakle, George
Wainscoate, George
Whitehead, Abraham
Wood, Catherine

Middlesex

Almon, Judith
Andrews, Charles
Baker, Daniel
Barrett, Frances wife of John
Barton, Martha
Bates alias Booth, Mary
Bennett, George
Berry, Jonathan
Boyd, Elizabeth wife of Terence

Brown, Christian
Buck, Thomas
Bym alias Bom, William
Capell, Sarah
Cartwright, Richard
Chaplin, Catherine
Chapman, Jacob
Cole, Charles
Copestakes, Hannah
Cordosa, Jacob - stopped
Davis, John
Davis, William
Douglass, Eleanor wife of John
Earl alias Day, William
Evans, Evey alias Evan
Flower, Eleanor
Foreman, Walter
Fuller, Sarah
Glinn, Patrick
Hamilton, John
Hartshorn, Susannah
Holmes alias Yates alias Smith, Mary
  - stopped
Hoskins, Ann
Hunt, Richard
Johnson, Mary
Kelly, John
Lluellin, David - 14 yrs
Maine, Charles
Maynard, Jane wife of Joseph
McKenzie, Christian
Merrick, Griffith
Mills, Sarah
Mitchell alias Procter, Christian
Mockridge, Mary wife of William
Morrison, Samuel
Price, James
Prick, Rachael
Procter, Mary
Rider, Ann
Rossum, Mary
Silver, John
Storer, Thomas
Sykes, Ann
Thomas, John
Wade, John
Ward, Joseph
Webb, Thomas
Weblin, Samuel
Wheeler, Susanna
White, Mary
Wilson, John

Windsor, Bacon
Woodward, Elizabeth

Jarrett, James
Miles, Mary

Sussex

Felons transported from London to Maryland by the *Neptune*, Capt. James Knight, in February 1744. (PRO: T53/41/419).

London

Blank, James
Blay, Richard
Boyce, Mary
Broughton, Thomas
Brown, William
Bulley, Henry
Burgess, Thomas
Cawdell, Mary
Collet, Lydia
Conoway, Matthew
Davis, Mary
Davis, John
Dean, Frances
Dennis, Roger
Eales, William
Fisk, Mary
Ford, James
Foster, Mary
Gardiner, Thomas
Gilbert, Thomas
Johnson, William
Judson, Ann
Keate, Thomas
Martin, John
Palmer, Rachael
Perryment, William
Pocock, Charles
Randall, William
Shaw, James
Smith, Thomas
Veale alias Webb, Jane
Wheatly, John
Williams, Thomas
Worgan, William

Middlesex

Adcock, Thomas
Alexander, Ann
Aspley alias Dalton, Jane
Bailey, Susannah
Baxter, Henry

Bean, Mary wife of William
Bird, Lydia
Bone, Ann
Brown, John
Brown, Thomas
Brown, William
Bunn, John
Cammock, Edward
Casey alias Gaffney, Patrick
Clarke, Ann
Clayton, Ann wife of William
Clough, John
Corker, Mary
Doody, Joseph
Douglas, Thomas
Elmore, Margaret wife of Samuel
Embling, John
Evans, Evey alias Evan
Ewen, John (QS)
Forsee, Elizabeth
Frost, Judith
Harvey, Susannah
Hinsman, Barbara
Holbrook, John
Jackson, Robert
Johnson alias Jackson
    alias Harrison, Ann
Joiner, Joseph
Jones, Penelope
Jones, Thomas
Keminett, Hannah
Leach, Joseph
Lewis, Thomas
Lewis, Ann wife of James
Marshall, Edward
McCoy, Benjamin
Miller alias Barefoot, Elizabeth
Mills, Isabella wife of Robert
Niblett, Joel
Norman, William
Palmer, Elizabeth
Parsons, Elizabeth
Penny, Thomas
Read, John

Richardson, Robert
Ricketts, William
Roberts, John, alias Langley, Edward
Rowe, Ann
Simons, Catherine
Skylight, Margaret
Smith, Christopher
Sonee, Ann
Stanley, James

Still, Richard
Swart, Michael
Todd, David
Tomlinson, Joseph
Warwick, Richard
Wild, Jane wife of Stephen
Willis, William
Wilson, Mary
Yearby, John

Felons transported by agreement of 30 March 1744 with John Buck of Bideford by the *Susannah* of Bideford, Capt. William Kenny, and registered in Kent Co. records 23 August 1744 (MSA: CR 42,840-8537 f. 124).

Devon

Bartlet, John
Bartlet, Nicholas
Berry, Robert - 14 yrs
Crossing, William - 14 yrs
Dart, William
Dyer, James - 14 yrs
Harris, John - 14 yrs
Huxtable, William - 14 yrs

Lane, John - 14 yrs
Martyn, William - 14 yrs
Pain, Mary - 14 yrs
Passenger, Jonathan - 14 yrs
Preston alias Budbrook, John - 14 yrs
Seamer, Nicholas
Tucker, John
Vicary, Hugh

Felons transported from London to Virginia by the *Justitia*, Capt. Jack Campbell, in May 1744. (PRO: T53/41/462).

Buckinghamshire

Davis, John
Eames, John - 14 yrs

Essex

Bailey, Simon
Evans, William
Hover, Samuel (QS)
Jones, Edward
Langley, Lydia
Morphew, John
Raw, Thomas - runaway
Smith, John
Turner, Samuel
Turvie, James
Wilson, Jasper
Wilson, Mary
Wood, John

Hertfordshire

Scother, Ann

Williams, John

Kent

Arnold, John
Carmuck, Patrick
Chisley, Tabitha
Dugmore, Sarah
Fielder, Richard
Gill, William
Hall, Richard
Jefferys, Benjamin
Joyner, Edward
Layton, Abraham
Powell, Thomas
Smith, Charles
Thorrington, John - 14 yrs

London

Cooper, Sarah
Dowles, Jacob
Evans, Thomas - runaway
Feagins, Nicholas

Geary, Eleanor - 14 yrs
Gosling, Josiah
Gumbleton, Humphrey
Hawkins, John
Howard, Robert
Hurt, Joseph
Lax, George
Poole, James
Shirley, Mary, alias Davis, Catherine
Simmonds, Sarah
Smith, John
Stansbury alias Boucher
  alias Burcher, Mary
  alias Margaret
Wild, Thomas

Middlesex

Andrews, George
Ball, Sarah
Barnett, Ann
Booth, Lydia
Budd, Ann
Callen, Eleanor
Cambell, Archibald
Challoner, George
Compton, Margaret
Creed, Henry
Dobbs, Thomas
Eaton, Elizabeth
Edwards alias Lareman, Elizabeth
Flint, David
Fowler, Mary
Gerrard, John
Gregory, James
Greswold, Joseph
Haycraft, James
Howard, Sarah
Hunt, Julius - 14 yrs
Inglish, Sarah
Jewers, Johanna

Jude, Michael - for life
Lloyd, John
Long, John
McDonnell, James
Mitchell, William
Page, Thomas
Phillips, Ann
Read alias Jeffryes, Susannah
Robinson, Elizabeth
Robinson, William
Saunders, Sarah
Smytheman, Samuel
Staples, William
Wainwick, Thomas
Wilson, George
Woodcock, Diana

Surrey

Beauchamp, John
Bonaretta, Anthony
Dagger, Mary - 14 yrs
French, Benjamin
Halliman, Mary
Haymer, Mary
Hill, Elizabeth
Kent, Ann
Kingdom, Arthur
McLaghlin, Henry
Mileist, Thomas
Price, Mary
Roundy, David - 14 yrs
Wall, Jane
Williams, Susan

Sussex

Browning, John
Dulvey, William
Forman, John
Seagrove, William

Felons transported from London to Maryland by the *Savannah*, Capt. James Dobbins, in October 1744. (PRO: T53/42/64).

Buckinghamshire

Coleman, Samuel - 14 yrs
Habberley, William - 14 yrs
Lewis, Josiah - 14 yrs

Essex

Butler, James - 14 yrs
Coney, Mark - 14 yrs
Flack, Richard - 14 yrs
Maddell, William - 14 yrs

Hertfordshire

Smith, Sarah

London

Bathaw, John
Betts, Lowry
Billingsley, Charles
Boraston, Edward
Deal alias Baker, Mary
Everett, James.
Nailor, Elizabeth
Piggott, Mary
Stansbury alias Stanberry, Mary
 alias Boucher alias Burcher, Margaret
Stewart, Sarah
Tims, Elizabeth wife of Joseph - 14 yrs
Wall, Mary
Wilder alias Hawkins, Ann

Middlesex

Bailey, Edward
Banham alias Greenwood, Carolina
Brown, Mary
Brownjohn, Cheney
Burk, Esther
Cleaver, Charles
Collett, Sarah
Copeland, Mary
Dixon, Catherine
Fordham, Alice
Fuller, Robert - 14 yrs
Hall, George

Haws, Catherine wife of William
Imbey, Mary
Jepton, Judith
Johnson, John - 14 yrs
Jones, William
King, Eleanor
Martin, James
Mills, Isabella
Monk, Martha
Monroe, Margaret
Orford, Mary
Powell, William
Pugh alias Harding, Elizabeth
Roach, Samuel
Rockett (Rooke), Robert - 14 yrs
Smith, Mary
Sullivan, Elizabeth
Swallow, Mary
Terry, Ann - for life
Tolloway, Elizabeth
Trotter, Abraham
Wandon alias Bannister, Richard
Waters, Mary
Webb alias Tooworth, Ann

Surrey

Browne, Thomas
Massingham, Charles

Sussex

Goacher, James
Stone, James

Felons transported from London to Virginia by the *Justitia*, Capt. John Johnstoun, in May 1745. (PRO: T53/42/138).

London

Anderson, Ann
Barber, Ann
Barker, Thomas
Bell, James
Bowyers, Catherine
Carter, Robert - for life
Cutler, Henry
Dalby, Mary
Davis, Mary
Deal, James
Falcon, Jacob

Farrow, John
Fitzwater, Joseph - for life
Fuller alias Pulley, Elizabeth
Galloway, James
Grimes alias Graham, Martha
Harman, John
Jones, Mary
Kennewall, Charles
King, David
Laws, John
Long, William
Meers alias Kirby, Margaret
Owen, Samuel

Peirson, John - for life
Price, John
Rich, Elizabeth
Shipper, William
Simmons, Anne
Smart, Mary
Smith, Jane alias Singing Jenny
Smith, John (2)
Sykes, John
Taylor, Susannah
Underhill, George
Webb, Henry
White, John
White, Henry
Widgeon, William
Young, Edward

Middlesex

Booth, Hannah

Brown, Elizabeth
Buckles, Dorothy
Cable, Isabella
Chapman, Peter
Fraizer, Elizabeth
Graham, Robert
Harrison, Ann
How, James
Jones, Ann
Jones, Mary
Kirk, Thomas
Launder, Philip
Linsey, Jane
Poulton, Samuel
Robinson, Andrew
Rosse, Hannah
Smith, John
Swawbrook alias Beakley, Magdalene
Tibbett, Elizabeth

Felons transported from London to Maryland by the *Italian Merchant*, Capt. Alexander Reid, in July 1745, (CLRO: London & LMA: Middlesex Bonds, PRO: Home Circuit records).

Essex

Bradley, Thomas
Cheventum, Thomas
Cooke, Henry
Dawkings alias Crispe, George
King, John
Nelson, William - 14 yrs
Smith, Daniel
Squirrell, Elizabeth
Stains, Benjamin
Stokes, John

Hertfordshire

Jarvis, Benjamin
Underwood, Jacob Fosbrook
Williams, James

Kent

Gwatkins, John
Naish, Susan
Nicholas, Robin
Norman, Anna Maria - runaway
North, Thomas
Salter, Samuel - runaway

Traffick, Jeremiah

London

Davis alias Boswell, Ann
Delander, Peter
Stavenaugh alias Howells, Elizabeth

Middlesex

Blackbourn, Elizabeth
Carter, William
Connell, Alexander
Haynes, John
Herring alias Brown, Catherine
Robinson, Rose
Simms, Henry

Surrey

Anderton, Eleanor
Burgess, John
Deal, Ann
Hood, John Jr.
Ledger, Thomas
Wright, Richard

Sussex

Leggatt, Thomas
Manser, Allen - 14 yrs

Felons transported from London to Maryland by the *Plain Dealer*, Capt. James Dobbins, in January 1746. (PRO: T53/42/138).

London

Bannister, George
Bannister, Mary
Barton, William
Beck, Mary
Bibbe, Sarah
Burne, Tobias
Carr, Elizabeth
Cason, Barnard.
Castelow, Thomas
Dix, Joseph
Doe, Mary
Doughty, Elizabeth
Edwards, Edward
Eves, Richard
Fitzgerald, Catherine
Ford, Thomas
Godby, Jasper
Grace, William
Hall, Susanna
Hancock, Elizabeth
Harrison, James
James, Joseph
Joyce, William
Leppard, James
Lone, Elizabeth
Morris, Jane
Pardo, Mary
Ranton, Richard
Rushby, Mary
Sollon, James
Staddow, John
Stanbury, Ann
Sutton, Thomas
Swinton, John
Westfield, Richard
Williamson, Edward
Williamson, James
Woollard, James

Middlesex

Abey, Thomas
Allen, John

Barton, John
Beason, William
Bramingham, Elizabeth
Brandling, Elizabeth
Brewin, William
Bride, Thomas
Burle, Jane
Caton alias Cathorne, Jane
Cave, Patrick - 14 yrs
Connor, Hugh - 14 yrs
Crew, Ann
Cunnington, Alice
Cust, Christopher
Danks, Mary
Davis, James
Dean, John
Demaine, Rebecca
Devine, Philip
Dundass, Elizabeth
Emtage, John
Fowler, Hester - 14 yrs
French, Alice
Gardner, Elizabeth
Glasswell, John
Gunnell, George
Hambridge, Richard
Hand, Patrick
Harris, Sarah
Haynes, Thomas
Horton, Richard - 14 yrs
Howell, Joseph
Hunt, John
Hyde, Elizabeth
Jones, Samuel - runaway
Knock, Thomas
Lawrett, Mary
Lincoln, Rose
Martin, John
Mason, John
Mays, Elizabeth
McLaughlin alias Mason
    alias Thomas, Mary
Morris, John
Newberry, Elizabeth wife of Thomas Jr.
Newman alias Smith, Thomas

Owen, Mary
Perkins, Ann
Perry, Ann
Phillips, Hannah
Pong, Lettice
Powell, Philip
Randall, Mary
Reed, Elizabeth
Robinson, John
Salmon, Richard
Scott, Jane

Seyers, John
Shaw, Mary
Smith, Margaret
Smith, Joseph
Stonehouse, William
Titmarsh, Susannah
Welsh, Thomas
Wheeler, Ralph
White, Elizabeth
Yowell, John
Zell, Thomas

Felons transported from London to Virginia (?) by the *Laura*, Capt. William Gracie, in April 1746. (CLRO: London & LMA: Middlesex Bonds).

London

Audless, Margaret
Crowther, Edward
Harris, Mary
Hurst, John
Murphy, Ann
Overbury, Robert
Parford, William
Robinson, Henry
Ross alias Bass, Jane
Scruton, Robert - 14 yrs
Sears, George
Webb, John

Middlesex

Bell, Mary - 14 yrs
Bennet, Eleanor
Bramston, John
Bullock, James
Burk, Catherine
Burne, George
Carter, Jane
Connell, Thomas - 14 yrs
Cooley, John
Darby, Ann
Davis, Thomas - 14 yrs
Dawson, Mary
Debidge, Ann
Edwards, Elizabeth wife of Joseph
Enwood, Mary
Evans, Catherine - 14 yrs
Farley, John
Field, Mary - 14 yrs

Foote, Elizabeth
Ford, Mary Ann
Gardner alias Bridgwater, Elizabeth
Grant, Susanna
Harris, Mary
Hobbs, Sarah
Hopwood, William
Howard, Ann
Hussey, Hester
Juson, John
Keith, Eleanor
Lanes, Elizabeth
Lloyd, Deborah - for life
Mason, Joseph - 14 yrs
McCornick, Adam
Miller, Daniel
O'Marsh, Catherine wife of James
 - 14 yrs
O'Marsh, James - 14 yrs
O'Marsh, Robert
O'Marsh, Thomas
Pagram, Mary
Smith, Ann
Summerton, Hester
Swan, Peter
Thomas, Ann
Thompson, Ann wife of Francis
Wade, Sarah wife of Solomon
Warden, William
Watson alias Madeira, Joshua
Whitfield, Barthia
Williams, Elizabeth
Wilson, Robert
Wright, Mary

111

Felons transported from London to Virginia by the *Mary*, Capt. John Johnstoun, in September 1746. (CLRO: London & LMA: Middlesex Bonds; PRO: Home Circuit records).

Essex

Baker, Joseph
Davis, Joseph
Goodchild, William
Theed, Richard - 14 yrs

Hertfordshire

Buckle, Daniel - 14 yrs
Snow, Robert - 14 yrs

Kent

Cole, James
Sadd, Thomas
Wellard, Thomas
Whetland, John

London

Dawson alias Dodson, John
Davis, Edward
Davis, Hannah
Watson, Ann
Finch, John
Carter, James

Middlesex

Anderson, Jane

Anderson, Thomas
Broughton, William
Brumley, Mary
Burn, Ann
Burn, William
Butler, Alice wife of William
Church, Elizabeth
Donnington, William
Ellis, Elizabeth
Freeman, John
Gardner, Samuel
Hoyles, William
Hurst, Hannah
King, Jane
Kipping, Mary alias wife of
    Edward Merrit - 14 yrs
Lowry, Catherine - 14 yrs
Ogleby, George
Searle, James
Smith, John
Thomas, Henry
Thornton, Susanna
Walters, Joseph
Williams, Elisha
Woolley alias Lawrence, Rebecca

Surrey

Crisp, Robert. - 14 yrs
McCahil, Owen - 14 yrs
Upchurch, John - 14 yrs

Felons transported from London to Virginia by the *George William*, Capt. James Dobbins, in January 1747. (CLRO: London & LMA: Middlesex Bonds).

London

Corp, Edward
Crockett, William
Davis, John
Deacon, Sarah
Hampton, John
Holloway alias Van Gadwey, Jacob
Hudd, Mary
Jones, Susanna
Levingston, Anna Maria
Lewen, William
Lowry, Edward

Marsh, Original
McLane, William
Pennell, Thomas
Robinson, Hannah
Simpson, Ann
Smith, Mary
Stracey, Ann
Theron alias Thorn, Isaac
Toasten alias Fennister, Mary
Warner, Richard
Webb, John
Webley, Ann

Middlesex

Adams, Mary
Bassett, Elizabeth
Burgess, Elizabeth wife of Samuel
Cannew, James
Cole, Judith
Dwyer, Mary wife of Matthew
Finch, Heneage
Godman, Elizabeth
Hart, Margaret wife of Daniel
Hill, Mary
Hudson, Jane
Jetter, John
Kasey, Thomas
Kelley, Ann
King, Mary
Kitchen, George

Lewis, Jane
Newell, William
Oakes, Thomas
Pidgeon, Mary wife of John
  alias Mary Evatt
Poulter, John - 14 yrs
Quickley, Bartholomew
Read, Susannah
Scholes, John
Sprightley, Hannah
Stannifer, Mary
Stewart, Alexander
Thomas, Henry - shipwrecked after
  sentence of May 1763
Tooley, Tool
Wheatley, Elizabeth
Williams, Elizabeth - runaway

Felons transported from London to Virginia by the *Laura*, Capt. William Gracie*, in July 1747. (CLRO: London & LMA: Middlesex Bonds; PRO: Home Circuit records).

Buckinghamshire

Brimley, John Jr.
Coleman, Thomas - 14 yrs
Isted, Edward

London

Baxson, Mordecai
Cape, Joseph
Courtney, Sarah
Dalfee, David
Darby, William
Griggs, Thomas
Groves, William
Harvey, Daniel
Hindley, William
Parsons, George
Powers, Thomas
Salmon, Richard
Taylor, Judith
West, Joseph

Middlesex

Aldridge, Robert
Anderson, Luke
Blackhood, John
Bright, William
Buckle, Benjamin

Butler, Thomas - runaway
Capell, Mary
Cobb, Samuel
Collings, John
Connelly, Patrick
Cooke, Mary
Edwards, Edward
Fletcher, William
Fulker, Mary
German, William
Goff, Elias
Gordon, Thomas
Gosdin, Mary
Gotray, Hugh
Grace, William
Green, John
Hobson, Thomas
Hussey, Mary
Jackson, Thomas
Jones, Ann
Lawin alias Lawlin, John
Lovett, Henry
Maud alias Pickington, Grace
Mercer, Elizabeth
Morgan, Jane
Notson alias Gibbons, Isabella
Oldfield, Margaret wife of Michael
  alias Grigg
Paine, Edward
Pankin, Paul

Prankitt, Robert
Sparks, Sarah
Stanley alias Brown, John
Stevens, Henry
Symonds, Vincent - runaway
Thompson, Joseph
Wilkins alias Philpott
  alias Awdrey, Jane

Wilkinson, Mary
Witherington, Henry
Woodward, John

Surrey

Mitchell, John
Warren, Margaret

*On this voyage Gracie was described as "a morose, surly person with a fierce temper" who frequently beat and threatened his crew. (PRO: HCA15/45).

Felons transported from London by the *St. George*, Capt. James Dobbins, in January 1748 and registered in Kent Co. records in March 1748. (PRO: T53/42/519; MSA: EI No. 8, ff. 404-408; updates list appearing in *To Maryland from Overseas* by Harry Wright Newman (GPC 1985).

Buckinghamshire

Taylor, John - a youth - 14 yrs

Essex

Clarke, Mary (QS)
Lennon alias Fyson, Thomas - 14 yrs
Mason, John - 14 yrs
Moule, Edward - 14 yrs
Mullings, William(QS)
Shreive, John - 14 yrs

Hampshire

Collins, John - 14 yrs
Harvie, John - 14 yrs
Jones, Samuel - 14 yrs
Jones, Thomas
Lawrence, Richard - 14 yrs
Massy, George - 14 yrs
Montgomery, Frances - 14 yrs
Rose, Edward - 14 yrs - runaway
Thacker, Jane - 14 yrs
White, Ann
Whitby, William - 14 yrs

Kent

Bunnett, William
Cooke, Nathaniel
Fairall, John
Heays, Mary (QS)
Prior, Samuel

London

Bagwell, Margaret
Ball, Elizabeth
Bennett, Elizabeth
Bennett, John
Bilby, William
Clarke, William
Coomes, Mary - died
Courtney, James
Craith, Bridget
Delaney, Dennis
Ellis, Jane
Franklin, Charles
Godby, Jasper
Hargrove, Thomas
Haughton, William
Jones, William
Jukes, Benjamin
Lamb, John
Lawrence, Nathaniel
Low, Edmund
Lowther, alias Reachead, Sarah - for life
Murray, Elizabeth
Read, Mary - died
Roberts, Hugh - runaway
Thompson, Susannah
Vaughan, Edward
Wright, Ann

Middlesex

Avery alias MacDonald, Patrick - died
Ayers, Ann

Baker, Mary
Barber, Mary
Boswell, Ann - 14 yrs
Bottles, Sarah
Brazen, Jane - died
Bruce, John
Carnes, Mary
Cooke, Thomas
Cormack, Mary
Crawford, Susannah
Cripps, John - 14 yrs
Crispe alias Ridge, Sarah
Cuddy, Sophia
Davis, John
Evans, Samuel
Fitzsimmonds, James
Fling, John
Flowers, Jane
Gregory, Ann
Groves, Ann
Harvey, John
Heath, Charles
Hodges alias Pinson, James
Holden, Thomas
Jacobs, Cornelius
Judge, Judith
Kendall, Mary
Kent, John
Killigrew, Hannah
Longden, Joseph
Magham, James
Matthews, Margaret
McQuire, Lackland
Mitchell, Elizabeth
Mitchell, George - died
Newman, William
Page, Ann alias Willis, Mary
Payne, Martha - 14 yrs
Pebworth alias Smith, Mary
Radwell, Robert -14 yrs
Read alias Sweep, John
Roberts, Charles
Seall, William
Strong, Ann

Studder, John
Swan, Priscilla - died
Tickner, Peter
Ward, Luke - died
Wellthresher, Joseph
Welsh, Ann
Welsh, John
White, Elizabeth
Williams, John
Williams, William
Wright, John - runaway

Norfolk

Shaw, Mary (QS)

Surrey

Cameron, John - 14 yrs
Gazey, Samuel
Harrison, William
Mitchell, James
Paddison, William
Wall, Mary

Sussex

Waters, Richard - 14 yrs

Warwickshire

Cleaver, Robert alias Temple, Thomas
  - previously transported in 1739
Hurlstone, Samuel
Jones, John
Webb, William - 14 yrs

Wiltshire

Chamberlaine, Richard - 14 yrs
Clerke, James - 14 yrs
Robbins, Matthew
Sawyer, James - 14 yrs
Sawyer, William

Felons transported from London to Virginia by the *Lichfield*, Capt. John Johnstoun, in June 1748. (CLRO: London & LMA: Middlesex Bonds; PRO: Home Circuit records).

Essex

Bell, John

Day, Zacariah
Halliston, William
Linsted, Thomas

Naylor, John
Platt, William
Robinson, John
Stanford, William
Tagg, Hester

Hertfordshire

Flack, George
Low, Thomas
Miller, Mary wife of Thomas

Kent

Akerman, Thomas
Baker, William
Cooper, John
Dinns, Sarah
Dunn, Elizabeth
Hoye, Mary
Hudson, William
March, James

London

Barrett, Ann
Blinkin, Thomas
Broadway, Edward
Chadwick, John (2)
Crafts, Thomas
Field, Ann
Frederick, John
Haddock, William
Hays, Elizabeth
Hill, Thomas
Hockley, Sarah
Howell, Francis
Irwin, Susanna
Jones, Cornelius
Keys alias Thornton, John
Knight, George
Lawrence, John
Levi, Jeremiah
Mackenzie, Penelope
Martin, Bryan
Matthews, William
Middleton, Thomas
Moore, William
Palmer, Ann
Parker, Samuel
Price, James
Prosey, William

Raynsdon, John
Sibre, Samuel
Simpson, William
Taylor, Francis
Ward, John
Winter, James

Middlesex

Ash, John
Barnes, John
Black, Joseph
Brannond, Catherine
Campbell, Hugh
Clarke, Mary
Collins, William
Cook, John - 14 yrs
Coyle, James
Coyle, Michael
Cuthbert, Ann
Dyal, Sarah
Evans, Jane
Exelby, Mary
Harringan, Neal
Harvey, John
Haynes, Edward
Hoare, William
Ivery, Bryan
Jacomo, James
Jones, John
King, Mary
Leadley, Robert
Lines, Margaret wife of Andrew
Long, Ann
Macklin, Thomas
Maybank. Elizabeth
McDonald, Ann
Morse, William
Moss, Peter
Owen, Elizabeth
Paul, Elizabeth
Paul, Gabriel
Pullenger, William
Rowland alias Rowlin, Hannah
Rumbow, Edward
Ryder, John
Ryley, Margaret
Saunders, Elizabeth
Scarrett, George
Silcock alias Chambers, Mary
Smith alias Ordery alias Pepper, Mary
Swinston, Francis

Taylor, Elizabeth - 14 yrs
Thomas, Ann
Thompson, William
Turnbull, William
Walker alias Johnson, Mary
Walker, John
Watson, Mary
Watts, Charles
Wells, John - 14 yrs
Wilcox, Thomas
Wiseman, James

Surrey

Muzzle, Joseph - 14 yrs
Phelps, Mary
Puin, Richard
Weston, John
Winter, Samuel

Sussex

Abrey, Thomas
Simpkin, Ruth

Felons transported from London to Virginia by the *Mary*, Capt. John Ramsay, in July 1748. (PRO: T53/43/136).

London

Blake, Daniel
Grafton, Henry, alias Taylor, Harry
Huggins, John
Jones, John
Le Valley
Miller, Robert
Mullings, Ann
Nicholls, William
Porter, Rebecca
Pugh, Ann
Rison, Martha
Strong, John - runaway
Waring, Ann
Williams, Thomas

Middlesex

Albert, George
Beadle, Mary
Boulter, William
Bourne, Catherine
Brooks alias Sharpless, Catherine
Brown, John
Buckley, Francis
Campbell, Catherine
Carne, Elizabeth
Chettum, William alias Samuel

Collins, William
Condren, Thomas (14 yrs)
Crone, Fergus
Dennison alias Lawler, Catherine
Dicker, Catherine
Fowles alias Fowler, Mary
Freeman, Mary
Haymour, Elizabeth
Higby, Mary
Hutchinson, Jane
Kelly, Mary
Kerr alias Hubbard, Elizabeth
Lawless, Mary Ann
Lloyd, John
Lowder, Richard
May alias Cross alias Darby, Mary
Munday, Frances
Myers, Mary
Palmer, Elizabeth
Rooke, Henry
Ryder, Mary - runaway
Sale, Mary
Simms, Jane
Smith, Susanna
Sutherland, Margaret
Thorne, Jane
Welsh, Thomas
White, Ann alias Elener

Felons transported from London to Virginia(?) by the *Laura*, Capt. William Gracie, in January 1749. (PRO: T53/43/190).

Essex

Bearman, Elizabeth

Bilby, William
Cousins, Mary
Leigh, William

117

Munt, Elizabeth
Smith, William
Stevens, Richard - 14 yrs

Hertfordshire

Burrows, George - 14 yrs
Chandler, Hester
Figgis, Mary
Harrison, Katherine
Holgate, William - 14 yrs
Lambert, William 14 yrs
Lowry, George
West, Roger - 14 yrs

Kent

Cheeseman, Richard - 14 yrs
Cornew, Thomas
Hales, John
Larkman, Edward
Prior, John
Venner, James
Viney, Edward
Walter, John
Wells, William

London

Brackett, Daniel
Bray, Thomas
Bushell, William
Cardon, Richard
Cooper, Thomas
Cox, Jane
Debee, Joseph
Fielder, Price
Hughes, Samuel
Kates, John
Marsh, Daniel
McGuire, Catherine
Peyton, George
Presgrove, Thomas
Price, Peter
Price, Robert
Richards, James
Rose, William
Seabrooke, Thomas
Simpkins, Hannah
Smith, Ann
Solomon, Abraham
Summers, John

Swaney, John
Talley, William
Taylor, William
Thompson, William

Middlesex

Allen, George
Arthur, Richard
Barrett alias Barrell, Lancelot
Baton, Thomas alias John
Bew alias Edwards, John
Bond, John
Brown, Alice
Brown, James
Brown, Mary
Campbell, John
Cherry, Henry
Clarke, John (2)
Collins, Michael
Coseret alias Banks, Rebecca
Crawford, Thomas
Cripps, Philip
Culley, Charles
Da Costa, Isaac Alvarez
Davis, John
Dixon, William
Downey, Daniel
Doyle, Catherine
Draper, William
Evans, John
Fitzgerald, Andrew,
    alias Parsons, James,
    alias Mackase, Bartholomew
Fowler alias Carter alias Clements,
    Elizabeth
Ganey, James
Gritton, William
Hamilton, William
Herbert, Mary
Huffman, Mary
Hughes, John
Johnson, Michael
Legross, John
Lynn alias Bond, Hester
Masterson, Thomas
Morris, John
Mumpman, Ann
Needham, Thomas
Nicholson, Ann
North, Thomas
Otter, Francis

Poland, Abraham
Richards, Mary
Roach, John
Robinson, John
Stevenson, Thomas
Swanson, James
Taylor, Mary
Thompson, Samuel
Thrift, Elizabeth
Turner, Ann
Turner, William
Underhill, Henry
Winepress, Catherine
Winfield, Ann

Surrey

Blades, Henry
Burton, Richard
Jurd, Mary
Patrick, Thomas
Pope, William
Wilson, Robert - 14 yrs

Sussex

Dunk, Edward
Read, Stephen - 14 yrs

Felons transported from London to Maryland by the *Lichfield*, Capt. John Johnstoun, in May 1749. (CLRO: London & LMA: Middlesex Bonds; PRO: Home Circuit records).

Buckinghamshire

Foskett, Henry
Grace alias Frazier, William
Johnson, William

Essex

Davett, Joseph
Gardner, Mary
Jenkins, Margaret (QS)
Jolly, Henry
Martin, William
Smith, Ann (QS)
Stephenson, John
White, Edward

Hertfordshire

Cappock, John
Everitt alias Everill, Andrew
Jones, John
Jones, Owen
Penn, John

Kent

Cane, James
Donnohow, David
Farmer, Edward
Hawes, William
Hooton, John
King, John

Langley, Elizabeth
Powning, John
Viney, Thomas - runaway
Wagger, Thomas

London

Batton, Mary
Butler, Abigail
Caswell, John
Chapman, John
Christian, Hannah
Collett alias Collard, Stephen
Commins, Elizabeth
Cooper, Elizabeth
Fawcett, James
Greenaway, Henry
Griffith, Thomas
Hales, Abraham
Hales, Roger
Hotton, John
Keene, Thomas
Kendrick, William
Leeson, Elizabeth
Lenthal, Samuel
Matthews, Hugh
McQuin, Daniel
Mildred, Hannah
Oldman, Robert
Pollard alias Gillett, Mary
Roductine, Hannah
Sherrard alias Harwood, Thomas
Smith, Thomas

119

Spurling, Elizabeth
Spurling, Nicholas
Stichbury, Isaac
Stiff, Abraham
Sullivan, Timothy
Thompson, James
Williams, Thomas

Middlesex

Allen, Dorothy
Atkinson, John
Avery, Jane
Barrett, William
Blesson, William
Blizerd, Joseph
Brasington, Samuel
Browne, James
Brown, John
Brown alias Morley, Mary
Burnett, Elizabeth
Cane, William
Carsey, Jeremiah
Clarke, Andrew
Clarke, Mary
Cole, Elizabeth
Collyer, Elizabeth
Cook, Richard
Croutch, Thomas
Dove, Elianor
Dumerick, George alias Napton, Francis
Elsegood, William
Fisher alias Casey, Alexander
Forster, John
Frindly, John
Gardener, Sarah
Green, Mary
Gregory, John
Halton, William
Hammond, Edward
Hatt, John
Hayden, Thomas
Henley, Mary
Hobson, Samuel
How, Thomas
Hudell alias Hoodell, Thomas
Jackson, John
Jones, Richard
Kain, Robert
King, Joseph
McLaughlin, Jeremiah
Melone, John

Millington, John
Mills, Emanuel
Morris, Margaret
Nutkins, Thomas
Odderway, James
Perry, Thomas
Phillips, John
Poker alias Rand alias Cole, John
Potts, Edmund
Raven, John - for life
Ryan, Richard
Rymas, Matthew
Sheaf, William
Slate, James
Slater, John
Smith, William
Spencer, Mary
Strong, Thomas
Taylor, William
Thomas, William
Thornton, John
Tracey, Dorothy
Tucker, Edward
Wade, John
Ward, Robert
Watson, Robert
Webber, William
Welch, Lawrence
Williams, John
Wilson, Joseph
Wilson, Robert

Surrey

Boxall, Robert
Carnes, Amos
Carter, Martha
Clark, David
Davis, Ann
Food, James
Gamble, Thomas
Gray, Christopher
Lingham, John
Partin, Thomas
Pinn, William (QS)
Pitt, Joseph
Riell, Robert - 14 yrs
Stone, Nicholas
Ward, Elizabeth
Williams, John - 14 yrs

Sussex

Cruttenden, Thomas - 14 yrs

Moseley, Joseph
Savage, Richard

Felons transported from London to Maryland by the *Thames*, Capt. James Dobbins, in August 1749. (CLRO: London & LMA: Middlesex bonds; PRO: Home Circuit records).

Buckinghamshire

Wooding, John - 14 yrs

Essex

Cuttridge, Thomas
Evans, Joseph
Finlay, Richard
Green, John - 14 yrs
Miller, Mary (QS)
Pady, Thomas
Seaborn, William
Shrimplin, John
Smith, Jane wife of Gabriel (QS)
Turner, John (QS)
Warren, Susanna (QS)
Weaver, Thomas

Hertfordshire

Hunt, Hannah wife of Joseph
Hunt, Joseph
Neal, Thomas - 14 yrs

Kent

Ashford, William
Barrett, Thomas
Bloomley, John
Bradley, John
Brockman, John
Dongey, William
Frost, Abraham
Parsons, Richard - 14 yrs
Skelton, Eleanor
Steed, Samuel - runaway
Thompson, Andrew
Venus, John
Vidgeon, Thomas

London

Avery, John

Beck, Richard
Brown, John
Conduit, John
Davidson, Catherine - for life - runaway
Griffin, Robert
Hall, Martha
Highmore, Richard
Howard, Richard
Jay, Richard
Johnson, George
Jones, Philip
Juncker, John Lewis
Lane, Thomas - 14 yrs
Lee, John
Low alias Jones alias Young
    alias Blinkhorne, John
McCarty, Lawrence - runaway
Mopps, Abraham
Obney, Robert
Phillips, Elizabeth
Plymouth, Susanna
Pope, William
Sharpe, Christopher
Smith, William
Tyler, John

Middlesex

Bates, William
Bavin, Thomas
Been, Timothy
Bradley, Hannah
Briggs, Sarah
Brown alias Thompson, James
Cooper, John
Darvey, Andrew
Dixon, Henry
Evans, Sarah
Gale, Dorothy
Goulston, Richard - for life
Hamilton, Jane
Hand, Elizabeth
Hill, Henry
Hill, James

Hinemore, Ann
Hopps, Anthony
Hudspitch (Hotchpitch), William
Huggins, Benjamin
Hutton, Samuel
Jackson, Bryan
Lacey, Martin - runaway
Leonard, Elizabeth
Lynch, Mary
McPherson, Ann
O'Brien, Thomas
Parish, George
Paxton, Charles
Riley, Mary
Rushing, Jane
Ryley, Sarah
Smith, Thomas
Spalding, Elizabeth
Taylor, John - for life
White, Thomas
Wise, Thomas

Surrey

Dickens, David
Dunk, Thomas
Fell, William - runaway
Field, Margaret
Hollows, Elizabeth
Kenneday, Bartholomew - 14 yrs
May, Richard
Pagans, Thomas
Perry, Peter
Rayner, John
Smith, Jane
Stenson, James alias William
Stubbs, Mary
Williams, Alice
Willshire, Thomas - 14 yrs
Young, James

Sussex

Boxall, James - 14 yrs
Rose, Stephen - 14 yrs
Smith, John

Felons transported from Bristol to Maryland by the *Chester*, Capt. William Sedgley, arrived 10 November 1749 and registered in Queen Anne's Co. records (MSA: MdHR 8854).

Herefordshire

Floyd, William
Jones, John
Pantall, Thomas - 14 yrs

Rainforth, George Jr.
Watts, Richard

Felons transported from London to Virginia (?) by the *Mary*, Capt. Leonard Gerrard, in October 1749. (CLRO: London & LMA: Middlesex Bonds).

London

Birch, John
Brown, Peter
Casey, John
Clayton, Thomas
Downes, Joseph
Hill alias Harrington, Edward
Hutchins, John
Kelly, Mary
MacLane, Jane
Mapleton, John
Miller alias Sargent, John
Mills, Mary
Moore, Charles

Needham, James
Peak, Sarah
Smith, Jonathan
Taylor, Margaret
Thomas, Griffith
Ventris, Benjamin
Whitmore, Lydia
Williams, John

Middlesex

Barclay, John
Bennett, Thomas
Brooks, Ann
Buly, John

122

Burnsides alias Downing, Michael
Carmichael, Mary
Crosby, John
Davidson, John
Dunfield, Edward
Forbes, Francis
Gascoyne, William
Goddard, John - 14 yrs
Green, William
Halfpenny, Peter
Harford, James
Hunt, Henry
Jewell, James
Jones, Phillis
Kempton, Thomas
Killigrew, Elizabeth

Lake, Lucy
Mackey, George
Martin, Sarah
Mills, Elford
Morris, Eleanor
Moseley, Charles
Nicholls, Emanuel
Pomfrett, Edward
Potter, George
Quin alias Bulger, Mary
Sullivan, Cornelius
Sullivan, Martin
Thompson, Samuel alias Crew, Simon
Waine, John
Whalock, James
Williams, Richard

Felons transported from London by the _Tryal_, Capt. John Johnstoun, in April 1750, arrived in Maryland in June 1750. (PRO: T1/340/20).

London

Alcon, Sarah
Bennett, Elizabeth (2)
Bennett, Sarah
Butcher, Judith
Cammell, George
Campbell, Peter - runaway
Clarke, William
Clowes, Elizabeth
Cooper, Thomas
Davis, William - for life
Dean, John
Deer, Richard
Evans, Timothy
Gerrard, Rebecca
Gwynn, Bryan
Hancock, Edward
Howard, Elizabeth
Howard, Mary
Hoyde, Philip
Huggett, Loftius
Mercer, James
Norbury, Hester
Parker, Joseph
Parker, Susanna
Payne, William
Poe, John - for life
Pollard, William
Reynolds, Constantine
Ryder, Jane
Senturelli, Joseph

Shores, Edward - for life
Smith, William
Stevens, John
Sutton, John
Swift, Jeremiah - runaway
Trimnell, Richard
Turner, William
Tyers, Sarah
Waller, John - for life
Ward, James
Wentworth, James
Whitaker, John
Williams, William

Middlesex

Adams, Thomas
Allen, George
Anson, Benjamin (QS)
Arnold, Sarah
Baker, Thomas (QS)
Bakewell, Thomas
Barefoot, Charles
Baston, James
Bavin, Thomas
Birkett, Samuel (QS)
Blackston, John
Bond, Nicholas
Bones, Elizabeth
Brown, Jane
Burn, Patrick - runaway
Busby, John (QS)

Chessam, Thomas
Collins, Ann
Cooper, Joseph
Crawford, Thomas - 14 yrs
Cruise, Peter
Curtis, Thomas
Da Costa, Antonio
Davis, Elizabeth
Dawsey, Patrick - runaway
Dighton, William (QS)
Dixon, Benjamin
Donnavan, Cornelius - 14 yrs
Evans, William
Eyles, Mary
Farrell, Francis - runaway
Fear, George
Fryer alias Turpin, John - 14 yrs
Gold, John
Grant, Christian
Hackney, John
Hall, John (QS)
Hammond, James - for life
Hammond, Mary
Hannah, William
Heydon, William
Hill, Mary
Holmes, Jane
Hurst, John
James, John (QS)
Joiner, William
Jones, James (QS)
Judah, Isaac - 14 yrs
Lane, James
Lawrence, William
Lovell, William (QS)
Lowry, Edward
Martin, John

McDaniel, Mary
McMahon alias Clarke, Benjamin
McUllister, Edward
Meadall, William
Merchant, William (QS)
Merriman, Thomas
Merriman, Thomas Jr.
Monro, Mary (QS)
Mooney, John - 14 yrs
Moore, Colin
Moore, John
Mullins, James
Munday, James
Murphy, Mary
Norris, Thomas (QS)
Proudfoot, Matthew
Quin, Margaret
Ragan, James (QS)
Ricketts, John - runaway
Sagemuller, John Diederick
Shepherd, William - 14 yrs
Simpkinson, Robert
Smith, Charles
Smith, Edward
Swan, Elizabeth
Swannock, John
Taafe, Elizabeth
Taylor, Samuel
Tunbridge, Samuel
Walter alias Wettie, Thomas
Wanless alias Newby, Elizabeth
White, John
Williams, Philip
Wilson alias Warren, Ann (QS)
Wolfington, Henry - for life
Wood, James
Wood, Robert

Felons transported from London to Maryland by the *Lichfield*, Capt. William Gracie, in May 1750. (PRO: T1/340/33).

Buckinghamshire

Adry, William
Davis, Richard

Essex

Aspell (Asplin), William (QS)
Banister, George
Buttenshaw, Thomas
Fuller, John

Goswell alias Gosling, James - for life
Harvey, Edward - 14 yrs
Hull, John
Jepson, John - for life
Jury, Ralph
Livermore, Mary - 14 yrs
Miles, William - 14 yrs
Partridge, Matthew (QS)
Saltmarsh, John (QS)
Small, Tobias (QS)
Smith, Henry (QS)

Hertfordshire

Bastin, William (QS)
Carter, Nathaniel
Clarke, James (QS)
Eaton, Charles (QS)
Hayse, John (QS)

Kent

Beverton, Simon
Bramstone alias Benham, Mary
Burk, William
Chaplow, James
Coleman, Isaa
Dunn, Amy
Dyer, James
Green, John - 14 yrs
Holland, Thomas
Jenner, Samuel
Joiner, Thomas
Joyce, James
Maplesden, Mary
Mills, John
Monroe, Joseph (QS)
Nicholls, John
Owen, William
Oyer, James
Portess, William
Rogers, Thomas - 14 yrs
Simpson, William - 14 yrs
Thomas, William

London

Anderson, Mary
Barnes, Edward
Beverley, William
Cornish, William
Crags alias Shaw, Thomas
Cross, James
Darlow, Thomas
Freeman, Ann
Hunt, Edward
Norton, James
Rawlett, William
Rich, Daniel
Rose, Thomas
Smith, Thomas
Storm, Michael
Stow, Jane
Stryce, Silver

Walker, William
Wetherford, Thomas
Windsor, William

Middlesex

Alexander, William
Ansley, John (QS)
Atkinson, Mary (QS)
Baggott, John
Bambrick, Richard
Barlat, Thomas (QS)
Blanthorn, James
Brown, Henry (QS)
Dawsey, James
Dunlapp, Jasper
Elliott, Richard
Eustead, William
Fenton, James
Fry, William - for life
Gordon, Frances
Gray, Thomas
Green, Thomas
Griffin, Peter (QS)
Hartley, James
Haydon, Thomas
Home, John (QS)
Hudson, John
Jefferys, John
Jones, James
Jones, Nehemiah
Kelly, Patrick (QS)
Kelley, Terence (QS)
Maidenought, Michael
Maria, James
Mead, Nightingale
Mosten, John
Palmer, Thomas
Perry, Joseph. M.
Phillips, Edward
Richens, John
Rogers, Philip
Simms, John
Smith, John (2)
Stanton, John - for life
Stephens, John Andrew
Stevens, William (QS)
Stichbury, Alexander
Sweetman, Edward
Thomas, John
Thorpe, John - for life
Watson, Elizabeth

Wright, Peter

Surrey

Atley, Christopher (QS)
Buckeridge, James (QS)
Darby, Roger (QS)
Dowdle, Thomas (QS)
Drewry, Jane - 14 yrs
Esthers, Sarah
Flack alias Jones, John - runaway
Ford, Jeremiah (QS)
Gambell, James
Glover, Thomas (QS)
Head, Anne (QS)
Heathfield, Thomas
Huggate, Richard
Inman, Millicent (QS)
Jennings, Samuel

Johnson, Mary (QS)
Lawrence, John (QS)
Mason, Edward (QS)
Metton, George (QS)
Phillips, Thomas (QS)
Prior, John - 14 yrs
Robinson, Thomas (QS)
Roning, John (QS)
Stead, Ann
Waymark, Sarah (QS)
Whitaker, Andrew
Williams, John (QS)

Sussex

Bollard, Richard
Read, John
Steel, Mary

Felons shipped by Thomas Benson Esq. of Northam in his ship *Catherine*, Capt. Peter Marshall, by agreements of June 1750 and registered in Queen Anne's Co. in November 1750. (MSA: MdHR 9043 - RT C ff. 466-475).

Bristol

Bouden, William
Davie, Philip
Griffiths, Mary wife of Griffith,
  cordwainer
Lightfoot, Arthur
Lodowick, Lewis
Pattin alias Perrin, Elizabeth
Tilletts, Samuel
Wells, Joseph
Woodward, John

Devon

Bucknole, Joseph (QS)
Clarke, John (QS)
Crudge, Margaret wife of Peter,
  feltmaker (QS)
Davis, Mary (QS)
Diment, Henry (QS)
Gould, Mary wife of William,
  weaver (QS)
Jeffery, Mary, spinster (QS)
Moses, Elizabeth wife of Richard,
  weaver (QS)
Smith, Catherine (QS)

Dorset

Fiford, William
Forse, Richard
Hawkins, Elizabeth - runaway
Noss alias Nurse, William - 14 yrs
Salisbury, Morris

Gloucestershire

Carey, James
Curtis, Henry
Dark, Joseph
Davidson, William
Dunn, Anne
Ellis, Ann wife of Edward - 14 yrs
Green, William (QS) - 14 yrs
Griffiths, John
Harmer, Kinard
Hobbs, Richard (QS)
Kirby, Richard
Lewis, Catherine
Oland, William
Spencer, John (QS)

Herefordshire

Gilbert, Thomas - 14 yrs

Hooper, William - 14 yrs
Ingram, Mordecai
Monk, Mary
Parlour, John - 14 yrs
Tomkins, William
Watton, John
Watts, Thomas - died

Monmouthshire

Davis, Charles
Jordan, Rachel - 14 yrs
Watkins, James

Somerset

Andrews, Amos - 14 yrs
Bendall, Thomas - 14 yrs
Boss, Robert

Brown, George (QS)
Bult, Robert
Chilcot, John
Martin, Hosea
Mercer, Jonas - 14 yrs
Street, William
Tackle, Abednego
Tackle, John
Thatcher, Abraham (QS)
Toms, John
Watts, William

Worcestershire

Askew, Jonathan
Brittain, Thomas
Rea, Matthew
Spragg, Abraham - 14 yrs
Wyatt, Richard - 14 yrs

Felons transported from London to Virginia (?) by unknown ship (*Mary?*), Capt.Leonard Gerrard, by bonds of 10 July 1750. (CLRO: London & LMA: Middlesex bonds).

London

Brightwell, Mary
Clarke, Thomas
Davies, John.
Harebottle, Elizabeth
Hart, John
Hodges, John
Jessey, Griffith
Jones, William
Kentt, John
Medham, Johyn
Mitchell, John
Redhead, Thomas
Rice, Elizabeth
Smith, Mary
Waller, Jane
Williams, Mary
Williamson, Robert
Willis, Dulick
Wilson, Thomas
Winter William

Middlesex

Allen, John
Aston, John
Bailey, Abraham

Bailey, John
Baker, William
Barker alias Baker, William
Boys, Mary
Butler alias Archer
    alias Ogden, Judith - 14 yrs
Coventry, Elizabeth
Cross, Charles
Curd, James
Drinkrow, John
Edwards, Elizabeth
Frazier, John
Gale, John
Green, Mary
Hawkins, John
Hill, Shadrick
Hilton, John
Hoskins, Esther
Huddle, Thomas
Hutchinson, William
Jenkins, Thomas
Kelly, Mary
King, William
Middleton, Michael
O'Brian, William
Puller, Joseph
Ryan, Mary - 14 yrs
Swaby, Joseph James

Tasker, William
Thomas, Richard
Thompson, Hester

Wilkinson, Edward
Williams, Philip
Wright, Abraham

Felons transported from London to Maryland by the *Rachael*, Capt. John Armstrong, in October 1750, arriving in December 1750. (PRO: T1/342/35)

Buckinghamshire

Cook, Thomas
Hollis, Mark
Holloway, John

Essex

Cowell, Joseph - 14 yrs
Jeggo, John
Mills alias Pizey, Henry - for life
Scott, William - for life
Sellersat alias Selerate, John
Shettleworth, Thomas
Smee, Robert - 14 yrs
Smith, John
Welch, Joseph - 14 yrs

Hertfordshire

Loggs, Henry - 14 yrs
Wiggs, Francis - 14 yrs

Kent

Adams, Benjamin
Baker, Benjamin - 14 yrs
Barton, John
Butters, William
Cleford, Thomas
Farleys, Henry - 14 yrs
Jackson, Joseph
Luckhurst, William
McKaw, Alexander
Randall, William
Walker, George

London

Cordoza, Samuel
Jones, Henry
Nicholls, George
Parker, Richard
Rickett, William
Spencer, James
Tappin, John

Middlesex

Badge, Sarah
Bailey, Susannah
Bateman, Peter
Bennett, Mary
Bradley, Joseph
Carroll, John - for life
Chambers, John
Coats, James (QS)
Cole, Richard
Duckett, John - 14 yrs
Fuller, Sarah
Glascow, Hannah
Grew, Joseph
Haughton, Adolphus James
Hawes, James
Hayes, James
Herryman, John
Heskett alias Hesketh, William
Lambeth, Ann
Leavers, Patience
Mascall, Mary
McArdell, Henry
Meal, Mary
Peck, Ann
Perry, George
Priest, Ann
Roe, John
Sherlock, Ralph
Shore, John
Stephens, John
Sullivan, Herbert (QS)
Taylor, Elizabeth
Trussin, Elizabeth wife of George
Veezey, Katherine
Wallis, Thomas - for life
Williams, John
Williams, Elizabeth (QS)
Yardley, Elizabeth
Yardley, Mary

Surrey

Annasant, Brillia

Bond, Joseph
Clark, John
Elliott, James - 14 yrs
Grant, Mary
Hampstead, Benjamin
Jeagles, William
Langley, William - 14 yrs
Lester, Elizabeth
Looms, Michael
Moor, James
Nicholls, Mary wife of John

Smallpass, Richard. - 14 yrs
Warner, William
Wilson, John

Sussex

Hale, William
Martin alias Martain, John - 14 yrs
McNara, Simon
Thompson, William - 14 yrs
Venice, Thomas - 14 yrs

Felons transported from London by the *Thames*, Capt. James Dobbins, in February 1751, arrived in Annapolis in May 1751. (CLRO: London & LMA: Middlesex bonds; gaol rolls for Surrey).

London

Allen, John
Buckley, Daniel
Burnell, Thomas
Burnham, John
Byall, John
Cook, John
Cosson, John
Cragy, Charles
Cunningham, Thomas
Daines, Edward
Douglas, Alexander
Durham, John
Evans, Edward
Fowler, Thomas
Gate, Stephen
Guest, Joseph
Hall, Thomas
Harris, William
Hayes, Thomas - runaway
Hodgson, William
James, Mary
Jones, Lamb
Jordan, Hugh
Kingston alias Brown, John
Leeman alias Smith, John
Little, Thomas
Love alias Lloyd, Peter - runaway
Meadows, Thomas
Meal, John
Munroe, Robert
Pattin, John
Potts, George
Smith, Joseph
Solomon, Robert alias Blind Isaac

Stevens, Henry
Trueman, Alice
Webber, Mary
Wilkes alias Biswell alias Griffiths, Mary
Williams, Thomas
Woodcock, Robert
Wyatt, William

Middlesex

Bosely, Thomas
Brown, John
Brown, Mary
Burn, Lawrence
Burridge, Robert - for life
Carr, Priscilla
Carroll, John
Chester, Mary
Colwell, Ufan
Connerly alias Connolly, John
Corrigan, Hugh
Cox, John
Currall, James
Curtis alias Richardson, Daniel
Dikes, Henry alias Clarke, James
Faulkner alias Steward, Jane
Fenton, William
Fordham, Jacob
Gorman, Sarah
Hardwick, John
Harrington, James
Harwood, John
Hatchet, Joseph
Hilliard, Ann
Hoar, Hannah
Holland alias Shepherd, Ann

Kay, Francis - for life
Lawson, John
Masterton, John
McCarter, Mary
Mills, Herman
Mulling, Patrick
Nicholls, Matthias - for life
Nutbrown, John
Nutbrown, Miles
Oadway alias Valentine, Mary
Orton alias Holton, John
Page, Judith
Parker, Mary
Price, William - 14 yrs - runaway
Pursley, John - 14 yrs
Sherlock, William
Smith, Elizabeth
Smith, James
Smith alias Brown, Mary
Terry, Elizabeth
Tucker, Thomas
Udall, John - runaway
Watson, William - 14 yrs
Wellam, Robert

Surrey*

Blackbourne, John (QS)
Butcher, Richard (QS)
Carr, William (QS)
Cook, Robert (QS)
Day, William (QS)
Edwards, Daniel Jr. (QS)
Goddard, William (QS)
Hall, John (QS)
Hanley, Peter (QS)
Herne, Thomas (QS)
Hipkin, Ann wife of Michael (QS)
Jefferson, John (QS)
Jiggle, William
Lloyd, John (QS)
Nobody alias Parsley, Mary (QS)
Plunkett, Robert (QS)
Rogers, Thomas (QS)
Rose, John (QS)
Sands, John (QS)
Shaw, Thomas (QS)
Spinks, Daniel (QS)
Winchurch, John (QS)

*According to T53/44/63 there were 23 Surrey felons aboard: this list includes those known to have been sentenced in Surrey in the appropriate period.

Felons transported from London to Maryland by the *Tryal*, Capt. John Johnstoun, in May 1751. (PRO: T1/346/29).

Buckinghamshire

Jenkins, Edward
Quelch, Moses

Essex

Bawcock, John
Boulter, Sarah
Brett, James
Brown, James
Cole, James - runaway
Dawkins, Richard
Garrard, Robert - 14 yrs
Mason, Richard
Pickering, John

Hertfordshire

Bassett, Joseph

Kent

Acland, George
Bowden, John
Boyle, James
Bremer, Jacob
Brown, Charles
Chapman, William
Claxton, William
Cooter, John
Cross, George
Dunn, James
Fullagar, John
Goldup, John
Henderson, William
Hillerton, Edward
Jackson, William
Johnson, Richard
Matthews, Thomas
Newbowl, George
Paramour, Phoebe

Pearson, John
Rainbird alias Garland, Joseph, - for life
  - runaway
Raybourn, Ann
Seaburn, Sarah
Smith, Thomas
Thorpe, Josiah
Wear, Samuel
Winch, Ellis
Wornoll, John
Wright, John - runaway

London

Barker, Mary
Beasley, John
Beaton, James
Bertie, George
Bisbee, James
Bowen, Charles
Cain alias Kayne, Patrick
Crisp, Thomas
Dunn, Hugh
Fison, Henry
Freeman, Samuel
Goddard, John
Gwynn, John
Hughes, John
Lee, William
Miles, Mary
Millett, Ann
Nicholls, Richard
Oakley, Thomas
Phillips, Edward
Plackett, John
Spackman, Charles
Spivey, James
Stanninot, William
Tindy, Richard
Wright, George

Middlesex

Adams, Mary
Aldridge, Susanna
Barber, Jane
Barker, Thomas
Bayley, Rachael
Bishop, William
Blake, Philip
Bowen, Mary
Brightman, William

Brown, Elizabeth
Brown, William
Bruce, Charles
Burch, Thomas (QS)
Burn, Thomas
Burling, Michael
Carter, Thomas
Coates, John
Cole, John
Colley alias Farmer, Ann
Cowdell, Thomas
Dart, Mary
Denslow, Mary
Dixon, Richard
Downing, John (QS)
Edwards, Margaret
Farrell, Thomas (QS)
Farris alias Farrow, James - 14 yrs
Freeman, Mary
Garrick, Arthur (QS)
Gaywood, John
Gibbons, William - died in Newgate
Green, Margaret (QS)
Grigg, William
Harvey, William
Hawson, Dennis
Horsey, Mary
Hurley, John (QS)
Innis, Walter
Jennings, Mary
Johns, Ann
Keith, John
Ling, Elizabeth - died in Newgate
Long, John (QS)
Marshall, James
Martin, John
Martin, Robert
Murphy, Jeremiah
Nesbitt, Elizabeth
Osborne, William
Paxton, Elizabeth
Peacock, Richard
Pearse, Andrew
Pitt alias Evans, Mary - died in Newgate
Pritchard, William
Pyner, Thomas - runaway
Rabnett, James
Ramsey, Ann
Richards, Stephen (QS)
Russell alias Kinsey, John
Ryan, Thomas - died in Newgate
Saunders, James

131

Smith, Solomon (QS)
Solomon, Emanuel
Talmige, John
Thorn, Robert
Walker, Letitia
Ward, Christopher
Wright, Mary

Rowse, John
Sinclair, William
Spittle, Robert
Vincent, Hezekiah
Walter, Thomas

Sussex

Surrey

Clark, John
Clay, Granger
Farmer, Robert
Forey, William
Johnson, John
Pink, Richard
Pulpitt, William
Saires, Thomas
Scarborough, Thomas
Willard, Nicholas

Andrews, Edward
Brown, James
Buck, George
Cooling, Thomas
Glibbery, John
Green, Joseph
Hollman, John
Lawson, Elizabeth
Oakley, Samuel

Felons transported from London to Virginia by the _Greyhound_, Capt. William Gracie, in September 1751. (PRO: T1/349/1).

Buckinghamshire

Dodd, Thomas
Evans, Edward
Keene, John
Kempster, John - 14 yrs
Kirby, John - 14 yrs

Essex

Bass, John (QS)
Cook, James - 14 yrs
Eastmead, John Clement - 14 yrs
Harris, John (QS)
Pillsworth, John (QS)
Steward, George

Hertfordshire

Bampton, George - 14 yrs
Croft, John - 14 yrs
Grindy, William - for life
Jones, William - 14 yrs
Lawrence, Martha - 14 yrs

Kent

Bailey, James
Brooks, Thomas

Cooley, Robert
Devereux, James
Fall, John - runaway
Gunner, Sarah
Lamsdall, Adam
Moate, John - 14 yrs
Perkins, William
Quittenden, Sarah
Rowland, Elizabeth
Simmons, William

London

Bellenger, Henry
Bellisford, William
Cross, Elizabeth
Davis alias Davison, Grace
Davy, Robert - for life
Gill, Richard
Hanshaw, William
Harding, James
Harleech, John
Howard, John
Jephson, John
Jones, Samuel (2)
Lee, John
Lewis, Daniel
McDonald, Archibald
Mills, Martha

Penrice, Lawrence
Richardson, Elizabeth
Strutton, William
Townsend, Elizabeth
Waters, Martha

Middlesex

Armstrong, Mary
Armstrong, Paul
Avergirl, Elizabeth (QS)
Bagshaw, Henry
Bath, William
Beard, Richard
Bennett, Elizabeth (2)
Bloom, David
Bowle, John
Brown, John
Cole alias Johnson, Mary (QS)
Crafts, Francis
Culpepper, Margaret
Davis, Elizabeth
Davis, Mary - but pardoned
Dempsey, Richard
Dodd, Samuel - 14 yrs
Donelly, John (QS)
Eves, William
Faulkner, Richard (QS)
Field, Hannah
Fisher, Christopher
Fisher, John
Fulford, John
Gardner, Richard
Gray, James (QS)
Handford, Martha
Harris, Frances (QS)
Hope, Thomas (QS)
Izard, Ann
Johnson, John
Jones, John
Jones, Silvester (QS)
Lyde, Hannah Rutter (QS)
Lynch, Disney (QS)
Meredith, Edward
Norman, Mary
O'Neal, Owen (QS)
Pierson, William
Rowley, Thomas
Smith, Sarah (QS)
Smith alias Breach, Thomas (QS)
Smith, William
Snellock, James

Steel, Richard
Steward, Daniel
Strong, John
Tallant, Patrick
Thomas, Hannah (QS)
Tythe, Mary (QS)
Walker, Richard
White, Alexander
White, Mary (QS)
Williams, Jane
Winnell, Thomas (QS)
Wright, Thomas
Young, John

Surrey

Alexander, James Jr. (QS)
Apted, Elizabeth
Baswicke, George (QS)
Bell, William (QS)
Benyon, William (QS)
Birdworth, Mary
Boatson, Michael
Bowers, Sarah
Boylan, William (QS)
Burge alias Skelton, Mary
Busby, Elizabeth (QS)
Chorey, John (QS)
Clark, Mary (QS)
Davis, John
Fisher, Joseph - 14 yrs
Goodye, John (QS)
Gough, Mary (QS)
Griffin, Harman (QS)
Harris, Martha (QS)
Harris, William (QS)
Harristick, Elizabeth (QS)
Jones, Mary (QS)
Kiteley, Benjamin
Lewis, Elizabeth (QS)
Lewis, Nathaniel (QS)
McDaniel alias McDonald,
    William (QS)
Morgan, William
Morse, Charles
Nisbett, William - 14 yrs
Peake, John
Penn, Matthew
Pocock, Robert
Reynolds, William
Roberts, Sarah (QS)
Samms, Alice (QS)

133

Smith, Samuel
Stanley, Thomas - for life
Timberwell, George (QS)
Turbett, Mary
Whitcliff, Richard (QS)
White, Elizabeth
White, Joseph

Yarmouth, Edward (QS)

Sussex

Cooke, Susanna
Huband, Matthew
Shore, Isaac
White, Thomas

Felons transported from London by the *Thames*, Capt. James Dobbins, in March 1752, arriving in Annapolis in April 1752. (CLRO: London and LMA: Middlesex bonds).

London

Albey, Joseph
Barker, Susanna
Bilson, William
Blee, John
Bolt, James
Bolton, John
Booth, Lucy
Bowles, Samuel
Brookes, William
Butcher, Susanna
Davis, Elizabeth - for life
Davis, John
Dixon alias Pope, Sarah
Dolls, James
Felton, John
Freeman, Thomas
Green, Robert
Hope, Matthew
Humphreys, Thomas
Johnson, Mary
Jones, John
Jones, Mary
Karrell, Joseph
Low, Samuel
Moore, Elizabeth
Parsley, Henry
Piper, Richard
Potter, William
Prior, Ann
Reynolds, William
Russell, Ann
South, John
West, Joshua
Winter, Catherine
Worrell, Francis
Wyatt, Thomas

Middlesex

Bacon, Samuel - for life
Bennett, John
Bickerton, John
Bissett, James
Brookes, Edward - for life
Brown, Mary
Clarke, Emanuel - for life
Conson, Ann
Coulsey, Thomas
Dollison, Thomas
Dunn, John
Eager, Samuel - for life
Elliott, William
Gilson, Arthur
Goodman, Joseph
Guy, John
Hicks alias Hilkes, John
Holland, Thomas
Hulston, Henry
Hunt, Mary wife of John - 14 yrs
Hunter, John - 14 yrs
Hutton, Susanna
Jebb, John - 14 yrs - runaway
King, Deborah
Lilly, John Patterson
Longham, Christian
Lovering, John
Luff, Robert
McClean, Eleanor
Merry, Richard
Morley, John
Newhouse, Cornelius - 14 yrs
Peart, Thomas
Purdue, Charles
Rakes, Weston - for life
Roach, James
Robinson, John

134

Robinson, Thomas - runaway
Ryley alias Bulger, Mary
Sherratt, Nathaniel
Simmons, Love
Smith, Benjamin - for life
Stoner, Francis
Tamplin, Anthony

Titten, Richard
Tyler, Joseph
Walthen, Jane
White, Mary
Williams, James
Willis, Sarah

Felons transported from London to Maryland by the *Lichfield*, Capt. Leonard Gerrard, in May 1752. (PRO: T1/348/8).

Buckinghamshire

Dod, John
Nethercliffe, William
Smith, John

Essex

Borcham, George (QS)
Crost alias Crowhurst, John
Freeman, Nathaniel
Ginn, Edward
Gowers, John (QS)
Jones alias Mortebois, Robert
King, James
Morris, Thomas
Stiles, William (QS)
Wiffen, John
Wright, Richard (QS)

Hertfordshire

Chapman, Charles
Harvey, James
Martin, Edward
Mead, Edward. - 14 yrs
Napkin, Hannah
Webster, William

Kent

Blackwood, Hamilton
Collier, Benjamin
Ditch, Lydia
Grimes, George
Laws, John
Petit, Thomas
Philpott, Henry
Pim, Thomas
Strood, Richard - 14 yrs
White, John - 14 yrs

London

Ainsworth, Michael
Allison, Robert
Bagot, Stephen
Barry, Barnard
Benjamin, Abraham
Brockley, Thomas
Carr, John
Cavendish, Margaret
Chittey, Simon
Cordoza, Aaron - 14 yrs
Debang, Hugh
Delaney, Mary
Fahee, Thomas
Gibson, Judith
Holden, John
Jennings, John
Jones, Lewis
Lego, Charles
Marshall, Martha
Martin, John
Nicholls, George
Parrott, Elizabeth
Pearson, Nathaniel
Rogers, William
Rowell, Francis
Scrivener, John
Shay, Jarvis alias Gervase
Smith, John
Thorne, John
Walker, Peter
Watkins, Marmaduke
Woolridge, Roger

Middlesex

Bannell alias Bland, Hannah
Banstead, Jane. (QS)
Barnes, Thomas
Beadle, William

Brome, Elizabeth
Brown, Mary
Bryan, John
Bullen, Richard
Burgiss, Joseph
Butterworth, Joseph
Carroll, Ann
Carter, Ann
Child, Edward
Compton, Walter
Connor, David (QS)
Cunningham, Ann
Doharty, Matthew
Emroe, Christopher (QS)
Endersby, Thomas - runaway
Forster, William
Frewin, Mary (QS)
Fry alias Hull, Ann (QS)
Goodin, Ann
Grady, Eleanor
Grant, Adam
Griffith, Emblin (QS)
Haley alias Poor, Jane
Hartley, John
Hilton, Ann
Houghton, James
Hughes, William - for life
Jeffreys, Benjamin
Kendrick, Ann
Lewis, John
Mace, William
Malone, John - runaway
Morestly alias Mosely, Joseph
Neale, William
Peate, John (QS)
Porter, John
Prosser, Thomas
Savage, Sarah

Smith, John (QS)
Upton, George (QS)
Wingcot, Philip (QS)

Surrey

Blackband, Elizabeth
Chapman, Jacob
Chapman, John
Clayton, John (QS)
Dacock, Thomas
Daws, Robert
Dodd, Elizabeth
Dunning, William -14 yrs
Edwards, John (QS)
Finder, Joseph (QS) - runaway
Foster, John
Gibson, Thomas - 14 yrs
Goddard, John (QS)
Gould, Elizabeth (QS)
Knight, John (QS)
Lennard, Margaret 14 yrs
Loseby, Peter
Miller, John
Parnell, Elizabeth
Peale, James
Rich, John
Simpson, Daniel 14 yrs
Sparrow, Joseph
Underwood, John

Sussex

Jarrett, William
Kent, Richard
McCoy, John
Scutt, John
Scutt, William

Felons assigned to Samuel Sedgley & Daniel Cheston of Bristol, transported in June 1752 by the *Bideford*, Capt. John Knill, arriving in Maryland in September 1752 & registered in Queen Anne's Co. records (MSA: MdHR 8854).

Worcestershire

Badger, Thomas
Crane, Francis
Felton, William

Hill, James
Lightbourne, Richard - 14 yrs - runaway

Felons transported from London to Maryland by the *Tryal*, Capt. John Johnstoun, in August 1752. (T1/348/18)

Buckinghamshire

Garrett, John - 14 yrs
Pargiter, William
Wilson, James - 14 yrs

Essex

Dixon, John
Eanis, Bryan - 14 yrs
Farraway, Robert
Hurt, John - 14 yrs
Lucey, James - 14 yrs
Perry, Martha (QS)
Radcliff, Joseph - 14 yrs
Rand, William - 14 yrs
Turner, John - 14 yrs
Warn, Richard

Hertfordshire

Radley, Joseph
Yeoman, John

Kent

Bailey, Thomas 14 yrs
Cooper, John
Davis, Ann
Hobbs, John
Hocklish, John
Hudnall, James
Keating, John
Nesbitt, James - 14 yrs
Pelling, John
Smith, John
Sturt, Thomas
Sutur, Thomas
Warner, John

London

Barnet, Joseph
Baythorn, William
Bewley, Mary
Biggs, Thomas
Burgess, Edward
Bush alias Bertie, Elizabeth
Bush, Margaret - 14 yrs

Cartwright, Matthew
Ford, Amelia
Hall, James - runaway
Knight, John - for life
Notere, Michael
Robinson, Catherine - 14 yrs
Robinson, William
Scolfield, John
Smith, Joseph
Welling, Richard
Wilson, William
Wind, Mary
Wright, Thomas

Middlesex

Allen, Phillipa
Barnes, Ezekiel
Bridgman, John
Burk, Ann
Callden, Robert
Carey, James
Child, Henry
Child, John
Clarke, William
Egerton alias Batt, Philip
Graham, George - runaway
Griffin, Martha
Hall, Mary (QS)
Hall, William
Hanna, John
Hollis, Alethea
Honour, William
Impey, Alice (QS)
Jennings, William
Jones, Mary
Keiling alias Sam, James
Landwick alias Lodowick, William
Man, Mary
Newman, Maria
Pearce, Sarah
Rock, Sarah
Rose, George
Sago, John
Seers, Bernard
Sheffield, Thomas
Stratton, Thomas
Tiffen, Joseph
Ward, Dorothy

Whitby, William
Wickham, Catherine

Surrey

Alcraft, Francis (QS)
Campbell, Charles - for life
Cannon, John (QS)
Cotteril, William
Cotton, William (QS)
Greenaway, Mary (QS)
Gumm, Ann
Havergirl, Nathaniel (QS)
Howell, William (QS)
Langsden, Mary - 14 yrs
Lundberg, Sven

Mitchell, Benjamin - 14 yrs
Morgan, Mary - 14 yrs
Peacock, William - 14 yrs
Powell, James
Stamper, Robert - 14 yrs
Strange alias Nailer, Mary (QS)
Thorowgood, George - 14 yrs
Waller, Elizabeth
White, Samuel

Sussex

Kellett, Charles - 14 yrs
Kinsett, Roger
Roades, William

Felons transported from Bristol by the *Chester*, Capt. John Lorain, in October 1752, arrived in Maryland in December 1752 & registered in Queen Anne's Co. records. (MSA: MdHR 8854).

Bristol

Hunt, Thomas, saddler - 14 yrs

Staffordshire

Blewitt, Charles
Boardman, Charles
Bowler, Hannah

Comberlidge, Thomas
Gibson, Joseph
Kelsall, Samuel - 14 yrs
Latham, Thomas
Lilly, Timothy - 14 yrs
Parks, William - 14 yrs
Rice, Nathaniel
Shoebotham, Thomas
Smithman alias Aston, Thomas

Felons transported from London to Maryland by the *Greyhound*, Capt. William Gracie, in December 1752 & registered in Maryland records on 22 July 1756. (PRO: T1/348/26; MSA: BT No. 1 ff. 1-2).

Buckinghamshire*

Cock, John

Kent*

Gibbons, John

London

Bowers, James*
Boyle, Mary
Brightwell, Elizabeth
Brooking, Samuel
Bullwinkle, Thomas
Clark, William
Clayton, Samuel

Curryer, William
Hiats, John*
Holford, Jane
Hutton, Richard
Knight, John
Knight, John - for life
Lacey, Joseph
Marshall, James*
Moody, John
Murray, Richard
Needs, John
Payce, James
Phenix, Caroll
Purser, Catherine
Rowland, Elizabeth
Smith, John
Solomon, David

Stennett, Absolom*
Thrift, James*
Tomlin, Mary
Ward, Catherine
Watkin, James*

Middlesex

Addis, Thomas
Arnold, Mary
Ash, Elizabeth
Aubery, John*
Baker, Henry
Barber, Susanna
Beazley, Richard*
Bell, Samuel
Biggs, Susanna
Bowman, John
Buckley, John - runaway
Bucktrout, Martha
Carroll alias Dutton, Andrew
Cartwright, Lucretia*
Castle, Eleanor
Clarke, John*
Cooper, Jordan
Crofts, William*
Dalton, John
Douglas, Robert*
Dupree, Ann
Dust, Samuel*
Edwards, Mary - 14 yrs
Edwards, Millicent - 14 yrs
Edwards, Ann
Fling, John
Ford, Richard*
Fourcausey, Peter
Garrett, Martha
Garrway, John*
Gore alias Purcell, John
Halfpenny, Michael
Haynes, William
Higgs, Susanna*
Holland, Mary
How, John
Hunsley, William (QS)*
Huxley, Mary
James, Thomas (QS)*
James, Edward

Welsh, John
Wiggen, William
Williams, Thomas
Wright, John.

Jolly, Samuel
Kelsy, William
Kemp, George
King, Margaret
Langenfilder, John
Levoyer alias Lovyer, Daniel
Lewis, Lewis
Little, Elizabeth
Manning, Richard
Matthews, William
Morris, Ruth
Nichols, Mary (QS)*
Ogilvy, George
Osborne, Sarah
Owen, William
Penpraise, James
Perry, Edward
Plowman, Robert
Pope, William
Prigg Elizabeth
Read, Hannah*
Richins, Jane
Roberts, Elizabeth
Rogers, Robert
Shields, Paul
Sutton, Samuel
Sweething, Nathaniel
Titchbourn, Ann - 14 yrs
Trenton, Edward
Walker, Isaac*
Walker, Richard
White, Sarah.
Wilkes, Knight (QS)*
Wilkinson, Mary (QS)*
Williams, Mary

Surrey*

Betts, John
Dutch, Ann
Robinson, Robert (QS)

*Not included in MSA record

139

Felons transported from London by the *Thames*, Capt. James Dobbins, in May 1753 arriving in Maryland in June 1753. (PRO: T1/351/17).

Buckinghamshire

Key, Thomas - 14 yrs
Pinner, Edward
Symonds, John
Tebby, John

Essex

Allen, Herman John (QS)
Boar alias Bourman, Robert,
   alias Norfolk Bob
Burroughs, John
Carver, Richard
Davy, Thomas
Hare, John
Hoy, Roger
Millers, James
Sheppard, Charles
Truss, John

Hertfordshire

Bellsford alias Bottsford, John
Burton, Mary - runaway
Thomas, John

Kent

Allen, Herman John
Beane, Robert
Bone, Edward
Brown, John
Farmer, William
Goodridge, Gilbert - runaway
Grosvenor, Richard
Holt, John
Knight, Thomas
Panckhurst, Thomas
Straw alias Shaw, Mary
Stringer, Mary
Stubbins, Hannah
Webdell, Thomas
Wickenden, David
Wright, John

London

Ashley, Thomas

Banks, Joseph
Batten, Edward
Belcher, Martyr
Blundell, Ann
Blundell, James
Butler, Mary
Clark, Mary
Cooke, James
Evans, John - runaway
Flemming, William
Francis, James
Harrison, Elizabeth
Hawes, Isaac
Hawes, Michael
Jetter, John Jr.
Johnson, Mary
Levy, Garret
Nelson, Ann
Osborne, Ann
Pierce, Elizabeth - 14 yrs - pardoned.
Reeves, Edmund
Ridge, Mary - 14 yrs
Rorke, John
Taylor, John
Thompson, James
Warner, John
Wilson, Edward

Middlesex

Anderson, Joshua
Bartlett, William
Batchelor, Jane
Blockumb, Peter
Blundell, George
Brigg, William (QS)
Brown, Mary (QS)
Buttersfield, William
Chiney, William (QS)
Clinton, John
Cooper, Thomas,
   alias Cope, James (QS)
Dennis, Thomas
Dickings, John (QS)
Egar, Silvester
Ellys, James
Grant, Joseph
Griffiths, Ann
Harper, Anthony - runaway

Harvey, Isabella
Hermitage, George
Higgins, Hannah (QS)
Johnson, Bridget
Jones, Elizabeth
Long, John (QS) - runaway
Lumley, John
Miles, John
Price, John
Quin, John (QS)
Richards, Margaret
Robinson, Barbara
Robinson, Joseph
Room, John
Simon, John
Simpson, John
Smith, Elizabeth
Smith alias Groves, John
Smith, Martha
Sommers, Joseph
Sommers, Sarah
Steel, Mary
Sterney, Susanna
Thompson, Elizabeth
Thorpe, John
Tippett, Abraham
Vinyard, Abraham
Walden (Waldron), William - runaway
Watling, John
Williams, Essex, alias Essex, William
Worrell, Frances

Surrey

Barnard, Ann (QS)
Barton, John (QS)

Best, John
Burgess, Nathaniel (QS)
Day, John (QS)
Fenleoo, Rachael (QS)
Guy, George
Huckell, Mary (QS)
Lane, Robert
Lawler, John
Lee, Benjamin (QS)
Lingard, Robert
Owen alias Belford, Elizabeth (QS)
Pardon, Thomas (QS)
Perkins, Richard
Rowland, John (QS)
Russell, Elizabeth
Severight, George
Smith, John (QS)
Smith, Richard (QS)
Stevens, Richard (QS) - runaway
Tabor, Philip (QS)
Wainwright, Esther
Walker, John (QS)
Wells, Valentine (QS)

Sussex

Bentley, Peter
Binsted, John
Brooker, Edward
Jones, Thomas
Patman, Edward
Reynolds, Thomas
Rogers, Edward
Shields, Michael
Smith, William

Felons transported from London to Virginia by the *Tryal*, Capt. John Johnstoun, in July 1753. (PRO: T1/353/29).

London

Bone, John
Cook, Charles
Cornhill, John
Curtis, Sarah
Dunn, Francis
Fife, Docia
Fillimore, Francis
Fish, Mary
Glover alias Lightfoot, Richard
Harding, Edward

Hartford, John
Heard, Archibald
Holstop, Joseph
Jarvis, John, alias Black Jack
Lightfoot, Richard
Metcalf, Elizabeth
Moore, James
Neale, Susannah
Newman, William
Onion, Hester - 14 yrs
Onion, Thomas
Paul, Benjamin

Peachy, Daniel
Peak, Frances
Price, John
Putten, Daniel
Richardson, Thomas
Riley, Philip
Robinson, Jeremiah
Russell, Sarah
Sheffield, Isaac - runaway
Smith, Thomas
Trow, John - runaway
Wiggins, John

Middlesex

Aspinall [Aspenwell], Richard (QS)
  but taken from ship
Atkins, Martha
Barclay, David
Barnes, Josiah
Barnfather, Samuel
Bartley, David - for life
Barton, Richard
Best, Elizabeth (QS)
Beverley, John
Birt, Robert
Blackwell alias Connor, Elizabeth
Branvile, Jane (QS)
Brookes, Jane
Brown, Mary
Butler, Eleanor (QS)
Butler, Richard (QS)
Carroll, Thomas
Cave, Felix (QS)
Clarey, Margaret (QS)
Collins, James
Cook, John
Cooley, Thomas (John)
Davis, Matthew
Derritt, Benjamin
Dobbins, Elizabeth
Drake, Ann (QS)
Dundas, James
Edgerley, Robert (QS)
Ellsey, Nicholas
Forbes, Isabella
Forrester, Ann
Freeman, John

Gainer alias Gehner, Sarah
Giles, John
Hall, Thomas
Hamon, John - 14 yrs
Hansom, James
Harrison alias Sarrison, Sarah
Hayley, Carbery
Hoadman, Martha
Holloway, John
Horn, Mary
Horne, Henry
Hunt, James
Johnson, Andrew
Johnson, Thomas
Lee alias Leeworthy, William
McDonald, Alexander
McDonnell, Mary
Middleton, William
Miller, Thomas
Milliner, William
Narder, James
Nugent, Patrick 14 yrs
Owens, William
Perkins, Mary
Rex alias Rix, Charles
Robinson, James
Selwood, Elizabeth
Smith, Edward
Smith alias Cox alias Brown, Mary
Standidge, Sarah
Steel, Richard
Stevens, Mary (QS)
Still, Richard
Swanson, Elizabeth
Thackeray, William
Toft, James
Underwood, John (QS)
Weaver, Thomas
Whitaker alias Slade, Mary

Surrey

Betts, John (QS)
Dutch, Ann (QS)
Harper, Christopher (QS)
Merry, James (QS)
Robinson, Robert

Felons transported from London to Virginia by the *Whiteing*, Capt. Matthew Johnson, in July 1753. (PRO: T1/358/1).

Essex

Campen, William
Chapman alias Fitch, William - 14 yrs
Filbrick, Henry (QS)
Hunt, Barbara
Jeffries, William (QS) - runaway
Mucklehone, James
Nightingale, William (QS)
Taverner, George
Ulph, Charles
Wicker, John
Wilkin, James

Hertfordshire

Dee, Richard - 14 yrs
Oliver, William - 14 yrs

Kent

Bevis, Simon - 14 yrs
Bluck, William
Brown, John - 14 yrs
Carrow, Mary
Carter, Joseph - 14 yrs
Dickenson, William
Filley, John
Fry, John
Jeakens, John
May, John - 14 yrs
Pittenden, John
Scarlett, William
Shelton, Edward
Smethurst, William
Webb, John
Wright, Thomas

London

Allen, Joseph
Baxter, John
Bisset, Alexander
Bridger, James
Chapman, Thomas
Cooper, Joseph
Cunningham, Joseph
Davis, Priscilla
Davis, Isabella
Hine, John
Homer, John
Ireland, Thomas
Israel, Sabate
Jones, Ann - runaway
Jones, Edward
Kendal, Samuel
Kummings, Thomas
McCormick, Francis
Mesquitta alias Jarro,
    Jacob Henriques
Monger, Sarah - 14 yrs
Nichol, Edward
Odew, Hester
Painter, Edward
Parkinson, James
Pearson, Ambrose
Rhimes, Mary
Roberts, Eleanor
Ruming, Thomas
Shepherd, Dorothy
Whaley, William
Whitmore, Francis

Middlesex

Atkinson, Richard
Bickerton, Thomas
Bignall, James
Blackburne, Catherine
Brooks, Thomas
Bruel, Frances
Bunyan, Ann
Clendon, Charles
Coultis, Thomas (QS)
Durham, Thomas
Ellis, Ann - for life
Fury alias Garvey, Mary
Gooding, Margaret (QS)
Hadley alias Adley, Mary
Holt, William
Humphryes, Ann
Kelly, Lothary
Kelly, Michael (QS)
Kirkwood, John
Lawson, Matthew (QS)
Lyons, Isaac
Mayne, John
Morgan, Thomas

143

Murphy, James
Murphy alias Edwards, Mary
Palmer, William
Price, John
Read, Michael
Richards, William
Sidaway, Samuel
Smith, Simon
Springett, Hester
Tagg, Daniel
Thomas, Mary
Tickner, Peter - for life
Wale, Mary
Walker, William
Wartell, Francis (QS)
Williams, Thomas

Surrey

Breeden, Edward (SQ)

Brown, John - 14 yrs
Burton, John (QS)
Dellow, Abraham (QS)
Emmerson, Henry (QS)
Green, Ann (QS)
Hayes, Robert - 14 yrs
Lundberg, Sven - 14 yrs
Robinson, Ann
Shepherd, Mary
Simpson, James
Tompkins, Henry - 14 yrs
Turner, Philip - 14 yrs

Sussex

Chasemore, Joseph
Gowden, Alexander
Phillips, Mary
Rogers, Henry (QS)
Sherryer, William

Felons shipped from London to Maryland by the *Greyhound*, Capt. Alexander Stewart, in February 1754 arriving in May 1754. (PRO: Home Circuit records).

Buckinghamshire

Harrold, John
Potter, Jeremiah
Reddall, John

Kent

Boggs, Robert
Hughs, John

Felons transported from London by the *Thames*, Capt.James Dobbins*, in March 1754, arriving in Annapolis in May 1754. (CLRO: London and LMA: Middlesex Bonds)

London

Angell, Isaac
Anthony alias Jennings, Mary
Ash, Hannah
Ashley, Ann
Bailey, Richard
Beetley alias Duggan, John
Beezley, Ann
Bray, Benjamin
Bullock, Catherine
Butler, George
Byde, Mary
Clarke, George
Dickins, Catherine
Edmonds, William
Fielder, Stephen

Godley, Joseph
Hastings, Martha
Howard, Margaret
Jones, Margaret
MacCormick, Ann
Mackenzie, Sarah alias Mary
Markman, James
Minett, Matthew
Mitchell, James
Monk, Ann
Moore, Robert
Newman, Ann
Nicholls, Walter - runaway
Pugh, Mary
Richmond, Mary
Riley, Michael
Robertson, John

Robinson, John
Skelt, John
Stapler, John
Stewart, John - runaway
Strong, Thomas
Tinsley, Ann
Waters, Thomas
Williams, Elizabeth
Winter, Samuel
Witham, Samuel

Middlesex

Adams, Philip
Allen, Edward - for life
Bamford, John (QS)
Barber, Robert
Barnes, Stephen - for life
Bedford, Walter
Bell, John
Brain, Elizabeth
Bronkee alias Bunker, Abraham
Brown alias Eler, Ann
Brown, Catherine
Brown, Elizabeth - 14 yrs
Bryant, John
Carney, Michael
Clarke, Ann
Connor, Mary
Conyers, Sarah
Cooke, Thomas
Cradock, Mary
Davis, Catherine
Davis, Matthew (QS)
Davis, Samuel
Dennis, William
Eaton, Elizabeth
Edgele alias Ellford, William
Emmott, William
Evans, James
Ford, Richard
Foreman, Mary
Foreman, Peter

Gervise, Gerrard
Hambleton, William
Hayes, Frances
Hearne, John
Hoare, Elizabeth
Humphreys, Elizabeth
Hunter, William (QS)
Hyan, William
Irons, William - for life
Jackson, James - for life
Jefferies, Luke
Jones, Ann
Jones, Mary
Kelly, Mary
Kempster, Elizabeth
Larmer, George
McNamer, Joseph (QS)
Mills alias Cassody, Elizabeth
Mingis, Martha
Nisbee alias Surrey, Susanna
Oliver, Thomas
Peat, Richard Denton
Pitts, Charles
Prosser, Samuel
Pugh, Daniel
Purney, Richard
Purvis, Ann - runaway
Radborn, John
Radborne alias Ambrose, Thomas
Rebecco alias Handford, Jane
Riley, Grace
Sherrard, John
Smith, Ann
Stowman, Ann
Taylor, Elizabeth alias Wiseman
Ward, John
Warner, Thomas - runaway
Watson, John
Weaver, Mary
Williams, Sarah
Witt, James
Woodland, Christopher

*James Dobbins died on the *Thames* a few days after leaving Maryland for England. (MG)

Felons transported from London by the *Tryal*, Capt. Isaac Johns*, in July 1754, arriving in Maryland in September 1754. (CLRO: London & LMA: Middlesex bonds & PRO: Home Circuit records).

Buckinghamshire

Harris, Elizabeth, spinster - 14 yrs
Harrold, John
Potter, Jeremiah
Reddall, John
Worley, Thomas - 14 yrs

Essex

Agnis, John (QS)
Benson, Benjamin - 14 yrs
Bowlton, Richard
Ellgood, Christopher (QS)
Exell, Ann
Gresham, Charles (QS)
Laver, Richard
Rust, William - 14 yrs
Siday, John
Turner, Thomas - 14 yrs
Warren, John (QS)
West, John (QS)

Hertfordshire

Byatt, Elizabeth
Cole, Robert
Cooper, John
Smith, John - 14 yrs

Kent

Bax, Jeremiah
Boggs, Robert (QS)
Clarke, William
Cowell, Caleb
Dunkin, Margaret
Hadlow, Hercules
Hall, William
Hughs, John (QS)
Mitchell, James
Moody, Samuel
Perkins, William
Ring, William
Saunders, John - 14 yrs
Tharpe, Joseph
Willins, Sarah

London

Bailey, Sarah
Carter, Elizabeth
Connor, Francis
Dunmole, Francis
Fagan, John
Gunnele, William
Heaverland, William
Laphan, James
Lee, James
Morris, John
Need, William
Oliver, William
Skate, Lucy
Walker alias Sparrow, Mary
Walker, John

Middlesex

Askew, Mary
Biggs, Thomas
Cardinale, Thomas
Carr, Ann
Carroll, Timothy
Cartright, Ann
Clarke, Mary
Cleham, Elizabeth
Cole, George - 14 yrs
Collins, Ann
Croshaw, Elizabeth
Cummings, Joseph
Dust, Francis
Ferring, Charles
Fitch, Edward
Forster, George
Fulham, Thomas
Gower, Philip
Handerson, John
Harwood, Elizabeth
Hine, Eleanor
Hitchman, Thomas
Jenkins, Thomas
Jennings, John
Kelly, Matthew
Knight, Walter
Low, Mary
Lucas, Rachael - 14 yrs

Maxfield, Mary
Monk, John
Page, John
Phillips, John
Pippin alias Pepper, Richard
Pugh, Hugh alias Hawkins, Henry
   - runaway
Ralph, John
Riley alias Barrett, Joseph
Riley alias Barrett, Mary - 14 yrs
Rock, John
Rose, Thomas
Saunders, William - runaway
Scott, Catherine
Selvie, George
Smith alias Hall, Elizabeth
Smith, Richard
Smith, Susanna
Tarrant, John
Taylor, Mary
Thompson, Mary
Tobin, James
West, Richard
Wilson, Hannah
Worrell, Francis - 14 yrs

Surrey

Batton, Francis
Bird, Matthew
Cheeke, William
Davies, Thomas
Frevitt, William
Ginn, Thomas (QS)
Gouldin, George - runaway
Grady, John
Gregory, Lile
Grose, Simon
Holt, Thomas
Hunter, William
Johnson, Robert (QS)
Joyner, John - 14 yrs
Sullivan, Catherine (QS)
Vinegar, Ann
Williams, Margaret

Sussex

Baker, William - runaway
Ballard, John
Sanders, Peter
Wright, John - 14 yrs

*Isaac Johns died 12 days out from London leaving a widow and child in Annapolis.
(MG)

**Felons transported from London to Virginia by the *Ruby*, Capt. Edward Ogle, in
October 1754.** (CLRO: London & LMA: Middlesex bonds; PRO: Home Circuit records).

Buckinghamshire

Branklyn, James
Collins, John - 14 yrs
Cox, John - 14 yrs
Cripps, Michael
Judge, Jane wife of William
Noble, Mark

Essex

Cloden, Garrett (QS)
Dawes, Thomas
Good, Mary
Goodwin, Daniel
Hill, John (QS)
Hill, Joseph (QS)
Howard, Edward (QS)
Lambert, Jeremiah alias Jemiah (QS)

Lambert, Philip (QS)
Lambert, William (QS)
Lilly, Margaret wife of William (QS)
Sparkes, Henry

Hertfordshire

Johnson, John -14 yrs
Morrice, Richard - 14 yrs
Tooley alias Tuley, John - 14 yrs
Tristram alias Tristrum, Joseph
Williams, John - 14 yrs
Wilson, Jeremiah

Kent

Bills, William - 14 yrs
Downing, William Biron - 14 yrs
Fear, John - 14 yrs

Harris, John
Hickman, Stephen
King, John
Meek, John
Murphy, William - 14 yrs
Thorburn, James
Johnson, Elizabeth alias Betty - 14 yrs

London

Bloss, Sarah
Collis, Thomas
Cooke, Mary
Davis, James
Dowling, Silas
Duncomb, Catherine
Farr, George
Fletcher, John
Foulks, Edward
Hamilton, Samuel
Harris, Daniel
Holden alias Lovegrove, Rebecca
Knapton, Robert
Lane, Thomas
Lewis, Ann - for life
Longbottom, Elizabeth
Murphy, Thomas
Rice, David
Smith, William
Taylor, Henry
Varron, Thomas
Verity, John
Walters, Elizabeth
Watton, James
Webb, Richard
Whitaker, John
Wilson, Mary
Wood, Paul

Middlesex

Baker alias Moore, Elizabeth
Brown, William
Buckland, Thomas
  alias Buckley, Humphrey
Clarke alias Griggs,
  Margaret - 14 yrs
Collier, John

Conner, Mary
Davies, John
Davis, Peter
Day, Susanna
Deemer, Jeremiah
Dukes, John
Dukes, Richard
Dunn, Mary
Foresight, John
Gordon, William
Gullick, William
Hall, Elizabeth
Harland, Frances
Hely, Joseph
Hinton, Timothy
Hobbs, Thomas
Jones, Elizabeth - for life
Knapp, James
Lediard, Ann
Mann, Edward alias William
Mooney, Richard
Pritchard, Elizabeth
Riley, John
Sanders, Mary
Simms, Elizabeth
  (alias wife of William Terry)
Slaughter, Mary
Smith, Elizabeth
State, Edward
Stoner, Sarah
Thompson, John
Watson, John
Webb, William

Surrey

Brown, Christian
Cooke, Sarah - 14 yrs
Dean, Richard
Downer, Elizabeth - 14 yrs
Weston, Mary.
White, Benjamin
Williamson, John

Sussex

Weston, George

Felons transported from London in February 1755 by the *Greyhound*, Capt. Alexander Stewart, arriving in Maryland in April 1755. (CLRO: London & LMA: Middlesex bonds).

London

Allen, Elizabeth
Allen, John
Ball, Benjamin
Berry, James
Burroughs, Samuel
Butler, Carolina
Cornwall, Elizabeth
Doyle, Philip
Fairbank, James - runaway
Gift, Elizabeth
Hammond, Elizabeth
Harling, Richard
Hughes, Edward
James, Thomas - for life - runaway
Jarvis, William
Marks, John
Moon als Mohun, Catherine
Peacock, William
Sparkes, Samuel
Tillie, James
Upton, Elizabeth
Vaughan, Thomas
Waddesley, John
Welch, Robert
Yeates, William

Middlesex

Adams, John (QS)
Barnes, Elizabeth (QS)
Boucher, Thomas (QS)
Bowen, William
Brown, John alias Henry
Cashbolt, John
Cassander, William
Christopher, John
Cole, James (QS)
Coney, George
Cooley, James (QS)

Cooper, Elizabeth
Cooper, Thomas
Dalton, Thomas
Dixon, Richard (QS)
Dorrell, Thomas (QS)
Dudley, Richard
Dyster, Edward
Eaton, Catherine
Gentry, Samuel
Godfrey, John (QS)
Goodwyn, Henry
Gretton, Cadman
Harbourn, Benjamin (QS)
Harris, Michael
Hone, Ann (QS)
Horton, Thomas
Hudson, William (QS)
Hughes, Ann (QS)
Hunt, Thomas (QS)
Ingmire, Robert
Jenvey, Peter
Jump, William
Malony, Daniel
Martin, Mary (QS)
Massey, Ann - 14 yrs
Massey, Sarah - 14 yrs
Mills, Thomas
Noon, John
Poulson, Elizabeth
Sacker, John alias Smith, William
Scarborough, James
Sheerman, William (QS)
Smith, Barwell
Southerby, Mary
Swift, Elizabeth
Tapling, John
Taylor, Alexander (QS)
Trowton, Robert (QS)
Williams, Susanna
Woolner, William

Felons transported from London to Maryland by the *Rose*, Capt. Thomas Slade, in May 1755 arriving in June 1755. (PRO: T1/261/39).

Essex

Aspindale, Peter

Bearman, William - 14 yrs
Brage, William (QS)
Carter, Robert

Davis, Sarah - runaway
Leach, Roger - 14 yrs
Murfey, Timothy
Stiggard, Mary (QS)
Ward, John
Wilson, James (QS)

Hertfordshire

Blunt, David
Grover, John
Shadbolt, William

Kent

Bates, John
Brooks, Thomas
Constable, John
Dorrington, Martha
Ellis, John
Harkney, Edward
Kelly, Peter
Leaver, Benjamin
Parks, Sampson
Savage, William
Smith, John
Tebbutt, William
Wilkeshire, William

London

Baker, Leonard
Cowley, John - 14 yrs
Dew, Joseph
Frigatee, Charles
Gardner, Thomas
Gray, Richard
Hoppit, William
Insell, Elizabeth
Jackson, Dorothy
Lowman, Michael
Martin, Thomas (alias
    Johnson, William) - runaway
Piercy alias Cooper, John
Pointer, John
Quimby, Peter
Ruggles, William
Thompson, Joseph
Todd, Sarah - for life
White, William
Williams, Elizabeth

Middlesex

Banks, William
Baxter, Hester
Bear alias Lacy, Elizabeth
Beckett, John (QS)
Brinkinshire, Richard
Brinkley, James
Bruff, John - runaway
Cheshire, John
Clarke, Ann
Connor, Terence
Dennis, John
Dobree, Elias
Farrell, Winifred
Finn, James
Fitzpatrick, Catherine (QS)
Fleck, John
Floyd, Thomas
Freeman, Elizabeth
Gaudon alias Garner, Elizabeth (QS)
Gayler, Thomas
Gill, Margaret
Gillman, John
Grimes, Robert (QS)
Hambleton, William - for life
Hasty, Ann
Hubbard, Catherine
Humphryes, Charles
James, Mary
Kennedy, Martin
King, Mary (QS)
King, Thomas
Lovell, Joseph
Metcalfe alias Smith, Thomas
Mills alias Liversidge, Elizabeth
Monk, Ann
Moore, Ann
Morrison, Lucy
Myers, William
Paice, Ashwood (QS)
Peck, Edward (QS)
Petty, Isabella
Powell, Joseph
Reculus, Lionel
Ricketts, John
Robertson, Ann
Robinson, Ann
Robinson, William
Ryley, Sarah (QS)
Scarlett, Catherine
Sears, Moses (QS)

Thorp, John (QS)
Weedon, James
Welch, John alias Thomas
Wells, Ann
White, Ann
Whitmell, William
Wilbourne, John
Wiseman, Margaret
Young, James - for life

Surrey

Blake, Charles
Bury, Mary
Cain, Morris

Cornwall, Mary - 14 yrs
Cuthbert, Samuel - 14 yrs
Davis, Christiana - 14 yrs
Delahunt, Rose (SQ)
Edmonds, John
Grainger, Joseph
Hale, Thomas
Pearce, Charles
Roby, Elizabeth
Samuel, Nathan
Stevenson, James - 14 yrs
Topps, Susanna
Turker, William
Turner, Elizabeth - 14 yrs
Tyler, John - 14 yrs

Felons transported from London to Maryland by the *Tryal*, Capt. William McGachin, in September 1755. (PRO: T1/361/67).

Buckinghamshire

Alberry, Thomas
Boswell, Thomas
Boswell, William
Cox, Thomas
Lake, John
Lyne, Thomas
Nottingham, James - runaway
Rowlet, John

Essex

Collins, John - 14 yrs
Collins, Thomas - 14 yrs
Harris, John
Skeggs, James - 14 yrs
Wyer, John - 14 yrs

Hertfordshire

Gurry, Richard - 14 yrs
Hanscombe, Thomas - for life
Willson, Thomas

Kent

Axleby, John - 14 yrs
Chittenden, Mary - 14 yrs
Davis, Philip - 14 yrs
Dugmore, Thomas (QS)
Jones, William (QS)

London

Anderson, Sarah
Bagg, Elizabeth
Barron, John
Barry, John
Bedford, Christopher
Bell, Mary
Bird, Susanna
Blackstone, Zebulon Thrift
Bowyer alias Scampey, William
  - for life
Burnett, John
Clarke, James
Cole, Thomas
Coulston, Thomas
Curtis, Catherine
Dayley alias Peterson, John
  alias Geohogan, Walter - for life
Diggenham, John
Grant, Sarah
Haywood, William
Heaton, John
Hollister, John
Hurst, James
Jacobs, Sarah
Johnson, Hester
Lyger, James
McCarty, David
McGlew, Patrick
Morris, Hannah
Mullins, James
Nelson, Eleanor

Paris, Daniel
Puckering, Edward
Redshaw alias Lacon, Sarah
Rice, William
Robinson, Mary
Scott, Ann
Scott, Thomas - for life
Smith, Mary - for life
Smith, Susanna
Sparkes, William
Stanley, John
Stevens, John
Turton, Mary
Vernall, Richard
Watson, Richard - for life
Welling, Thomas
Westcote, Thomas
Williamson, William - runaway

Middlesex

Ashby, John
Barrett, Mary
Bland, Ambrose (QS)
Bodden, Agnes (QS) but also noted as
   transported in 1756 by *Greyhound*
Butler, Elizabeth
Clarke, Thomas
Conquest, John
Cooke, Ann
Cooke, William
Darlow alias Barlow, William - for life
Davis, Margaret
Fagan, James
Fuller, Rebecca
Goddard, Mary
Godson, Charles
Graves, Elizabeth
Griffiths, Richard - 14 yrs
Groom, William
Hatt, Grace
Higham, Farwell (QS)
Hust, Ann
Jackson, William
Johnson, John (QS)

Jordan, Bridget
Lewis, Mary
Mackey, Patrick
Newby, Sarah (QS)
Norris, Frances
Plummer, Mary
Price, John
Rade, Thomas
Read, Thomas
Sands, Ann
Sedgwicke, John
Sherridan, Catherine
Smith, John (QS)
Stempston, John
Stevens, Amelia
Stevens, John
Swift, Samuel
Ward, Dorothy (QS)
Ward, Elizabeth
Wilson, John
Windell, Elizabeth
Wood, Jane
Woodbegood alias Robins, Mary

Surrey

Bell, Mary
Byass, Daniel
Cheshire, John
Coombes, William
Delahunt, Rose
Fielding, Catherine
Humphryes, John - 14 yrs
Johnson, Hester
McCarty, David
Steele, Joseph
Tame, John
Trivet, Mary
Tugman, James
Wheymark, Elizabeth

Sussex

Jenner, Samuel - 14 yrs
Savage, John - 14 yrs

Felons transported from London to Maryland by the *Greyhound*, Capt. Alexander Stewart, in January 1756 arriving in April 1756. (PRO: T1/367/2).

Hertfordshire

Peacock, Thomas

Titmouse, Francis

Kent

Walker, John (QS)- runaway

London

Barnes, Thomas
Barnett, Sarah
Bentley, Samuel
Bills, William
Binsted, Mary
Carroll, John - 14 yrs
Clayton, John
Cleverton, Ann
Collins, Elizabeth
Cooley, Margaret
Davis, Thomas
Duncastle, Robert
Eaton, Martha
Finnimore, Joseph
Fynes, Margery
Gould, William
Gray, Elizabeth
Hayes, Thomas
Hipworth, John
Ingoll, John
Lampard, Thomas
Marshall, Rachael
McDonald, Margaret
Myers, John
Myers, William
Nicholls alias Cryer, Jane
Palmer, Mary
Peirson, John
Phillips, Ann
Rawthorne, John
Reed, Joseph
Shervill, John, alias Tom Thumb
Strafford, Susanna
Welch, James
Wingrove, John

Middlesex

Appleby, Thomas (QS)
Armstrong, Thomas
Banks, Randall
Billian, James - for life
Blunt alias Butler, James
Booden, Agnes (QS)
Brady, Catherine (QS)
Brocklebank, Jonathan

Bryan, James
Burton, Francis
Carr, Mary
Cartwright, Joseph
Chinnery, Rebecca
Coltman, Judith
Cornbury, Richard - pardoned
Davids, Abraham
Davids, David
Dellmore, Elizabeth
Dodd, Mary
Dyson, William (QS)
Ferguson, John
Foowles, Jane
Frederick alias Johannes, Daniel
Fryett, Robert
Grierson, Rev. John - 14 yrs
  - died on passage
Groom, William
Hall, Samuel (QS)
Harris, James (QS)
Harris, John
Haskins, Thomas
Hull, Eleanor
Jones, Thomas (QS)
Lambeth, Joseph
Lamprey, Sarah
Leve, Daniel
Mullens, Thomas
Murdock, Alexander
Nash, Matthew
O'Bryan, Eleanor
Porter, Mary
Pottle, James (QS)
Randall, Elizabeth
Ready, Peter
Rees, John - runaway
Seares, George - runaway
Smith, Edward
Smith, Elizabeth
Smith, Humphry (QS)
Smith, John
Southeran alias Keys, Elizabeth
Sparrow, Robert
Stafford, Ann
Stevens, Joseph
Weston, John
Whiteman, Ann
Yeates, Elizabeth

Surrey

Bedford, Christian (QS)
Foster, Thomas (QS)
Hill, Robert (QS)

Holt, William (QS)
Mail, Edmund (QS)
Martin, James (QS)
Riley, James. (QS)
Wakeling, John (QS)

Felons transported from London to Maryland by the _Lyon_, Capt. James Dyer, in June 1756, arrived in Annapolis in August 1756. (PRO: T1/365/98; MG).

Essex

Boone, Jeremiah (QS)
Cobble, Priscilla (QS)
Cooper, Thomas
Cubberd, Anthony (QS)
Cubberd, William (QS)
Finch, William
Morris, Robert (QS)
Stebbing, Thomas - 14 yrs
Upson, Mary
Ward, Francis 14 yrs
Warner, William
Woodland, Lydia

Hertfordshire

Graham, Ann

Kent

Adams, John
Cryer, Richard - 14 yrs
Dugmore, Thomas
Elliot, Mary
Geale, Elizabeth
Jones, William
King, John - runaway
Lavan, Hannah
Mullins, Matthew
Smith, Benjamin
Walker, John
Ware, John - runaway

London

Abrahams, Alexander - 14 yrs
Ayers, John
Brangham, Mary
Brassell, Daniel
Buckhurst, Elizabeth
Coates, Benjamin
Eagan, William

Ellis, Elizabeth
Floyd, Arthur
Fuller, John
Izard, Abraham
Jones, David
Lee, Martha
Levi, Hyam
Levi, David
Miller, John
Montgomery, Eleanor
Palmer, Sarah
Plunket, James
Richardson, William
Smith, James
Speed, Mary
Stephenson, Susanna
Thompson, John
Toy, Samuel
Ventris, John
White, George

Middlesex

Bargier, Paul
Benson, Thomas
Benton, John
Brown, Elizabeth
Carter, William (QS)
Casey, Isabella
Cockup, Mary
Coram, John - 14 yrs
Costello, Honor
Davies, William
Dudley, Edward
Endsor, Edward
Fitzgerald, Walter
Germain, Elizabeth
Gill, Elizabeth
Grubb, William
Harvey, Richard
Horne, Henry
Hyde, Thomas
Jones, William

Jones, Sarah
Kemp, John
Kingston, Mary
Lee, Sarah
Login, William - runaway
Marriott (Meritt), Edward (QS)
 - runaway
Martin, Charles
Munday, Richard
Nevell, John
Page, John
Pease, John
Perry, Thomas (QS)
Quin, Winifred
Rousser, Lewis
Royston, Elizabeth
Sampson, Richard
Taylor, Esther

Townley, Mary
Trevis, Philip
Wigmore, John
Williams, Thomas
Wood, John
Wright alias Wilkinson, Elizabeth

Surrey

Boreman, Elizabeth
Brasier, John - 14 yrs
Coates, Benjamin (QS)
Jones, Edward - but pardoned
Smith, William - 14 yrs
Thompson, James - 14 yrs
Tonkyn, John - for life
Trevith, Mary
Witton, William

Felons transported from London to Virginia by the *Barnard*, Capt. Philip Weatherall, in October 1756. (CLRO: London bond, LMA: Middlesex Sessions & PRO: Home Circuit records).

Buckinghamshire

Biggs, John - 14 yrs
Dawkins, John - 14 yrs
Parish, Benjamin
Virgo, Thomas - 14 yrs
Willis, John

Essex

Clay, John
Monk, George - 14 yrs
Warriker, Abraham - 14 yrs

Hertfordshire

Burn, Tanglis
Tree, Robert - 14 yrs
Woodward, Elizabeth

Kent

Ashby, John - 14 yrs
Beaumont, William
Brown, Ann
Greaves, Ann
Humphrey, William - 14 yrs
Jones, John

Large, Thomas
Slater, Isaac
Swinyard, Edward
Thomas, Richard

London

Evans, John
Gordon, John
Hall, Richard
Hart, Michael
Heath, Mary
Leatherstone, Hannah
Levi, Israel
McHalfpenn, James
Page, Jane
Rawlings, John
Williams, Elizabeth
Williams, William - 14 yrs

Middlesex

Briggs, Mary
Buckeridge, Ruth
Chambers, Margaret
Cole, George
Conway, Ann wife of John
Davies, William
Davis, Elizabeth

Day, Elizabeth
Dean, Ann
East, Jane
Eve, John
Fife, William
Fletcher, Eleanor
Gill, John
Griffin, Edward
Gutteridge, Charles
Higgins, Matthew
Hodgman, Edward
Holl alias Bowen, Elizabeth
Horner, Robert
Howell, Margaret
Jameson, John
Jefferys, Elizabeth
Jones, Catherine
Jones, Henry
Keith, Joseph
Kelsey, John
Knott, Mary
Lanson, Catherine
Little, Daniel - for life
Matthews, Clement wife of Michael
Moores, John - for life
Moores, Thomas - for life
Morgan, Sarah
Mulloy, Mary
Newman alias Howard, Bridget
Norris, John
Rivers, Elizabeth
Saint, John Egerton
Scott, James
Shelock, James - for life

Sibthorpe, William
Stubbs, Ann
Stubbs, Frances wife of John
Stubbs, John
Sutherland, Margaret
Thomas, William
Walker, Richard
Ward alias English, Elizabeth
Waters, Elizabeth
Watts, William - for life
Wilkinson, John, clerk - 14 yrs
Wilson alias Wilkinson, Mary
Wright, George
Young, Mary

Surrey

Appleton, Mary
Ausley, Henry
Blackwell, William - 14 yrs
Brown, Francis - 14 yrs
Davis, William
Gardiner, William
Grimsby, Richard
Holmes, Ann
Hunt, Susannah
McArter, Alexander John
Richardson, Joseph - 14 yrs
Smith, George
Wallis, Ann

Sussex

Roberts, George - 14 yrs

Felons transported from London to Maryland by the *Tryal*, Capt. Mills, in March 1757 arriving Patapsco in June 1757. (CLRO: London & LMA: Middlesex Calendars; PRO: T53/46/110).

London

Abraham, Moses
Butler, Charles
Carroll, Jane.
Cay, Elizabeth
Davis, David - for life
Foster, John
Griffiths, Mary
Holland, Thomas
Hughes, John - for life
Jones, Daniel
King, William

Knotsmell alias Shelton, Elizabeth
Martin, Mary
Peck, Mary
Savage, James
Sawyer, Charles
Ware, Edward
Wells, William
Williams, Susanna
Willis, Lydia

Middlesex

Allard, Paul

Barnett, William
Baythorne, James - for life
Clarke, Leonard
Cooke, George
Eagle, Edward
George, Elizabeth wife of Edward
Gorman, Lawrence
Griffith, James - runaway
Hart, William - for life
Higgins, William - for life - runaway
Howland, John - runaway
Jones, Mary
King, Elizabeth

Langley, George - for life
McNemara, Mary wife of James
Pevett, Elizabeth
Pritchard, Martha
Probart, William
Prosser, James - for life
Ridout, Thomas - for life
Saunders, Catherine
Smith alias Richardson, Mary
Timperley, Robert - 14 yrs
Troward, Edward
Watkins, Hannah
Woods, Edward - 14 yrs

*Alexander Scott, former Captain, drowned in Falmouth on outward voyage (MG)

Felons transported from London to Maryland by the *Thetis*, Capt. Matthew Craymer*, in September 1757, arriving at Annapolis in December 1757. (PRO: T1/378/64).

Buckinghamshire

Brett, William
Chester alias Lewis, Elizabeth
Gilbee, Ahaz
Goodall, Thomas
Hutton, Richard - 14 yrs
Leverit, James
Poon, Peter - 14 yrs
Richardson, Charles
Rutland, Joseph - 14 yrs

Essex

Ballantine, William
Cole, Richard (QS)
Green, Joseph
Mead, John (QS) - but pardoned
Probuts, William (QS)
Ross, John
Strong, Peter - 14 yrs - runaway
Stubbing, John

Hertfordshire

Dundass, John, alias Gordon, James
 - 14 yrs
Little, Keziah
Newman, Thomas - 14 yrs

Kent

Bonner, William
Dooley, Nathaniel
Fisher, Sarah
Fowler, Thomas
Freeman, John
Garrett, Elizabeth
Kidder, Edward,
 alias Alchin, John (QS)
Smith, John (2)
Smithers, Elizabeth
Ticehurst, Thomas (QS)
Wheatley, Mary
White, Susanna
Winterbottom, Margaret

London

Allen, Mary
Bedwell, James
Bourne alias Knowland, Catherine
Boyd, Robert
Caldwell, William
Cannon, Thomas
Curry, Michael
Dimsdale, Rachael
Dumble, Thomas
Easton, Samuel
Finch, Thomas
Flatt, John
Fordham, Hannah

Gascoyne alias Connor, Sarah
Godard, James
Green, Henry
Griffiths, Catherine
Grimstead, William
Hall, Robert
Horley, Robert
Johnson, Turner
Kelly, Miles
McDannel, James
Murgatroyd, Joseph
Narroway, William
Oppenhein, Jacob
Plank, Sarah
Smith, John
Taylor, Solomon
Thornton, Thomas
Tyers, Richard
Wiesenthall, Charles Frederick
Williams, Richard - runaway
Wilson, Henry

Middlesex

Ashton, James, clerk
Baythorne, James - for life
Birch, Esther
Broughton, Elizabeth wife of Thomas
Brown, John
Bynion, Thomas (QS)
Cartwright, George
Chalmers, Margaret
Chester, Mary, widow
Coleman, Mary Ann
Conduit, Mary
Connington, Lewis
Cooper, James
Courtney, Elizabeth wife of William
Davison, Jane
Day, Thomas - 14 yrs
Duffin, Edward
Dwyer, Mary, alias Ryland, Eleanor
Elkins, Mary wife of William,
  alias wife of John Wood
Elkins, James
Felton, Mary
Fiefield alias Pyefield, Susannah
Flanigan, Richard
Gilford, William
Gorgonna, John Baptista
Graham alias Grimes, John
Green, Jane

Handby, John
Harrison, Elizabeth
Hayman, William
Heathcote, Isaac (QS)
Higgonson, William
Hutton, Ann wife of John
Jacobs, Michael
Jefferyes, Mary
Jenks, Christopher
Johnson, Elizabeth
Johnson, John
Jones, Elizabeth
Jones, John
Jones, Sarah
Lee, Daniel
Lennard, James (QS)
Lucas, Ann
Maddison, Sarah
Manton, Mary
Matthews, Richard
Mead, George
Miller, Samuel
Mooring alias Grey, William
Morris, Sarah
Nockliss, Mary
Palmer alias Connor, Hester
  wife of John
Peirson, Diana
Perry, Priscilla
Riley, Thomas
Saunders, Richard
Savage, Elizabeth
Simonds, Ann
Singleton, Edward
Smith, Jane
Smith, John
Smith, Sarah
Stewart, Mary
Sutton, John
Symonds, William
Tapper, Joseph
Wall, Ann, spinster
Ward, Ann
Wetherell, John
Williams, Mary wife of John
Woollen, Ann

Surrey

Andrews, William - runaway
Colvell, William
Dalton, Thomas - 14 yrs

158

Davis, Michael - 14 yrs
Good, William
Hounsby, William
Jones, William - 14 yrs
Joseph, Moses - 14 yrs
King, Ann wife of John (QS)
Maze, Benjamin
Peacock, Elizabeth
Percival, Thomas
Rice, Mary

Ridge, Andrew - 14 yrs
Wilson, James

Sussex

Ayling alias Pullin, John - 14 yrs
Boxall, Henry
Jones, Robert - runaway
Pilcher, William (QS)
Rutley, Robert - 14 yrs

*The former Captain, James Edmunds, and 28 convicts died on passage.

Felons transported from London to Maryland by the *Dragon*, Capt. William McGachin, in March 1758. (PRO: T1/387/17).

London

Ardern, Robert
Banks, Joseph
Baruh, Abraham
Booker, Richard
Bromfield, James
Brooker, Jane
Campbell, Elizabeth
Day, Mary
Dyer, Elizabeth
Farrell, Peter
Foxon, William
Gosling, Mary
Griffith, Ann
Holmes, Frederick
Huckenhull, Mary Jr
Jones, William
Kennard, Samuel
Lion, Thomas
Richards, Sarah
Seagrave, John
Smith, Samuel
Walker, Israel
Webb, Samuel - runaway
Wilder, Sarah
Wilder, William
Williams, Mary

London (King's Bench)

Banks, Joseph
Farrell, Peter
Smith, Samuel

Middlesex

Arnold, Mary
Bagdurf, Christopher
Biggs, Thomas (QS)
Boston, Beverly
Bowen, Ann
Cheriton, Elizabeth
Clark, Thomas
Coupland, William
Craven, John
Doherty, John (QS)
Duncan, Elizabeth wife of John
Eaton, Lawrence (QS)
Farnum, Lawrence
Franklyn, Samuel
Gilham, William
Godfrey, Elizabeth
Gregory, Ann
Hall, John
Hall, George
Hickey, Jane
Holmes, William
Honey, Sarah (QS)
Humphries, Robert
Hutchinson, William - runaway
Holly, Edward
Kenny, Luke
Letter, Elizabeth
Lockin, Richard
Loman, Robert
Louder, Jonathan
Low, John
Maddocks, Martha
Matthews alias Cole, Ann,
    alias wife of Thomas Tobeings

159

Moody, John - for life
Moore, Ann
Murphil, John Lawrence
Newton, Thomas - 14 yrs
Newton, John
Palmer, Catherine
Pentycost, Eleanor wife of John
Rhodes, John - runaway
Rose, Thomas
Savage, John
Scott, Mary
Skinner, Ann
Stratton alias Strutton, William
Thatcher, Elizabeth
Tilman, Martha
Titchborne, Elizabeth wife of Henry
Watkins, Elizabeth
Weaver, John
Wells alias Davis, Catherine

Wilkinson, Mary alias Watkins
Witherington, Jane

Surrey

Ball, John (QS)
Cooke, Mary (QS)
Davis, Jane (QS)
Fearson, Ann
Foster, Mary (QS)
Grinley, Ann
Harrison, George (QS)
Isaacs, Solomon (QS)
Lewis, Sarah (QS)
Pearson, Ann
Richards, Francis (QS) - runaway
Spriggs, Stephen (QS)
Weaver, Elizabeth (QS)

Felons transported from London to Baltimore by the *Lux*, Capt. Wilcox, in April 1758. (PRO: Sheriffs' Cravings).

Derbyshire

Adlington, George
Burton, William
Flinders, William
Gregory, John - 14 yrs
Hagg, Paul

Shelton, Jonah
Wood, Peter - 14 yrs

Felons transported from London to Maryland by the *Tryal*, Capt. Nicholas Andrew, in September 1758. (PRO: T1/387/29 & 41).

Buckinghamshire

Gifford, William
Kebble, Richard - 14 yrs
Lidgley, John
Topping, Henry - 14 yrs

Essex

Butcher, William
Cole, Sarah (QS)
Constable, Thomas (QS)
Cox, Hannah
Dean, Sarah
Dorman, Timothy (QS) - runaway
Green alias Tiptee, Bathsheba (QS)
Lambert, Thomas (QS)

Lydiatt, Jane
Martin, Benjamin (QS)
Osborn, John
Osborne alias Chisnell, Martha (QS)
Pitchey, George - 14 yrs
Potter, Sarah (QS) - 14 yrs
Poulton, George (QS)
Sabin, Robert (QS)
Saxon, George (QS) - runaway
Starr, John (QS)
Stock, Samuel
Stolery, Brice - 14 yrs

Hertfordshire

Bowman, John

Kent

Brittain, James - 14 yrs
Burton, Elizabeth (QS)
Dane, Francis
Freemore, John (QS)
Gray, Elizabeth
Harrison, Nathaniel - 14 yrs
Kelly, Cecilly
Lindley, William - runaway
Riley, John
Robinson, Bridget (QS)
Seymour, George - runaway
Stanely, William
Stupple, John
Tapsell, Mary
Thorne, John
Trubshaw, Ann
Weston, George
Winter, Margaret (QS)

London

Bellisford, William
Bricklebank alias Quin, Mary
Bruenna, Margaret
Buckland, John
Chamberlain, William
Coffield, William
Frost, John
Goodey, Henry
Jones, Thomas
Margrave, John
Martindale, John
Matthews, Maria
Merritt alias Jones alias Wright, Ann
Richards, Edward
Rustin, Mary
Savoy, Gabriel - 14 yrs
Shackleton, Edward
Singer, Elliot
Styers, Thomas
Thornton, Sarah
Turner, Thomas
Woodey, Thomas

Middlesex

Allen, Elizabeth - for life
Banks, Andrew (QS)
Barker, Christian wife of John
Barret, Mary (QS)

Baxter alias Jones, Mary,
  alias Black Moll - for life
Beale, John
Benham, Richard - for life
Bloomer, William
Bray, Robert
Brown, Thomas, alias Lanham, Henry
Burroughs, John - runaway
Cameron, Margaret
Carney, Mary - for life
Cole, George
Cowcraft, John (QS)
Darnell, William
Davis, Robert - but pardoned
Dunning, Mary
Finley, Robert
Greaghan, John
Haddington, John (QS)
Hamilton, Arthur
Hodgson, Jane
Humphrys, Edward - for life
Hurst, Ann
Iron, Aaron
Johnson, Ann wife of John
Jones alias Baxter, Mary
Jones, Sarah
Latter, John
Maine, Mary - for life
Marriott, Edward
Matts, Roger (QS)
Mead, Charles
Meadows alias Willes, Elizabeth
  - for life
Moody, John - for life
Morein, John - runaway
Paul, William (QS)
Poor, Arthur (QS)
Price, John (QS)
Rice, Elizabeth wife of John
Riley, Philip - for life
Stephens, Daniel
Urquhart, William
Wales, James - for life
Worster alias Worcester, Andrew
Yates, Sarah (QS)

Surrey

Best, William
Burk, Frances
Butcher, Mary
Cartwright, Thomas

Coster, Richard
Debuck, Mary
Gibbons alias Gibbeson, Samuel
 - but taken from ship
Green, Joseph - 14 yrs
Haydon, Richard
Hook, Thomas
Ingram, Mary
Jackson, Mary
Mordecai, Moses
Nixon, Robert - 14 yrs
Pierce, Mary
Pugh, Hugh - runaway

Silver, William - 14 yrs
Smith, John (QS) - but pardoned
West, Matthew
Wood, William - 14 yrs

Sussex

Cramp, William
Dyke, Moses - runaway
Mason, Thomas
Pearson, James
Reynolds, Richard
Stewart, Dorothy

Felons transported from London to Maryland by *The Brothers*, Capt. Alan Boyd, in December 1758. (PRO: T1/340/159).

Essex

Darken, Isaac - 14 yrs
Gibson, William
Green, Thomas - 14 yrs
Hammond, Elizabeth
Jacobs, Michael - 14 yrs
Marsh, Nathaniel
Rickets, Thomas - 14 yrs
Rickets, William - 14 yrs
Wright, William - 14 yrs

Hertfordshire

Allam, John
Chandler, John (QS)
Ellis, Sarah (QS)
Gladwin, John - 14 yrs
Grange, Eunice - 14 yrs
Harris, Christopher
Howard, Eignon (QS)
Warbey, Edward - 14 yrs

Kent

Atkinson, John - 14 yrs
Baumer, William - 14 yrs
Bradley, William - 14 yrs
Davis, Elizabeth
Hunt, William - 14 yrs
Lavinder, Elizabeth
Shepheard, John
Smith, Thomas - 14 yrs
Snell, Thomas - 14 yrs
Stevenson, William

Williams, James - runaway

London

Ashbrook, Hannah
Awbrey, William
Barrett, Edmund
Barry, Frances
Barton, Henry
Brown, John
Buckland, Walter - 14 yrs
Buckley, Mary
Bunney, Bartholomew
Chester, Richard
Dabey, William
Dickins, Edward
Francis, James
Holland, Sarah
Lawrence, Elizabeth
Lee, William
McDonnack, Edward
Moon, Thomas
Payne, John
Petty alias Pettit, Ann - 14 yrs
Pinnock, Henry
Reynolds, Isaac
Richards, Lucy
Rowsell, John
Smith, William
Stedman, Samuel
Swinton, John
Talborn, Elizabeth
Tanklin, John
Timms, John
Witherington, Elizabeth

Wright, Martin - runaway

Middlesex

Ash, Richard
Battle, James
Bell, Ann
Burk, Margaret
Burnaby, Carew
Butler, Isabella wife of Thomas
Cotterell, Elizabeth (QS)
Davis, Ann
Davis, John
Drawwater, Michael
Durham, Elizabeth
Eadon, Thomas
Fenley, Mary
Finch, Sarah
Fish, James
Flannigan, Matthew
Fox, Samuel
Gee, Edward
Glynn, Abigail
Heron, Henry
Innis, David
Johnson, Elizabeth
Lee, Rebecca

Lehook, Mary
Liddell, Elizabeth
Linch, Michael
Lindsey, Mary
Lyon, William
Moore, William
Neal, Paul - 14 yrs
Sadler alias Cartwright, Ralph
Smith, Mary
Webb, William (QS)
Williams, Edward - but pardoned
Withers, Sarah (QS)

Surrey

Daniel, Elizabeth (QS)
Douglas, Rebecca (QS)
Jenkins, William Glover
Rivers alias Scott, Benjamin (QS)
Thompson, Jane wife of John (QS)

Sussex

Bellchamber, Elizabeth - 14 yrs
Daniel, William
Goldring, Thomas - 14 yrs

Felons transported from London to Maryland by the *Thetis*, Capt. Matthew Craymer, in April 1759 arriving in July 1759. (PRO: T1/391/79).

Buckinghamshire

Crawley, John - 14 yrs
Crawley, Richard - 14 yrs
Grosvenor, Thomas - 14 yrs
Langston, William
Peake (Peck), George
Prentice, William
Ranson, William
Ross, Mary
Smith, William - 14 yrs
Winter, Thomas

Essex

Bones, Robert
Caryson, Sarah
Chalkley, Ann (QS)
Chipperfield, James - 14 yrs
Clements, John
Cockley, William - 14 yrs

Deekes, Joseph (QS)
Drake, Mary
Edwards, Thomas - 14 yrs
Erith, Jeffery (QS) - but pardoned
Ginn, Edward
Hunt, James - 14 yrs - runaway
Jones, James
Nott, William Sr. - 14 yrs
Nott, William Jr. - 14 yrs
Waskett, Mary Sr.
Waskett, Mary Jr.
Waskett, William

Hertfordshire

Adams, Sarah - 14 yrs
Garment, William
Stephens, John

Kent

Harden, William
Eaton, Mary
Tyrell, Elizabeth - 14 yrs

London

Askew alias Askiss, Catherine
Bennett, John
Bowden, Mary
Broadhead, Thomas
Cornew, William
Dutton, Jane
Garland, Sarah
Green, Sarah
Jenkins alias Bateman, Elizabeth
Kendall, Ann
Painter, Sarah
Painter, Thomas
Swinney, Ann

Middlesex

Bell, William
Blaze, Joseph
Brown, Elizabeth
Casey, John
Cleaver, Edward
Cox, Winifred
Daland, Eleanor wife of Lawrence
Dunthorne, Samuel
England, Elizabeth
Feathers, Henry - 14 yrs
Fish, John - runaway
Ford, Richard
Frazier, Samuel (QS)
Giles alias Friday, Ann
Goff, Martha wife of John - 14 yrs
Haynes, William
Heath, John
Jones, John (QS)
Laws, Mary
Levi, John (QS)
Lewis, Christopher
Lovett, Mary
Moore, Sarah

Neale, Connell
Pindar, Elizabeth
Ray alias Lewis, William,
    alias Cockran, James
Scott, Celia
Sharp, Elizabeth - 14 yrs
Smith, John
Tracey, Catherine
Ward, Mary, alias Holmes, Hannah
Watkins alias Ware, Margaret
Willis, Elizabeth - 14 yrs
Willis, James
Wilson, William

Surrey

Aires, James
Baker, James
Brown, John (QS)
Chisselden, Edward (QS)
Duel, Martha
Gaddish, James
Gahagan, Farrant (QS)
Harrison, Henry
Heathcote, Lydia - 14 yrs
Heathcote, Thomas
Johnson, Elizabeth
Kendall, Thomas
Kitson, James (QS)
Monk, Elizabeth
Moore, Timothy (QS)
Murphy, Garrett (QS)
Newsted, Abigail
Powell, Edward - 14 yrs
Price, Henry (QS)
Strudell, Michael
Turner, George - 14 yrs - runaway
Williams, George

Sussex

Eldridge, John
Foster, George - runaway
Till, Martha
West, John - 14 yrs

164

Felons transported from London to Maryland by the *Phoenix*, Capt. William McGachin, in December 1759 arriving in January 1760. (PRO: T1/401/133; CLRO: London & LMA: Middlesex Bonds).

Essex

Darby, Elizabeth (QS)
Eves, John
Jackson, George - 14 yrs
Sutton, Edward

Hertfordshire

Govey, George - 14 yrs
Levings, Edward

Kent

Green, Joseph
Hickman, John
Lane, Sarah
Nicks, John - runaway
Thomas, William
Weeks, Susanna

London

Armstead, Hannah
Bates, Thomas
Bennett, Ann
Brayner, Mary
Burton, Jane
Buswell, Stephen
Chavin, Elizabeth
Crowther, John
Dolling, Mary
Fernandez, Lewis
Hall, George
Hoskins, Thomas
Hughes, Elizabeth
Hughes, John
Hulls, Mary
Johnson, John
Kenne, Catherine
Lee, John
Lloyd, William - 14 yrs
Morris, Elizabeth
Morris, Richard
Neale, William
Paul, Mary
Pomfrey, Elizabeth
Pope, William

Powis, Elizabeth
Ridgeway, John
Ryecroft, Henry
Saunders, Ann
Sherwood, John
Shute, Hannah
Simpson, Elizabeth
Smith, Susannah
Standeford, William
Taylor, Thomas
Terry, Samuel
Thackerill, Edward - for life
Thurston, Mary - 14 yrs
Tomlinson, John
Waite, Thomas
White, John

Middlesex

Abbott, George
Arnold, Susannah
Arundell, Thomas (QS)
Baker alias Lutterell, James
Barber, John
Bayley, Ann
Berry, Richard
Boston, Mary wife of David
Brown, Mary (QS)
Bryan, Elizabeth
Burrell, Elizabeth
Butterfield, Mary
Cale alias Brown, Elizabeth
Campbell, Sarah wife of Duncombe
Cannon, Ann
Cater, Sarah wife of Solomon
Charlton, Jane
Connell, Ann
Connell, Catherine
Cooper, Mary
Cotterel, Sarah wife of John
Cowen, John
Crawford, Mary
Crockford, John
Darbin alias Broom, Mary
Darby, James
Dickinson, Joseph
Eagan, Catherine
Farrah, James

Forth, Richard
Gibson, Jonathan
Gill, Thomas
Glover, Mary
Goldsmith, Ann
Green, John (QS)
Harding, Ann
Harris, Eleanor
Haseldine, Grace
Hewitt, Thomas - pardoned
Holford, Thomas
Horseley, John
Larner, Elizabeth
Lewis, Ann
Lloyd, Dorothy wife of Thomas
Ludlam, Thomas
Mason, Peter
McGrath, Margaret
Meyer, Christopher
Morgan, John
Norris, Letitia (QS)
Ockleford, Mary
Outwood, Richard
Peters, Solomon
Pitfield, Sarah
Price, Samuel (QS)
Ricketts, Elizabeth
Robinson, Robert

Scott, Mary
Silver, Isaac
Speight, Christopher
Swingwood, James
Thompson, Elizabeth
Toms, James
Townsend, Jacob
Turner, Mary
Wallis, Eleanor
Weech, Rebecca
Went, Elizabeth
White, Mary
Williams, John
Wright, John
Young, Elizabeth

Surrey

Chavin, Elizabeth (QS)
Newberry, Robert - 14 yrs
Reed, Martin - 14 yrs - pardoned
Snow, Erasmus John.
Tibbs, John - 14 yrs

Sussex

Fuller, Robert - 14 yrs

Felons transported from London to Maryland by the *Friendship*, Capt. Dougal McDougal, in March 1760 arriving in June 1760. (PRO: T1/401/135).

London

Ambery, John - runaway
Baker, John - runaway
Beaucline, Elizabeth
Blackmore, James
Dixon, Jesse
Dixon, Zachariah
Eardley, Margery
Edwards, Mary
Hickman, Richard
Holmes, Joshua
Morgan, David
Saunders, Lucretia
Schau, Claus Johnson
Smith, John
Smith, Robert
Solomon, Saunders
Tedar, Joseph
Thompson, Alexander

Yearwood alias Haywood, Joseph

Middlesex

Brown, John (QS)
Burch, John
Burnish, Jane
Clark, Alice
Cordall, Mary
Cowdrey, Ann wife of Richard
Daily, Daniel
Davis, Rachel
Davis, William
Driver, Hopkins
Feary, Ann
Gater, Alexander
Harland, Jane
Hewet, Ann wife of Thomas
Johnson, Edward
Jones, Alice

Jones, Thomas
Marland, Henry
Marsh, Walter
McGueire, Margaret
Murphy, Margaret
Pardon, Sarah
Pearce, James (QS)

Powell, Charles (QS)
Saunders, William
Scott, William (QS)
Smith, Thomas
Stevens, Ann
Symonds, John (QS)
Wilcox, Mary

Felons transported from London to Maryland by the *Thetis*, Capt. Matthew Craymer, in April 1760 arriving in June 1760. (PRO: T1/401/137)

Essex

Kilgour, Alexander
Lent, Thomas
Mead, Thomas Jr.
Read, Henry
Shonk, John - 14 yrs
Smith, Ann (QS)
Thomas, John - 14 yrs - runaway
Wigsted, John

Kent

Brown, Richard 14 yrs
Haley, Patrick
Turner, William
Tyrell, Elizabeth - 14 yrs

Surrey

Georgeson, James (QS)
Hammond, Elizabeth wife of John (QS)
Laws, Ann (QS)
Lyfolly, Richard (QS)
Phillips, Joseph (QS) - 14 yrs
Price, John (QS)
Rogers, Sarah - runaway
Turner, George - 14 yrs
Wheeler, James
Wright, Elizabeth

Sussex

Jenkins, Frances - 14 yrs
Rutley, Robert - 14 yrs
Varndell, John

Felons transported from London to Maryland by the *Phoenix*, Capt. William McGachin, in October 1760, arriving in January 1761. (CLRO: London Bond , LMA: Middlesex Sessions and PRO: Home Circuit records).

Buckinghamshire

Cranwell alias Cranaway, John - 14 yrs
Darey, Mary

Essex

Barker, Isaac - 14 yrs
Conn, John - 14 yrs
Gibbon, John - 14 yrs
Mead, Thomas - 14 yrs
Pye, William - 14 yrs
Reed, Hannah - 14 yrs

Hertfordshire

Sable, John

Kent

Baker, John
Barrington, Mary - 14 yrs - runaway
Bexter, John - 14 yrs
Dailey, Charles
Pankhurst, Thomas - 14 yrs
Smith, Jeremiah

London

Bowen, William
Carle, Thomas - runaway
Crackles, Thomas
Dempsey, Pearce
Driver, John
Dunn, Catherine
Fisher, John

167

Gibbs, William
Gill, George
Grant, Mary
Hickson, Benjamin
Houghton, William
Howard, Ann
Jones, Mary
Melvin, Richard
Preston, Ann
Richards, Margaret
Risley, William
Ryder, William
Scott, Judith
Shaen, William
Staveley, Elizabeth
Taylor, Thomas
Thompson, Mary

Middlesex

Allen, Roger
Allen, Thomas - pardoned
Anderson, Francis
Anderson, George
Barrett, Elizabeth
Basey, Ann
Birch, Moses
Bird, Eleanor
Briggs, Thomas
Brooks alias Delany, Mary
Burn, Mary
Carr, Elizabeth - but stopped
Clewes, Mary
Collins, Hugh
Couch, Elianor
Crump, Francis
Davies, Sarah - but stopped
Davis, William
Dennison, John
Dixon, Jane
Donnelly, Patrick - runaway
Edgley (alias Hamilton), Ann
Erwin, Esther
Field, William

Flintham, Mary
Harper, Ann
Hopkins, Elizabeth
Hughes, Catherine wife of Jacob
Hughes, Deborah
Hughes, John
Hullock, Ann
Jackson, James
King, Margaret
Lacey, John
Lindsey, Catherine
Littler, Abigail
Long, Sarah
Martin, Andrew
McCall, Elizabeth
Neilson, Neil
Nowell, Lamprey
Oatley, Margaret
Parker, Ann
Paterson alias Anderson
  alias Isedale, Isabella
Potter, Charles
Powell, Eleanor
Rose, Jacob
Saunders, Hannah
Savage, Bartholomew - runaway
Smith, Margaret
Smith, Mary
Stabler, John
Thompson, Richard - pardoned
Ward, Ann
Wardley, Francis
Whiteman, Sarah
Wright, John

Surrey

Amor, William (QS)
Barrett, Nathaniel - 14 yrs
Christy, Elizabeth - 14 yrs
McCartney, Patrick (QS)
Payne, Edward - 14 yrs
Stevens, Edward - 14 yrs

Felons transported from London to Maryland by the _Neptune_, Capt. Benjamin Dawson, in March 1761, arriving in May 1761. (CLRO: London Bond & LMA: Middlesex Sessions records).

London

Berry, Ann

Burton, Abraham
Campion, Robert - pardoned
Clark, Alice

Coe, Anthony
Darton, Amelia alias Millicent
Deacon, Elizabeth
Foster, Edward - pardoned
Gaywood, William
Glyn, Richard
Green, John
Gunnell, John
Hall, Isaac - pardoned
Hoar, Thomas
Holloway, Alice
Matthews, James - pardoned
Mowls, Ann
Newport, John - pardoned
Norris, Richard
Peacock, Jeremiah
Pearce, Thomas
Shears, Mary
Shelton, James
Smithson, John - pardoned
Thompson, Alice - pardoned
Williams, Elizabeth
Youman, Susanna

Middlesex

Arnold, Samuel
Bannister, George
Bush, Ann
Cook, Anne

Davis, John
Fogarty, Mary
Francis, Samuel - stopped
Graham, Patrick
Handford alias Gordon, Richard
Harrison, William
Hunter, Joseph - pardoned
Jones, John - pardoned
Kegan, Robert - pardoned
Kelly, Ann
Kelly, Matthew
King, Daniel
King, Eleanor wife of James
Lane, Sarah wife of Benjamin
Long, Mary
Manning, John - pardoned
Mansfield, Elizabeth wife of Robert
Manton, Samuel
Manton, Thomas
O'Brien, Loramy
Pearce, Thomas
Pettit, Sarah
Peyton, Ann wife of Richard
Sampson, James
Schlutingt, Claus - pardoned
Simpson, Jonathan - pardoned
Tuniola, Margaret
Wallington, Ann
Warner, John - pardoned

Felons transported from London to Maryland by the *Dolphin*, Capt. Dougal McDougal, in April 1761 arriving in June 1761. (CLRO: London Bond, LMA: Middlesex Sessions papers; PRO: Home Circuit records).

Essex

Gason, William - pardoned
Knights, Sarah
Osborne, Mary (QS) - runaway
Pollard, Andrew
Shelley, Philip - 14 yrs
Smith, Thomas - pardoned
Swan, Robert

Kent

Pattenden, John
Pollard, John - pardoned
Ralph, Thomas - pardoned
Davis, William - pardoned

London

Clifton, Thomas - pardoned
Lewin, William - pardoned
Peake, Dorothy
Preston, Thomas
White, Elizabeth

Middlesex

Cromb, Ann - stopped
Cuthbertson, John - stopped
Dowland, Margaret
Drinkwater, Elizabeth
Ewin, John
Flannagan, Andrew
Graham, Sarah

Hand, Harriot
Harwood, Sarah
Hoddy, Richard
Pateman, Ann wife of John
Price, William
Seymour, Ann
Smith, Terence
Swan, Mary

Surrey

Dawson, Ann
Edwards, Anthony
Geary, Jane
Griffiths, Elizabeth
Morse, Dinah
Pantry, Robert - pardoned
South, Samuel (QS)
Taylor, Thomas - pardoned

Felons transported from London to Maryland by the *Maryland Packet*, Capt. Alexander Ramsay, in October 1761 arriving in January 1762. (CLRO: London Bond, LMA: Middlesex Sessions & PRO: Home Circuit records).

Buckinghamshire

Barton, John - 14 yrs
Fowler, Elizabeth - 14 yrs
Harding, Edward
Harding, Richard
Reynolds, William

Essex

Barlow, John - 14 yrs
Bury, William - 14 yrs
Hosler, William - 14 yrs
King, William - 14 yrs
Smith, Mary (QS)
Uggles, Richard - 14 yrs
Willers, Robert

Kent

Hawks, Thomas - runaway
Jennings, Henry
Palmer, Bridget
Turner, Samuel

London

Bell, James
Burdet, John - pardoned
Cade alias Bennett, John - pardoned
Carrington, Daniel - to transport himself
Chambers, Mary
Emblen, James - pardoned
Hall, William
Hitchings, Richard - pardoned
Jones alias Jonas, Elias
Lloyd, Eleanor

Moses, Joseph - pardoned
Perrin, Sarah
Pritchard, Ann
Quincey, John - pardoned
Sanders, Lucy
Smith, Charles - pardoned
Squires, Mary
Thompson, Mary
Woodward, Elizabeth

Middlesex

Anderson, Rachael
Barnard, Thomas
Bates, Susannah
Beaumont, Elizabeth wife of Thomas
Brown, Elizabeth
Calyham, John
Clay, Elizabeth
Collins, Ann
Compton, Mary
Daffy, Isabella
Egerton, Isaac
Ferguson, John - pardoned
Fogarty, Patrick
Gendrier, Francis
Goulding, Charles - pardoned
Green alias Collyer alias Waller, Mary
Griffiths, Eleanor
Harrison alias Johnson
  alias Williamson, Ann
Head, James - pardoned
Hennick, Rachael
Hughes, Mary
Ingram, Elizabeth wife of John
Johnson, Matthew - pardoned
Kane, Jane wife of Edward

Lewis, Ann
Mason, William
Mathews, Thomas - pardoned
Middleditch, Eleanor
Miller, Andrew
Morgan, David - for life - pardoned
Nixon alias Holt alias Robinson, Ann
Ogden, John
Quin, Thomas - pardoned
Shaw, Jane
Sheffield, Joseph - pardoned
Sockett, Andrew

Tap, Elizabeth
Trussell, Ann
Tunicliff, Ann
Watkins, Richard - pardoned
Welch, Martha alias Edwards, Mary
Wilson, Edward alias Joseph

Surrey

Howard, James (QS) - pardoned
Pricklow, John (QS) - pardoned
Truelock, Giles (QS) - runaway

transported from London to Maryland by the *Dolphin*, Capt. Matthew Craymer, in April 1762. (PRO: T1/418/265).

London

Adams, James
Allen, James - runaway
Bartlom, Edward
Brady, Mary - runaway
Brooksby, Samuel
Bryant, Richard - runaway
Bulger, Mary - for life
Chaffey, James
Coolet, Mary
Crouch alias Crouchefer, Mary
Dowdell, William - pardoned
Elliott, John - pardoned
Floyd, Mary
Green, Thomas - pardoned
Hickey, Cicily
Hughes, Mary
Incell alias Ilsen, William - pardoned
Jaques, George - pardoned
Kitching, Mary
McDonald, Ann
Moll, Francisco - pardoned
Moneypenny, Hugh - pardoned
Moses, Jacob
Nathan, Bernard
Paris, John - pardoned
Smith, Sarah
Urvoy, Toussaint Felix - pardoned
Welch, Richard
Williams, David - pardoned

Middlesex

Anderson, Rachael
Arnot, Mary

Baker, Thomas - pardoned
Beard, John (QS) - pardoned
Bloor, James
Bunney alias Stowe, Mary Anne
 - for life
Caston, Mary
Chambers, Mary
Clements alias Smith, Elizabeth
 - for life
Collins alias Clarke, Ann
Crosby, Thomas (QS)
Davenport, Mary
Duxon, Hannah
Everett, William - pardoned
Fitzwalter, Mark
Fleming, Elizabeth
Fleming, Lettice
Flinn, Barnard - pardoned
Flinn, Thomas
Forshea alias Southward, Eleanor
Fountain, Mary
Gendrier, Francis
Gilson, Thomas
Griffiths, Eleanor
Henning, Jane
Hughes, Mary
Izack, Samuel - pardoned
James, George - pardoned
Kimber, Mary
Langston, Robert - pardoned
Middleton alias Hutchinson, Mary
Morris, Mary - for life
Parsons, Mary
Plessis, Nicholas - pardoned
Price alias Humphries, Mary
Puttyford, John - pardoned

Quinn, Thomas - pardoned
Roach, Elizabeth wife of John
Roach, John - pardoned
Robinson, Henry
Scrivenor, George
Shelton, Hannah
Sherman, Rachael
Smith, James
Smith, Sarah
Smith, William
Sollowin alias Quin, Margaret - for life
Stiff, John - pardoned

Stubbs, Ann
Vere, Cecily - for life
Watkins, Richard - pardoned
Williams, Ann
Wiseley, Thomas - pardoned
Woodhouse, Thomas - pardoned
Young, Jane wife of John (QS)

Surrey

Jackson, Elizabeth (QS)

Felons transported from London to Virginia by the *Neptune*, Capt. Benjamin Dawson, in April 1762. (PRO: T1/418/267).

Essex

Brown, William (QS)
Collison alias Collis, William
 - pardoned
Finch, Elizabeth (QS)
Rayner, William (QS)
Smith, Elizabeth
Wright, Ann (QS)

Hertfordshire

Baker, Francis
Powell, Anthony - pardoned

Kent

Allum, Catherine
Andrews, William - pardoned
Daw, Thomas
Evans, Thomas - 14 yrs - runaway
Knowland, William

London

Cohen, Isaac
Graham, William
Jones, Mary
Matthews, Catherine Rebecca
Moseley, Hannah
Robinson, Christopher
Smith, Francis

Smith, John
Smith, Sarah

Middlesex

Birk, Eleanor
Clarke, Sarah
Denston, Isabella
Lamb, Sarah
Snell, Bejamin, alias Rice, Dick
South, Samuel
Stather, William
Stevens, Catherine
Topping, Joyce wife of Edward

Surrey

Alett, John (QS) - pardoned
England, Elizabeth
Greentree, Isabella
Lilly, John (QS) - pardoned
Mackrell alias Jordan, Sarah (QS)
Powell, John - pardoned
Russell, John - pardoned
West, Sarah (QS)

Sussex

Brooks, Thomas

Felons transported from London to Virginia by the *Prince William*, Capt. Dougal McDougal, in November 1762. (PRO: T1/418/360).

Essex

Godfrey, Thomas - for life
Green alias Smith, Edward (QS)
Hudling, Hugh (QS)
Sanders, Henry
Seale, Matthias
Taylor, Ann
Thorpe, William - 14 yrs

Kent

Arthur, Hannah - 14 yrs
Beverton, Simon (QS)
Colchin, John
Griggs, John - runaway
Lee, Thomas - 14 yrs
White, William - 14 yrs- pardoned

London

Barber, Elizabeth - 14 yrs
Barnes, William - 14 yrs
Clinch, William - pardoned
Crawley, Daniel
Davis, Edward
Dawson, Mary Ann
    wife of George (QS)
Dixon, John
Elgar, William
Geare, Henry
Gilham, Peter
Johnson, Ann
Lattimore, Stephen
Popplewell, Mary wife of Thomas (QS)
Rawlins, Nathaniel
Robinson, Michael - pardoned
Rustead, Richard
Sweetman, Richard Matthew (QS)
Thorne, William
Tisdale, Rebecca
Waddington, Alice
Wade, John
Young, Hugh John

Middlesex

Adams, Elizabeth
Adams, Hannah

Addams, John (QS)
Arrowsmith, Mary
Ashford, Thomas
Atkins, Joseph (QS)
Baker alias Black, Ann
Baker, Elizabeth
Benson, Francis
Black, Robert
Blake, Mary
Bradshaw, Andrew (QS)
Brand, Zachariah
Brocklehurst or Brackleyhurst,
    William - pardoned
Brookes alias Taylor, Agnes
Cary, William - pardoned
Clarke, Arthur - pardoned
Cockran, Mary
Davies, Edward
Duke, Catherine
Fenwick, Ann
Giles, William
Harrison, William
Hassell, Ann
Hind, Richard
James, John (QS)
Jones, Jeremiah
King, Mary
Leary, Margaret
Levy, Brina
Mallows, Sarah
Mandeville, Penelope
Morgan, William
Page, Mary
Perry alias McLaughland, Hannah
Powell, Richard
Powell, Robert
Rice, Elizabeth wife of James
Robinson, Mary (2)
Scott, William
Seaward, Ann wife of Roger
Simmons, Sarah (QS)
Solomon, Isaac - pardoned
Thompson alias Brown, Mary
Vandervenvell, Jan Jonas - runaway
Walker, Sarah
Watts, William
Welch, Mary wife of John
Wilkinson, Elizabeth
Williams, James, alias Parrott, Thomas

Surrey

Clarke, Elizabeth
Draper, Elizabeth (QS)

Fullagate, Edward - 14 yrs
Hersey, Martha
Skinner, Ann (QS)

Felons transported from London to Maryland by the *Neptune*, Capt. Colin Somervell, in April 1763. (PRO: T1/423/236).

Cheshire*

Smith, James

Devon*

Marsh, George
Sadler, Joseph

London

Allen, James - runaway
Baines, Richard
Bradford, Elizabeth
Brocker, John
Bromwich, Samuel
Burgess, Thomas
Clarke, Burton
Derbin, Joseph
Eason, William
Edwards, Mary
Follit, William
Hale, Matthew
Haynes, Catherine
Haynes, James
Oates, Elizabeth
Richmond, Ann
Smith, Alice
Sykes, Elizabeth
Wells, John
Wilkinson,. George - runaway
Wilmot, Elizabeth
Wright, James

Middlesex

Barnett, Susan
Berry, Hester
Bounds, Thomas
Brown, John
Butcher, James
Carroll, Patrick - runaway
Clark alias Lenorchan, Ann
Clements, Ann

Dowson, Martha
Elliott, Martha
Flexham, William
Gray alias Graves, Jane (QS)
Holden, James
Kennick, John
Lacruce, John
Le Grand, Lewis
Lutwich, William
Meals, Cassandra
Messenger, Elizabeth
Moore, Daniel
Morin, Rogers
Nash, Ann
Nicholls, Richard (QS)
Pass, Joshua
Patterson, James
Read, Ann
Renshaw, Henry
Smith, David (QS)
Smith, Honor
Snell, Bejamin, alias Rice, Dick
South, Samuel
Stather, William
Stevens, Catherine
Swift, Eleanor (QS)
Tasker, Grace
Turner, Samuel
Wade alias Demfries, Ann
West, John
Wise, Thomas
Wood, William

Shropshire

Giles, Richard*

Somerset*

Bourne, Charles
Cole, Thomas
Miller, Joseph
Rowe, George

Surrey

Baxter, William (QS)
Bibben, Ann (QS)
Booker, Thomas (QS)
Downey, Thomas (QS)
Gregory, Richard (QS)
Hurst, Nathaniel

Wiltshire*

Mulbens, Joseph
Rutt, Christopher

Worcestershire*

Bailey, Jane

* Originally transported from Bristol by the *Maryland Packet*, Capt. Alexander Ramsay, in October 1761, intercepted by a French vessel but retaken by an English warship: the recaptured felons now transported again to serve their terms.

Felons transported from London to Maryland by the *Dolphin*, Capt. Matthew Craymer, in May 1763. (CLRO: CLRO: London & LMA: Middlesex Bonds; PRO: Home Circuit records).

Buckinghamshire

Bradbury, John - pardoned
Griffin, Thomas
Phipps, James
Richardson, John
Vice, Thomas

Essex

Bland, Thomas
Brewer, Richard (QS)
Brockwell, Thomas
Cook, William - 14 yrs
Harris, Richard
Jackson, George (QS)
Knight, William
Lobly, Joshua (QS)
Onion, Thomas
Scott, Nicholas
Sorrell, Joseph
Turnbull, John
Turrell, John
Westley, Samuel
White, Sarah

Hertfordshire

Barnet, Joseph
Gillett, William
Moody, John
Simpson, James
Smith, William Watkins
Taylor, Elias

Kent

Andrews, James
Bell, Thomas - 14 yrs
Frasier, Sarah
Parr, Thomas
Shrons, Godfrey
Walker, Richard
Ward, Edward (QS)

London

Addison, Robert
Baynham, Henry
Davis, Joseph
Hughes, Jane
Johnson, James
Luthwait, John
O'Neal, Charles
Paston, James - pardoned
Seddon, John
Simpson, John
Thomas, John
Waters, Thomas

Middlesex

Anderson, James - runaway
Barnet, Stair
Bryan, James
Cooke, Miles - runaway
Donaldson, James - runaway
Donnelly, Bryan
Hunter, John - runaway

Jefferies, Jane
Jennings, Christopher
King, Andrew
Murray, Robert
Orton, Thomas
Richards, Elizabeth wife of Henry
Robinson, William
Smith, Richard
Ward, William

Surrey

Cox, William
Doggett, Jacob (QS)
Mullens, Mary (QS)
Philpot, Mary
Pugh, Simon (QS) - runaway
Read, Elizabeth
Rudkin, Edward
Smith, Mary
Warden, Richard Morse
Watson, Thomas - runaway

Felons transported from London to Virginia by the _Beverly_, Capt. Robert Allen, in August 1763. (CLRO: London Bond, LMA: Middlesex Sessions & PRO: Home Circuit records).

London

Autonreith, William - for life
Barker, Elizabeth
Brinklow, John
Brugmore, Lucy
Burn, Patrick
Costello, Robert - 14 yrs
Doolan, John
Eeg, Hans - for life
Fairburn, Robert
Faulkner, Ann
Foy, James
Garnon, Judith
Gilbert alias Sparkes, Samuel
Goldsmith, Elizabeth
Gouge, Richard
Green, Francis
Griffin, Mary
Kelly, Andrew
Lewis, Bartholomew
Lewis, John
Lyon, Elizabeth alias Esther - 14 yrs
Miller, Lawrence
Morgan, John
Moses, Jacob
Robinson, Michael
Ryan, Thomas
Thorpe, James
Upton, Edward
Warrington, Mary
Wright, Elizabeth
Wright, Henry

Middlesex

Aldwell, John, alias Jack above Ground
Allen, Roger
Atkinson, Robert
Baylis, Joseph
Brade, James
Burton, Catherine
Carver, Ann
Casey, John
Collins, Hugh
Collins, William
Colnet, Isaac
Eagle, Edward - runaway
English, William - runaway
Forrester, John
Gouldin, Pearcy
Gray, William
Humphry, Elizabeth
Hunt, Catherine
Jebens, Moses
Jones, Mary
Kenzer, John
Low, Thomas
Marsh, John
Marshall, Elias
Morgan, William
Murphy, Mary wife of John
Myford, Elizabeth
Nicholls, William
Owen, Hugh
Pittam, John
Pracey, Thomas
Price, Edward
Smith, Mary

Smith, William
Thomas, Catherine
Welch, Mary

Wetherall, Jane wife of Thomas
Wilkes, Isaac

Felons transported from London to Maryland by the *Neptune*, Capt. Colin Somervell, in December 1763. (PRO: T1/422/23).

Buckinghamshire

Burkett, Thomas
Burrold, Thomas
Simmons, Robert

Kent

Campbell, James
Chapman, William - 14 yrs
Court, James
Hayward, Joseph
Horden, John
Martin, James
Miles, Christian
Milner, Thomas (QS) - runaway
Plum, Frederick - 14 yrs
Ralph, John
Shipley, George
Waterman, Michael
Williams, John (QS) - runaway

London

Allen, John
Alsop, John
Ashton, Arthur
Barnard, Joseph
Barrett, Richard
Brookes, Richard
Chamberlain, Mary
Clarke, John
Cobey, Sarah
Cole, Thomas
Crispin, Robert
Dugmore, Sarah - 14 yrs
Featherstone, Ann
Field, John
Flant, John (QS)
Gabriel, Solomon - runaway
Halsey, James
Hearn, John
Johnson, Ann
Leipman, Levi
Morgan, Charles

Morris, Edward
Nicklow, Elizabeth (QS)
Palmer, James
Pawley, George
Pennithorne, Peter
Potter alias Pollard, Richard, alias
   McGee, Andrew - 14 yrs
Ross, Alexander
Stevens, John
Thompson, Ann
Tomkins, John
Tucker, George - runaway
Watson, Isabella - runaway
Wheatland, Mary
White, George

Middlesex

Armstrong, William (QS)
Birch, Mary
Brown, Jocelyn (QS)
Brown, John
Brown, William
Caen, Patrick
Callaghan, Gerhard
Clarke, Sarah
Collins, Edmund (QS) - runaway
Corbett, John
Daxon, James (QS)
Edgar, Ann
Erick, Hans
Evans, John - runaway
Florence, Francis
Giffoy, Charles (QS)
Hall, William - runaway
Hardimore, Rebecca
Harris, Margaret
Hattersley, William
Hobbs, James
Hooper, Robert
Huff, Mary wife of William
Kelly, James
Kelly, Matthias

Kirklin, Mary - 14 yrs
Langley, William
Lock, Elizabeth
Lutwich, William
Madden, Edward
Marshall, Lydia
Mates, Joseph
Nicholson, Edmund
Nugent, William (QS)
Perkins, Benjamin (QS)
Procter, Elizabeth
Read, Christian, alias wife of
   William Barrow
Rosseter, Samuel
Rowland, Thomas (QS)
Simmonds, Thomas - runaway
Smart, Sarah
Smith, John
Stockdale, Elizabeth - 14 yrs
Symonds, Thomas (QS)
Tully, Susanna wife of William
Wallis, Henry
Whiting, Thomas

Williams, George
Williams, John
Wood, Thomas

Surrey

Ainsty, John
Chappell, Benjamin
Cranley, Joseph (QS)
Dekin, Thomas (QS) - pardoned
English, Christian (QS)
Hammond, William (QS)
Jackson, John - 14 yrs
Life alias Roberts, Robert
McGuffin, Alexander (QS)
Miller, William
Rogers, John
Trump, James
Wolfe, Joseph (QS) - 14 yrs

Sussex

Lewis, John James

Felons transported from London to Maryland by the _Tryal_, Capt. William McGachin, in March 1764. (PRO: T1/429/147)

London

Anderton, William
Bishop, Giles
Boland, James
Brown, Thomas
Bunyard, James
Clancey, Daniel
Cobert, John
Codey, Richard
Cohen, Jacob
Connaway, William
Cooke, Richard
Cooke, Thomas
Cotes, Eleanor
Dean, John - for life
Dean, Thomas
Drew, John
Dukes, Isaac
Evans, Robert
Farthing, Mary
Flood, Daniel
Hathen, Daniel
Heather, Mary
Hitchins, Richard

Ireland, Richard
Jaume, Francois
Johnston, James
Jones, Elizabeth
Jones, Thomas
Kennedy, Philip
Lee, Edward
Lestadau, John
Levi, Jacob
Lowe, John
McKonnelly, Michael
Newman, Michael
Nooney, James
Pearce, Charles
Phillips, Mary
Rimmington, John
Shadwell, John - but to transport
   himself
Smith, James - pardoned
Smith, John (2)
Wallin, John

Middlesex

Abraham alias Scampey, Philip

Barrett, John - for life - runaway
Baswell alias Bazwell, Jonathan
Beales, Jane wife of John
Bird, John
Blake alias Buckley, Jane
Bodger, Thomas
Brown, John - for life
Brown, John
Brown, Mary
Brown, Thomas
Bunker, Martha (QS)
Butterfield, Thomas
Byass, Andrew
Campbell, Duncan
Carpenter alias Huckle, John
Colvall, Thomas
Comyns, Lawrence
Connelly, Edward
Cormack, Christopher
Crocker, John (QS)
Dale, Thomas
Daley, Charles (QS)
David, William - for life
Davis, Edward
Davis alias Baker, Thomas
Dean, Jane - pardoned
Dugdell, Henry
Edinburgh, John 14 yrs
Edwards, Edward
Element, Thomas
Ellis, John (QS)
Farrell, Margaret (QS)
Fell, Elizabeth
Fielden, Thomas
Francis, Thomas
Frazier, James
Glascow, Elizabeth
Green, Thomas
Gully, Michael
Haines, Isaiah - pardoned
Hall, William
Hamilton, Henry
Hanlow alias Handle, William
Harding, John
Hogan, John
Hogan, Sebastian - for life
Holloway, Mary wife of Anthony
  - 14 yrs
Howland, Ann
Huckaby, William (QS)
Humphry, Thomas
Hunt, John - for life

Jarman, Daniel
Johnson, Joseph - 14 yrs
Johnson, Thomas (QS)
Jones, Isaac
Jones, William
Kelly, George - for life
Kennedy, Michael - for life
King, Ann
Lally, John
Layforton, Anthony
Lee, John
Liddle, John (QS)
Limarez, John
Lovelace, Edward (QS)
Matcham, Henry
Matthews, Andrew
Matthews, John (QS)
Mayo, Thomas
McDougal, James
McGinnis, John (QS)
Munday, Richard
Murphy, James
Musters alias Pawles, Munday
Nokes, James
Norton alias Notman alias Miller, Mary
O'Brien, Jane alias Katherine
Parker, John
Pauldock alias Balldock, William
Pearce, Gilbert
Preston, William James
Ryan, Daniel
Shales, Daniel - for life
Small, Robert
Smallman, John
Smith, Mary
Smith, Sarah
Spratley alias Featherstone, Millicent
Stephens, Thomas
Stride, Joseph - for life
Swaine, James (QS)
Tanner alias Taylor alias Williams
  alias Dodson, Mary
Taylor, George
Taylor alias Turner, Joseph
Tenpenny, Nathaniel
Towers, John
Usher, Isaac
Wallis, John
Warrington, Elizabeth
Waters, Sarah
Wilkinson, John
Williams, Eleanor

179

Williams, Mary - for life
Wilson, John
Winfield, William

Surrey

Bassett, Andrew (QS)
Blundell, Charles (QS)
Burchett, Thomas (QS)
Cook, Thomas (QS)
  - to transport himself
Davis, Ann (QS)
Evans, William (QS)

Farrell, James (QS)
Funge, William (QS)
Gasking, Richard alias John (QS)
Martin, Mary
Plane, Moses (QS)
Plane, Thomas (QS)
Slote, John (QS)
Smeeton, John (QS)
Taubman, Thomas (QS)
Tillewar, James (QS)
Urwin, James
White, John (QS)

Felons transported from London to Virginia by the *Dolphin*, Capt. Dougal McDougal, in Jun 1764. (PRO: T1/429/148).

Buckinghamshire

Biggs, Robert Jr.
Cock, Richard - 14 yrs
Edwin, Francis - runaway
Williamson, Shadrack

Essex

Chilson, Brown - 14 yrs
Green alias Man, Sarah
Hall, Joseph
Hazlewood, Jacob
Howell, William
Pitcher, Martha
Prescott, Mary - pardoned
Wilson, John

Hertfordshire

Chappel, William (QS)
Cleverly, John
Curtis, James
Cutmore, Joshua
Cutmore, William
Haines, Joseph - runaway
Herne, John (QS)
Humphreys, Thomas (QS)
Murton, William
Woodward, Thomas (QS)
Wright, Lucretia wife of John (QS)

Kent

Batchelor, James

Best, Thomas (QS) - runaway
Bradley, Francis
Bryant, Thomas - 14 yrs
Carod, Henry (QS)
Clarke, John
Douglas, William
Eldridge, John
Graves, James - 14 yrs
Grigg, Elizabeth
Hubbard, John - runaway
Jacob, Ann
Jones, David
Jordan, William - runaway
Martin, Jonathan
McCarty, Darby
McGennes, William
Middleton, Ann
Morris, James
Rapson, Thomas
Roberts, Charles
Sherer, John
Staddon, William
Taylor, William - 14 yrs
Watts, John
Williams, David

London

Burnett, Thomas
Byrne, John
Collins, Benjamin
Daniel, Joseph
Fosset, Henry
Hayes alias Trail, Christian
Hoasse, Philip alias John

Hopps, Joseph
Hyam, Emanuel
Jackson, Thomas
Levy, Michael
Maer, Alexander - pardoned
Paine, John
Palmer, Alice
Paul, Benjamin
Rowland, John
Solomon, Barnard
Thomas, John

Middlesex

Applin, Robert
Banks, Charles
Barnes, Elizabeth
Blair, Mary
Blamire, Stephen
Bowles, Thomas
Brown, John
Bunce, Richard
Cadman, Warner
Chambers, John
Cobane, Rachael wife of Joseph
Cox, Mary
Cunningham, John
Cutler, Edmund
Darling, Thomas
Deprose, Mary
Dolan, John (QS)
Doran, Edward
Forden, William
Fowler, Elizabeth wife of David - 14 yrs
  - pardoned
Fraser alias Friswell
  alias Treswell,Loring John (QS)
Hurley, Patrick - runaway
Johnson, James
Jolly, Luke
Jones, Mary (2)
Kingston, George
Lamdale, Walter
Langley, Mary
Lawrane, Domingo (QS)
Levins, Isaac
Lewen, William
Lynch, Eleanor - pardoned
Matthews, Thomas - runaway

McCabe, Sarah
Mullins, John (QS)
Murphy, Edward
Mutlow, Sarah
Perrey, Mary Frances
Perry alias Penny,
  Elizabeth wife of William
Ramsey, George alias John
Roberts, Richard
Robinson, Blaze
Robinson, Mary
Sheridan, John
Sidnell, John
Smith, Jane
Swift, Richard - 14 yrs
Taylor, John (QS)
Taylor, John
Torrince, Abraham
Trembley, Corney - runaway
Welch, Robert
Woodcock, John

Surrey

Adams, William (QS)
Almack, William (QS)
Cook, Archibald (QS)
Dorey, John (QS)
Frampton, Joseph
Frazer, Charlotte - pardoned
Handysides, William (QS)
Jones, Thomas - 14 yrs
Knowling, Mary (QS)
Lee alias White alias Young, John (QS)
Lord, Mary - 14 yrs
Richardson, Thomas
Stafford, Nathaniel (QS) - runaway
Tillison, William (QS)
Verdon, Joseph - 14 yrs
Ward, Robert (QS)
Watson, William

Sussex

Fowler, Richard
Hall, William
Hammond, John
Hughes, Arthur

181

Felons transported from London to Virginia by the *Justitia*, Capt. Colin Somervell, in September 1764. (PRO: T1/429/147).

Buckinghamshire

Collins, Richard
Edwards, Richard - 14 yrs
Putnam, James - pardoned

Essex

Bowie, George
Foker, John - 14 yrs
Grange, William
Newman alias Biggs, Jane
Perryn, John
Rider, William - 14 yrs
Watson, John
Wheatfield, George

Hertfordshire

Hunt, Robert - 14 yrs
Murfey, William
Soleby, Thomas
Watkins, Richard

Kent

Atkinson, John - 14 yrs
Beverton, Simon (QS)
Coleman, John
Crowhurst, John - 14 yrs
Hurst, James
Lash, Joseph - 14 yrs
Lewis, Richard (QS)
Louis, Francis
McQuin alias McQueen
  alias Johnson, John (QS)
Nesbitt, James
Smith, Joseph
Smith, Thomas (QS)
Strude, William - 14 yrs
Taylor, Elizabeth
Tyer, John - 14 yrs
Williams, George - 14 yrs - runaway
Young, Stephen

London

Beadon, John
Bendall, Thomas

Benjamin, Isaac
Bond alias Clark, Richard
Brackstone, Thomas (King's Bench)
Brewer, Patrick
Brooks, James - 14 yrs
Brown, John
Brown, William - for life
Cooke, Edward
Cooper, Elizabeth
Crane, William
Crook, Francis - pardoned
Curtis, Samuel
Death, William
Dollard, William
Drummond, Sarah
Elgar, Mary
Faulkner, Jane - for life
Fawcet, John
Geary, John
Germain, Henry
Gray, Walter
Groves, William
Harman, Richard
Hart, John
Hockerdy, Philip
Holliday, William
Hyde, Sarah
Jenner, Charles
Jewes, Richard
Kilburn, Jeremiah
Loseby, Thomas
Miller, William
Onion, Edward
Orrox, Elizabeth - pardoned
Penn, Susanna
Pilmer, William
Sampson, Michael - for life
Smith, James
Smith, John (2)
Smith, William
Vaughan, William
Ward, Celia
Webb, John
West, John
Whitehead, William
Wilkinson, Francis
Wilkinson, William
Williams, Susanna
Williamson, Anthony

Middlesex

Allen, Grace
Andrews, John (QS)
Baker, Benjamin
Baker, Susannah - pardoned
Barden, John
Barry, Edward
Bellis, Henry
Bevas, Richard
Billet, William
Blake, Edward
Boyland alias Baylin, John
Burn, Judith
Byrne, James (QS)
Carey, William (QS)
Cassell, James
Cassady, Laurence (QS)
Clarke, Elizabeth (QS)
Coen, Sarah
Comerford, James
Conkin, George
Corrigan, James (QS)
Davis, John (QS)
Davis, Joseph (QS)
Dilly, Alice
Dover, Ann
Dunn, Richard
Edwards, Ann
Edwards, Mary (QS)
Etteridge, Thomas
Evans, Philip
Fairwell, Anthony
Fanside, Ann
Farmer, Matthew
Faulkner, James
Fenley, John
Flaytey, Thomas
Fowler, Thomas
Foy, Patrick (QS)
Frazer, Daniel (QS)
Goddard, Eleanor
Gray, Richard
Gregory alias Crane, Lucy (QS)
Harris, John
Harris, Sarah
Harrison, George
Haslegrove, John
Hemming, John (QS)
Hill, John - runaway
Hillier, John
Hodgson, John

Iliffe, Margaret
Jenkins, William
Jones, Edward (QS)
Jones, Matthew
Kane, Arthur
Keith, Alexander (QS)
Keith, Thomas (QS)
Lavess, Samuel
Linakin, Mary
Lovell, John
Macrin, Mary
Manning alias Mannen, James
Manning, William
Massavet, Conrad
May, Eleanor
May, Samuel
McClelland, John
McDaniel, Hugh
Miller, John (2)
Moody, William
Morris, John
Nash, Sarah (QS)
Nightingale, Matthew (QS)
Nugent, Philip
Oliver, William
Ong, James (QS)
Ooler, James
Osborne, Elizabeth
Parkhouse alias Douglas, Isabella
Peace alias Edwards, Edward (QS)
Pomfret, Elizabeth wife of William
Poole, Robert
Preston, Thomas
Pullein, John - 14 yrs
Reynolds, John (QS)
Riley, John (QS)
Robinson, Edward
Ross, Esther wife of Edward
Rouse, Sarah
Rowley, William
Sampson, Richard
Smith, Charles
Smith, Stephen (QS)
Stanley, Peter
Steele, Richard
Taylor, John
Thompson, Daniel
Thornton, Christopher (QS)
Wade, Margaret
Walker, John
Watkins, Mary
Wharton, James

White, Catherine
White, Elizabeth (QS)
Wickham, Matthew (QS)
Woodman, Phillis (QS)

Surrey

Bates, John
Billings, John
Cartridge, John
Coates, John (QS)

Davidson, George
Davis, Edward
Fossett, Joseph (QS)
Grant, William
Griffiths, James (QS)
Hood, John - 14 yrs
Hunt, William
Jaques alias Jakes, William
McCloud, Elizabeth (QS)
Odele, Edward - 14 yrs
Silvester, Richard - 14 yrs

Felons transported from London to Virginia by the *Tryal*, Capt. John Errington, in February 1765. (PRO: T1/437/17)

London

Abrahams, Jonas
Barnes, John
Colley, James
Crosgell, John
Davis, Joseph
Dowle, Samuel
Farrer, George
Felton, Mary
Foster, John
Foulger, John
Imer, Richard
Isaacs alias Solomons, Solomon
Jones, Thomas
Mallett, John
McCall, James
McCartney, Patrick
McGuire, Matthew
Morgan, William
Nunn, William
Ritchie, Peter
Robinson, William
Ross, Andrew - 14 yrs
Ross, William - 14 yrs
Scullfer, William
Shadwell, John
Simpson, John
Smith, Benjamin
Smith, Richard
Stiner, Jacob
Watkins, Martha
White, Michael
Young, Frederick

Middlesex

Barlow, Samuel - pardoned
Barry, Elizabeth
Beaden, Thomas
Bland, John
Burn, James
Burton, Richard
Callwell, Charles
Carey, William
Carroll, Eleanor
Clarke, Catherine
Cohan, Joseph
Connell, Alexander
Cooper, James
Davenport, William
Devoux, Stephen
Donnevan, John
Driver, William
Dyer, Elizabeth
Ellis, Edward
Evans, Morris - runaway
Farrell, Francis
Farrell, John
Gill, William
Goodwin, Solomon
Heaton, John
Higgins, John - runaway
Hilliard, Thomas
Hinds, Thomas
Hockley, Thomas
Hooper, Elizabeth
Hussey, John
Hussey, Samuel
Janes alias Jones, Joseph
Johnson, Ann
Johnson, James

Jones, Simon
Jones, William
Kago, King alias Williams, John
Laugham, Nicholas
Lawton, Moses
Lewis, Jane
Linney, Charles
Magee, John
Marlock, John
Mason, Benjamin
Maund alias Philpott, John - runaway
McDonald, Christopher
McFarland, Catherine
Mist, John
Morris, John - runaway
Nicholson, Patrick
Pearce, Morris
Pinchin alias White, John
Platt, Joseph
Pow, Frederick
Powell, Robert
Power, William
Raredon, Bartholomew
Regan, Mary
Riley, Ann
Roberts, Elizabeth
Roney, Alice wife of John - 14 yrs
Rotchford, Thomas

Saintree, John
Saverin, John
Seagrave, James
Silsby, James
Sims, Joseph
Squires, William
Stallard, William
Thomas, John - runaway
Tophurst, Francis
Turner, James
Vender, Mary wife of Samuel
   alias Mary Stone
Wallis, John
Ward, Edward
Ward, Mary
Welbeloved, John
West, James - runaway

Surrey

Coolley, Thomas (QS)
Foot, Joseph (QS)
Grantham, Henry (QS)
Wilkinson, Thomas (QS)

Sussex

Raise, William

Felons transported from London to Virginia by the *Ann*, Capt. Christopher Reed, in April 1765. (PRO: T1/437/22).

Buckinghamshire

Ainsworth alias Hains, Robert - runaway
Cripps, Nathaniel - but stopped
Goodspeed, Mary
Silk, John
Worral, Thomas

Essex

Cheshire, Anne
Gall, Samuel
Hunt, Robert
Perry, Richard
Scott, George (QS)

Hertfordshire

Crawley, Joseph

Dodd, Robert
Piggott, John - 14 yrs
Roberts, Richard
Uncle, Benjamin Jr. (QS)

Kent

Batt, Samuel
Haynes, Richard
Hills, Matthew
Hills, William
Holman, Thomas (QS)
Know, John Jr.
Lander, John (QS) - pardoned
Macquire, Henry
Pain, Stephen
Payne, William - 14 yrs
Piper, Elizabeth
Smith, John
Sutton alias Jutton, James (QS)

Vaughan, Henry - 14 yrs
Webb, Andrew

London

Barker, John
Batty, William
Brown, Thomas
Bunnell, Mary
Burgin, John
Burk, John - runaway
Burne, John
Carroll, John
Carroll, Mary wife of John
Cooke, John
Dobey, James - runaway
Dukes, Elizabeth
Dutton, George
Edwards, Margaret
Evans, John - runaway
Fish, Thomas
Garrett, Philip
Harris, Mary
Harrison, Humphrey
Heron, John
Hines, Elizabeth
Howorth, William
Kirk, Thomas - runaway
Long, Thomas
Matthews, John
McKenzie, Alexander
Mitchell, Sarah
Morris, Benjamin
Murdock, John
Murrell alias Brooks
   alias Sneechall, Sarah
Randall, John
Richardson, William
Roberts, John
Robinson, Joseph
Saunders, Elizabeth
Seares, William
Spearin, James
Thompson, Thomas
Turner, William
Wackett, Joseph
Walker, Thomas
Wallis, George
Williams, Eleanor
Wilson, Thomas
Wood, James

Middlesex

Bannister, Richard
Booth, Henry
Britton, Samuel - pardoned
Burk, Frances wife of Edward
Carrol alias Carlow, John
Carroll alias Macgee, Mary
Chapman, Thomas
Combes, Charles
Courtney, Patrick - 14 yrs
Dagenhart, John
Dalton, Michael
Downes, John
Drummer, Sarah
Fulham, Edward (QS)
Hall, Ann
Homell, Elizabeth
Hornsbee alias Hornsby, William
Johnson, Eleanor
Kealty, William
Kellick, John (QS) - pardoned
Lovell, Richard - 14 yrs
Magin, Charles
Mainwaring, James (QS)
McDermot, Timothy
McGee, Catherine
Muckleroy, Bartholomew
Murphy, Lawrence - 14 yrs
Norman, Elizabeth
Norton, Mary
O'Neal, James
Ogden, John
Pedder, Charles (QS)
Price, Elizabeth
Rice, Alexander
Richardson, Martha
Robinson, Thomas
Root, George - pardoned
Row alias Roe, William
Ryan, John
Ryan, Mary wife of John
Shearman, Elizabeth
Sinnott, Richard
Smith, Luke
Smith, William (QS)
Sparrow, Joseph
Steele, Joseph
Stone, John
Stringer, Joseph
Swinney, James Rigley
Tanner, Christopher William

Tanner, George - 14 yrs
Taylor, Edward
Thomas, John
Tooley, Mary
Whitfield, Thomas

Surrey

Andrews, Robert (QS)
Bagley, Edward (QS)
Clark, Mary (QS)
Cohogh, Thomas (QS)
Crew, William
Culmore, Joseph (QS) - pardoned
Field, Sarah
Fleming, John (QS)
Fox, Richard
Freemantle, John (QS)
Graham, Mary
Green, Edward (QS)

Harris, William (QS)
Hill, Richard (QS)
Horan, James (QS)
Jones, Thomas
King, William (QS)
Linch, John (QS)
Norris, Richard - 14 yrs
Prawl, Thomas (QS)
Rose, William (QS)
Saunders, John (QS)
Scott, Elizabeth (QS)
Smith, James - 14 yrs
Williams, Henry (QS)
Winch, John (QS)

Sussex

Corke, Arthur - 14 yrs
Farley, John - 14 yrs
Jones, Robert

Felons transported from London to Virginia by the *Justitia*, Capt. Colin Somervell, in September 1765. (PRO: T1/437/28).

Buckinghamshire

Cripps, Nathaniel
Worral, Thomas - 14 yrs

Essex

Barnard, Edward - 14 yrs

Hertfordshire

Balm, John - 14 yrs
Hunt, William
Titmus, William (QS)

Kent

Barker, Samuel - 14 yrs - pardoned
Beeching, Thomas
Bennett, Charlotte
Herod, George
Holt, John
Noble, George (QS)
Place, William
Williams, Elizabeth

London

Birch, John
Cooke, William
Curtis, John
Davis, Eleazar
Dean alias Cook, Thomas
Farrell, James
Gale, Christopher
Hare, Richard
Hart, Walter
King, James
Langham, Joseph - pardoned
Littleton, Joseph
Lovell, Catherine
Moring, Elias
Nichols, Jonathan - pardoned
Radley, Thomas
Reeves, John
Salisbury, William
Smith, Henry
Spicer, George
Spragg, John
Stanmore, Elizabeth
Swinney, Edmund
Watkins, John
Watkins, William
Wiggan, Joseph

Wing, Daniel
Wolfe, Saunders

Middlesex

Artery, James
Berry, Edward (QS)
Bingley, John
Blane, Joseph (QS)
Bolton, Hannah
Boucher, Stephen
Bright, William
Bryan, John
Bucklinghorn, Sarah
Clarke, Robert
Colston, John
Connor, Daniel
Cowley, Mary wife of George
Cowper, James
Crawley, James
Cross, Thomas alias John alias Robert
Davis, William
Devine, Thomas
Donvilla, Victoire
Dougle, Margaret
Dove, John (QS)
Dumond, Charlotte (QS)
Dunn, Edward
Dust, Samuel
Ealey alias Keeley, William
Erkeen, Thomas
Eyes, John
Fluty, John
Gammon, Richard
Gates alias Yeates, George (QS)
Grant, John
Green, Mary (QS)
Harris, Thomas alias Richard
Hatchman, John
Hawket, James
Hemmings, James (QS)
Holland, Joseph - 14 yrs
Holmes, Elizabeth
Johnson, Davison (QS)
Jackson, Thomas
Jones alias Williams, Edward
Jones, Mary wife of John (QS)
Joslyn, Jane
Lawrence, Henry
Lewis, William - pardoned
Malcomb, Robert
Manley, Richard

Mears, Richard
Mitchell alias Hutchinson, Robert
Monkhouse, Jane wife of William,
     alias Jane Murray
Morris, Thomas
Morrison, Effa
Munden, James
Nichollus, Elizabeth
O'Brien, William
Orme, Andrew
Palmerstone, Henry
Peyton, Edward (QS)
Platton, Samuel
Prince, William
Pritchard alias Oadley, Sarah
Purser, Richard
Quin, Patrick
Quin, William (QS)
Rance, Richard
Rees, John
Richards, Ann wife of Jenkins
Riley, Richard
Robinson, John
Robinson, Sarah
Rook, William
Russell, Hannah
Savell, Ann, widow,
     alias Brown, Thomas (*sic*)
Scarborough, Lawrence
Sharborn, John
Simmonds, John
Smith, John
Smith alias Dunn, Mary
Smith, William (2)
Stanley alias Alder, Ann
     - ordered to remain in England
Swift, Ann wife of James,
     alias Ann May, spinster
Tate, Rosamond
Tate, William
Till, William - to transport himself
Trueman, William
Vincent, John
Walters, Elizabeth
Walters, Redfern (QS)
Weeks, James
Wellins, John
Wilcox alias Cox, Thomas
Wilkinson, George
Wittam, John
Wood, Mary wife of Richard

Surrey

Bassett, Alexander (QS)
Brown, John
Cooper, William
Davis, Richard
Durham, John - 14 yrs
Fisher, Isaac (QS)
Gregory, Mary (QS)
Jenkins, Hannah - 14 yrs
Longstaff, William

Shakleton, Thomas - 14 yrs
Smith alias Dixon, Ann (QS)
Solomons, Rachael (QS)
Thomas, John (QS) - runaway
Waters, Leonard (QS)

Sussex

Hammond, Thomas
Swaine, William - 14 yrs

Felons transported from London to Virginia by the *Tryal*, Capt. John Errington, in January 1766. (PRO: T1/449/126)

Hertfordshire

Crouch, John (QS)
Hawley, Joseph (QS)
Smith, John (QS)

Kent

Davis, Philip (QS)
Mahony, Michael (QS)
Wood, William (QS)

London

Abraham, Meyer - 14 yrs
Anderton, Thomas
Atkins, Thomas
Bird, William Reynolds
Connell, Ann
Davis, Samuel
Deale, Richard
Dunn, William - for life
Gelvin, William
Godwin, Mary
Goulding, Peter - runaway
Gounley, Jane (King's Bench)
Gregory alias Walter, Hannah
Haley, Cornelius
Hatton, Richard
Henshaw, John - pardoned
Hill, Ann
Jackson, Mary - pardoned
James, William
Jenkins, Ann
Jones, John
McCullock, William
Palmer, John

Robinson, John - for life
Shepherd, Thomas
Smith, James
Stone, William
Temple, John
Whitfield, Joshua
Wilkes alias Bolton, Catherine

Middlesex

Abbott, William - for life - runaway
Adams, Peter
Bagnon alias Berville
  alias Lewis, Philip
Barlow, Sarah (QS)
Barnfield, Isaac
Bignell alias Brown, John
Bird, Thomas
Boreham, Thomas
Brigs alias Ablet, John
Broderick, Joseph (QS)
Brown alias Hillman, Elizabeth
Bryde, Eleanor
Bull, Jane - pardoned
Burn, William
Byfield, Robert
Calvert, Mary (QS)
Carnes, Arundell (QS)
Clean, William
Clifford, Ann
Coleman, Esther
Crew, John - runaway
Davis, Thomas
Denell, Pearce (QS)
Durden, Mary (QS)
Edwards, Mary - 14 yrs
English, Mary - 14 yrs - runaway

Evans alias Harris, John
Evans, Mary Jane
Eyles, Martha
Fletcher, Thomas - 14 yrs
French, George
Geyrin, Hannah
Gill, Thomas
Goad, Thomas
Godwin, Richard
Gould, Elizabeth
Hall, John
Hands, John - for life
Hatch, Daniel
Healey, Elizabeth
Hill, George
Howard, Jenkin
Hughes, Nathaniel
Innis, James
Johnson, Charles
Johnson, Thomas
Levy, Henry (QS)
Linsey, William
Little, Thomas - 14 yrs
Mackrell, Edward
Maloye, Lawrence
McNeil, Henry
Minty, Mary
Nevill, Eleanor
Ovins alias O'Brien, Mary
Parker, Jonathan
Price, James
Print alias Price, Sarah
Pritchard, John
Rawlington, Elizabeth
Robinson, John
Ross, Ann

Sharp, Eleanor
Shaw, Walter
Shields, Dennis
Smith, Ann
Smith, Lyon
Stanfield alias Ogden, Elizabeth
Stephens, Thomas
Stott, Elizabeth wife of Henry
Sullivan, John - for life
Tovey, Ann
Treviss, John
Trueman, Jane
Turner, Sarah, alias Bryan, Ann
Vacheron, Antoine
Weston, Margaret
Whytall, William
Wright, John - runaway

Surrey

Bartlett, James (QS)
Blackburn, William (QS)
Hale, Thomas (QS)
Haley, Margaret, widow (QS)
Jackson, Isaac (QS)
Jones, John (QS)
Lowell, John (QS)
McFeet, John (QS)
Moore, Thomas (QS)
Noakes, Jeremiah. (QS)
Oakam, James (QS)
Parris, Mary (QS)
Raven, Thomas (QS) - runaway
Roe, John (QS)
Taylor, Joseph (QS)
Winchelsea, Donbarty (QS)

Felons transported from London to Maryland by the *Ann*, Capt. Christopher Reed, in April 1766. (PRO: T1/449/19).

Buckinghamshire

Carey, John (QS)
Dimock, Peter - 14 yrs
Fellows, Richard
Fuller, John - 14 yrs
Hanwell, William (QS)
Lea, John
Plummeridge, Edward
Radwell, Bernard (QS)
Stop, John - 14 yrs

Essex

Bilson, Benjamin
Butcher, James
Cornish, William
Debman, William (QS)
Downes, Thomas
Fairing, Daniel
Higham, Elizabeth (QS)
Johnson, Samuel (QS)
Lawrence, Jacob

McLaughlin alias McLinglin,
  Michael (QS)
Meade, Thomas - 14 yrs
Pearson, Joseph - 14 yrs

Hertfordshire

Brown, William (QS)
Dimmock, William - 14 yrs
Fowler, William
Ingram, Jacob (QS)

Kent

Anderson, Henry
Bailey, Thomas
Bedleston, George
Feathers, Samuel
Frame, Mary
Fulham, Margaret (QS)
Harris, Henry
Hills, Matthew
McKensie, Andrew
Parsons, Robert
Penny, William
Portland, James
Pratt, John - runaway
Reed, Anthony
Wiles, Charles

London

Braine, Joseph
Cartwright, John
Clarke alias Hamilton, Barbara
Comyns, James
Corp, Thomas
Cotterell, James
Crawford, William
Everett, James
Fitzgerald, Michael
Fitzgerald, Andrew - for life
Freeman, John
Graham, William - runaway
Haines, John - to transport himself
Hall, William
Harris, William
How, William
Jacob, Elizabeth
Kemp, Thomas
Kirby, Mary
Lamball, John

Levy, Solomon
Mason, Elizabeth
McInnes, John
Murphy, James
Phillips, Richard
Robinson, George
Saunders alias Thompson, Elizabeth
Scandon, John
Smith, Mary
Stafford, John
Talbott, Benjamin
White, Charles
White, William - runaway

Middlesex

Agar, Frank
Ash, John
Bales alias Brown alias Gough, Eleanor
Bannerman, John
Berryman, Thomas
Bolus, Elizabeth
Borne, Joseph
Brown, Mary - 14 yrs
Burnham, James
Burroughs, William (QS)
Byrne, Garrett
Cambell, Mary
Carrivan alias Kerrivan, Edward
Chapel, Alice
Chizley, Owen
Clarke, John (QS)
Corbet, Henry
Crafter, John
Dale, Thomas
Davis, John
Dawson, John (QS)
Donnolly, John - pardoned
Drodge, Henry
Dun, Mathew
Evans, John
Everett alias Wright, John (QS)
Fendley, Charles
Foy, Rose
Gordon, Ann
Graham, Joseph (QS)
Graham, William
Hind, Charles (QS)
Hodgson, William - 14 yrs
Hollis, Vincent
Hopwood alias Orpwood, John (QS)
Hunter, Christian

191

Lambeth, Joseph
Lane, William
McKensie, Susanna
Merchant, John
Miller, Thomas
Monter, Sarah
Morley, Ann wife of Joseph,
  alias Ann Wylett, spinster
Mundle, John
Oxen, William (QS)
Penson, William
Phillips, Hannah
Quelsh, William (QS)
Reardon, John
Richards, Edward
Richards, Frederick - pardoned
Richardson, John
Riviere, Lewis
Rutherford, John
Seymour, Benjamin Ambrose (QS)
Smith, John, alias Newcombe, Robert
Solomons alias Abrahams, Samuel (QS)
Stephens, Joseph
Stephens, William
Swanskin, John (QS)
Swift, William
Thorley, Jane (QS)
Thorp, John (QS)
Tipping, Francis
Trayford, Thomas (QS)
Tricket, Edward - 14 yrs - runaway
Triest, Peter
Tucker, Gregory (QS)
Turner, Mary

Turner, Elizabeth (QS)
Upgood, John
Walker, John
Welch, John
Wells, Joshua
West, John
White, Christopher - runaway
Williams, Mary
Williamson, Eleanor
Woodin, John
Wright alias Brown, Mary
Yates, Susannah

Surrey

Brent, Samuel
Brown, Simon
Colson, Robert - 14 yrs
Edge, William (QS)
Fitzgerald, James (QS)
Goater, John
Hill, John
Howard, William (QS)
Joyner, William
Ovins, Gilbert - for life
Traverse, John

Sussex

Blachford, Thomas alias William - 14
yrs
Gardiner, Philis - 14 yrs
Winslett, John - 14 yrs
Winslett, Samuel - 14 yrs

Felons transported from London to Virginia by the *Justitia*, Capt. Colin Somervell, in September 1766. (PRO: T1/450/96).

Buckinghamshire

Fellows, Henry - 14 yrs
Howard, Samuel - 14 yrs
Jones, Roger - 14 yrs
Kelsey, John - for life

Essex

Blackburne, John - 14 yrs
Clark, John (QS)
Elder, Joshua
Forster, Thomas (QS)
Jay, Elizabeth

Lilley, William
Parker, Mary (QS)
Taylor, William - 14 yrs
Tiverton, Joseph - 14 yrs
Watkins, Walter - 14 yrs

Hertfordshire

Gower, Thomas - 14 yrs
Miller, Ganzelius
Montgomery, John (QS)
Mould, Jeremiah
White alias Towser, George - 14 yrs

Kent

Allen, George
Bousden, John - 14 yrs
Butler, John
Clarke, Thomas
Dugmore, John - for life
Green, Edward - 14 yrs
Heath, Robert - 14 yrs
Hills, Matthew - for life
Hudson, Philip (QS)
Jennings, alias Smith alias Pennings
  alias Waters, Abel
Lockeskegg, Thomas - for life
Pullen, Joseph - 14 yrs
Tisely, John - for life
Tolhurst, John - 14 yrs
Webber, Robert - 14 yrs
Williams, William - 14 yrs

London

Bannister, Mark
Bent, Daniel
Bow, John
Burgis, William
Butler, Margaret
Clarke, William
Crompton, Ann
Davis, John (2)
Davis, James
Dunn, Elizabeth - for life
Garrett, Gilbert
Griffin, Robert - 14 yrs
Haynes, John
Innes, George - to transport himself
Jones, John
Langham, Joseph - pardoned
McIntosh, William
Moody, Samuel
Munns, Joshua
Newman, James
Pitt, George
Renshaw, Isabella - pardoned
Rygman, John
Salisbury, Ann
Shakespear, William
Shields, Henry
Smith, James
Webb, John

Middlesex

Ackron, Godfrey
Aldridge, John - for life
Allen, Mary - pardoned
Anderson, Benjamin
Angess, William - runaway
Arnold, Rebecca
Ashford, Ralph (QS)
Ayres, Mary - 14 yrs
Benton, Ann
Bevan, John - 14 yrs
Birch, Edward (QS)
Bletsley, William
Blott, Mary
Bradford, John (QS)
Bradshaw alias Smith, Robert
Bridgman, Ann
Brigland, James (QS)
Brown, Frances
Burford, Samuel
Burke, Alexander
Burton, John
Cardigan, Mary
Charbilies, Maria Louisa
Chassereau, Pearce John Anthony
Child, John
Currell, Elizabeth,
  alias wife of Thomas Keithly
Curtis, Deborah
Davis, Charles
Davis, William - 14 yrs
Day, Edward
Denby, Samuel
Docker, John (QS)
Downs, John
Duffey, Andrew
Elliott, Robert - pardoned
Evans, John (QS)
Foster, Rose
French, Gasper alias Baptiste
Froud, Jane - for life
Gardiner, Jane
Gooding, William
Gordon, John
Gorgrave, Richard
Hammond, Richard
Hatton alias Hutton, Elizabeth (QS)
Healey, Edward
Hoopham, John
Inks, John (QS)
Inks, William (QS)

Jackson, Sarah (QS)
Jacob, Thomas, alias Thomas, Jacob
Jenkins, Mathew
Knight, Mary
Lermount, John
Linnigin, John
Lodge, Thomas (QS)
Lucy, William (QS)
Male, Robert
Maloney, Thomas
Matthews, Darby
May, Celius (QS)
Miller, John
Moore, Robert (QS)
Murphy, Patrick
Mussen, James
Nicholls, Joseph
Nixon, Susanna
O'Brien, William
Oliver, Evan (QS)
Parfect, Robert
Parker, Catherine
Parker, Hannah
Parry, Thomas (QS)
Partridge, Richard (QS)
Pelter, James
Phillips, John (QS)
Pitman, Mary
Pleasants, Charles
Plumber, Samuel
Porter, Margaret (QS)
Read, Robert (QS)
Reddin, James
Redmond, Francis
Ross, Elizabeth
Ryder, William
Salter, Charles (QS)
Simmonds, William (QS)
Smith, Joseph
Soukes, Rowland

Stewart, Charles (QS)
Surry, John
Talbot, John
Taylor, John
Turner, Joseph
Vasthold, Martin
Walker, Robert
Walters, John
Watkins, Mary
Watkinson, Alice (QS)
Weaver, Richard
Whitaker, David (QS)
White, Mary
Wilford, Joseph
Williams, Thomas

Surrey

Andrew, John (QS)
Burch, William
Clayton, Thomas (QS)
Dewell, Thomas (QS)
Green, Joseph - 14 yrs - runaway
Hamper, William (QS)
Horner, John - 14 yrs
Hull, Ann
Johnson, Samuel
Martin, John (QS)
Millams, George
Pitt, John (QS)
Rose, James (QS)
Smith, James (QS)
Wilson, Benjamin (QS)

Sussex

Kemp, Cornelius - 14 yrs
Marwick, John - 14 yrs
Reynolds, John

Felons transported from London to Virginia by the *Tryal*, Capt. John Somervell, in January 1767. (PRO: T1/460/48).

Hertfordshire

Barlow, Thomas (QS)

Kent

Mahony, Michael (QS) - runaway

London

Adams, Edward
Barrell, Thomas
Bradley, Thomas
Brown, James
Carroll, Patrick
Cohen, Abraham

194

Dowle, Mary
Hague, Susanna
Hawes, Edward
Jackson, Mary - pardoned
Law, Margaret
Madding, Hannah
McNamara, Timothy
Miller, John - pardoned
Mills, Samuel
Molney, Peter
Moore, John
Morley, Joseph
Moses, Samuel
Olive, John
Pead, Joseph
Siseland, William
Smith, William
Southall, Elizabeth
Southerland, Jane
Walton, Margaret
Wilkinson, John
Wright, Charles

Middlesex

Atkins, George
Atkins, Thomas
Barne, Elizabeth
Bell, Thomas (QS)
Blowers, Benjamin
Bourke alias Carr, Thomas
Bowden, Thomas (QS)
Bowyer, Francis (QS)
Branch, Elizabeth
Bremingham, George (QS)
Britton, Samuel (QS)
Bruce, George (QS)
Burton, John
Carney, Margaret
Castle, Ann
Ceaton, John (QS)
Clark, John (QS)
Coleman, Daniel
Cooper, John
Crawford, Thomas (QS)
Crispin, Ann
Davis, Catherine
Davis, William
Donnelly, John
Downing, Robert
Dye alias Dyde, Michael (QS)
  - pardoned

Dyer, John
Edwards, Edward (QS)
Egan, William
Egerton, Peter
Falkner, Mary
Farrell, Peter
Flood, Judith
Fox, Eleanor
Gadbury, John
Gorman, Edward
Granger, Esther
Gray, Catharine
Gwynn, John (QS)
Hempstead, John (QS)
Hindes, George
Hinkes, Thomas
Holden, Thomas (QS)
Holliday, Thomas (QS)
How, Isabella
Hull, Benjamin
Jenkins, Edward
Johnson alias Ingram, James - runaway
Jones, Mary
Jones, Richard
Jones, Thomas
Kelly, Patrick (QS)
Kennedy, Timothy
Lemange, Peter (QS)
Lockhart, Thomas (QS) - runaway
Loxham, Elizabeth, alias Gatson, Jane
Maley, Patrick (QS)
Markland, John (QS)
Martin, Andrew - pardoned
Merchant, Elizabeth
Mitton, Mary
Neptune, Ann
Newman, John Thomas
Nunn, Elizabeth
Owen, Jane wife of John
Peake, Samuel
Potter, John (QS)
Powell, Eleanor
Pratt, Sarah
Rice, William (QS)
Roberts, John (QS)
Rutter, Thomas - pardoned
Scanderett, Henry - pardoned
Smith, Richard
Sprigmore alias Caddell, Elizabeth (QS)
Stanley, William (QS)
Stewart, James
Strode, Edward

Strutt, Elizabeth,
   alias wife of John Boseden
Sutton, William
Taylor, Charles (QS)
Taylor, William (2)
Tennant, Judith (QS)
Tomlinson, Michael (QS)
Triggs, Elizabeth
Turner, Thomas (QS)
Vincent, Samuel (QS)
Walker, John
Wallace, George
Watson, John (QS)
Watts, John
Webb, Thomas
Webley, Henry
Wenden, James
White, Ann
White, Mary Ann
Whittaker, Mary Ann (QS)
Wilton, James
Wright, John

Surrey

Arnold, John (QS)
Berry, James (QS)
Blizard, John (QS)
Bulger, Judith wife of James (QS)
Chevening, James
   alias Reynolds, Richard
Clements, Thomas (QS)
Coulter, Mary (QS)
Curby, Paul (QS)
Dawson, Nancy alias Elizabeth
Dunford, Thomas (QS)
Howlat, Madis John (QS)
Johnson, William (QS)
Lawless, Mary wife of John (QS)
Mull, James (QS)
Price alias Sterry, Richard (QS)
Waker, Edward (QS)
Welch, James (QS)
Williams, William (QS) - runaway

Felons transported from London by the *Thornton*, Capt. Christopher Reed, in May 1767, arriving at Elk Ridge Landing, Maryland in July 1767. (PRO: T1/460/4 & 55).

Buckinghamshire

Baily, William
Brading, John
Fokes, John
Goody, Richard
Kingham, John - runaway
Rolt, John
Smith, John - 14 yrs - runaway
Smith, Joseph - for life - runaway
Smith, William - 14 yrs - runaway
Thompson, Jeremiah
Wiggington, William

Essex

Bussell, William - 14 yrs
Button, David (QS)
Chaplin, William
Finnis, William
Fitzgerald, Thomas
Gill, Hezziah
Grimson, Samuel - 14 yrs
Hart, Thomas - 14 yrs
Harvey, Martha - 14 yrs

Hopkins, James
Moss, Jarvis (QS)
Norton, George

Hertfordshire

Bates, John (QS)
Rolfe, John (QS)
Taylor, James - 14 yrs - pardoned

Kent

Archdeacon, John
Barratt, Sarah
Brown, Thomas
Carter, Richard
Constable, Sarah
Edmonds, William
Horson, Thomas
Hues, Thomas
Lee, John - 14 yrs
Lee, Sarah - 14 yrs
Lotta, Stephen - 14 yrs
Perrott, Roger
Smith, Thomas

Stace, Thomas
Stevens, Thomas
Watson, Christopher
White, George - 14 yrs

London

Bottin, John - runaway
Bradshaw, William.
Butler, John.
Cap, Thomas.
Chaff, Patrick.
Claxton, George.
Clifford, William.
Fearn, Elizabeth
Gilliard, William Thompson - runaway
Glass, Enoch.
Green, Matthew
Hasker, John
Hatfield, Susanna
Hewitt, John
Hudson, Skinner.
Hynes, John Martin
Kitchener, Mary
Laird, Christopher
Lowe, John
Mason, William.
Matthews, Sarah
Miller, Thomas Zachariah
Mitchell, John.
Owen, John
Parry, Thomas.
Price, Ann.
Richardson, William.
Skeele, William
Stafford, Ann.
White, Mary
Williams, Thomas
Wise, Edward
Wright, Charles.

Middlesex

Allison, Samuel
Bartlett, Mary
Beesmore, Elizabeth (QS)
Bibb, Michael (QS)
Black, Henry
Blake alias Groves, Ann (QS)
Boast, Sarah
Brannon, John (QS)
Cape, John

Carroll, John
Chapman, Joseph (QS)
Churchill, John (QS)
Clark, James
Cole, John
Connor, Patrick
Cooper, George - pardoned
Cooper, John
Dilkill, Mary
Donnelly, Thomas
Dorman, Elizabeth
Downe, Charles
Dunn, Horton
Edwards, John
Field, Matthew (QS)
Fletcher, John
Force, James (QS)
Ford, John
Gardiner, Elizabeth (QS)
Hall, Eleanor (QS)
Hall, Sarah
Hamilton, Margaret wife of Charles
Henley, James (QS)
Herbert, Charles (QS)
Hill, John
Holloway, George (QS)
House, Thomas (QS)
Jones, Thomas (QS)
Jones, Thomas
King, Michael (QS)
Linton, Samuel (QS)
Lowe, Rosanna (QS)
Maddox, John (QS)
Mainwairing, Charles
McCasey, William (QS)
Merritt, Charles
Miles, Mary - 14 yrs
Miller, Charles
Montgomery, George Frederick (QS)
Moore, William (QS)
Moss, Francis (QS)
Price alias Thrift alias Church, Peter
Redriff, John
Reynolds, Miles
Rich, William
Saville, Thomas
Scandrett, Henry (QS) - pardoned
Sherman alias Clayton, Susannah
Smith, Joseph alias Thomas
Spencer, Jane wife of William
Sprague, Michael - 14 yrs
Stewart, John

197

Stokes, Robert
Sullinge, Edward
Sullinge, Richard
Tatler, Joseph (QS)
Thompson, James (QS)
Toole, James (QS)
Toombes, John (QS)
Turner, Frances
Walden, Susanna (QS)
Webber, John
Whims, Thomas (QS)
Wildman, John
Wilkinson, John
Williams, David (QS)
Williams, Frances wife of Rice
Williams, Hannah
Williams, Thomas (QS)
Willoughby, Thomas
Wilson, Elizabeth
Young, Thomas

Surrey

Alsop, John
Alsop, Joseph
Atkins, Richard (QS)
Carter, Dennis
Faulkner, Joseph
Gwyn, James (QS)
Mitchell, Dorothy - 14 yrs
Moody, James of Newington (QS)
   - 14 yrs
Moore, William Sr. - 14 yrs
Moore, William Jr. - 14 yrs
Richards, John - 14 yrs
Sayers, William
Toovey, John
Waite, Richard (QS)
Wilkinson, William

Sussex

Card, Peter - for life
Carter, John
Catt, Curtis - 14 yrs
Surgeon, John - 14 yrs

Felons transported from London to Virginia by the *Justitia*, Capt. Colin Somervell, in September 1767. (PRO: T1/456/23).

Buckinghamshire

Adkins, William
Alcock alias Hawks alias Hawkins, John
Clarke, John
Grubb, William
Hale, George
Humphreys, Thomas
Joice, Benjamin
Rutter, George
Smith, Susanna

Essex

Argent, Ann (QS)
Capp, John
Clarke, John (QS)
Cosins, John - 14 yrs
Debart, Joseph - 14 yrs
Grimwood, Thomas - 14 yrs
Harrord alias Henrord, Edward - 14 yrs
Heald, John
Hobbs, William - 14 yrs

Lord, John - 14 yrs
Pewter, John - 14 yrs
Phillips, Edward
Powell, William
Rank, Martin
Richards, Anthony - runaway
Saunders, Henry
Shillingford, Jacob - 14 yrs
Ward, Thomas - 14 yrs

Hertfordshire

Arnold, George
Castle, William (QS)
Hodges, Francis - 14 yrs
McKoan, James (QS)
Page, Joseph (QS)
Samuel, Thomas - 14 yrs
Thorowgood, Mary
Tibbworth, Susannah
Walpole, Edward

Kent

Brambleby, William Henry - 14 yrs
Free, John
Fullager, Elizabeth
Taylor, John
Vine, James
Watt, William
Wilson, Thomas - 14 yrs

London

Alexander, William - runaway
Barew, Moses
Brewer, Ann
Bryon, John
Clarke, Ann
Clark, Richard
Clements, James
Coant, John
Cockle, John
Cormick, Michael
Cowen, Israel - 14 yrs
Dadsley, William
Dixon, Thomas
Doyle, William
Gunn, John
Harris, John
Hart alias Carter, Elizabeth
Hincks, Sarah
Hull, Isaac
Johnson, Robert - runaway
Jones, Elizabeth
Mackey, George
Mann, James
Manning, Elizabeth
Mills, Thomas
Morgan, Elizabeth
Page, Ann
Peake, Thomas - 14 yrs
Peck, Mary - for life
Phineas, Joseph
Rippon, Henry
Russell, Ann
Saunders, William
Silvester, John
Sleath, Joseph
Smith, Thomas (2)
Spindler, Richard
Townsend, Thomas
Turner, Daniel
Vickars, Robert

Walford, Thomas
Walker, Ann
Westwood, William
Williams, Edward - runaway
Wilson, George
Winter, John

Middlesex

Adams alias Haydon, Ann
Adams, Thomas
Ashford, Elizabeth
Aylsbury, Thomas - pardoned
Benham, John - for life
Boyce, Elizabeth
Bratton, Richard
Brown, Francis
Brown alias Delapp, Jane
Burne, Patrick (QS)
Butler, John (QS)
Carr, John (QS)
Clark, Ann (QS)
Clodd, Robert (QS)
Collins, Samuel - for life
Collins, William - 14 yrs
Connor, Mary (QS)
Connor, Thomas
Cooksey, John (QS)
Cox, William
Craydon, Elizabeth
Curray alias McGrath, Elizabeth
Dalton, Sarah wife of James
Dartee, Bartholomew
Dawson, Thomas
Delany, Martha alias Margaret
Dixon, Elizabeth (QS)
Dolland, Elizabeth
Donally, Henry
Doyle, Michael - pardoned
Dunning, Mary wife of William (QS)
Everee, John
Farrell, Michael
Fisher, John
Gibbons, Mary
Goodson, Catherine - pardoned
Gray, William
Green, Ann (QS)
Griffiths, William - for life
Harris, John - 14 yrs
Helenford, Phillip
Hill, John
Hinds, Thomas (QS)

Hobbs, Daniel - for life
House, Mary
Hudson, Benjamin
Hull, Edward, alias Doleman, John
Hurst, Christopher (QS)
Jaycocks, Thomas - 14 yrs
    - to transport himself
Jefferys, William (QS)
Johnson, Henry - for life - runaway
Jones, Martha
Jones, William
Knutson, Hans
Ladd, Elizabeth
Lawrence, Thomas
Leach, Richard - for life
Letteridge, Samuel
Mallett, William
McDaniel, Daniel
Mills, Mary
Milton, Henry (QS)
Morehane, Joseph - for life
Nicholson, William
Nicolls, Elizabeth (QS)
Patience, John (QS)
Pattison, William
Pitman, John
Preston, Charles
Reaudolph, Mary
Reid, David
Richardson, Thomas
Roberts, David - 14 yrs
Saunders, Catherine
Serjeant, Elizabeth (QS)
Simpson, James - 14 yrs
Smith, Ann
Smith alias Nordis, Catherine
Smith, James

Smith, Thomas - for life
Spines, Thomas - for life
Stoddard, Martha wife of Peter
Taylor, James (QS)
Thompson, Zachariah (QS)
Vince, John - pardoned
Warwick, Thomas (QS)
Williams, John
Wilson, John (QS)
Wise, Thomas
Wright, Mary

Rutland

Freeman, Thomas
Kemp, Edward

Surrey

Carter, Richard
Clarke, James
Dolly, James (QS)
Ellis, John - 14 yrs
Hood, Esther - 14 yrs
Moorey, John
Payne, Richard (QS)
Wigmore, Catherine (QS)
Wood, Zachariah (QS)
York, John

Sussex

Greenfield, John - 14 yrs
Harwood, John
Haynes, Henry - 14 yrs
Sweetman, John - 14 yrs

Felons transported from London to Virginia by the *Neptune*, Capt. James Arbuckle, in January 1768. (PRO: T1/465/386).

Kent

Small, Thomas (QS)

London

Arnold, Rowland
Austin, John
Ballard, John
Bishop, Lucas
Bliss, William

Blundell, James
Bowers, Thomas
Brown, Joseph
Brown, Mary wife of Benjamin
Bryan, James
Clarke, Charlotte, spinster
Collins, Joseph
Cunningham, James (2)
Cuthbert, William
Dailey, John
Deane, Daniel

Edwards, John
Elliott, Samuel
Fanton, Mary, widow
Flint, Richard
Green, Anthony
Henshaw, John
Hodges, John
Holythorne, Thomas - 14 yrs
Johnson, John
Jones, Elizabeth
Lawrence, Jane wife of Robert
Lawson, William
Lees, George
Marshall, John
McCrew, John
Morris, Catherine wife of Richard
Myers, Ann
Nesbitt, William
Newman, Thomas
Parker, Joseph
Pentecost alias Pentecross, James
Phillips, John
Richardson, William
Rose, Henry
Skelton, Susannah, spinster
Smith, Mary
Stanley, John
Stephens, Mary
Territt, William
Thomas, Elizabeth, widow
Tillett, William
Turvey, Joseph
Warner, Thomas
Watkins, William
Woolls, William
Young, James

Middlesex

Ball, John
Beale, John
Bess alias Best, James
Bird, Thomas
Brackett, Mary
Brandham, Richard
Broadhead, Caleb
Bully, Susanna (QS)
Cane alias Wayne, William
Cane, Abraham
Carty, Timothy (QS)
Chilcott, James
Clisby, William

Cordall alias Cowdell, Richard
Courtney, John (QS)
Crowe, Daniel
Davis, Richard
Doil alias Doyle, Bartholomew - died
Dollimore, Thomas
Doyle alias Heydon, Michael
Eades, George - pardoned
Eaton, George (QS)
Empson, Daniel (QS)
Ewen, John (QS) - runaway
Farmer, Ann
Gibson, John (2)
Hall, Arnold - pardoned
Harrington, Thomas
Harvey, Ann
Hayward, Joseph
Henley, Mathew
Henry, Mary
Hoare, Elizabeth (QS)
Hodges, Mary (QS)
Hudson, Thomas
Hunderboome, Thomas
Hunt, Margaret (QS)
Kay, James
Kelly, Hugh (QS)
Kelly, Thomas
King, Bridget
King, George (QS)
Kitson, Mary - pardoned
Lantwell, Bernard (QS)
Layton, Judith
Leith, John
Lewis, Thomas
Linney, William - 14 yrs
Lloyd, Thomas
Lockhart, Benjamin (QS)
Love, James
Manning, Mary - 14 yrs
May, Richard
McAway, William
McDone, Ephraim
McDowell, James
Miller alias Crockstone, John
Nornevill, John (QS)
Nottingham, William
Nowles, John
Owen, Benjamin
Pape, Robert
Phillips, Thomas - runaway
Redman, Mary
Richardson, Charles (QS)

Ross, Charles (QS)
Seymour, John
Sharwell, John
Sheldon, Thomas
Simpson, John
Smout, John
Steele, William (QS)
Stevens, Joseph alias Richard
Still, Andrew
Stringer, William
Thornham, Thomas (QS)
Towers, James
Trafford, Charles
Walker, John

Wheeler, Ann (QS)
Wigginson, Peter
Williams, Elizabeth (QS)
Williams, Henry
Worral, Margaret Ann
Wykes, Richard

Surrey

Grovier, John (QS)
Long, Isaac (QS)
Welland, Richard (QS)
Wheeler, Richard (QS)

Felons transported from London to Maryland by the *Thornton*, Capt. Christopher Reed, in April 1768. (PRO: T1/465/391).

Buckinghamshire

Egleton, William
Fountaine, William
Gilby, Henry
Gilby, Thomas
Hussey, James
Jarvis, Jacob
Probert, William
Roanes, Samuel
Wikes, Francis

Essex

Butcher, Isaac
Button, David (QS)
Corder, Thomas - 14 yrs
Cracknal, William - 14 yrs
Green, Edward - 14 yrs
Green, William - 14 yrs
Harrington, Charles - for life
Heard, James - 14 yrs
Moss, Jarvis (QS)
Pennock, William - 14 yrs
Phillips, John - 14 yrs
Pomfret, Henry - 14 yrs
Tomlin, William - 14 yrs

Hertfordshire

Adams, Francis - 14 yrs
Ariss, John - 14 yrs
Betts, William - 14 yrs
Field, Peter - 14 yrs

Gill, Thomas (QS)
Hard, Dyer - 14 yrs
Harrop, John - 14 yrs
Knight, William (QS)
Warner, William - 14 yrs
Wood, John (QS)

Kent

Adams, William - 14 yrs
Banks, Joseph - 14 yrs
Batten, William - 14 yrs
Brownfield, Elizabeth - 14 yrs
Carter, Robert - for life
Gordon, John
Green, Margaret
Hartley, William - 14 yrs
Humphrey, John - 14 yrs - runaway
Lawrence, William - 14 yrs
Moseley, Paul (QS)
Oram, Ann - 14 yrs
Page, Richard
Penn, Amy - 14 yrs
Porter, William - 14 yrs
Smith, Richard
Tool, David - runaway
West, John (QS)
Woodman, William

London

Adams, James
Baker, Richard
Brown, John

202

Buller, James
Burn, James
Callogan, James
Carter, Elizabeth
Cook, Henry
Daniels, Benny
Dixon, Jane wife of Christopher
Dixon, John
Griffiths, Ann
Johnson, William
Levy, Henry
Mitchell, Thomas
Pharaoh, Thomas
Ranger, Luke
Roberts, John - runaway
Rogers, Francis
Shepherd, William
Short, George
Spackman, Rebecca
Taylor, William (2)
Thorpe, Richard
Vevers alias Bever, John
Wilson, Jane

Middlesex

Bailey, James - runaway
Berry, Ann
Blissett, George
Brice, Elizabeth
Brown, Charles
Burbridge, Thomas
Burford, Joseph (George)
Casey alias Clarke, John
Clifford, Ann
Collop, Thomas
Crosby, James (QS)
Dewy, Richard (QS)
Dodd, Richard
French, Peter
Giles, John
Gordon, Elizabeth wife of John
Green, Richard (QS)
Griffiths, Thomas - 14 yrs
Harding, Michael
Harvey, John
Hill, Thomas
Howard, Thomas (QS)
Hughes, Henry
Johnson, David - runaway
Johnson, Phillip
Jones, William

Keley, Jane
King, Thomas
Kingston, George (QS)
Knight, Charles
Ludlow, Henry, aged 11 - pardoned
Manahay, William (QS)
Miller, David alias John
Monk alias Williams, John
Neal, John
Nugent, John (QS)
Peterson, William
Phillips, John
Price, Richard (QS)
Probert, Thomas (QS)
Richardson, Richard
Roberts, William
Robinson, Thomas
Robinson, William
Sale, Thomas (QS)
Simmons, William - runaway
Smith, Alexander
Smith, Alice (QS)
Smith, James (QS)
Smith, Joseph
Stamps, William
Stephens, William
Stife, Richard (QS)
Taylor, Robert
Todd, William (QS)
Toole, Thomas
Trotman, George (QS)
Upton, John (QS)
Walker, James (QS)
Whiffen, John
Wilford, Hannah (QS)
Williams, Henry
Williams, John (QS)
Wood, Ann (QS)
Wright, James

Surrey

Ashmore, Charles (QS)
Beadle, Richard (QS)
Binnifield, John (QS)
Boswell, Jane (QS)
Bramsby, William
Briton, John (QS)
Brown, John (QS)
Capps, James (QS)
Cole, John - 14 yrs
Creed, James - 14 yrs

203

Dawson, Joseph (QS) - pardoned
Ellis, William
Evans, Elizabeth (QS)
Fowler, John - runaway
Gee, Jeremiah - 14 yrs
Graves, Thomas- 14 yrs
Griffiths, Thomas - 14 yrs - pardoned
King, Isaac (QS)
Linakin, John
Lockhart, John (QS)
Porter, Francis
Porter, Thomas (QS)
Rambell, Lewis (QS)
Roberts, John (QS)
Smith, Benjamin - 14 yrs

Stone, John
Tremble, George - pardoned
Wayte, Thomas - 14 yrs
Willis, Jacob
Wilson, Thomas (QS)
Wood, Thomas (QS)

Sussex

Bartholomew, Edmund - 14 yrs
Elliot, Edmund
Martin, John - 14 yrs
Page, Thomas - 14 yrs
Tidey, William - 14 yrs

Felons transported from London to Virginia by the *Tryal*, Capt. Dougal McDougal, in June 1768. (PRO: T1/465/400).

Hertfordshire

Dunk, William - for life

London

Beacham, Rebecca
Beck, Matthew
Bell, Thomas
Berklise, Rachael
Cave, Richard
Delay, Richard
Draper, Thomas
Elry, John
Evans, Benjamin
Field, Stephen
Griggs alias White, James
Hardy, Andrew
Heywood, John
Kelly, Thomas
Manning, James
Martin, John
Purney, Thomas
Reading, George
Rock, Mary, widow
Stars, John
Thomas, Edmond
Thompson, John
Trainer, John
Walker, George
Williamson, David

Middlesex

Ambler, George
Anthony, Mary
Ash, John
Atherley, Susannah
Benny alias Bennett, John (QS) - stopped
Berry, Thomas
Bignell, Gibson
Bridgeford, Elizabeth
Brooks, Thomas
Brown, Edward (QS)
Brown, Elizabeth
Burn, Ann
Christian, Catherine (QS)
Connor, James (QS)
Crow alias Farrell, Margaret
Cunningham, Joseph
Currin, James
Deane, Daniel (QS)
Doran, John
Doyle, Mary
Doyle, Patrick
Ellis, Mary
Enoch, William
Fisher, William
Gibson, Elizabeth
Greggs, Sarah
Gwillim, Lewis - to transport himself
Hoskins alias Haskins, Elizabeth
Howard, Elizabeth
Hughes alias Lewis, John

Jemison, Eleanor (QS)
Jemitt, Green
Johnson, Michael (QS)
Johnson, Sarah (QS)
Johnson, William
Lacore, Mary
Lloyd, Griffith (QS)
Lotan, Francis
Martin, John
Mason alias Nicholls, Elizabeth
Mathews, Paul (QS)
McDonald, James (QS)
McGirk, James
Merchant, Robert (QS)
Morgan, Thomas
O'Brien, Edward (QS)
Pearson, Edward (QS)
Porter, John (QS)
Pump, Jeremiah
Rainsfrow, Thomas
Rice, Elizabeth (QS)
Slaving, Elizabeth
Smith, Anthony
Smith, Charlotte
Smith, John (QS)

Spencer, John
Stapleton, Thomas - runaway
Steel, William
Taplin, John
Taylor, John
Teppell, Mary
Tinley, John
Trippitt, William
Turner, John (QS)
Udith, James
Wade, Joseph
Ware, Robert (QS)
Waters, John
Wells, Paul William
Whitlow, William (QS)
Willis, Benjamin

Surrey

Gwynn, Joseph (QS)
Hunt, John (QS)
McCaib, John (QS)
Vallis, Stephen (QS)
Ward, William - 14 yrs
Williams, Pleasant (QS)

Felons transported to Maryland by the *Randolph*, Capt. John W. Price, in September 1768. (PRO: Western Circuit Order Books & Dorset RO MS).

Devon

Barter, Mark
Davey, William
Granger, Richard
Greenslade, William
Hitchcock, Mary
Jorden, William

Dorset

Symes, John (QS)
Pennick, Joseph

Hampshire

Budden, Elias
Davis, John
Farrell, James

Hickey, David
Kitto, William
Read, William
Rumbold, Thomas (QS)
Whitemesh, John

Somerset

Ward, James, alias Ryan, Jeremiah

Wiltshire

Gingel, Dinah
Hillier, John
Hopes, John
Jefferies, John
Smith, Thomas
Sparrable alias Sparribell, Isaac

Felons transported from London to Virginia by the *Justitia*, Capt. Thomas Somervell, in October 1768. (PRO: T1/465/407).

Buckinghamshire

Brampton, John
Cosby, John
Heden, John
Moores, Richard
Seckington, James - 14 yrs
Smith, James

Essex

Delight, John (QS)
Downs alias Hakins, Benjamin (QS)
Hakins alias Downs, Benjamin (QS)
Harris, Elizabeth Maria - 14 yrs
Hills, Thomas (QS)
Mason, John - 14 yrs
Mitchell, George
Moore, John - 14 yrs
Scarfe, Jeremiah
Walker, Timothy - 14 yrs

Hertfordshire

Bibby, William (QS)
Covington, Richard - 14 yrs
Greenham, Richard (QS)
Levit, William - 14 yrs

Kent

Austen, Richard (QS)
Beckett, George (QS)
Crittenden, Thomas
Green, John (2)
How, Edward
How, James - 14 yrs
Jennings, Thomas (QS)
Kelley, Richard
Marston, William - for life
Parker, Francis - 14 yrs
Podmore, George - for life
Terry, Stephen - 14 yrs
West, Thomas (QS)

London

Abbott, John - for life
Cox, Jeremiah

Davis, Charles - for life
Eades, Ann
Garton, William
Gay, Charles
Haley, Jane
Jones, Rowland
Knight, Mary
Melleory, Thomas
Mitchiner, Thomas - for life
Morgan, Charles
Norris, James
Offer, John
Page, John - for life
Pinchest, John
Pipson, John
Reavell, Sophia
Robinson, Ann - 14 yrs
Saunders, Ann
Spencer, Moses
Stearn, Joseph
Turpin, John
Vaughan, Thomas
Vickers, William
Whittaker, James
Yates alias Ates, Joseph

Middlesex

Abby, William (QS)
Alders, John - for life
Allen, Dorothy
Barnet, John
Bedford, Catherine
Benjamin, Joseph (QS)
Benny alias Bennett, John
Bignall, George
Bird, John - pardoned
Bohannan, James - for life
Bowen, Elizabeth
Brannon, Nicholas (QS)
Bulger, John (QS)
Byrne, John (QS)
Cayley, William - for life
Clare, George (QS)
Clarke, Philip - 14 yrs
Collins, John
Connor, Thomas (QS)
Conscollen, Mary
Cox, James

Dagnell, Elizabeth (QS)
De Beaufort, Leonard Peter Casalor
Derby, Isaac
Dupree, John
Elkin, John
Fox, Mary
Gardiner, Susannah wife of Luke
Goodge, Charles
Gordon, Alexander
Grantham, John (QS)
Greenwood, George (QS)
Griffiths, John
Hamilton, alias Scholar, William
Hargins, Mathias
Ingram, John
James, Thomas - for life - runaway
Jarlett, John
Jennison, John (QS)
Johnson, William - for life
Joy, William (QS)
Kelly, Thomas (QS)
Kirk, Sarah
Kite, Robert
Lewis, John - pardoned
Major, James(QS)
Marks, Esther
Matthews, Margaret (QS)
Miller, Thomas
Moreland, John (QS)
O'Brien, Dennis (QS)
Pangriffiths, Thomas James
Rackley, James
Ransom, Elizabeth
Slavin, Cornelius - 14 yrs
Smith, John - 14 yrs

Steward, William
Tinsey, John - for life
Tudor, Samuel - for life - runaway
Turner, Ann Harvey - for life
Tyne, Sarah
Webb, Joseph - 14 yrs
Welch, Henry (QS)
Welsh, Samuel (QS)
White, John
Williams, Thomas (QS)
Windsor, Thomas
Wood, Edward
Wooldridge, William

Surrey

Belfour alias Belford, John
Bell, James - for life
Bullen, James - 14 yrs
Evans, Susannah
Fulgeram, Thomas - for life
Jennings, John - runaway
Mooney, Nicholas
Mullins, Richard - for life
Purchase, William - 14 yrs
Rudge, Eleanor
Terry, Thomas
Thompson, William - 14 yrs
Thompson, John - 14 yrs

Sussex

Paies, Robert - 14 yrs
White, James - 14 yrs

Felons transported from London to Virginia by the *Thornton*, Capt. Christopher Reed, in February 1769. (PRO: T1/470/21).

Kent

Bowler, Jonathan (QS)
Ellis, Richard (QS)
Gibbs, John (QS)

London

Adley, Elizabeth
Bailey, Ann
Barew, Solomon
Blanch, John
Bradley, James

Cane alias Cain, Edward
Clarke, William
Colvill, John
Cox, Edward
Flanady, Margaret
Foster, John
Green, John
Hardy, Richard
Higgins, Joseph
Hines, James
Hines, Jane
Isaac, Lazarus
Lane alias Roberts, Sarah - pardoned

207

Lawrence, William
Leay alias Lee, Joseph
Lucas, George
McDonald, Roger
Mills, Alexander, alias Wiltshire, David
Morey, James
Oyley alias Dyley, Marik
Pain, Thomas
Parker, William
Pearslow, John
Polin, William
Purney, John
Read, John - runaway
Roe, John
Ross, Alexander
Thompson, James
Thorman, Thomas
Wright, Mary

Middlesex

Andrews, William
Antrobus, John
Astley, Esther
Bartram, Mary
Bennett, Hooper
Berrisford, Mary
Buck, Mary (QS)
Burridge, William (QS)
Burton, Benjamin
Cane, Thomas (QS)
Carr, Sarah (QS)
Carter, Mary (QS)
Chattell, Thomas (QS)
Churchill, John (QS)
Clarke, Catherine
Clarke, John
Connolly, Cornelius
Cooper, Eleanor (QS)
Coventry, Charles (QS)
Cowen, Eleanor (QS)
Curtis, James
Dawes, Thomas
Doxey, Eleanor (QS)
Drake, Robert (QS)
Dunn, John (QS)
Ealey, Easter (QS)
Elkin, John (QS)
Fitzpatrick, Francis
Flint, Mary Ann wife of Thomas
Gawdry, John (QS)
Gayler alias Galin, James

Greaves, Elizabeth - pardoned
Guildford alias Wood, Margaret
Gurton alias Kirton, Anthony (QS)
Harris, William
Harwood alias Howard, John (QS)
Herring, Mary
Hinchley, Mary
Hopegood, Mary - 14 yrs
Hutchins, John (QS)
Kaye, Abraham
King, James (QS)
Knight, John
Laroche, Constantine
Lewis, John
Lewis, John (QS)
Lilley, William (QS)
Linnard, Richard
Lucas, George
Malloy, Mary (QS)
Mantle, John
McDonald, Charles - runaway
McGinnis, Judith (QS)
McGowing, John
Metcalfe, Thomas
Moratt alias Milley, John (QS)
Nash, Susannah
Nash, Diana (QS)
Newcombe, Frances - 14 yrs
Newey, John (QS)
Newton, William (QS)
Norton, John (QS) - runaway
Oakley, George (QS) - runaway
Perrott, William
Perry, William - runaway
Phillips, Isaac
Phillips, James (QS)
Phillips, Samuel (QS)
Pitman, Thomas
Pollard, Elizabeth (QS)
Preston, Johanna
Price, Ann (QS)
Price, John
Pritchard, Arnold
Purlement, Elizabeth wife of William
Roberts, John (QS)
Robinson, Brittain
Rossar, Thomas (QS)
Sedgware alias Fowler, Margaret
Sherrard, Bernard (QS)
Short, Richard (QS)
Sise, Sarah (QS)
Smith, John (QS)

Stokes, Margaret
Terry, George (QS)
True, John
Twyner, John
Ward, John
Ward, William
Warwick, James (QS)
Welldon, George
Williamson, Mary
Wilson, Thomas
Wiltshire, John

Surrey

Abraham, John (QS) - pardoned
Bond, Charles (QS)
Cawley, John (QS)
Chisseldine, Edward (QS)

Draper, Thomas (QS)
Dyal, Hannah (QS)
Elliott, John (QS)
Fish, James (QS)
Gardiner, John (QS)
Griffiths, Thomas (QS) - pardoned
Hadden, Laurence (QS)
Hagan, Michael (QS)
Harris, James (QS)
Harris, William (QS)
Jackson, Richard (QS)
Nicholls, Walter (QS)
Sheene, George (QS)
Sheppard, William (QS)
Smith, James (QS)
Veriner, James (QS)
Woollard, William (QS)

Felons transported from London to Maryland by the *Tryal*, Capt. Dougal McDougal, in April 1769. (PRO: T1/470/10).

Buckinghamshire

Inns, John
Jenkins, Joseph
Kitchen alias Kitchener, John
Wild, Peter

Essex

Boon, Joseph
Curtis, Susannah
Hales, David
Lacey, Thomas - runaway
Lambden, John - for life
Serjeant, John
Silvester, John
Warren, James
Watson, Thomas - 14 yrs
Woolley, Robert
Wright, George

Hertfordshire

Robinson, John
Winch, Isaac

Kent

Acton, John - for life
Brown, James

Brown, Joseph - 14 yrs
Caspen, William (QS)
Chapman, James - 14 yrs
Clifford, Edward - for life
Copus, John
Dowtch, Robert - 14 yrs
Howson, John - 14 yrs
Imeson, John
Leeson, John
Matthews, Daniel - for life
Perry, Simon - 14 yrs
Pilkington, Thomas - 14 yrs
Simmonds, Edward - for life - runaway
White, James - 14 yrs
Winn, Sampson

London

Aldsworth, Samuel - runaway
Birch, Ann - pardoned
Charter, John
Davis, John
Evans, Elizabeth - pardoned
Houten, William
Jackson, James
Lawrence, James
Locke, Isaac
Michael, Sarah
Miles, Elizabeth
Mordicai, Samuel

Moses, Jacob
Pegg, William
Reynolds, George
Swift, John
Task, Deborah
Thomas, Edward

Middlesex

Ashford, Elizabeth (QS)
Baldwin, Thomas
Barfoot, John
Bine, Stephen
Brown, Daniel (QS)
Burgess, Elizabeth
Church, Abraham
Coffee alias Coffield, Ann (QS)
Conway, Thomas (QS)
Cox, Elizabeth (QS)
Crocker, Thomas
Currant alias Corrand, John
Davis, John
De Bruyer, Henry (QS)
Dixon, Jonathan
Doyle, Sylvester (QS)
Dunn, Richard (QS)
Edge, William
Felter, Ann
Fisher, Samuel (QS)
Fletcher, John
Ford, Samuel
Gathwaite, William
Hedges, William - pardoned
Hussey, Catherine
Knope, George (QS)
Lawley, Mary (QS)
Lewis, John
North, Thomas (QS)
Paris, Robert (QS)

Price, Robert (QS)
Regan, Bartholomew (QS)
Smithson, William
Spicer, Jane
Stead, James
Sutton, Thomas
Tiernon, Joseph (QS)
Waldon, Edward
Ward, Joseph
Wardin, John
Williams, Susan

Surrey

Broadbridge, Elizabeth
Dalby, Daniel
Foot, Esau - 14 yrs
Forsith, John, alias Berkley, William
    - for life
Green, William (QS)
Humber, William (QS)
Jack, James - 14 yrs
Jerrachino, Abraham
Lockett, Benjamin
Lovely, Martha
Sawyer, John - 14 yrs
Thornton, Mary (QS)
Turner, John - runaway
Turner, William - 14 yrs
Wood, William - 14 yrs

Sussex

Chantler, Nathaniel, alias Chandler,
    William - 14 yrs
Hyder, Stephen (QS)
Parsons, Thomas
Pierson, Joseph - 14 yrs
Venn, Jane

Felons transported from London to Maryland (?) by the *Douglas*, Mr. William Beckenridge, in August 1769.. (PRO: T1/670/1).

Essex

Broad, James - 14 yrs
Day, William
Douyer, Peter - 14 yrs
Duffield, Jacob - 14 yrs
Eades, James - 14 yrs
Gardner, John
Holmes, Henry - 14 yrs

Patmore, Benjamin
Sampson, John
Sarjeant, George (QS)
Smith, Gideon - 14 yrs

Hertfordshire

Loveday, Thomas (QS)

Kent

Channam alias Cannam, William
Cornwall, Richard
Gray, Thomas
Gray, James - 14 yrs
Jeffery, Thomas - 14 yrs

London

Belcher, Sarah
Bluckfield, Joseph
Catling, James
Cheyney, John
Clay, William
Delwyn, William
Dick alias Dickenson, George - 14 yrs
Erouselle, Philip - pardoned
Harding, Mary
Harris, William
Hill, William
Howard, Henry
Johnson alias Farr, Alice
Kynaston, Mary
Lary, Mary
Manton alias Strutton alias Smith, Sarah
Mills, Michael
Nicholls, William
Payne, George
Poole, George
Proctor, Sarah
Sage, Thomas (QS)
Shuler, John
Smith, Eleanor
Smith, John
Spicer, Thomas
Steward, John
Wallis, James - 14 yrs
Wilson, Alexander - 14 yrs
Wilson, John

Middlesex

Baker, John - 14 yrs
Beatley, Thomas (QS)
Bird, John
Bottens, Robert
Bryan, Thomas
Burges, William (QS)
Burk, Andrew - 14 yrs
Burn, Patrick - 14 yrs
Burnett, John - 14 yrs

Bush, Francis - 14 yrs
Butler, John - 14 yrs
Carryl, Winifred - 14 yrs
Cooper, James - 14 yrs
Craycraft, Samuel - 14 yrs
Crew, Charles
Dallaway, Matthew - 14 yrs
Davis, John
Dick, Jane - 14 yrs
Dobbins, Joseph
Dollison, James - 14 yrs
Duggan, Joseph (QS)
Evans alias Dyer, John
Fanning, James
Fennell, John
Gray, Thomas - 14 yrs
Grinald, Thomas
Hanson, Henry
Harris, Reuben
Hay, Collin
Higgs, William (QS) - pardoned
Hixton alias Axall, Thomas (QS)
Hope, Stephen - 14 yrs
House, John - 14 yrs
Jones, Thomas - 14 yrs
King, George (QS)
Law, John - pardoned
Lawrence, John - 14 yrs - runaway
Leech, John (QS)
Levy, Samuel - 14 yrs
Lions, Barnaby
Loome, John
Loveland, Daniel (QS)
Malloes, Robert - 14 yrs
Martin, Bartholomew
McDonald alias McDorell, Andrew
Medley, Peter - 14 yrs
Mersey, William
Moore, John - 14 yrs
Moreton, James
Morgan, Eleanor wife of John,
    alias Eleanor Walker, spinster - 14 yrs
Morris alias Hambleton, John - 14 yrs
Odell, Elizabeth - 14 yrs
Parker, John (QS)
Parsingham alias Parsons, John
Perkins, Ann - for life
Perry, William - 14 yrs
Rock, Edward (QS)
Rowdon, Sarah
Shakespear, Samuel (QS)
Singer, Robert

Smith, John (QS)
Spink, Robert
Strutt, Sarah
Tindell alias Norman, Henry
Towell, Thomas
Trippett, Joseph
Walldeck, Joseph
Warden, James
Waters, Moses
Watts, Margaret - 14 yrs
Wilkes, Charles - 14 yrs
Williams, Edward (QS)
Williams, Robert
Woodthey, John - 14 yrs
Wright, John (QS)

Surrey

Brown, William - 14 yrs
Carr, Elizabeth
Dalton, John - 14 yrs
Griffiths, James - 14 yrs
Hammond, Joseph (QS)
Johns, Thomas (QS)
Jones, John
Mitchell, James
Ransome, William (QS)
Steers, John
Turner, Elizabeth (QS)
Turner, Joseph (QS)
Winstanley, Francis (QS) - for life

Felons transported from London to Virginia by the *Justitia*, Capt. Colin Somervell, in February 1770. (PRO: T1/478/1).

Hertfordshire

Watts, John (QS) - runaway
Young, James (QS)

Kent

Hammond, Richard - for life
Knight, Joseph (QS)
Louiza, Elizabeth (QS)
Smith, Thomas (QS)

London

Babb, Thomas
Bagnell, William
Bailey, Samuel - runaway
Bell, Robert
Bradshaw, Elizabeth
Burridge, Charles
Carroll, John
Cave, John
Cave, Thomas
Clements, Richard
Croft, Matthew
Dean, James
Finnick, Francis - pardoned
Fraser, George
Gardiner, Sarah
Gibbons, Samuel
Hemmery alias Horton, Robert
Holmes, Sarah

Howsden, Benjamin
Ireland, Elizabeth
Law, Thomas
Martin, Henry alias William
Mitchel, Samuel
Pindar, Rachael
Robinson, John
Rowlins, James
Simpson, James
Smith, Joseph - sold to
    Andrew Buchanan
Smith, Robert - to transport himself
Thomas, John
Williams, John

Middlesex

Alderman, Richard
Baker, John (QS)
Baker, William (QS)
Barnet, Abraham
Barrett, Ann
Baxter, Sarah
Biddis, Jane
Biggs, Reuben - for life
Blanchfield, John (QS)
Bozey alias Bland, Golden
Brown, Elizabeth
Castle, Susanna (QS)
Catton, John
Caustin, Paul
Clarke, John

Cook, John (2)
Cooper, Samuel Joseph
Croucher, George
Dallow, Martha, spinster,
  alias Tomlins, widow
Davies, Thomas (QS)
Davis, Jane
Dealy alias Dayly, William
Dean, John
Dowland, William (QS)
Drury, Timothy - runaway
Duggin, William
Dyer, Thomas (QS) - runaway
Eason, Samuel
Ebbit, Ann wife of Oliver
Edghill, Thomas
Ellwood, John
Emmery, John (QS)
Fenton, Bartholomew
Fitzpatrick, William
Fleming, Susanna
Gibbard, Sarah wife of Henry,
  alias Mary Jones, spinster
Gill, Mary
Hall, Thomas
Hardwicke, Charles
Head, William
Hughes, Edward
Hymes, Michael
Ireland, William - pardoned
Johnson, Joseph
Kennedy, Edward (QS)
Keysell, George
Kidder, Ann - pardoned
Knope, Hannah wife of George
Lagden, Robert

Levi, Emanuel (QS)
Lewis, Christopher
Light, Esther
Lovell, James (QS)
Lowry, Ann (QS)
Maddocks, Martha wife of William
Mahan, Joseph - 14 yrs
Mashman, James
McAway, Stephen
Mellon, Edward
Neale, Richard
North, Edward (QS)
Nowell, Esther (QS)
Pisano, Joseph
Price alias Pessey, David
Reading, Lambeth (QS) - pardoned
Roberts, John
Scott alias Piggot, John
Smith, Catherine
Spruce, Apswell (QS)
Stapleton, William
Stroud, Ann
Sumner, Margaret
Trimble, John - 14 yrs
Trimble, William
Wall, George
Walldeck, Joseph - 14 yrs
White, Mary
Willis, Jane (QS)
Young, Martha

Surrey

Evans, Evan (QS)
Robinson, Thomas (QS)
Wotton, Thomas (QS)

Felons transported from London to Maryland by the *Thornton*, Capt. Dougal McDougal, in May 1770. (PRO: T1/478/93).

Buckinghamshire

Baker, William
Benbow, Thomas
Cato, John
Davis, Thomas
Hartwell, John
Oakly, Thomas
Parnham, Thomas
Parry, Thomas
Sear, Thomas

Essex

Attridge, William - 14 yrs
Biass, James
Evins, Henry
Hampil, John - 14 yrs
Harvey, Jonathan
Hasham, John - for life
Inch alias Lee, Ann
Inch, John - for life
May, Henry
Middleton, Elizabeth

Paine, Peter
Pride, Shadrake
Quantrill, Prettyman - 14 yrs
Shelley, Susannah
Solomon, Alley - 14 yrs
Thompson, James
Wood, George - 14 yrs

Hertfordshire

Abbey, John
Day, John - for life
Day, Thomas - for life
Hicks, Rebecca - 14 yrs
Hicks, Silvia - 14 yrs
Horner, Thomas - 21 yrs

Kent

Calvert, William
Dixon, John - for life
Donald, William (QS)
Honey, John Jr.
Marlow, William
Thornally, Francis
Trott, Richard - for life
Waller, William

London

Barber, Thomas
Bateman, Samuel
Blunder, Sarah
Bowell, John
Clarke, Richard (QS)
Dunn, Thomas
Gough, Rose wife of Francis
Gould, Jane
Harris, James
Harris, Mary
Harris, Thomas
Harwood, Mary
Hatsett, Thomas
Haywood, William
Hebb, Matthew
Hill, John - runaway
Lamotte, Isaac
Martin, John
Martin, Matthew - pardoned
Oakley, Benjamin
Osborn, William
Peters, Abraham - runaway

Pratt, Roger
Price, John
Reynolds, Edward - to transport himself
Richardson, Jane wife of Joseph
Robinson, James (QS)
Smith, James
Smith, Louisa
Sparkes, Charles
Stafford, John
Trigg, Daniel
Withers, John

Middlesex

Abraham alias Abrahams, John
- for life - runaway
Baker, Thomas (QS)
Balding, Judith - 14 yrs
Bellamy, John (QS)
Benjamin, Benjamin (QS)
Busby, Christopher - for life
Butler, Willam
Carroll, Hugh
Carter, Richard - 14 yrs
Cary alias Rooke, Susannah
Chapple, Elizabeth
Church, Benjamin
Clark, William - 14 yrs - pardoned
Claxton alias Darling
alias Underwood, Ann - for life
Cotteral, James
Cox, John
Craig, Charles (QS)
Creamer, John - 14 yrs
Crowder, George - 14 yrs
Cunningham, Jane
Davidson, Mary - 14 yrs
Duncan, John
Durant, Elizabeth wife of Benjamin,
alias Shewing, Elizabeth, spinster
Fanting, Lewis
Ferguson, John (QS)
Fife, James
Folkes, John
Francis, Hannah wife of William
Gascoyne, Elizabeth (QS)
Gosling, Thomas - pardoned
Griffis, James (QS)
Griffiths, Thomas
Hall, Edward (QS) - runaway
Hall, Jonathan - for life
Harrison, William

214

Hawther, Mary
Haycock, Sarah - for life
Hayton, Ann
Hickson, Mathew
Hill, Sarah
Hindmarsh, John - 14 yrs
Jones, Benjamin - for life
Jones, Sarah
Kennedy, Mathew - for life
Legrand, John Rodolph
Linsey, Thomas
Lister, John - for life
Lungreen, Anders Hendrick - for life
Makepeace, Elizabeth wife of Stephen
McCannon, Frederick (QS)
Miller, Nicholas (QS)
Mitchells, Jacob
Montgomery, Margaret
Murphy, John
Newson, John - pardoned
Nicholls, Joseph - for life
Nott, Randall (QS)
Pemberton, Isaac - for life
Petman, John
Powney, William
Priest, John - for life
Pyne, Charles - to transport himself
Randall, John - 14 yrs
Rawlinson alias Jones, Mary
Staples, Ann wife of Robert
Strutt, Daniel - 14 yrs
Symonds, John - 14 yrs
Tipping, Thomas - runaway
Troy, William - for life
Unwin, Francis
Waller, Elizabeth
Ward, Thomas (QS)
Warrecker, William - for life - runaway
Watkins, Benjamin
Watkins, William (QS)
Watson, John, alias Davies, William

- for life
Webster, John Michael (QS)
Whitely alias Ward, Mary
Wild, Edward
Yardley, John
Young, George (QS)

Surrey

Adams alias Bandy, Richard
Anderson, Christian
Baker, John - runaway
Bennett, Edward - for life
Boon, Moses (QS)
Brace alias Braca, Samuel (QS)
Brown, John - 14 yrs
Bryan, John - 3 yrs
Day, Benjamin - for life
Deval, George (QS)
Eldridge, John - 14 yrs
Frankland, Samuel (QS)
Greenwell, Acton (QS) - pardoned
Hownsome, William - 14 yrs
Jackson, Anthony - runaway
Kelly, Catherine
Mathews, Pater (QS)
McGennis, Thomas - 14 yrs
Oakley, Benjamin
Pissey, John
Powditch, George (QS)
Ross, Margaret (QS)
Simmonds, William - 14 yrs - runaway
Smith, James (QS)
Steward, James
Tresler, John
Wade, Michael (QS)

Sussex

Kenrick, Henry (QS)
Peadle alias Read, Richard

Felons transported from London to Maryland by the *Scarsdale*, Capt. Christopher Reed, in July 1770. (PRO: T1/478/80).

Buckinghamshire

Wilkinson, Henry

Hertfordshire

Gibbard, Thomas (QS)

Mordrum, Henry (QS)
Stroud, Richard (QS)
Watts, Thomas (QS)

London

Allan, James

215

Armond, John
Baker, Dorothy, widow
Berry, William
Bird, Thomas
Carne, Peter
Cole, William
Craft, John
Davies, Jacob
Dear, Naphthali
Dixon, Robert
Dove, William
Elias, Thomas
Emanuel, Aaron
Fenton, William - pardoned
Frazer, Margaret
Gale, Robert
Green, Joseph
Green, Elizabeth
Hanson, Mary
Hargrave, Nathaniel
Higginson, Joseph - runaway
Horne, Mary
Hyland, Michael
Jackson, Robert
Jenkins, Thomas
Lee, Joseph
Lemon, David
Levy, Lazarus
Mahoney, Florence
Martin, Sarah, spinster
Milston, Thomas
Moss, Sarah wife of William
Myer alias Meale, Abraham
Payne, Burry
Pearce, James
Powell, James
Regan, Andrew
Richardson, Alexander
Solomon, Hyam
Taylor, Thomas
Turnam, Thomas (QS)
Valvin, Robert
Welch, Thomas
Williams, William
Wright, Ann wife of John
Wright, David

Middlesex

Adams, Elizabeth
Alloway, Mary
Ashford, Samuel

Atherton, James - for life
Atherton, John
Barnes, Sarah
Batchelor, Peter - runaway
Bennett, John
Benson, James
Berry, Edward
Bevan, Thomas - for life
Bird, John
Bisset, Robert
Bower, John
Brown, Jane
Brown, John
Browning, John
Burton, Joseph
Butler, William
Camber, William (QS)
Cane, Thomas
Carter, Ann
Chapman, Joseph alias Richard (QS)
Chatterley, Charles - for life
Child, Sarah
Cly, Henry
Coaly, John
Collins, John
Comfort alias Comford, Francis
Cook, John
Cooke, Thomas
Cox, Joseph
Coyn, James
Davis, Elizabeth
Davis, William
Deacon, John
Delaforce, Joseph - for life
Dobbs, Thomas
Donnala, Michael
Dunn alias Matthews, Paul
Dyer, Samuel
Edwards, John, alias Howard, Edward
Edwards, Bridget wife of Philip
Ellis, Sarah
Fordham, Thomas
Garnons, William - for life
Goodwin, Catherine
Gould, Joseph
Graham, Peter - 14 yrs
Green, Thomas
Gregory, Edward
Haddock, John
Holmes, Edward - 14 yrs
Humphrys, John
Hunt, Rebecca

Iveson, William
Jackson, William
Jagger, John - 14 yrs
Jilks, William
Jones, Thomas
Keeling, Andrew
Kellihorn, John
Kelly, George
Kelsworth, John
Knight, John
Lappington, Elizabeth
Larkworthy, James
Lawson, Samuel
Lee, James
Linney, John
Lyon, Moses
Marckle, Christopher - 14 yrs
Matthews, John (QS)
McDonald, James
McKew, Henry
Memory, George
Milbank, John - for life
Mitchell, William
Monro, John - for life
Morris, John
Newland, James - for life
Page, Sarah
Peele, Thomas
Pratt, William
Pritchard, James (QS)
Puddle, Hannah - 14 yrs
Purdem, Thomas
Reeves, Robert
Regis, Vittorio

Richards, Elizabeth
Riddle, Hannah
Riges, Victory
Ryder, James
Simms, James
Smith, Samuel
Soddi, Elizabeth - 14 ys
Speed, Simon
Staines, William
Staniford, Walter
Taffe, Henry
Talbot, Elizabeth
Taylor, William - pardoned
Thacker, William
Thompson, Joseph
Tilks, William
Tomlin, Richard
Twyford, Henry
Watson, Robert - to transport himself
Wharton alias Thomas, William
- for life
Wheatley alias Whitney, Mary
- pardoned
Wilkins, Thomas (QS)
Wilson, Joseph
Worn, Edward

Surrey

Carter, Anthony (QS)
Clark, John (QS)
Siney, John - for life
Sparks, Edward (QS)

Felons transported from Bristol by the *Trotman*, Capt. Joseph Blickenden, and registered in Baltimore Co. records in December 1770. (MSA: CR 40,516 f. 9).

Bedfordshire

Godfrey, Elizabeth: sold to Abraham Ensor - recognizance f. 35.

Herefordshire

Price, William: sold to Abraham Ensor - recognizance f. 35.

Huntingdonshire

Wilkinson, Elijah [Elisha]: escaped in London

Leicestershire

Thompson, Samuel: sold to Abraham Ensor - recognizance f. 34.

London

Lucas, George: sold to George Lytle - also listed as transported by *Thornton* 1769
- runaway

Northamptonshire

Brooks, William: sold to Jeremiah Johnson - recognizance f. 33.
Draper, Thomas: sold to John Cockey - recognizance f. 32.
Wright, Samuel: sold to Philip Chamberlain

Nottinghamshire

Forth [Firth], James: sold to Daniel Shaw

Surrey

Hamilton, William: escaped in London

Yorkshire

Alcroft, John: sold to Nicholas Norwood
Allerton, Robert: escaped in London
Baker [Barker], Christopher: escaped in London
Carr, George: sold to William Randall - recognizance f. 30.
Dalby, William: sold to John Cockey - recognizance f. 33.
Dunning, Ann: sold to William Hunter
Lambert, Samuel: sold to Larkin Randall
Moore, William (alias Robert): sold to Stephen Gill Jr. - recognizance f. 25.
Morris, John: sold to Charles Baker
Moburn, George: sold to ---- Amos
Owen, William: sold to John Price Jr. - recognizance f. 26.
Pierson, Mary (QS): sold to John Males
Richardson, William: sold to Thomas Cole Sr. - recognizance f. 25.
Smith, Benjamin: sold to Jonathan Plowman - recognizance f. 30.
Tunningley [Tunnely], John: sold to Mordecai Price son of John
Unthank, Daniel: sold to Aquila Price - recognizance f. 28. - runaway
Whitfield, Richard: escaped in London
Wilson, John: sold to Ezekiel Bosley - recognizance f. 38.

Unidentified

Allen, Ann: sold to William Barney - recognizance f. 28.
Allen, William: sold to Charles Howard
Brown, John: sold to William Baker
Foster?, Mary: sold to John Gill Jr. - recognizance f. 25.
Goodman, Richard: sold to Aquila Price - recognizance f. 27.
Howard?, William: sold to George Hammond
Johnson, John: sold to James Baker - runaway

Felons transported [also by the *Trotman*?] on the account of William Stevenson and William Randolph, merchants, arriving in Maryland on 6 December and registered in Baltimore Co. records on 12 December 1770 (CR 40,516):

Bristol

Hume, Dennison
Thomas, Francis

Cheshire

Moores, Mary
Newell, Daniel
Scowlcroft, William - 14 yrs

Devon

Major, Hannah
Nicholson, Anthony (QS)
Salway, John (QS)

Herefordshire

Hitch, Thomas
Bowles, Thomas
Craddock, Elizabeth

Shropshire

Higgs, John
Pugh, Joan

Somerset

Gibbons, Charles

Staffordshire

Sherrard, George
Smith, Mary

Warwickshire

Allen, Mary
Bromidge, James
  - but put ashore in Bristol
Hadden, John
Hinks, Thomas
Lee, Thomas
Rotheram, Joseph - 14 yrs
Tysoe, James - 14 yrs
Williams, James
Wootton, Margaret

Worcestershire

Taylor, Edward
Baylis, Abraham

Felons transported from London to Virginia by the *Justitia*, Capt. Colin Somervell, in December 1770. (PRO: T1/483/90).

Buckinghamshire

Dobbs, Joseph
King, John

Essex

Hills, Thomas - 14 yrs

Hertfordshire

Lee, John (QS)

Kent

Blaxland, William - for life
Burbridge, William (QS)

Carey, George (QS) - pardoned
Carr, William - for life
Corbin, Robert (QS)
Craddock, William
Howard, Denchier
Lorrimer, Richard Francis - for life
Mitcham, William
Sharpe, Robert (QS)
Williams alias Beauman, Sarah (QS)

London

Allen, James
Barber, Mary
Bede, Thomas
Billing, John
Bird alias Boyle, Samuel

Boyer, William
Brookfield, Joseph
Bunce, James
Carroll, John
Chapman, Joseph
Cock, Eleanor
Coleman, Rose
Connolly, James
Connolly, Margaret
Cowen, Aaron
Dangerfield, Samuel
Delamar, Edward
Doyle, Francis
Eaton, Grace
Flocker, John
French, Thomas
Glyn, James
Hart, Isaac - runaway
Jones, Henry - pardoned
Kenny, Mary
Landekin, Thomas
Law, William - runaway
Malcah, Abraham - pardoned
Moore, William
Moy, Richard
Plunket, Mary
Price, Joseph
Reason, Bartholomew
Restall, George
Smith, Robert - to transport himself
Tatham, Thomas - 14 yrs
Thompson, Thomas
Underwood, John - 14 yrs
Ward, John
Willett, Humphry

Middlesex

Biddleston, Jonathan
Birk, Peter
Bland, Thomas (QS) - pardoned
Bracey, John
Brown, Bartholomew - pardoned
Brown, Elizabeth wife of William
Burrows, Margaret, widow,
    alias wife of John
Butterom, Elizabeth
Carey, Henry
Castle, Elizabeth wife of Richard
Clarke, William
Clinch, Elizabeth
Cole, James

Conroy, John
Crow, Alice
Dacey, Mary (QS)
Darby, Thomas
Fettyplace, George
Gee, Richard
Gibson, William
Grayhurst, Mary
Green, Elizabeth
Harrison, Robert (QS)
Henley, William
Hutchinson, Mary
Jones, Simon
Kennedy, Robert
Kinchley, Peter
Knowland, Katherine
Langford, Elizabeth
Lloyd, Richard (QS)
Mathews, Harriot
McDaniel, Ann
Meadows, Eleanor
Munk, Jane
Murray, Brien (QS)
Murray, John
Neal, John (QS)
Odell, Edward (QS)
Page, Elizabeth
Parker, Robert - pardoned
Pearce, James
Pretty, Eleanor
Pretty, Sarah
Querri, Richard
Rutlidge, Thomas - pardoned
Seymour, Elizabeth
Singleton, Ann
Smith, Richard - 14 yrs
Tovey, Hannah (QS)
Turner, John (QS)
Walmsley, Philip
Warner, Elizabeth
Watts, Mary
Whitney, John
Windon, Elizabeth
Witchett, Elizabeth (QS)
Young, Deborah (QS)

Surrey

Brown, John
Dryberry, Thomas
Eaton alias Royal, Elizabeth
Finney, William - for life

220

Froud, James - for life
Hoar, Thomas - pardoned
Murphy, Thomas
Robinson, John - 14 yrs
Steers, William - 14 yrs

Sutton, John - for life
Tigh, Henry
Turner, Jane
Vincent, John
Wilson, Maria wife of George

Felons transported from London by the *Thornton*, Capt. Dougal McDougal, in May 1771 and registered in Anne Arundel Co. records on 16 July 1771. (PRO: T1/483/47; MSA: CR 40,516).

Buckinghamshire

Barber, Thomas Jr.*
Bradley, Thomas - runaway
Henson, John*
Saxton (Sexton), John
Wooton, Paul*

Essex

Collyer, John - runaway
Hurry, Ann

Hertfordshire

Dixon, William
Foster, John (QS)
Rowles, Daniel
Taylor, William (QS)

Kent

Allen, Elizabeth
Bury, James
Carter, William (QS)
Chilman, George Jr. (QS)
Cook, Elizabeth (QS)
Dewine, William - 14 yrs
Downe, William
Farnaby, Ralph
Green, John (QS)
Hearnden, Thomas
Humphrey, Edward - 14 yrs - runaway
Hutchford, Elizabeth
Jessup, Thomas - 14 yrs
Reynolds, Ann
Sampson, Jonathan
Wharton, William - 14 yrs
Wood, Thomas

London

Abrahams, Jacob
Cavenagh, Hannah
Crook, William - sold to Joshua Bond
Desbrieres, Rose Langlais
Edwards, Thomas
 - sold to Ephraim Steward
Johnson, Robert
Marshall, Elizabeth
Moore, John
Moreton, Christopher
Muckaway, Thomas
Pearce, William
Sanders, Benjamin alias Abraham
Siday, Elizabeth wife of William
 - 14 yrs
Smith, Edward
 - sold to Ephraim Steward
Sproson, John
Sullivan, John
Tudor, Frances
Welch, John
Wood, Solomon

Middlesex

Abel, Thomas - runaway
Ashman, Charles - sold to
 John Whitacre Jr. (MSA)
Barfield alias Bradfield, Ann
Beach, John
Beddington, Edward
Benson, George (QS)
Booth, Ann - pardoned
Cordosa, Jacob (QS) - pardoned
Diaper, John
Erskine alias Maxwell alias Hamilton,
 Thomas - to transport himself
Farthing, John
Field, James - sold to William Selman
 - runaway

Gannon, John
Gannon, Michael* - 14 yrs
Goodwin, Mary
Haggerty, Matthew
Harvey, Sarah
Hawke, William* - 14 yrs - runaway
Herne, Mary*
Hopcroft, Robert
Jackson, James
Jacobs, Jacob* - 14 yrs
James, Thomas
Jenkinson, Paul
Johnson, John
Jones, Elizabeth
Kent, Grace
Lakin, Isabella
Largent, Frances
Lashley, Joseph
Lescallott, William*
Livesson, John
Lockwood, Mary
May, Susannah
McGuire, Martin
Merchant, Joseph - pardoned
Miller, Maximilian
Murray, Matthew
Muston, Richard Joseph
Pardon, Catherine (QS)* - runaway
Pullen, Richard (QS)
Raby, William
Randall, Ann
Pardon, Catherine (QS)*
Ready, Thomas (QS)* - runaway
Roberts, Mary
Sargent, Frances*
Sawyer, Charles (QS)* - runaway
Serjeant, Thomas

Smith, Edward
Solomons, Solomon
Sowden, Michael
Suledge, Samuel
Thomas, James*
Thornton alias Thornhill, Benjamin
Trevis, John (QS)
Walker, Thomas
Watson, James William - pardoned
Welch, Michael
Wood, Mary*

Surrey

Beaumont, William (QS)
Gold, Mary
Roberts, John* - 14 yrs
Woodfield, Jane - 14 yrs
Woodfield, Maria
Bear, Richard*
Bullen, James* - 14 yrs
Lyon, Jacob*
Paterson, Peter*
Penny, Benjamin*
Pether, John* - 14 yrs - runaway
Revel, James*
Ryley, Ann - pardoned
Stone, Hercules*
Taylor, Joseph*
Williams, Mary*

Sussex

Parkhurst, James - 14 yrs
Baily, Robert*
Catt, William*
Gardiner, John*

*Not on LC

Felons transported by William Stevenson and William Randolph, merchants, from Bristol to Maryland and registered in Baltimore Co. records on 17 June 1771 (MSA: CR 40,516 ff. 37-44).

Cheshire

Burchall, Thomas

Devon

Batten, John
Haggott, John

Hallett, William - for life
Matthews, James
Patty, John (QS)
Wilson, John

Gloucestershire

Richards, John (QS)

Shropshire

Evans, Edward - 14 yrs
Smith, Peter - 14 yrs
Smith, Elias (QS)
Thomas, Margaret - 14 yrs

Somerset

Moore, John alias Stone, Samuel

Worcestershire

Forbes, James - for life

Felons transported by William Stevenson and William Randolph, merchants, from Bristol to Maryland and registered in Baltimore Co. records on 3 July 1771 (MSA: CR 40,516 ff. 48-82).

Cheshire

Bold alias Blimstone, Robert
  - recognizance f. 89.
Jones, Joseph

Cornwall

Baker, Susanna (QS)
Hill, Jane (QS)
Sweetman, Thomas (QS)
Tippett, Jane

Devon

Andrews, Mary
Baker alias Sawcer, William - 14 yrs
Bennett, Alexander - 14 yrs
  - recognizance f. 87.
Bowden alias Pike, Arthur (QS)
Brown, Robert
Clarke, Phillis
Davy, Ann - for life
Edy, William alias Pascoe, Joseph
  - 14 yrs
Gosling, Samuel - 14 yrs
  - recognizance f. 88
Knight, John - for life
Pengelly, Thomas - for life
Rowland, Thomas
Tuck, Henry

Dorset

Bown, Sarah - 14 yrs
Custard, Thomas (QS)
Foxall, Elizabeth - 14 yrs
  - recognizance f. 89
Galpin, William
Guppy, John

Marsh, George - 14 yrs
Read, Ann - 14 yrs
Weed, Samuel (QS)

Herefordshire

Badham, Edward - 14 yrs - runaway
Brace, Daniel
Brace, Richard
Griffiths, Thomas
Hall, Elizabeth - 14 yrs
Hunt alias Symonds, William - 14 yrs
Morris, William - recognizance f. 90

Monmouthshire

Jones, Mary

Shropshire

Baker, Elizabeth

Somerset

Bellamy, John
Coles, Jonathan - 14 yrs
Farncombe alias Vencombe, Henry
  - 14 yrs
Mills, Robert
Mopsey, Ann - for life
Norman, Philip
Strickland, George - for life

Staffordshire

Brookes Richard alias Badger
Jervis, William - 14 yrs
Manifold alias Merry, Joseph (QS) -
  runaway
Nuthall, Thomas - 14 yrs

223

Warwickshire

Bayliss, Richard - 14 yrs
Beards, Joseph
Buckley, Elizabeth
Clews, Richard
Davison, Ralph
Dickinson, William
Leach, Solomon
Newey, John
Pinfield, John - runaway
Strange, Thomas

Wiltshire

Lacey, William - 14 yrs
Lawrence, William
Pinnigar, Joseph
Wadhams, William

Worcestershire

Matthews, William
Winnall, Elizabeth

Felons transported from London to Virginia by the *Scarsdale*, Capt. Christopher Reed, in July 1771. (PRO: T1/483/60).

Kent

Russell, Nicholas (QS)

London

Aldridge, Richard
Alexander, Solomon
Arons, Benie
Baylis, John
Brett, John - runaway
Bullock, William
Caton, Ann
Cleghorn, Robert
Coward, James - pardoned
Davis, Thomas - 14 yrs
Dawson, George
Dousy, Innace
Eagles, Edward
East, Charles
Ferrand, Sarah
Foster, James - 14 yrs
Green, William - 14 yrs
Griffin, John - 14 yrs
Griffiths, John
Hall, Thomas
Hancock, James
Holland, John
Hughes, John
Humphrays, Gumpay
Hunter, David
Hurst, Sarah - pardoned
Jones, David
Jones, Mary (2)
Jones, Margaret
Kelly, William

Lane, Thomas
Le Groves, William
Levi, Solomon
Lockitt alias Brock, Mary
Lowe, William
Lucas, Thomas
Lyons, Joseph
McFeast, Mary
McLane, David
Mitchell, John
Newland, William
Payne, Benjamin
Pinnick, Ann - 14 yrs
Read, Mary
Robinson, Henry - 14 yrs
Smith, Sarah
Wallace, Lawrence
Ward, Joseph - runaway

Middlesex

Adcock, William
Allen, Elizabeth (QS)
Ashton, James (QS)
Baker, Charles - for life
Banks, Ann - runaway
Barew, Abraham
Barns, Ann
Barns, Mary
Bateman, Harriot
Bayley alias Bayless, Nathaniel
Beaver, Ann - pardoned
Berry, James (QS)
Bland, William (QS)
Boston, Mary
Boyce, Thomas

Brace, George
Brazier, Susannah (QS)
Brown, Thomas
Burt, Thomas
Butcher, Richard - for life
Cain, Richard (QS)
Callagan alias Gallagher, Charles
  - for life
Campbell, Duncan, alias Douglas,
  John Hunter (QS)
Carey, George
Clarke, William
Clarke alias Farrell, John - 14 yrs
Clayton, Joseph (QS)
Clemmenshaw, Elizabeth
  wife of Thomas
Cocklin, Jane
Cohen, Henry (QS)
Crow, Thomas
Dawson, James
Day, William - runaway
Dolman, John
Earle, John
Eastman, Edward
Emmet, Richard
Etherington, Terence
Folwell, Mary
Francis, John
Freckleton, Catherine
Frostick alias Harris, Ruth,
  alias Jones, Mary
Gargle, Elizabeth
Gew, John
Groom, Jonathan (QS)
Hackett, Peter
Hancock, Susannah
Harbridge, John (QS)
Hardy, Samuel
Harrington, Jeremiah (QS)
Harris, Mary
Hawkins, Mary
Hook, Richard
Howard alias Hayward, John (QS)
Hunter, James (QS)
Ibbert, Charles
Ingram, Mary
Jackson, James
Johnson, John
Jones, Henry
Jones, Mary
Jones, Richard
Kennedy, Matthew - for life

Kennedy, Patrick
Kenny, Patrick
Kenny, William
Kinghorn, James
Knowles, Thomas
Larcher, Joseph
Leveridge, John - 14 yrs
Levy, Moses Simon
Mahoney, Thomas (QS)
Mannon, Mary
Marshall, Scoter
McDonald, John - for life
McGee, Mary
Mitchell, Ralph
Morris, Thomas
Murphy, John
Murphy, Patrick (QS)
Musgrave, Andrew
Natt, John
Parker, Robert
Parr, John (QS)
Payne, Elizabeth (QS)
Peddington, John
Pollard, John (QS) - runaway
Polock, James
Porter, Solomon (QS)
Powell, Sarah
Price, Thomas - for life
Putnam, Mary wife of John
Radford, Sarah wife of Samuel
Salt, William (QS)
Shin alias Slim, Abraham (QS)
  - pardoned
Sibthorpe, Ann (QS)
Smith, Jane
Smith alias Coffery, Thomas
Smith, William
Steel, William (QS)
Swanscombe, Richard
Thomas, Thomas
Throup, James - to transport himself
Turvel, Ann
Vigures, James
Virgine, Catherine (QS)
Walker, Martha
Walters, John (QS)
Watts, Ann
Welch, Hannah
Welch, James (QS)
Wells, Granby Thomas
West, William
Westcoate, Peter

Wheeler, Thomas
White, George
Wilson, John
Wilson, Mary

Surrey

Brooker, Richard - for life
Lassam, Ann wife of Richard (QS)
Mullens, Daniel (QS)

Felons transported by William Stevenson and William Randolph, merchants, [by the *Restoration*, Capt. James Thomas] from Bristol to Maryland and registered in Baltimore Co. records on 23 Oct 1771 (MSA: CR 40,516 ff. 90-118; NGSQ).

Bristol

Butt, William - 14 yrs
Millidge, Mary
Seal, Ann - 14 yrs
Treharn, Margaret

Davis, Edward - 14 yrs
Davis, Richard - 14 yrs
Phillips, Evan - 14 yrs
Roberts, Hugh
Twiss, Elizabeth
Twiss, Mary wife of William

Cheshire

McCartney, George

Devon

Earle alias Saunders, Nicholas
Freney, Elizabeth (QS)
Haynes, Thomas
Luscombe, John (QS)

Somerset

Iverson, Peter
Mitchell, John
Perriman, Betty
Skull alias Scull, William - 14 yrs
Sugar, Edward (QS)
Woolcott, George

Dorset

Oldis, Sarah - 14 yrs

Staffordshire

Cook, Charles alias Holm, George alias
Peel, James
Dangerfield, Samuel
Dickenson, Robert - 14 yrs
Foster, Henry
Jevon, Daniel
Rushton, Thomas
Thornway, James - 14 yrs
Wilkes, Thomas (QS)
Wood, Mary (QS)

Gloucestershire

Dickenson, Amy
Jockam, John
Millard, Thomas
Moss, Charles

Herefordshire

Downes, James
Jenkins, Thomas - 14 yrs

Warwickshire

Cross, William
Eaton, Mary wife of George
Jackson, Mary
Nash, Mary
Phillips, John - for life
Roper, James
Rudge, William (QS) - runaway
Ruston, Alice

Monmouthshire

John, William - 14 yrs
Jones, Henry - 14 yrs

Shropshire

Bennett, George - 14 yrs

226

Worcestershire

Dudley, Joseph
Field, Mary

Hinton, John - runaway
Jones, Edward
Southall, Joseph

Felons transported from London to Virginia by the *Justitia*, Capt. Neil Gillis, in January 1772. (PRO: T1/483/47).

Essex

Francis, John - 14 yrs
Lingley, Elizabeth
March, George - 14 yrs
Smith, Joseph
Wakeling, John - 14 yrs

Hertfordshire

Banks, William - 14 yrs
Field, John - 14 yrs
Herrington, Roger
Rowles, Daniel - 14 yrs

Kent

Acres, Aaron (QS)
Acres, Samuel (QS)
Armstrong, John - 14 yrs
Ghent, Timothy (QS)
Labeur, Francis (QS)
Stannard, Stephen (QS) - pardoned

London

Anderson, Luke
Angus, Robert - pardoned
Austin, Alice
Barnes, Samuel
Bowler, John - pardoned
Clare, Benjamin
Clark, John
Cooke, Stephen
Cox, John
Davis, Jane
Dennison, Richard
Dowley, Richard
Eleazer, Jacob - respited
Evans, Edward
Eyre, John (Esq) - died in Va
Ferguson, Robert
Field, Mary
Gray, James

Grimstead, William
Hall, William
Hammack, Edward - pardoned
Harding, John
Hardy, Duncan
Hawkins, Mary
Hoare, William Grenville
Howlett, William
Hughes, William
Humphreys, Lewis
Hunter, Anthony
Knight, James
Levy, Elias
Levy, Henry
Levy, Judah
Lluellin, John
Loveday, Joseph - runaway
Maffett, Samuel
Miller, Daniel
Mills, Joseph
Mitchell, James
Moody, John
Paris, John
Peele, James
Perrot, John
Phillips, Joseph
Porter, Daniel
Roberts, Charles
Russell, Joseph
Showell, Thomas
Solomons, Lazarus
Spinks, Thomas
Stowell, George
Summerhayes, Ann - 14 yrs
Taylor, Edward
Ward, Ann
Watson, Anthony
West, Ann
Westbrook, William
White, Edward
White, John
Young, Ann - pardoned

Middlesex

Abraham, Judith wife of Solomon
   - pardoned
Akerman, Ann
Allen, William
Aspland, William
Backarac alias Abrahams
   alias Isaacs, Lyon
Bale, George
Barrett, John
Bayliss, William
Bean, Mary wife of John
Bedkin, Henry
Bevington, Francis (QS)
Bigglestone, Richard
Blackwell, Deborah - pardoned
Blundy, Charles (QS)
Bolton, Sarah (QS)
Booth, William (QS) - runaway
Brace, John
Bryant, Patrick
Burges, Thomas - pardoned
Butterfield, Ann wife of William
Cain, John, alias Blakeney, William
Cannon, Michael (QS)
Carroll, Jane wife of Peter
Carter, John
Castle, John - respited
Chattenau, Anthony
Cobham, James
Coblin, William (QS)
Coleman, Richard
Cooper alias Foster, Sarah
Cox, Sarah
Craven, Francis
Creamer alias McCarty, Michael
Danks, Mary
Davison, John
Dodd, Thomas
Doncaster, Elizabeth
Dupere, Ann
Earl, Nathaniel (QS)
Edgers, Mary
Edwards, William (QS)
Edwards, Richard
Evans, James (QS)
Farrell, Peter
Fileman, Philip (QS)
Fisher, Thomas
Forster, Mary
Francis, Dorothy (QS)

Gibson, James (QS)
Glover, James
Gordon, Margaret (QS)
Hall, Mary wife of John - 14 yrs
Hanes, Thomas
Harman, John (QS)
Harpin, Elizabeth
Hawes, Thomas - pardoned
Haydon, John - runaway
Henley, Ardell
Herbert, Thomas - runaway
Higgins, Ann
Hill, Elijah - runaway
Hill, Elizabeth
Hipsey, Elizabeth
Holloway, Robert
Hughes, John
Ireland, Edward
Jones, James
Jones, John
Jones, William
Kennedy, Michael
Keys, Thomas (QS)
Kinner, Thomas (QS) - pardoned
Knott, John
Lancaster, Mary
Leppingwell, James
Littlejohn, Elizabeth
Maddens, Samuel
Marchinton, Matthew
Matthews, Eleanor
May, James, alias Mills, Emanuel
McDonald, Rachael
McGuire, Dennis (QS)
Metcalf, James (QS)
Metcalf, William (QS)
Millett, Mary
Missiter, Richard
Mitchell, John
Mitchell, William
Moor, Nicholas
Murphy, John
Neil alias O'Neil, Cornelius
Nelson, Peter (QS)
Newman, Nash (QS)
Niccoli alias Niccolin, William
Ogilby, Thomas
Overton, John (QS)
Payne, William - 14 yrs
Phillips, Thomas
Porson, Sarah
Prescott, George (QS)

Price, Edward
Price, Peter (QS)
Pritchard, Sarah
Quinn, Thomas
Read, John
Reason, William
Rice, Stephen (QS)
Rich, Samuel
Roberts, William
Saunders, Lion (QS)
Saville, John
Shaw, John
Smith, Thomas.
Smith, William (QS)
Stevens, John
Stream, John (QS) - pardoned
Sullivan, James
Thomas, Ann
Tireman, John
Turvey, William
Walker, Francis
Wall, Mary
Ward, Elizabeth wife of Thomas
Ward, Thomas - 14 yrs
Warren, Thomas (QS)
Weaver, William
Webber, John (QS)
Welch, Elizabeth
Wharton, Thomas - runaway
Wilkinson, James

Wilson, Mary (QS)
Wooley, Richard (QS)
Wyld, John

Surrey

Bradley, Andrew
Callaghan, Thomas (QS)
Carter, Robert - 14 yrs
Clark, Joseph
Deane, William (QS)
Evans, George - for life
Fox, William - 14 yrs
Fry, John - for life
Hollings, Robert
Jenkins, William (QS) - runaway
Jones, John (QS)
McKenzie, John
Moss, Thomas
Parrott, John Jr. - 14 yrs
Richardson, William - 14 yrs
Smith, Ann (QS) - 14 yrs
Strudwick, Thomas - 14 yrs
White, Thomas - for life
Wood, John - 14 yrs

Sussex

Pearce, Edward
Smith, Henry, alias Johnson, William

Felons transported from London to Virginia by the _Thornton_, Capt. John Kidd, in April 1772. (PRO: T1/490/75).

Buckinghamshire

Kent, Richard
Mires, Thomas
Williams, Ann

Essex

Alcock alias Taylor, Robert - 14 yrs
Chesterman, Thomas - 14 yrs
Gooch, John
Hale, Richard - 14 yrs
Hall, William
Lawe, William - 14 yrs
Stopps, Thomas
Telsted, Mark
Turner, Samuel
Whitecake, John - 14 yrs

Willes, Theodore

Hertfordshire

Barnes, William - 14 yrs
Bennett, John - 14 yrs
Robnut, Edward
Todd, James - 14 yrs
White alias Jennings, William

Kent

Barner, Henry - 14 yrs
Bingham, Elizabeth
Bluck, William
Calles alias Careless, Robert
Clubb, Alexander - for life - runaway
Cole, George - 14 yrs

Day, Robert - 14 yrs
Herring, Elizabeth (QS)
Ingram, Joseph - for life - runaway
Knight, Peter (QS) - runaway
Mansen, Thomas (QS)
Smith, Elizabeth
Toms, Edward - for life
Walker, Ann
Whalon, Pevice
White, Randall alias William
- 14 yrs

London

Barnes, William
Bates, William - 14 yrs
Bland, William
Brown, Ann
Coleman, John
Collett, John
Cooke, Peter
Dunnet, John
Edwards, Henry
Exall, Susannah
Golding, Richard
Greeves, Robert
Herbert, Benjamin - pardoned
Hind, David - runaway
Hurst, Mary
La Ross, John - pardoned
Martin, William
May, Samuel
Messeter, Hannah
Morgan, James
Newland, James
Phillips, Levy
Pollard, Mary
Ringing, John
Sells, James
Shaw, Samuel
Smith, John
Stevens, George
Talmy alias Felmy, John
  alias Blind Jack the Kidnapper
Thomas, Richard
Welch, Edward
Wilcocks, Robert
Williams, William

Middlesex

Almond, John

Altop, Thomas
Angle, Ann
Banks, David
Barrett, Edward (QS) - pardoned
Beeks, Sarah - 14 yrs
Bishop, John
Brewer, Henry (QS)
Broadwood, James - pardoned
Brown, Ann
Brown, William Trueman
Burbridge, Thomas
Carter alias Gasford, Samuel
  - for life - runaway
Cavenagh, Thomas
  - to transport himself
Clark, James
Cotter, Eleanor
Cross, Elizabeth
Cullen, John (QS)
Davis, John (QS)
Davis, John
Davis, Rebecca
Dowley, Lawrence
Fenley, Patrick
Flendell, Joseph - 14 yrs
Fletcher, Joseph
Ford, John (QS)
Forster, Joseph (QS)
Freshwater, Sarah
Godbolt, James - for life
Griffiths, George
Gulley, Richard - pardoned
Hart, William
Hines, John (QS)
Hunt, James
Hurdley, John - pardoned
Jenkins, Thomas - 14 yrs
Jennings, James
Jones, Mary (QS)
Jordan, Joseph
Keefs, Rose - 14 yrs
Kilbert, John - 14 yrs
Kirk, John
Landon, Isaac
Lewis, John - 14 yrs
Linnick alias Baker, Robert
Lish, Thomas
Lloyd, Joseph (QS)
London, Charlotte (QS)
Lyon, Charles - 14 yrs
Lyons, Catherine
McCloud, William (QS)

Millard, John
Miller, Maximilian
Morgan, Sarah (QS)
Murphy alias Knight, Mary
Pearce, Richard - 14 yrs
Rogers, Michael
Russell, David (QS)
Saythuss, James, alias Dumb Jemmy
Seymour, William
Skelton, Mary (QS)
Smith, Edward
Smith, Joseph
Smith, Rebecca
Street, Ann
Sutcliff, Margaret (QS)
Thwaites, William - for life
Trives, Robert
Trotter, James
Wade, Joseph - 14 yrs- runaway
Walker, Robert
Ward alias Parker, Thomas
Ward, William alias John - runaway
West, John
Wilton, Samuel
Woodley, Benjamin
Young, Henry (QS)
Young alias Smith, John

Surrey

Bawcutt, William
Carty, Peter
Chapman, Thomas - 14 yrs
Hunt, John - 14 yrs
Jackson, John - 14 yrs
Levy, Abraham
Lewis, Joseph (QS)
Nicholson, William (QS) - runaway
Pearcey, Charles - 14 yrs
Randall, Thomas - 14 yrs
Shepherd, William
Smith, Joseph
Smith, William - 14 yrs - runaway
Sutherland, John - 14 yrs
Taylor, William
Weldon, Robert William - runaway
Wilkins, Thomas - 14 yrs

Sussex

Bartlett, Hannah wife of George
(QS)
Bennett, William
Pellett, John (QS)

Felons transported by William Stevenson and William Randolph, merchants, from Bristol to Maryland and registered in Baltimore Co. records on 24 July 1772. (MSA: CR 40,516 ff. 123-184).

Devon

Armstrong, Charles
Bennett alias Baker, Thomas
Bowden, William alias Hill, John
Davy, Thomas - 14 yrs
Early, Ann
Goff, Richard - 14 yrs
Gothard, John Jr. - 14 yrs
Gothard, Sarah - 14 yrs
Hancock, William (QS)
Hancock, John (QS)
Harris, John (QS) - runaway
 - recognizance f. 191.
Holmes, John Jr.
Jury, Richard
Mager, John
Morrish, William
Newberry, John
 - recognizance f. 194.

Patterson, Robert (QS)
Russell, John of Exeter
Willcocks, Henry
Williams, Michael
Worth, Andrew (QS)

Dorset

Abell, William
Bennett, Walter
Bennett, William
Brown, Edward
Harbin, Joseph
Harding, James
Harding, Robert
Harris, George
Lush, William
Morris, Ann wife of William - 14 yrs
Slake, John

231

Gloucestershire

Dayley, Thomas
Fluck, Richard
Fream, John
Howell, John
Keen, Richrd
Knight, John
Lusty, Anrew (QS)
Marsh, Edward
Revers Robert
Roberts, Henry
Slye, Robert
Turk, Esau

Herefordshire

Bird, Anthony
Brookes alias Brooker, Susanna
Paling, Thomas
Pritchard alias Williams, William
Thomas, Robert - 14 yrs

Monmouthshire

Carter, Joseph
Harris, George
Williams, Thomas

Shropshire

Bennett, Thomas
Boot, Daniel
Davies, John
Johnson, Thomas
Jones, Jane
Kitchen, Samuel - 14 yrs
Lambath, Ephraim
Mansell, Samuel
Robertson, John
Wilkinson, Thomas
Williams, Mary

Somerset

Atwool, Thomas
Bennett, Henry
Bince, William

Chamberlain, Samuel
Cox, Ann - 14 yrs
Gard, Christopher (QS)
Gillard, George
Harvey, Thomas (QS)
Jeffery, Francis - 14 yrs
Manners, William (QS)
Marsham, James - 14 yrs
Sharp, Thomas (QS)
Stevens, Robert
Stock, Ann

Staffordshire

Brown, John
Heatley, Ralph - 14 yrs - runaway
Nabbs, Thomas
Parker, Mary - runaway
Reynolds, Thomas - 14 yrs
Richardson, John - runaway
Savage, George - 14 yrs
Smith, William
Steel, Joseph - 14 yrs
Wright, William - 14 yrs

Wiltshire

Brookes, George
    - recognizance f. 197.
Brown, Mary wife of Henry
Burrel, George alias Black George
    alias Othello
Glass, Henry - 14 yrs
Hurst, George
Martin, Richard - 14 yrs
Maton, Ann - 14 yrs
Parrott, John - for life
Poulsum, Mary
Spratt, Sarah
Tuck, Philip - died
Winter, Thomas (QS)

Worcestershire

Evans, Samuel
Gatfield, Margaret
Griffiths (alias Turner), Mary

232

Felons transported from London to Virginia by the *Grange Bay*, Capt. Neil Somerville, in July 1772. (PRO: T1/490/68).

Hertfordshire

Burgess, Thomas (QS)
Cocks, James (QS)
Penn, Matthew - for life

Kent

Colefoot, John (QS)
Pyall, David (QS)

Pyall, John (QS)
Ryley, James (QS)

Surrey

Acton, Thomas - for life
Lomas, Samuel (QS)
Mason, Edward (QS)
Webb, John (QS)

Felons transported from London to Virginia by the *Tayloe*, Capt. Dougal McDougal, in July 1772. (PRO: T1/490/62).

London

Adams, Thomas
Allen, David
Allie, Antonio
Barclay, Henry
Barrett, James
Bedford, William
Brady, Ann - 14 yrs
Brandett, Eleanor
Bristol, John
Brown alias MacDonald, James
Commings, John
Downton, George
Dudley, Joshua
Ford, Charles
Gregory, James
Hancock, James - for life
Hayes, Elizabeth (QS)
Healey, John - pardoned
Hill, Thomas
Holyman, Richard
Lucas, James
Lyons, Abraham
Lyons, John - 14 yrs
Masters, Thomas
Mathews, Elizabeth
Molson, Joseph
Price, Thomas
Raymond, John
Samuel, Samuel
Spours, John
Steel, Charles
Warsdale, Francis
West, Luke

Middlesex

Adams alias Stanley, Thomas - 14 yrs
Ashley, Ann
Ayres, Robert
Baldwin, Charlotte
Barry, Edward - 14 yrs
Blackgrove, John
Blunkill, William
Blunt, Jane wife of William
Bouch, John (QS)
Bowers, John - 14 yrs
Bowman, Joseph alias James - 14 yrs
Bowyer, Thomas - pardoned
Bransgrove, Edward - 14 yrs
Brayne, Mary - 14 yrs
Brown, Elizabeth (QS)
Burton, George
Cain, Job (QS)
Cain, Nathaniel
Carryl, John (QS)
Cartwright, James
Chapperlin, Mary
Clayton, James
Clayton, John (QS)
Cole, James (QS)
Cook, John
Cook, Thomas - pardoned
Collins, John, alias Jones, Thomas
Conway, John (QS)
Cook, Bridget
Cook, John
Cox, Benjamin
Crofts, Thomas
Crow, John

233

Davis, William
Dawson, John - runaway
Day, John
Drake, William
Effen, Elizabeth
Elliot, Eleanor
Evans, Catherine
Fellamy, Elizabeth (QS)
Flint, John (QS)
Folling, Cecilia (QS)
Fryer, William
Gainer, Thomas
Garbutt, Richard
Gardiner, Mark (QS)
George, William
Gilbert alias Phillips, James John
Gom, James
Greatrix, Samuel
Green alias Greenaway, Joseph
Gunn, Mary
Hall, Richard
Hayes, Elizabeth (QS)
Hicks alias White, Ann
Hitchcock, John - 14 yrs
Hodd, Thomas
Holmes, Thomas
Hudson, Ann
Hunt, John (QS)
Jewell, William (QS) - runaway
Johnson, Samuel
Jones, Edward - 14 yrs
Jones, Elizabeth
Jones, Thomas
Josephs, Nathan (QS)
Kendrick, James (QS)
King, Elizabeth
Kirke, Thomas
Lairey alias Laurey, Jeremiah
Leech, Andrew
Lewis, Daniel (QS)
Liptrap, Isaac - 14 yrs
Lumm, Joseph - 14 yrs
Major, James (QS)
Manly alias Mansby, William
  - 14 yrs - runaway
Manning, Edward
Marshall, William (2)
Mascada, Francis, alias Car, Peras,
  alias Da Silva, Joseph - for life
Mason, John
McDuff, John (QS)

Middleton, Alexander
Miller, Edward (QS)
Mitchell, Adam (QS)
Mitchell, James (QS)
Murphy, Edward (QS)
Page, Thomas - 14 yrs
Paine, Henry (QS)
Peverley, Rebecca (QS)
Piggott, Mary (QS)
Price, Hugh (QS)
Price, Mary (QS)
Price, Simon
Procter, William
Rance, Mary
Rayton, Joseph (QS)
Richards, Richard (QS)
Robinson alias Roberts, William (QS)
Robinson, William (QS)
Rook, Thomas
Row, Edward (QS)
Rowling, Thomas (QS)
Ryer, James
Saul, Henry
Sharpless alias Hall, John
Sherrar, William (QS)
Smith, Richard (QS)
Spicer, Elizabeth
Stevens, James (QS)
Stokes, William (QS)
Thorne, Daniel - 14 yrs
Tudor, Hervey alias Slingsby
Upham, Thomas (QS)
Vainwright, John (QS)
Vender, Thomas
Wallis, Robert
Ward, Thomas (QS)
Waters, John - 14 yrs - pardoned
Webster, Mary
Welch, Andrew - 14 yrs
Wells, Jeremiah - 14 yrs
Whiley, John (QS)
Whitfield, Henry
Wiggins, Mary (QS)
Williamhurst, Alice (QS)
Williams, Elizabeth
Wilson, Jane (QS)
Wilson, Richard
Yorkshire, Thomas (QS)
Young, Elizabeth
Younger, Thomas - pardoned

Felons transported by William Stevenson and William Randolph, merchants, from Bristol to Maryland and registered in Baltimore Co. records on 21 December 1772. (MSA: CR 40,516 ff.208-233).

Cheshire

Elliot, Michael

Cornwall

Chapman, Richard (QS)
Easam, James - 14 yrs
Eastlake, Pascoe (QS)
Lyne, Benedictus (QS)

Devon

Beacham, George - 14 yrs - runaway
Binn, Mary
Hall, William
Hole, John - 14 yrs
Kent, Stephen
Langdon, Ann (QS)
Smith, George (QS)

Dorset

Whiffen, Joseph (QS)

Gloucestershire

Austin, Robert (QS)

Hampshire

Gibbons, William
Kidd, John
Linnerton, George
Matthews, Moses

Herefordshire

Swindles, John - recognizance f. 239.

Monmouthshire

Williams, Jones

Shropshire

Fletcher, George (QS)

Somerset

Barnett, Betty wife of William - 14 yrs
Collins, William
Daniel, John
Legg, Catharine (QS)
Ley, Robert (QS)
Seward, James - 14 yrs
Shears, Leonard
Snailum, Thomas (QS)
Tilsey alias Edwards, Mary (QS)
Warburton, William

Staffordshire

Billingham, Thomas
Ford, William
Holdturn (Holden), Thomas
    - recognizance f..239.
Knowles, Clement - runaway
Lloyd, Thomas (QS)
Rock, Joseph
Smith, John

Warwickshire

Bagot, Ann
Biddle, John
Boff, John
Bryan, Stephen aliasThomas
Cashmore, Edward
Craft, John - 14 yrs
Eaves, Edward - 14 yrs
Edgerton, Ann wife of Thomas
    - runaway
Heritage, Sarah wife of Richard
Hunt, William
Mogg, John
Parkes, Joseph
Piercy, Charles
Reddall, Mary wife of Samuel
Rowley, Ann
Suffolk, Richard - runaway
Webb, Thomas
Webster, John

Wiltshire   Alford, Nathaniel (QS)

Felons transported from London to Virginia by the *Justitia*, Capt. Finlay Gray, in January 1773. (CLRO: London & LMA: Middlesex Bonds; Home Circuit records).

Buckinghamshire

Essex, Richard
Sipthorp, Alexander

Essex

Allen, Samuel
Deeks, Thomas
Donnahaugh, Dennis
Hillingworth, Richard
Ottley, Susannah
Scudder, John

Hertfordshire

Bradley, Thomas
Puttenham alias Putnam, William

Kent

Callihan, John (QS)
Carpenter, Joseph
Constable, Sarah (QS)
Gordon, John - for life
Hogden, Nehemiah
Jones, Elizabeth (QS)
Reeves, Joseph - runaway
Rolph, Thomas
Steel, John - runaway
Tucker, Emanuel (QS)

London

Apps, Thomas
Asher, Isaac
Atwood, Hannah
Blake, Jane
Brown, Joseph
Collins, Thomas
Dickens, John
Dubden, Valentine
Fielding, John
Harrad, Martha
Hindes, Terence
Jones, David

Jones, Robert - to transport himself
Leary, John - 14 yrs
Litners, Thomas
May, Peter
Nurse, Catherine
Pearce, John - pardoned
Porter, William
Pratt, Thomas - runaway
Risdale, William
Row, William
Silvey, Aaron
Smith, Martha
Tucker, Joseph - pardoned
Walker, Alice - runaway
Wall, Charles
Wilkins, Thomas
Williams, Thomas

Middlesex

Aistrop, Robert - 14 yrs
Allwright, Richard
Andrews, Mary
Arlinge, Francis
Assent, James - 14 yrs
Bartram, Anthony (QS)
Bateman als Bates, Thomas (QS)
Baxter, James (QS)
Best, Richard
Birks, John
Blackburn, Benjamin - 14 yrs
Bonniface, William
Boyle, Alice
Burling, Thomas
Burton, Edmund - 14 yrs
Butcher, Thomas
Byrne, Arthur
Carmody, Michael (QS)
Chandler, Joseph (QS) - pardoned
Cherry, Elias - pardoned
Clark, Mary
Cole, Richard - 14 yrs
Coleman, Henry
Collins, John
Collins, Richard
Cook, George

Coster, William
Cox, Peter (QS)
Curd, Christopher
Davis, Sarah - 14 yrs
Davis, Thomas
Dempsey, James - for life
Dooley alias Dowley, William (QS)
Duffey, James
Dunn, John
Durden, Benjamin
Eaton, Ann - pardoned
Evans, Elias (QS)
Evans, William
Farrell, John - runaway
Fitzgerald, James
French, David
Fryers, John - 14 yrs
Grayley, Francis
Green, Henry
Green, William
Greenwood, Elizabeth
Hadley, David
Haslip, Thomas
Hatch, William - pardoned
Haughton, Elizabeth
Hicks, Elizabeth
Holmes, Richard
Howard, Henry
Hurst, Henry - runaway
James, William
Johnson, Benjamin - 14 yrs
Johnson, William
Jolland, Elizabeth wife of Robert
Jolland, John
Jones, Deborah
Jones, John
Jordan, Sarah,
    alias wife of Samuel Blythe
Kem alias Butcher, George - 14 yrs
Kilke, Esther
Kirkman, Sarah
Ladle, Michael
Lamb, John
Leo, John (John William)
Lever, James
Levy, Solomon - 14 yrs
Lewis, Francis
Masey, Thomas - 14 yrs
McKenzie, Eleanor
Morton, Mary wife of Robert
Naylor, Susannah
Nixon, Francis

O'Conner, Timothy
Parker, William
Plumer, William (QS)
Poulton, Isaac - 14 yrs
Powell, Eleanor
Redwood, William - pardoned
Rhodes, Samuel
Richards, William
Riley, John (QS)
Roberts, Richard
Rogers, John - 14 yrs
Rye, George
Rymer, George
Servant, Mary
Sheldon, Mary
Silver, Ann - 14 yrs
Simons, Abraham
Simons, Simon
Smith, Mary
Smith, William
Solomon, Aaron
Spencer, Mary
Spires, William
Steale, William - runaway
Stint, Richard
Taylor, Abraham (QS)
Taylor, James (QS)
Truebridge, Mary
Turner, William (QS)
Wade, Sarah
Walker, Thomas (QS)
Ward, John
Wardens, James
Welch, Philip - pardoned
White, Margaret
Wilds, Hannah
Williams, Lewis - 14 yrs
Wise, Ann
Wood alias Johnson
    alias Smith, Elizabeth*
Wood, John - runaway

Surrey

Brown, Thomas
Eaton, John - runaway
Fitness, Eden
Hughes, Joseph (QS)
Pobgee, William - runaway
Priest, Thomas
Rhodes, Thomas
Robb, Peter - runaway

Rolls, John
Shearing, Mary
Taylor, James
Thrift, John - runaway
Turtle, William Sr.
Wells, Thomas (QS)

Sussex

Jeffery, Mary
Patterson, William
Penfold, Thomas
Wilson, Samuel

*Sentenced but not on bond

Felons transported by William Stevenson and William Randolph, merchants, from Bristol to Maryland and registered in Baltimore Co. records on 10 April 1773. (MSA: CR 40,516 ff. 241-273).

Cornwall

Blackford, William
Congdon, Elizabeth wife of Faithful
Hayne, Philip - 14 yrs
Hoyle, John (QS)
Strong, John - 14 yrs - runaway
Witheridge, Stephen (QS)

Gloucestershire

Atkins, George (QS)
Beard, Samuel
Bird, William
Esbury, James (QS)
Flower, James (QS)
Greenwood, Thomas - 14 yrs - runaway
Hemming, William
Jarrett, George (QS)
Jones, Richard
Nelmes, Mary
Newth, Thomas (QS)
Price, Mary
Rooke, Richard Jr. - for life
Shepperd, Philip (QS)
Taylor, Thomas
Townsend, Thomas - 14 yrs
Tyler, Edward - 14 yrs
 - recognizance f. 241.
Wilkins, Mary - for life

Williams, Thomas - for life

Monmouthshire

Griffith, William
Hopkins, Thomas (QS)
Williams, Jervis

Somerset

Best, George - 14 yrs
Bew, Robert (QS)
Conybeare, Ann (QS) - 14 yrs
Cox, James - 14 yrs
Harris, James - 14 yrs
Symes, Joseph - 14 yrs
Thomas, James (QS)
Webb, James (QS)
Weller, Sarah
Willis, Richard (QS)

Worcestershire

Brewton, Thomas - 14 yrs
Cox, William
Glover, Benjamin
Hanley, Edward
Smith, Daniel
Smith, Samuel
Tedstill, Christopher

Felons transported by William Stevenson and William Randolph, merchants, from Bristol to Maryland and registered in Baltimore Co. records on 22 June 1773. (MSA: CR 40,516 ff. 277-341).

Cheshire

Greenacres, Ann

Powell, Sarah wife of William (QS)

Cornwall

Clements, Samuel Felix
Harefoot alias Halford, John
Harvey, Edward
Harvey, Richard - 14 yrs
Heathier, William
Jewel, William
Mallick, John
Matthews alias Davies
   alias Davey,William
Mitchell alias Gillard, Scipio
Oatie, William
Odger, William
Puncheon, Lawrence
Uren alias Calebna, Jane

Devon

Caddugan, Philip (QS)
Marsh, William - 14 yrs
Reed, Mary (QS)
Squire, William - 14 yrs

Dorset

Ball, John Sr.
Foot, Simon
Goddard, James Jr. - runaway
House, James
Pound, John - 14 yrs
Trimby, Stephen - 14 yrs

Gloucestershire

Bennett, Thomas - 14 yrs
Chew, William - 14 yrs
Drayton, Samuel - 14 yrs
Eastbury, James
Evans, Samuel - 14 yrs
Garne, Thomas - 14 yrs
Newth, Thomas (QS)
Smith, James - 14 yrs
Soul, Thomas - 14 yrs
Wilkes, William
Williams, Jarrett - 14 yrs

Hampshire

Bagwell, Mary
Barns, Due - 14 yrs
Blackmore, Robert

Bower alias Bowens, Oliver
Bradley, Charles
Burke, William
Cook, William - pardoned
Fisher, Joseph
Ford, Thomas
Hawkins, John
Hebb, Thomas
Laws, George
Mott, Richard - 14 yrs
Randall, Thomas - pardoned
Reed, John
Thomson, James
Vernoll, George - 14 yrs - runaway
Warre, William Jr.
Whoulfrey, John

Herefordshire

Baker, William
Davis, Luke - 14 yrs
Gritton, John
Isaac, John
Jones, George
Parle, James
Thomas, James

Monmouthshire

Evans, William (QS)
Godwin, William
Kenvin, Evan

Shropshire

Brinsford, Thomas - 14 yrs
Davis, Thomas - 14 yrs
Lloyd, Matthew - 14 yrs
Smith, Thomas - 14 yrs
Tipton, Francis - 14 yrs
Williams, Edward - 14 yrs - runaway
Williams, Richard

Somerset

Burge, Thomas Jr.
Collins, John
Cox, John
Ellery, John
Fear, Edmund - for life
Fuller, Thomas alias Smith alias
Shorter, William - 14 yrs - runaway

Hardwick, John - 14 yrs
Lush, William
Powell, John
Rich, Samuel
Shortoe, George
Sidwell, Jonathan
Slocombe, Isaac - 14 yrs
Smith, George

Staffordshire

Biddesford, Thomas
Blackmore alias Blackman, William
Burrows, Richard - 14 yrs
Colley, Joseph - 14 yrs
Evans alias Burgess, John - pardoned
Greenhough, Thomas
Hardware, Charles - 14 yrs
Killman, Joseph
Town alias Towle alias Towe
  alias Craddock, James - 14 yrs
Wood, Robert (QS)
Woodhall, Edward

Warwickshire

Andrews, Thomas - 14 yrs
Bate, Benjamin
Birch, Richard - for life
Mason, Charles

Taylor, William
Taylor, Jane wife of John
Tuckey, John

Wiltshire

Cook, Joseph
Cundit, John (QS)
Draper, Simon
Draper, Thomas
Grist, Charles.
Hicks, William - bond by Elias Barniby.
Jordan, Thomas
Long alias Bartelott, Robert - for life
Martin, Henry (QS)
Morgan alias Slade, Moses.
Pitt, William Moss - 14 yrs - runaway
Ridgely alias Bartelott, George - for life
White, John
Wiltshire, James (QS)
Basil alias Boswell, Timothy - runaway

Worcestershire

Basil alias Boswell, Henry - runaway
Phillips, Benjamin
Powis, Samuel - runaway
Shepherd, Charles - for life
Stephens, Thomas - for life
Thornbury, Mary

Felons transported from London by the *Thornton*, Capt. John Kidd, in May 1773 & registered in Anne Arundel Co. records on 3 July 1773. (CLRO: London & LMA: Middlesex Bonds; MSA: CR 40,516 ff. 16-33)

Buckinghamshire

Bignell, Joseph
Wadcase, Richard

Essex

Allen, John - 14 yrs
Fell, Edward - 14 yrs
Holten, Benjamin - 14 yrs
Kemp, George - 14 yrs
Ladd, John - 14 yrs
Montford, Robert
Sack, John Jr. - 14 yrs
Taylor, Michael Thomas - for life
Walden, James
Wilson, Elizabeth - 14 yrs

Hertfordshire

Clements, Mark - 14 yrs
Crawley, Jacob
Cutler, Thomas alias Weedon
Honeybond, William -14 yrs
Pickett, Henry - for life
Williams, John - 14 yrs

Kent

Blanchett, William (QS) - runaway
Burwell, Richard alias Nash, John
  - 14 yrs
Clarke, Edmund - for life
Dawley, Francis
Drayson, Gabriel

240

Ewens, William - 14 yrs
Frazer, Henry - runaway
Harris, Ann
Hatton, William - for life
Hope, William
Lewis, William - 14 yrs
Maddox, Elizabeth
Nash, William
Pattson, John - 14 yrs
Payne, William - 14 yrs
Smith, Henry
Sneesby, Richard
Uden, William - for life
Whitewood, John (QS)
Wilkins, Phebe

London

Armstrong, George - runaway
Armstrong, Robert - runaway
Ayris, William (QS)
Batty, James
Carter, James
Collins, Timothy
Cotterell, William
Davis, William
Daw, Michael
Duncan, John
Franklin, Thomas
Glin (Glyn), Sarah
Johnson, David
Kilroy, Bernard
Lazarus, Isaac
Plumb, John - pardoned
Reed alias Sumner, Margaret
Rhodes, Thomas
Singleton, Bridget - pardoned
Slinney, Bridget
Smithers, Ann - pardoned
Summers, Thomas
Walker, Mary
Whitehead, Henry

Middlesex

Baker, John
Baldwin, John (QS)
Bartram, Anthony (QS)
Benn, William
Bilth, James (QS)
Bird, Thomas
Boyde, James

Branston, John (QS)
Burn, Timothy
Burnham, John (QS)
Burrill, Thomas
Carney, John (QS)
Casey, Mary
Cayton, William
Chameron, Mary Catherine
Cole, John (QS)
Corpe, Richard - pardoned
Dalton, William
Darling, Robert
Davis, Elizabeth
Denman, Robert
Dunn, Patrick
Eades, John
East alias Wiggington, John (QS)
    - pardoned
Evans, Elizabeth (QS)
Every, Mary wife of John
Fitzgerald, Eleanor - runaway
Flood, Frances (QS)
Goodwin, Mary
Greatwood, James
Gregory, Catherine
Hagan, Mary
Haggett, William
Hamilton, John
Harcourt, Mary (QS)
Herring, Henry
Hobbs, James
Hollis, William alias Berk, Thomas
    - pardoned
Hudson, John
Johnson, Timothy (QS)
Jones, John (2)
Jones, Sarah
King, Richard
Kitchenside, Abraham
Lawson, Isabella
Lever, James
Locup, Mary (QS)
Lowe, Samuel - pardoned
Lymes, Herman
Marian, Nicholas
Mash, John
Melvin, Elliot (QS)
Nimmo, John (QS)
Osborn, Joseph
O'Neil, Charles (QS)
Palmer, Henry
Powell, John (QS)

Price, Sarah (QS)
Prior, Hannah (QS)
Radford, John
Reeves, Richard
Rigby, James (QS)
Robinson, John (QS)
Schults, Gotolph (QS)
Smith, Mary
Smith, William (2)
Stamford, James (QS)
Stone, James
Sullivan, Dennis
Tapp, Henry (QS)
Warren, Birtle
Whitehead, John
Willett, Ann
Witherspoon, Robert (QS)
Wood, Mary

Field, William (QS)
Garnett, John (QS)
Gravett, James (QS)
Hogg, Andrew (QS)
Isaacs, James - 14 yrs
Jones, John (QS)
Lenard, John (QS)
Morris, James (QS) - pardoned
Pyner, William (QS)
Roe, Hannah - 14 yrs
Simmons, Nicholas
Smith, Catherine - 14 yrs
Strudwick, George - 14 yrs
Thompson, Andrew (QS)
Turrell, Mary
Unrich, Rosina (QS)
Wilcox, John - 14 yrs
Worsfold, Thomas (QS)

Surrey

Sussex

Confield, Thomas (QS)
Dockerday, William (QS)

Trossill, William

Felons transported from Newcastle upon Tyne to Maryland by the *Adventure*, Capt. Wharton Wilson, in March 1773 and registered in Baltimore Co. records on 23 June 1773. (MSA: CR 40,516 ff. 354-360).

Durham

Northumberland

Adamson, Susannah wife of George
Atkinson, William (QS)
Chapman, William (QS)
Dodds, John
Harrison, William (QS) - runaway
Hodgson, John
Nixon, Margaret
Stewart, Margaret (QS)
Walker, Edmund (QS)
Walls, Dorothy

Blackburn, Thomas (QS)
Brown, Robert
Brown, William
Gibson, Isabel, spinster
Hart, Margaret (QS)
Innis, Ann (QS)
Lawson, John (QS)
Newton, George (QS)
Patterson, Robert
Robson, George
Sidey, Jane (QS)
Todd alias Smith, William
Wilson, Andrew (QS)
Wilson, James (QS) - runaway
Young, John (QS)

Felons transported from London by the *Hanover Planter*, Captain William McCulloch, in May 1773 & registered in Anne Arundel Co. records on 29 July 1773 (MSA: CR 40, 516 ff. 36-40).

London

Austin, Isaac
Boswell, Samuel
Brown, Richard - pardoned
Carragan, James
Compton, James
Connolly, Dennis
Dunn, Patrick
Dyer, Angelo
Emerton, John
Frickens, Mary
Gunn, Catherine
Halford, Joseph
Hughes, William - 14 yrs
Ingram, Elizabeth
Kipling, Robert - pardoned
Oliver, Mary
Read, Christian
Shean, James
Smith, Richard
Wyatt, John

Middlesex

Abbott, Ann
Abbott, Mary wife of John - pardoned
Atkinson, John - pardoned
Bagnall, John - runaway
Beazor, John
Beazor, Richard
Beeton, Maryon (Margaret)
Bevan, Matthew
Bilby, Richard
Bond, Thomas
Booth, William
Bray, James
Breakspear, Jane wife of John
  - pardoned
Bryan, Catherine
Bryant, Rowland (QS)
Cardiff, Thomas
Cato, William (QS)
Caton, Nicholas (QS)
Christopher, John
Coleman, John
Copes, John - 14 yrs
Corner, Richard
Davis, John Evan (QS)
Dean, Samuel
Devett, James
Dickens, Thomas (QS)

Dixon, John
Dowling, Richard
Duft, Hugh (QS)
Elinian, Robert (QS)
Farroll, John (QS)
Fisher, Joseph (QS)
Fossett, John
Francis, Phene - pardoned
Gill, Catherine
Godstone, William
Green, Robert
Grey, Henrietta (QS)
Griffin, John (QS)
Griffith alias Hatch, Ann
Griffiths, John (QS)
Groves, Sarah wife of John - pardoned
Harding, Francis (QS)
Harding, William
Herbert, William - pardoned
Hill, Mary (QS)
Hill, William (QS) - runaway
Holmes, Isaac
Humphrys, Samuel
Jones, Matthias
Jones, Thomas (QS)
Kennedy, James
Knight, John (QS) - runaway
Lawrence, John (QS)
Lewis, John (QS)
Lloyd, Sarah
Maddox, Elizabeth
Martin, James
Mason, Amey (QS)
McKInney, Thomas (QS)
Mercier, Francis
Mereden, Joseph
Mutkirke, William
Newings, Letitia (wife of John)
North, John - pardoned
Parish, Thomas (QS)
Procter, John
Roach, Richard (QS)
Rutlege, Thomas
Sheirs, Richard (QS)
Shields, Mary
Silvester, Thomas (QS) - pardoned
Simmons alias Symonds, John
Smith, William
Southam, Thomas (QS)
Spicer, Jonathan
Sullivan, Isabella (QS)
Sykes, Nathaniel (QS)

Taylor, Samuel (QS) - pardoned
Trainer, Patrick
Wale, William
Wallis, Margaret (QS)
Waters, William
West, Henry

Whitefoot, Thomas
Widgeon, Sarah (QS)
Williams, John (QS)
Williams, Thomas (2) (QS)
Wilson, James
Wilson, John

Felons transported from London to Virginia by the *Tayloe*, Capt. John Ogilvy, in July 1773. (CLRO: London Sessions records, LMA: Middlesex Bond & PRO: Home Circuit records).

Buckinghamshire

Duckett, Richard
Durham, Ralph
Simcock, Theophilus

Essex

Mansfield, Peter (QS)
Taylor, Thomas - for life
Pickell, Henry - for life

Kent

Alexander, William (QS)

London

Bannister, Mary
Barker, Joseph - runaway
Bird, John
Carter, Mary
Cherry, William
Covnett, John
Davis, Thomas
Forster, Mary
Grainger, Francis - for being at large
Hall, Mary
Jones, William
Lewes, Abraham
Marshall, Edward
Martin, Thomas
Morris, William
Murphy, Eleanor
Plodd, John Henry
Porter, Mary
Richards alias Monk, Joseph
Rossiter, Elizabeth
Shute, John Jr.
Styles, William

Waterhouse, Elizabeth wife of John
  - pardoned
Wood, Michael

Middlesex

Abrahams, Levy
Archer, Isaac
Archer, John
Asher. Levi
Bailey, John
Barrett, William
Beard alias Butcher, Charlotte
Benjamin, Samuel
Bird, John
Blaney alias Evans, William
Boothman, Jonathan - runaway
Burn, Thomas
Butler, Edward - runaway
Cherry, Elias - pardoned
Chresty, James
Cook, John
Craven, Edward
Davis, Ann
Dennison, Thomas
Dunbar, Jonathan
Duncomb, John
Etheridge, Sarah
Evans, Charles
Fitzmorris, John
Forbes, John
Fowler, John
Gahagan, John - for life
Garrett, Bartholomew
George, Richard
Goffee, John
Grant, Margaret wife of John
Groves, William
Haughton, William
Havilock, John - pardoned
Hide, Elizabeth wife of William

244

Jennings, George
Jones, Mary
Jones, Sarah
Lade, Edward
Levy, Jacob
Llewellin, Elizabeth
Lock, John
Lone, John
Lushby, William
Macarty, James
Malone, Abraham
Meakham, Samuel
Merchant, Stephen Jr.
Miller, Thomas
Mills, Eleanor wife of William
Monk, Joseph
Parnell, Nurse
Parsons, Margaret
Phillips, John
Plaistow, Samuel
Preston, Paul - runaway
Pritchard, John
Ring, Richard
Sage, James
Smith, John
Smith, Joseph
Smith, Mary
Starling, Edward
Strahan, Robert

Swann, Christie
Talbot, Mary
Thompson, Grace
Topham, Sarah
Vaughan, John
Vickers, John
Walklin, Thomas
Walters, John - for life
Warby, James
Warwick, Christopher
Waters, Catherine
Watson, Francis
Webb, Jane
Williams, Mary
Williams, William - to transport himself

Surrey

Bailey, John - for life
Butler, John - for life
Canfield, Thomas (QS)
Grant, Alexander
Holbert, Margaret (QS)
Jones, John (QS)
Lawrence, John (QS)
Lewis, Elizabeth (QS)
Lowance, John (QS)
Martin, Oliver - for life - runaway
Thompson, John (QS) - runaway

Felons transported from London to Virginia by the *Justitia*, Capt. Finlay Gray, in January 1774. (CLRO: London & LMA: Middlesex Bonds).

Buckinghamshire

Beal, Samuel (QS) - 5 yrs
Bavington, Ann
Biggs, Stephen
Burrell, Thomas - for life
Packer, Daniel
Stonell, Richard
Wallis, John

Essex

Bishop, Roger (QS)
Brown, John
Gates, Samuel (QS)
Taylor, Thomas - for life

Hertfordshire

Bates, William
Brown, James
Edwards, John
Read, Robert
Shrobb, Edward
Wheeler, William

Kent

Cleveland, John
Hazell, Robert (QS)
Holden, Richard
Smith, John

London

Abrahams, Sarah

245

Austin alias Veil, Ann
Bray, Timothy
Broadas, Joseph
Butler, Joseph
Chilton, John
Coleman, Edward - pardoned
Cumber, James
Davis, William
Duggan, Thomas
Dunning, Alexander - pardoned
Enwood, John
Field, Ann
Garnes, Lewis
Grainger, Francis - 14 yrs - runaway
Hall, John
Harden, John
Hog, Catherine
Hussey, Mary
Johnson, Christopher
Jones, Elizabeth
Kelly, James - pardoned
King, John
Leeson, Esther
Middleton, William
Moses, Solomon
Newman, Edward - pardoned
Newton, George (QS) - runaway
Norris, Francis
Porte, Henry
Ragan, William
Seal, John
Shepherd, Conrad - pardoned
Smith, Sarah
Solomon, Barnard - 14 yrs
Varnial, Mary
Ward, Margaret
Watson, Richard
Wilson, Joseph
Young, Elizabeth

Middlesex

Abbot, Mary
Agar, William
Allam, Ann
Alsop, Margaret
Beck, John
Bounce, Sarah
Bradley, Richard
Brindley, Elizabeth
Broad, Robert
Brown, Andrew

Brown, Ann
Brown, George
Bryant, Michael
Bull, Susanna
Burnham, Mary
Chatham, Ann
Collins, Alice
Cuthbert, James - pardoned
Dailey, Ann
Dales, Robert
Daley, Mary
Davidson, William
Davis, Elizabeth
Dawson, Timothy
Delaney, Mary
Devereux, James
Fagan, Catherine
Fanjoy, William
Fletcher, William
Godby, Ann wife of Jasper
Gould, Mary
Grear, Ann
Hall, Thomas
Harrison, Ann
Hart, Matthew
Heath, Alexander
Hinds, William
Hoffein, Goddard - pardoned
Hyatt, Elizabeth
Jaffray, Lewis
James, William
Johnson, Ann
Jones, Thomas
Keatly, Thomas
Kirby, Thomas
Kirk, John
Leverett, James - pardoned
Lewis, Frank alias Francis
Liddle, Isabella
Marriott, Samuel
McDaniel, Elizabeth
Milson, Thomas
Montgomery, Alexander
Norton, Mary wife of George
O'Brien, William
Patch, John
Price, Thomas
Redwood, William
Rivers, Robert
Robinson, Benjamin - pardoned
Robinson, John
Rowles, Thomas

Savage, Henry
Scarborough, James - runaway
Seaman, Jane wife of William
Short, Philip - 14 yrs
Simberlen alias Simberell, Francis
Simons alias Simmons, John
Smith, Mary
Talbot, Francis - for life
Thomas, Charles
Tugwell, Elizabeth
Twanney, John
Walker, Robert - for life
Ward, John
Watson, George
Welch, Susannah
Wentworth, Elizabeth
Williams alias McKenzie,
 William - 14 yrs
Wilson, Edward
Worth alias Bibby, Mary
Younger, James

Davy, John
Duffield, William
Grant, Alexander (QS)
Handley, James
Heathcote, Lydia - 14 yrs - runaway
Heathcote, Robert - 14 yrs
Holbert, Margaret (QS)
Hollis, Richard
King, Edward
Lawrence, John (QS)
Lewis, Elizabeth (QS)
Marshall, William - for life
Pullen, Samuel
Read, Elizabeth
Robinson, William
Smith, Elizabeth (QS) - pardoned
Stedman, William
Teddy, John
Wheeler, Mary - 14 yrs
Wingrove, John - for life
Withall, Thomas

Surrey

Bull, John
Burchett, John (QS)
Clarkson, Richard

Sussex

Bulbeck, Thomas
Wakefield, Thomas

Felons transported from London by the *Thornton*, Captain John Kidd, in May 1774 & registered in Anne Arundel Co. records on 23 July 1774. (MSA: CR 40,516 ff. 41-72):

Essex

Algate, Mary
Cheney, William
Davis, Charles - 14 yrs
Dawkins, Thomas
Everett, Joseph
Ford, Patrick
Fordham, Thomas
Jepp, William
Kendall, Thomas
Litchfield, John
Mann, Mary
Pettitt, Sarah
Prescott, Mary (QS)
Sparrow, Robert alias Alliston,
 Ambrose
Wadley, Elizabeth
Wells, William

Hertfordshire

Aylett alias Pallett, William
Baldwin, Samuel (QS)
Billis, John
Flint, John - 14 yrs
Kempster, John - 14 yrs
Randall, Richard
Rice, John - runaway

Kent

Allmond, Richard
Bird, John alias Holton, Griffith (QS)
Cox, Charles
Farrell, Peter
Fenn alias Welham, James - for life
Ford, Ann
Hopkins, John
Mount, Jonas

Parry, John - for life
Pope, John
Roberts, Richard
Smith, Mary
Streak, Francis

London

Abrahams alias Solomons, Joseph
Armstrong, Mary
Blake, John
Brown alias Scott, Hannah
Brown, John
Brown, William
Chapman, Samuel
Clark, Elijah
David, Daniel
Davis, William
Dodson, John
Edgley, Mary Magdalen
Foller, Robert - pardoned
Fox, Mary
Furrier, Ann
Gullaken, James
Hanby, Thomas
Hill, Robert
Jenkins, William
Jones, Jane
Lacey, Michael
Larner, Ann - pardoned
Lyon, Moses
Moore, William
Nary, Andrew
Norton, John
Owens, William
Pearce, Thomas - pardoned
Perrier, Peter
Powell, Jeremiah.
Price, James
Probeart, Thomas
Russell, William
Sampson, Thomas - 14 yrs
Simonds, Elizabeth
Smith, William
Solomon, Joshua
Steele, Mary
Tyler, Mary
Wakeling, Samuel
Watson, James
West, John

Middlesex

Adamson, Margaret wife of Thomas
Aldridge, Mary (QS)
Allday, Thomas (QS)
Archer, William - pardoned
Armstrong, Mary
Ashworth, John (QS)
Ball, William
Barnes, John (QS)
Barrett, James
Barry, Ann
Bean, Daniel - pardoned
Bennett, Ann
Billings, John
Blissed, Guido
Bodden, Samuel
Bonney, Julia (Judith) (QS) - pardoned
Bowles (Bowels), Elizabeth
Bright, Thomas - pardoned
Brown, Mark - pardoned
Burdell, James
Butcher, John
Campbell, Robert
Childs, William - runaway
Clark, James
Clark, John
Clewley, Joseph
Cook, John
Cooley, John - runaway
Cotton, William
Counsellor, Jacob
Davis, Jane
Davis, Mary
Davison, John
Dawson, John
Decelie, Samuel (QS)
Dewitt, Elizabeth
Dickinson, Guy (QS)
Duffee, James (QS)
Duffy, Michael (QS)
Evans, Henry (QS)
Flannagan, William
Flood, Matthew (QS)
Flower, Samuel (QS)
Fosker, William (QS)
Garth, James
Gee, John
Godfrey, William
Gordon, Richard
Gould, Elizabeth
Griffiths, James

Gross, Sarah
Hall, William
Harding, George (QS)
Harvey, Charles (QS)
Hawkins, Reubin (QS)
Heasman, George
Hibberd, William
Higginbottom, Thomas
Hind, Mary
Hobbs, Robert (QS)
Horton, Thomas
Hughes, William
Hunt, Samuel (QS)
Hurly, John
Jones, Ann
Jones, Mary (QS)
Jones, Mary
Kemp, Hannah (QS)
Lane, William
Laremore, Daniel (QS) - pardoned
Latimore, Andrew (QS)
Lee, John
Lelleongreen, Frederick
Leonard, William - pardoned
Lewis, Elizab
Lewis, Henry (QS)
Lewis, Mary
Maccoy alias Smith, Sarah (QS)
Maclochlen, Cornelius
Marshall, John
Mattocks, John
McGanley, James (QS)
McGuire, Catherine
Moore, Jane
Moore, William
Morgan, John alias Morris, Thomas
Nicholson, George
Norbury, Elizabeth - pardoned
Nowland, Eleanor
Orchard, Thomas (QS)
Parish, James (QS)
Pickering, John (QS)
Platt, John
Pugh, John William - pardoned
Read, Francis (QS)
Rice, Mary
Richardson, John
Richmond, John (QS)
Richmond, William
Rigby, Nicholas
Robinson, Jane - pardoned
Robinson, John

Rowland, John (QS)
Sage, Robert (QS)
Sampson, William
Sandys, Samuel
Scully, Ann
Sell, William
Sheen, William
Sheppard, Robert - pardoned
Smith, Ann
Smith, Henry
Smith, Henry (QS)
Smith, Robert (QS)
Sparrow alias Parrott, John (QS)
Stanford, Elizabeth
Stringer, Peter
Thompson, Joseph
Tibballs, Samuel
Trusty, John
Wade, Sarah
Walker, Thomas (QS)
Wall, George
Wapshot, James (QS)
Wardell, Leonard
Warren, John
Wheeler, William
Wild, John - hanged in 1775
Woodward, James
Wright, John (QS)

Surrey

Adams, John (QS)
Bailiss, John (QS)
Barnes alias Carrol, Bridget (QS)
Burnham, Solomon
Carter, Robert (QS)
Coles, Benjamin (QS)
Combes, James (QS)
Ellis, George
Fore, George (QS)
George, William
Goldhawk, Amey (QS)
Morris, Daniel - for life
Morris, Thomas - 14 yrs
Noble, Jonathan (QS)
Overan, John (QS)
Peter, William. (QS)
Scarlett, Stephen
Smith, Elizabeth - pardoned
Squires, James
Vallum, John. (QS)
Vernon, Henry

249

Wright, Samuel - runaway

Sussex

Avenell, John
Brown, James

Dabbs, John
Hull, William (QS)
Read, John
Stacey, Robert
Tyler, William
Young, John Eldridge

Felons transported from Bristol to Maryland by William Stevenson and William Randolph, merchants, and registered in Baltimore Co. records on 15 July 1774 (CR 40,516, ff. 370-380).

Dorset

Francis, John (QS)
Redman, John
Snook, Thomas (QS)
Sparrow, John
Wherrett, John
Williams, John - runaway

Shropshire

Ferriday, Edward.
Hughes, John
Price, Daniel.
Rhodenhurst, Mary
Taylor, Ann
Williams, Elizabeth

Wiltshire

Avery, Thomas.
Burford, Thomas
Comley, Thomas
Hughes, John
Little, William (QS)
Major alias Markerson, Walter
Mounty alias Mountague, William
Nodder, Sarah
Nolligg, Ephraim
Nolly, Sarah (QS)
Pipp, Joseph
Read, Nicholas
Wright, Charles

- entries apparently unfinished after f. 380.

Felons transported from London to Virginia by the *Tayloe*, Capt. John Ogilvie, in July 1774. (CLRO: London & LMA: Middlesex Bonds).

London

Abrahams, Moses
Aldridge, William
Ashford, William - 14 yrs
Austin, Isaac
Burnett, William - 14 yrs
Corderoy, Robert
Davis, Mary
Dovetrie, James
Field, Ann - 14 yrs
Gibson, Samuel
Hanby, Richard
Isdell, William
Jones, Robert
Littleboy, John
Marshall, Thomas
Morland, Eleanor

Parkes, Giles
Phillips, Elizabeth
Phillips, Moses
Roberts, Thomas
Skatt, Timothy Featherstonehaugh
  - to transport himself
Sowden, Benjamin
Tomlin, John
Walker, Alice - 14 yrs
Wilson, Ann - runaway
Withall, Thomas - 14 yrs

Middlesex

Allies, John
Atkins alias Atkinson, Susannah
Baldwin, Thomas
Banning, James

250

Barker, Mary
Bateman, Sarah
Bridgman, Susannah
Burn, Jeremiah
Charles, John
Chevys. George
Clarke alias Green, Ann
Collier, Sarah wife of John
Connerly, Eleanor
Constable, Elizabeth wife of Samuel
Coster, Joshua
Doggarty, Patrick
Doughty, Philip
Dyer, Margaret
Eason, John
Everett, Joseph - 14 yrs
Garrett, Richard - for life
Glesby, Ann
Godfrey, Benjamin
Gray alias Graves, Jane
Green, Charles
Hall, Frances
Harris, George
Hawes, George
Herne alias Horne, Pooling
  - runaway
Hobler, Mary
Hopkins, Thomas
Houghton (Haughton), William - 14 yrs
Hurcan alias Hurkham, Thomas
Jefferson, John - pardoned
Jones, William (2)

Kelly, Ann
Leer, Abraham
Loton, Ann
Maid, Jane
Martin, Benjamin
McDaniel, James - 14 yrs
McKan, John
Mecum, John
Medcalf, Joseph - 14 yrs
Mince, John alias Peter
Monk, Ann
Monro, Margaret
Morgan, Thomas
Neal, Daniel
Nowland, Henry
Pitt, Richard
Prior, ElizabethRidley, John
Shields, Patrick
Shirley, John - 14 yrs
Simons, David
Singer, Michael
Singer, Thomas
Smith, Sarah
Stephenson, Ann
Suggs alias Preston, Mary
Taylor, John
Thane, James Wallis
Thompson, John
Walsom, Thomas - runaway
Ward, John
Waters, Thomas
Whitehouse, James - 14 yrs

Indented servants [*sic* but mostly transported felons] **transported from Bristol by the** *William*, **Capt. James Thomas, in October 1774 on the account of Messrs. Stevenson, Randolph & Cheston, arriving in Maryland in December 1774** (MSA: Cheston-Galloway papers).

Bristol

Davis, William:
  sold to Thomas Johnson Jr.

Cheshire

Rice, William - 14 yrs:
  sold to James Hutchings

Cornwall

Jennings, Richard - 14 yrs:
  sold to James & Joshua Howard

Jewell, Lawrence
  sold to James Hutchings
Simmons, William:
  sold to James Hodges
Solomon (alias Wolfe), Benjamin:
  sold to James Hutchings

Dorset

Flippen [Fleppen], John:
  sold to Richard Jacob
Miles, Bryan - 14 yrs:
  sold to Lancelot Warfield

251

Smith, John:
  sold to James Hutchings

Gloucestershire

Catanack, William - for life:
  sold to James Hutchings
Hooper, Josiah:
  sold to Thomas Johnson Jr.
Lisle, William:
  sold to James Hutchings
Meek, William - 14 yrs:
  sold to Roger Pomfrey
Trotman, John:
  sold to Dorrey Jacob

Hampshire

Boxwell (alias Baxall), William:
  sold to James Hutchings
Cook, William:
  sold to William Lux
Phillips, James:
  sold to John Stork
Reynolds, Thomas:
  sold to Harry Dorsey Gough
Seagar, Thomas:
  sold to James Hutchings
Sheppard, William:
  sold to James Hutchings - runaway
White, John:
  sold to James Hutchings

Herefordshire

Bickerton, George - 14 yrs:
  sold to James Frazer - runaway
Delahay, John: (paid cash)

Monmouthshire

Everton (Overton), John:
  sold to James Hutchings
George, Philip:
  sold to James Hutchings
George, Thomas:
  sold to James Hutchings
George, William - 14 yrs:
  sold to Thomas Johnson Jr.
Griffiths, William:
  sold to Thomas Johnson Jr.

Hughes, William (Sr.):
  sold to James Hutchings
Hughes, William:
  sold to James Hutchings
James, William - for life:
  sold to Ely Bailey
Perry (Parry), John:
  sold to William Lux
Williams, Evan:
  sold to James & Joshua Howard

Northamptonshire

May, Thomas - 14 yrs:
  sold to Harry Dorsey Gough

Oxfordshire

Broomfield, Thomas - 14 yrs:
  sold to Abram Vanbibber
Crips, Dianah:
  sold to John Robert Holliday
Herritage, Thomas:
  sold to James Hutchings
Hinds, John - 14 yrs:
  sold to James Hutchings
Humphreys, James:
  sold to Vincent Trapnell
Lardner, John:
  sold to John Elder
Sawyer, Francis (Frances):
  sold to James Hutchings

Shropshire

Bird, John:
  sold to John Gordon
Broadfield, William:
  sold to Brittingham Dickinson
Davis, Thomas:
  sold to James Hutchings
Evans, Richard:
  sold to Thomas Rams(?)
Gregory, Henry:
  sold to Thomas Johnson Jr.
Harper, John:
  sold to John Philpot
Lawrence, William - 14 yrs:
  sold to Arthur Bryan
Roberts, James - 14 yrs:
  sold to James Walker
Roberts, Edward - 14 yrs:

sold to John Walker
Taylor, Thomas - 14 yrs:
sold to Rodolph Hook

Somerset

Martin, John:
sold to James Hutchings
Phillips, Thomas:
sold to James Hutchings
Scott, William:
sold to James Hutchings

Staffordshire

Dawson, Richard: (paid cash)
Evans, William (alias Hamilton):
sold to Henry Howard
Fowkes, Edward:
sold to Thomas Johnson Jr.
Hough, Hugh:
sold to John McCabe
Jones, John:
sold to Harry Dorsey Gough
Lakin, Francis:
sold to John Christopher
Laken (Lakin), Robert:
sold to Thomas Dorsey
Powell, Evan - for life:
sold to James & Joshua Howard
Seagar (alias Boxer), Benjamin:
sold to Aubrey Richardson
Sylvester, Richard - 14 yrs:
sold to Elisha Warfield - runaway
Tunks (Tonks), William - 14 yrs:
sold to James Hutchings
Turner (alias Borroughs), William
- 14 yrs: sold to James Hutchings
Wright, Benjamin - 14 yrs:
sold to James & Joshua Howard
- runaway

Warwickshire

Betts, William:
sold to Frederick Myers
Stevens, Thomas:
sold to James Hutchings
Thomson, William:
sold to James Hutchings
Buckly, Timothy:
sold to James Hutchings

Foyle, William:
sold to Henry Penny

Worcestershire

Mias (Miers), Emanuel - 14 yrs:
sold to James Hutchings
Parker, Joseph: (paid cash) - runaway
Smith, Elizabeth:
sold to Thomas Smyth

Unidentified

Beacham, Joseph:
sold to James Hutchings
Bowden, Robert:
sold to James Hutchings
Clark, Honor:
sold to James & Josha Howard
Clarke, Thomas: (paid cash)
Clark, William:
sold to James & Joshua Howard
Drew, Elizabeth:
sold to James Bennett
Evans, William:
sold to Thomas Johnson Jr.
Finch, Thomas:
sold to James & Joshua Howard
Gardner, George:
sold to James Hutchings
Harper, Hannah [wife of John
Harper above?]
sold to John Philpot
Harrison, James:
sold to James Hutchings
Hinds, Elizabeth [wife of John
Hinds above?]:
sold to James Hutchings
Howard, Margaret:
sold to John Cooper
James, William:
sold to Bartholomew Balderston
Jervis, John:
sold to Vincent Trapnell
Jones, Margaret:
sold to James Hutchings
Jones, William
[3 candidates of this name]:
sold to Richard Rode
Morris, Hugh:
sold to Hon. Benj. Calvert - runaway

Quarman, John:
   sold to James Hutchings
Richards, Richard:
   sold to Henry Howard
Smith, Mathias:
   sold to James Hutchings

Stone, Isaac:
   sold to James Hutchings
Symons, William:
   sold to Thomas Dorsey
Zavier, Samuel:
   sold to Thomas Johnson Jr.

Felons transported from London to Virginia by the *Justitia*, Capt. John Kidd, in December 1774. (CLRO: London & LMA: Middlesex Bonds).

London

Adkins, Sarah
Alsom, William
Atkinson, Thomas
Ayres, John
Beam, William
Beeson, James
Bell, Hannah - pardoned
Bergenhow, Peter
Bowman, Samuel
Brown, Thomas
Butterfield, Abraham
Carey, Margaret
Cook, Alexander
Cotton, Joshua
Duffin, Ann
Elder, Andrew
Emanuel, Ralph - runaway
Eustice, Thomas
Fenley, Henry
Flathers, Edward
Gunn, John
Gusseny, Abraham
Harris, John
Hart, Arabella
Hart, Thomas
Hodges, John
Jones, Richard
Jones, William
Kennaty, William
Kennedy, Peter
Lee, William
Linford, Samuel
Magrave, Ralph
Oldbury, Mark
Peirse, William - runaway
Peto, Thomas
Phillips, Benjamin
Pollett, William
Pullen, Charles - pardoned
Robertson, John - 14 yrs

Ruffhead, William
Sharkey, Lewis
Smith, William
Templer, James
Trantum, Samuel
Ward, William
Welch, James
White, William
Wright, Edward
Wright, James

Middlesex

Ambrose, Ann
Austin, Bryant (QS)
Bailey alias Bowden, Susannah
Booth, Elizabeth
Brannon, Michael - for life
Broadbent, Richard (QS)
Bryant, Samuel (QS)
Burbridge, Elizabeth
Cannon, Bridget (QS)
Clark, Thomas (QS)
Collier, William - 14 yrs
Collop, George
Cooper, John
Daikins, Anna Maria
Daily, John (QS)
Davids, Joseph (QS)
Dillon, John
Dixon, Eleanor
Doggett, Joseph
Dooley, Laurence (QS)
Dotterell, William (QS)
Ducret, John Victoire
Dunn, Barnaby (QS)
Edwards, John
Edwards, Robert
Elber, Henry
Ellis, Thomas
Fenby, Thomas
Fossett, Edward - pardoned

French, William
Fukes, Thomas (QS)
Gaffy, Mary (QS)
George, William
Gilman, Thomas
Greeve, Elizabeth Harriot (QS)
Griffiths, Morris (QS)
Hawes, George
Hazard, William (QS)
Higgins, William
Hipditch, William - runaway
Ironmonger, Robert (QS)
Jilson, Richard
Jones alias Maunder, Henry
Jones, William
Kelly, Patrick
King alias Williams, Sarah
Lambeth, Thomas (QS)
Legay, Lewis
Lequint, Lewis
Levy, Mordecai (QS)
Lewis, Fabius
Lishman, Jane
Lockett alias Lockington
  alias Wilson, Charles - for life
Martin, Thomas (QS)
McCullogh, Margaret
Newton, William (QS)
Nicholls, Edward
North, William (QS)
Phipps, Edward

Popplewell, Joseph
  - to transport himself
Presstand, George (QS)
Price, Elizabeth wife of Samuel
Pyner, John (QS)
Richards, Charles (QS)
Roache, Eleanor - 14 yrs
Scott, Thomas - runaway
Sears, Mary Ann
Shaw, Charles - 14 yrs
Smith, Hannah (2)
Smith, John
Stevenson, Arthur
Storey, William
Thompson, Elizabeth
Tidbury, Joseph - 14 yrs
Tomlins, George
Tranter, Mary
Venner, Isaac (QS)
Ward, Samuel (QS)
Warrington, William
Watkins, John
Watson, Henry Drake
Welch, Henry
Wellbrand alias Welbred
  alias Summers, Mary
Wheatley, George (QS)
White alias Rigglesworth, William
  - pardoned
Wigley, Elizabeth - 14 yrs
Williams, Lewis

Felons transported from Bristol in the *Elizabeth*, Capt. Thomas Spencer in April 1775 on the account of Messrs. Stevenson, Randolph & Cheston, arriving in Maryland in June 1775. (MSA: Cheston-Galloway papers).

Dorset

King, Charles:
  sold to Francis Deakens
Leaves, Samuel - 14 yrs:
  sold to Waters & Gartrall
Mathews, Sarah - 14 yrs:
  sold to Francis Deakens
Randall (Rendall), Judith:
  (paid cash)

Gloucestershire

Goodsell (Godsall), James:
  sold to Waters & Gartrall

Guy, William - 14 yrs:
  sold to Samuel Dorsey Jr.
Hawkins, William - 14 yrs:
  sold to Waters & Gartrall
Hyatt, William - 14 yrs:
  sold to Capt. Chas Ridgely & Co.
Mabbett, Anthony:
  sold to Waters & Gartrall
Morgan, Mary - 14 yrs:
  sold to George Galaspy
Smith, Gabriel - 14 yrs:
  sold to Henry Stevenson Sr.
Watson, Thomas:
  sold to Francis Deakens
Weston, William:
  sold to Samuel Dorsey Jr.

Williams, Thomas - 14 yrs:
sold to Waters & Gartrall - runaway

Hampshire

Bayley, Elias - for life:
sold to William Perry
Benham, Samuel:
sold to Samuel Dorsey Jr.
Bennet, Michael:
sold to James Franklin
Bishop, Henry:
sold to Capt. Chas Ridgely & Co.
Forder, Henry:
sold to Samuel Dorsey Jr.
Frumantle (Freemantle), William
- 14 yrs: sold to Thomas B. Hands
Goodall, William (Elias) - 14 yrs:
sold to Henry Stevenson Sr.
Goodwell (Goodall), Joseph
- 14 yrs: sold to Waters & Gartrall
Lodge, Job:
sold to Abednego Baker
Moses, William:
sold to Capt. Chas Ridgely & Co.
North, James:
sold to Francis Deakens
Yalden, John:
sold to Daniel Carter

Herefordshire

Gummer, Thomas - 14 yrs:
sold to Samuel Dorsey Jr. - runaway
Harris, Robert - 14 yrs:
sold to James Franklin - runaway
Parry, James:
sold to Samuel Dorsey Jr.

Monmouthshire

Lewis, John:
sold to Samuel Dorsey Jr.

Oxfordshire

Crags (Creg), Thomas:
sold to Samuel Dorsey Jr.
Garrett, Mary:
sold to Capt. Chas Ridgely & Co.
Meal (Male), Samuel:
sold to Capt. Chas Ridgely & Co.

Weston, Thomas:
sold to Samuel Dorsey Jr.
Wiggins, James:
sold to Capt. Chas Ridgely & Co.

Shropshire

Harris, Silvanus:
sold to Waters & Gartrall
Jones, John:
sold to Francis Deakens
Phillips, John (alias Jones, Philip):
sold to John Israel
Thomas, Samuel:
sold to Waters & Gartrall

Somerset

Barrington, Thomas:
sold to Waters & Gartrall
Bishop, Mary:
sold to Francis Deakens
Clements, Edward:
sold to Andrew Hammond
Gold, John:
sold to Samuel Dorsey Jr.
Greenland, Edward - 14 yrs:
sold to Samuel Dorsey Jr.
Johnson, William:
sold to Capt. Chas Ridgely & Co.
Masters, Andrew - 14 yrs:
sold to Capt. Chas Ridgely & Co.
- runaway
Pedder (Pether), Thomas - 14 yrs:
(paid cash) - runaway
Shears, Thomas:
sold to Francis Deakens

Staffordshire

Biddulph, John:
sold to Samuel Dorsey Jr.
Foster, James:
sold to Samuel Dorsey Jr.
Hall, William - 14 yrs:
sold to John Cockey Owings
Thornley, John - 14 yrs:
sold to Stephen Price

Warwickshire

Blair, Mary:
sold to Francis Deakens
Button, Mary - 14 yrs:
sold to Francis Deakens
Cadman, James:
sold to Vincent Trapnell
Crowder, Joseph:
sold to Waters & Gartrall
Edwards, Rosannah:
sold to Waters & Gartrall
Elliot, Enoc:
sold to Francis Deakens
Greenaway, Ann:
sold to Capt. Chas Ridgely & Co.
Handley, John:
sold to Waters & Gartrall
Hobson, Mary: (paid cash)
Inkley, William:
sold to John Cockey Owings
Morgan, William:
sold to Francis Deakens
Smith, Thomas:
sold to Gartrall & Roberts
Webb, William - 14 yrs:
sold to Samuel Dorsey Jr.
Willis, John:
sold to Capt. Chas. Ridgely & Co.

Wiltshire

Day, Wilber (William}:
sold to Daniel Carter
Falkner, John:
sold to Francis Deakens
Lafford (Lawford), Sarah:
sold to Francis Deakens
Stanley (Standley), Humphrey
- 14 yrs: sold to Samuel Dorsey Jr.
Wotton, James:
sold to Francis Deakens

Worcestershire

Duck (alias Bolton), John - 14 yrs:
sold to William Perry
Hall, Joseph - 14 yrs:
sold to Vincent Trapnell
Kittle (Kettle), William - 14 yrs:
sold to John Walker

Salter, Thomas:
sold to Francis Deakens
Saunders, Barley:
sold to Francis Deakens
Southing (Southan), William:
sold to Francis Deakens
Till, John:
sold to Caleb Owings - runaway
Whitehouse, Joseph:
sold to Francis Deakens
Williams, John - 14 yrs:
sold to James Franklin

Unidentified

Bazely, John:
sold to Francis Deakens
Bolter, Edward:
sold to Gartrall & Roberts
Clay, Joseph:
sold to Francis Deakens
Codry, John:
sold to Samuel Dorsey Jr.
Ember, Matthew:
sold to John Page
Follett, James:
sold to Francis Deakens
Gibbons, Thomas:
sold to Capt. Chas Ridgely & Co.
Greeny, Charles:
sold to Abraham Hicks
Hands, William:
sold to George Haile
Haynes, Thomas:
sold to Capt. Chas Ridgely & Co.
Jilks, Mary:
sold to Francis Deakens
Jones, John Morgan:
sold to Mark Alexander Harris
McCombe, John:
sold to Francis Deakens
McLoglin, Mary:
sold to Francis Deakens
Osborne, James:
sold to John Cockey Owings
Pewford, Joseph:
sold to Capt. Chas Ridgely & Co.
Powell, Evan:
sold to Samuel Dorsey Jr.
Rice, William:
sold to Samuel Dorsey Jr.

Safford, Benjamin:
  sold to Waters & Gartrall
Samuel, John:
  sold to Francis Deakens
Stern, John:
  sold to Thomas Samuel Pole
Tapper, James:

  sold to Francis Deakens
Veazey, Thomas:
  sold to John Israel
Weakley, John:
  sold to Samuel Dorsey Jr.
Woodall, Elias:
  sold to Samuel Dorsey Jr.

Felons transported from London to Maryland by the *Thornton*, Captain Finlay Gray, in May 1775 & registered in Anne Arundel Co. records in July 1775 (MSA: CR 40,516 ff. 74-88).

Buckinghamshire

Batterson, John
Beaver, John - 14 yrs
Buckingham, Joseph
Buckingham, Thomas
Chambers, William - 14 yrs
Clarke, Richard
Cooke, Stephen
Johnson, Robert - runaway
Kempton, Thomas
Kinder, John
Morris, John
Powell, Susanna
West, James
Wilding, Henry - 14 yrs - runaway

Essex

Carter, John - 14 yrs
Carter, Philip - 14 yrs
Colbrath, John
Eppingstall, John
Everett, James
Flack, William - 14 yrs
Flemming, Thomas - 14 yrs
Garrison, Elizabeth
Hales, James
Jackson, William
Jennings, William - 14 yrs
Kelly, Francis
Madle, Joseph
Mead alias Watts, John alias Baker,
  Rowland - 14 yrs
Mole, Thomas
Mott, Joseph
Nottage, John
Orgar, Edward
Rawles, Joseph
Stammers, John - 14 yrs

Hertfordshire

Cole, John
Cramphorn, William
Edwards, Thomas
Hall, William - runaway
Medcalf, William - for life
Penington, John (QS)
Pudiphat, Samuel
Smith, John alias Hickman, Smith
Ward, Edward - 14 yrs

Kent

Baker, George - 14 yrs
Barnes, Benjamin (QS)
Bryant, Ann
Buck, John
Clarke, William
Cooper, Thomas
Dodd, Robert - for life
Doyle, Margaret
Gilham, Richard
Glover, John -14 yrs
Grimshire, Josiah - 14 yrs
Hinton, Thomas (QS)
Johnson, Thomas
Lakey, Hannah - 14 yrs
Langley, John - 14 yrs
Lucas, Steven - pardoned
Marshall, Henry
Moore, Peter - 14 yrs
Mount, John - 14 yrs
Neaton, Edward
Newell, John
Norwood, Robert - for life
Palmer, John (QS)
Patmore, Benjamin
Race, Charles (QS)
Reeves, Joseph - for life

Stevens, John - 14 yrs
Thompson, Edward
Wells, Edward (QS)

London

Angus, Daniel
Bird, John
Butts, William
Carpenter, Martha - pardoned
Daniel, Thomas
Field, Hannah
Hartman, William
Hawkins, William - pardoned
Hickman, Seymour
Johnson, Ann
Joseph, Henry - 14 yrs
Knight, Thomas
McClough, Daniel
Millikin, Mark
Needham, William
Nisbett, Richard
Rogers, John
Seller, William
Simpson, Ann
Staples, Matthe
Thomas, John - runaway
Warden, Arthur
Watts, Thomas

Middlesex

Allen, John
Austin, Henry
Bailey, Francis - pardoned
Banfield, Richard
Best, John (QS)
Blandell, Eleanor
Bradford, Richard (QS)
Bradshaw, William
Browning, Joseph
Burnham, John (QS)
Cane, Robert (QS)
Carr, Lewis
Casey, John (QS)
Chapman, Stephen
Chinn, Robert (QS)
Clayton, William
Cohen, John (QS)
Coker, John (QS)
Cooke, Charles
Corbet, James

Cox, Peter (QS)
Crompton, James
Daubigney, Alexander
Dawson, Mary
Dugard, John
Dugard, Abraham
Elder, Alexander
Ellis, Elizabeth
Every, Robert (QS)
Farthing, Charles (QS)
Flint, Richard - pardoned
Freeman, James (QS)
Fry, Richard (QS) - pardoned
Garrett, Joseph
Gilchrist, Henry (QS)
Gough, James
Hainsworth, Benjamin
Harris, William
Hart, Joseph (QS)
Hicks, George (QS)
Hide, John (QS)
Hoare alias Brown
    alias Kirkman, Elizabeth
Holland, William
Holmes, Rebecca wife of James
Hooper, Mary
Howard, John
Hughes, John
Hurst, Elizabeth wife of Emanuel
James, Diana wife of William
Jones, James (QS)
Lambert, Thomas
Lescallie, William (QS)
Lewis, Robert
Linton, Henry
Lumley, Thomas (QS)
Matthews, William
Molloy, Roger (QS)
Morgan, Richard
Munt, Jane - for life
Murphy, James
Nicholson alias Nichols, Daniel
Ogborn, Robert (QS)
Othen, Samuel
Parker, Elizabeth
Pettin, Ann wife of Robert
Pinkstone, Thomas - for life
Richmond, Edward (QS)
Rooker, William
Shelton, John (QS)
Singleton, Bridget
Slight, John (QS)

259

Smith, Elizabeth
Spencer, Edward
Stanton, James
Storey, James (QS)
Sutton, Joseph (QS)
Thomas, William
Tucker, James (QS)
Tufnell, John (QS)
Ward, Patrick
Ward, Thomas
White, John (QS)
Whitworth, Alice
Wigmore, Catherine
Willey, Elizabeth (QS)
Wright, William (QS)

Surrey

Arnold, Richard
Bailey, Richard (QS)
Barnes alias Carrol, Bridget
Billens, William - for life
Bishop, George
Blandford, William - for life
Bowker, John (QS)
Coster, James - for life
Coxhill, Henry Joseph
Delany, Richard - 14 yrs
Dorman, George (QS) - runaway
Elliott, Thomas
Elson, Henry
Goldhawk, Amey (QS)
Harding, William - 14 yrs
Harris, Ann wife of Edward - 14 yrs

Hayward, Thomas - pardoned
Hill, Shadrack (QS)
Hoare, Henry - for life
Hughes, Abraham - 14 yrs
Humphreys, James - for life
Jenkins, John
Jones, Jane - pardoned
Jones, Thomas
Kenzie, Mary (QS)
Mulford, David
Perry, James (QS)
Petter, William (QS)
Pritchards, John (QS)
Stent, Thomas
Stevens, William - 14 yrs
Stothers, John (QS)
Taylor, Thomas
Upham, Robert - 14 yrs
Vellum, John (QS)
Webb, John - 14 yrs
Williams, Mary
Wingrove, John

Sussex

Boxall, John
Bridger, John
Clarke, John
Morris, Batchelor
Read, Mary wife of Archibald - 14 yrs
Richardson, Nicholas
Shelley, John
Steer, Thomas

Convict & indented servants transported from Bristol by the *Isabella*, Capt. James Thomas. in May 1775 on the account of Messrs. Stevenson, Randolph & Cheston, arriving in Maryland in July 1775. (MSA: Cheston-Galloway papers).

Bristol

Bigwood, James:
  sold to Gartrall & Roberts
Bolton, Ann:
  sold to Waters & Gartrall
Bridgeman, Francis (Swanston):
  sold to Waters & Gartrall
Cooper, George:
  sold to Waters & Gartrall
Jones, Ann:
  sold to Bazil Ridgely

Lidyard, Sarah (wife of John):
  (paid cash)
Slade, Samuel:
  sold to Waters & Gartrall
Tucker, William:
  sold to Waters & Gartrall
Webber, John:
  sold to Waters & Gartrall
Williams, Judith:
  sold to Waters & Gartrall

Cornwall

John, Thomas:
  sold to Waters & Gartrall
Moyle, Richard:
  sold to George Scott

Monmouthshire

Hulonce (alias Hulins), Thomas
  - 14 yrs: sold to Bazil Ridgely

Shropshire

Aston, Jane (wife of Walter):
  sold to Richard Moals
  "An unfortunate poor woman ... to
  be found a kind humane master."

Warwickshire

Barker, Samuel:
  sold to Waters & Gartrall
Burrows, Benjamin:
  sold to Waters & Gartrall
Tew, William:
  convict but paid his passage

Unidentified

Adrington, Richard:
  sold to Samuel Dorsey Jr.
Andrews, Edward:
  sold to John Walker
Blackford, Thomas:
  sold to Thomas Samuel Pole
Clavier, William: (paid cash)
Davis, John:
  sold to Waters & Gartrall
Frost, Job:
  sold to Nathan Jacobs
Hipps, James: (paid cash)
Jones, Charity
  [wife of Timothy below?]:
  sold to John Welch
Jones, Timothy:
  sold to John Welch
Kenney, Charlotte:
  sold to James Young
McCarty, Bridget:
  sold to Elizabeth Harrison
Rigg, George: (paid cash)
Russ, Thomas:
  sold to Henry Howard

Felons transported from London to Maryland by the *Saltspring*, Capt.John Ogilvie, in July 1775. (CLRO: London & LMA: Middlesex Bonds).

London

Bailey, John
Barrett, Peter
Berry, Alice
Bryant, Samuel
Castle, John
Chalkley, Thomas
Clift, Thomas
Donaldson, William
Dowday, John
Downes, Charles
Franklin, Catherine
Garner, Leda
Goldsmith, Samuel
Grindall, Joseph
Harrison, William
Hart, Fanny
Hawke, Richard - 14 yrs - runaway
Hitchcock, Edward
Lynch, John

Manhall, Elizabeth
Miller, Margaret
Norton, Thomas
Pagett, Edward
Pixley, Thomas
Rice, William
Richardson, Richard
Smith, James
Smith, John - 14 yrs
Smith, Mary
Topping, John - runaway
Tuffnal, James
Westhall, Henry
Wilkins, John

Middlesex

Armer, John - 14 yrs
Avery, Mary
Barrett, William - 14 yrs
Benoit, Joseph

Berry, Margaret
Blackmore, Edmond
Bowers, Robert
Burdell, James
Butler, William
Chapman, Stephen
Clifton, William - 14 yrs
Cooper, Charles
Cross, Samuel - 14 yrs
Crowder, Thomas
Daley, Rose
Dunn, James
Edwards alias Jones, Ann
Emanuel, Samuel
Emon, David
Evans, Thomas
Gibbons, Walter
Gregory, Daniel - 14 yrs
Hackney, William
Hainsworth, James
Harcot, Peter
Harden, Elizabeth - pardoned
Harris, James
Herbert, William - 14 yrs
Hill, Mary
Hines, John - 14 yrs

Hoffman, Mary wife of John - pardoned
Horton, Joseph - 14 yrs
Howard, William
Hunt, Francis - 14 yrs
Hurd, William
James, James
Jones alias Ravell, Edward - 14 yrs
Lee alias Levy, Ann
Lloyd, Joseph - 14 yrs
Lovett, Mary
Maybrick, Charles, alias Jones, John
Mitchell, Susannah
Newton, James
Nutter, Elizabeth
Oxtoby, William - 14 yrs
Pollard, Mary
Rogers, Charles - 14 yrs
Sharpley, James
Stewart, James - 14 yrs
Storer, Samuel - 14 yrs
Taylor, Sarah
Terry, Mary wife of James
Thompson, Ann
Ward, Samuel
Wilson, Margaret
Woolley, William

Felons transported from London to Maryland by the *Justitia*, Capt.John Kidd, in February 1776. (CLRO: London & LMA: Middlesex Bonds).

London

Angus, William
Ash, David
Barber, William
Biggs, Samuel
Blay, John
Bowman, William
Bryant, Thomas
Guy, Sarah
Gwillam, John
Harley, John
Harrad, Mary
Harris, Peter
Heath, Philip
Lynch, Edward
Mackintosh, James
Mann, James
McDaniel, James
Mitchell, William
Sell, Richard
Smith, John

Smith, Mary
Solomons, Levy
Spencer, Aaron
Unthank, Joseph
Woodhead, Charles

Middlesex

Bargo, Sarah wife of John
Bassett, Elisha
Binns, Mary
Black, Andrew
Black, Eleanor wife of William
Burleigh, Thomas (QS)
Burridge, Archibald (QS)
Bushman, Armenia (QS)
Campion, Hyder
Clarke, Sarah
Cook, Thomas
Court, Eleanor
Cox, John
Cuthbert, George

Davis, Benjamin (QS)
Diamond, Mary
East, Daniel
Emmerson, Ann
Fagan, John
Ford, John
Gordon, James
Gosling, William
Hawkins, Richard
Henderson, Jane
Jenkins, John
Jones, Edward
Jones, Joseph

London, John
McGinnis, Charles
Nelson, Thomas
Ogle, Eleanor - 14 yrs
Pilbean, John
Povey, Thomas (QS)
Roley alias Moronie, John
Rowland, Philip
Shears, Isaac
Smith, Mary
Turner, Elizabeth
Wootton alias Hudson, Alice
Wynn, John

Felons sentenced in 1782-1783 to be "transported according to the Statutes in that Case made", consigned to George Moore of London, merchant, and by him to George Salmon (of Baltimore, merchant); transported by the *Swift*, Capt. Thomas Pamp, and registered in Baltimore Co. records on 31 December 1783 (MSA: CR 40,516, f.383-389):

London

Barnsley, Joseph
Bean, John
Bull, John
Burgess, John
Burke, Catherine
Busby, William
Collier, Nathaniel
Goo---, Ann
Griffiths, Elizabeth
Hastings, William
Hawkins, William
Jacobs, Samuel
Lancher, Joseph
North, Catherine
Perry, John
Saltonstall, Richard
Sewell, Richard
Winton alias Winter, Thomas
Wood, John

Middlesex

Allen, Samuel
Anderson, Edward
Andrews, Mary
Bage, George
Bailey, Daniel
Barew, Lawrence
Beattie?, William
Blatherhose, William

Boyle, Mark
Brown, Thomas
Bryan, Thomas
Corledge, William
Dannage, Joseph
Davis, William
Dudfield, Thomas
Fisher, John
Gaffney, Michael
Gould, Thomas
Graves, Mary
Grove, Benjamin
Groves, John
Hall, William
Hammond, Thomas
Hast, David
Hast, Virginia.
Henley, Thomas
Highby, Samuel
Howard, John
Hulme?, Richard
Inglesent, Martha
Jenkins, John
Jones, John
Keeling, Charles
Kellam alias Keeling, John Herbert.
Kilpack, David
King, Margaret
Lacey, William
Lasgent, John
Lasoach, Baptist
Legg, Solomon

Levy, Hart
Littlepage, Thomas
Lyon, Robert - runaway
McDaniel, Thomas
McOwen, Owen
Mees, John
Neal, John
Newton, William
Partridge, Richard
Paylin, Frederick
William
Phasoo, Joseph alias Barnard
Read, Samuel
Savory, John
Thomas, Charles
Tomkins, William
Trusty, Christopher
Tugwell, Thomas
Walker, Mary
Wallis, Samuel
White, John
White, Mary
Williams, Ellis
Williams, Henry
Williams, John
Williams alias Eady, Mary
Wilson, Thomas alias Hart, Henry
Wright, Reuben

FELON RUNAWAYS 1734 - 1788

Entries marked with an asterisk appear in *Complete Book of Emigrants in Bondage.*

Abbott, William, 22. From John Adamson, FR Co Md. (MG 12 Jun 1766, 12 & 26 May 1768).*

Abrahams, John, 23. From Francis Mercier. (MJ 16 Sep & 7 Oct 1777).*

Acres, Charles, 35, 5'8". From James Smith, BA Co Ironworks Md . Has been in the colonies before. (PAG 26 Sep 1765).

Acton, William, English, 28, joiner. From Gamaliel Butler, Annapolis. (MG 15 Jan & 4 Mar 1756).

Adams, George, 35, farmer, good scholar. From John Murray, BA Co Md (MG 10 Aug 1769; from Nicholas Britton (MG 5 Jly 1770).

Adams, John, 24, 5'8". From David Lindsatt, QA Co Md (PAG 7 Sep 1769).

Adams, William. From John Hood Jr., AA Co Md. (MG 9 Feb 1779).

Adginton (Edgerton) Ann (wife of Thomas), English, good spinner. From Roger Brooke, MO Co Md. (MG 3 & 24 Jun 1777).*

Adley, Joseph, 30. From Abraham Woodward & Gilbert Yealdhall, AA Co Md. (MG 30 Apr 1772).

Adwell, Richard (1767). *See* Cross, Bartholomew.

Ager, Thomas, English, 24, 5'4". From Charles Howard, BA Co Md. Has run before. (PAG 7 Jly 1773).

Aikens, John, from West of England, 30, team driver for some years. From Caleb Dorsey, AA Co Md. (MG 19 Apr & 10 May 1770).

Aires, Charles, 35, writes well. From James Smith, Kingsbury Furnace, BA Co Md. (MG 24 Oct 1765).

Akister, Thomas, from Yorkshire. From Benj Merryman & John Orrick, BA Co Md. (MG 24 Aug 1775 - 7 Mar 1776).

Alder, John, English. From Philip Hamond, AA Co Md. (MG 6 Sep - 4 Oct 1753).

Aldred, Giles, 25, weaver, Welsh accent. From John Leitch, PE Co Va. (VG 18 Mar 1773).

Allen, James, English, cooper. From Thos Waters, FR Co Md. (MG 1 & 8 Sep 1763).

Allsworth, Samuel, 22, 5'6", gunstocker. From Samuel Poole, of AA Co Md. (PAG 31 May 1770).

Allum, Thomas, 38, shoemaker. From Joshua Hall, BA Co Md. (MG 21 & 28 Oct 1777).

Amburry, John. From Wm Hobbs, AA Co Md. (MG 30 Jly 1761).*

Ancell, John, English, 30, 5'6". From Thomas Colgate, BA Co Md. (PAG 21 Aug 1766)

Andersby, Thomas, English, 20. From Thos Adams, PG Co Md. (MG 25 Jan 1753).

Anderson, James, English, 32, 5'5". From Capt. Craymer, ship captain, at Baltimore. (MG 11 Aug - 1 Sep 1763; PAG 18 Aug 1763).*

Anderson, John, born Leicestershire, brickmaker. From Benedict Calvert, Annapolis. (MG 10 Jun - 1 Jly 1756)

Anderson, William, English, 36. From George Clark, KE Co Md. (MG 8 - 22 May 1766).

Andrews, Joseph, Italian, 27, 5'8", speaks good English & some French. From David Gorsuch & John Ensor Jr. BA Co Md. (MG 18 Apr 1765, PAG 25 Apr 1765).

Andrews, William, an old man. From the snow *Trial.* (MG 15 Feb - 1 Mar 1759).*

Angess, William Daniel, 22, shoemaker. From John Francis & Clement Trigg, Bladenburg Md. (MG 11 Jun 1767).*

Archdeacon, William, 49, tall. From Wm Dimmitt, BA Co Md. (PAG 2 Sep 1742).*

Archer, Benjamin, English, of St. Ives, Cornwall, 22, hatter. From Wm Lux of BA Co Md. (MG 26 Apr - 24 May 1764, PAG 3 May 1764).

Armstrong, George, English, 30, 5'5". From Wm Jones of BA Co Md (PAG 1 Sep 1773).*

265

RUNAWAYS

Ashford, Thomas, 5'10", called "the farmer". From D. Dulany, TA Co Md. (MG 16 - 30 Sep 1746; PAG 30 Oct 1746).
Ashworth, Allis (Ellis), Yorkshire man, 30, weaver. From Matthias Wisnor, BA Co Md. (MG13 Oct - 10 Nov 1774).
Askott, Thomas, English, speaks West Country dialect. From John Kent, Elk Ridge Furnace Md. (MG 16 Jun - 30 Aug 1759).
Atkins, John, English, 6', butcher. From Wm Steward, KE Co Md. (PAG 25 Jun 1752).*
Attix, George (1770). *See* Hall.

Bachelor, Peter, English, 23. From Joseph Strother CU Co Va. (VG 4 Jly 1771).*
Badham, Edward, 17. From Robt Owen & Edwd Penn, FR Co Md. (MG 25 Jly - 1 Aug 1776).*
Badley, Thomas, 50, 5'6". From Alexis Lemmon, Baltimore Ironworks. (PAG 5 Sep 1771).
Bagnall, John, 20, born London, tin plate worker, arrived Nov 1771 by *Alexandria*. From Roger Beckwith, RI Co Va. (VG 30 Jly 1772).
Bagnall, John, English, 21. From Wm Hill, Baltimore Town. (PAG 1 Sep 1773).*
Bailey, Anne. From John Orme, Georgetown Md. (MG 11 & 18 Apr 1771).
Bailey, James, 21, blacksmith. From Samuel Wade Magruder & Benedict Craiger, FR Co Md. (MG 20 Jly 1769).*
Bailey, John, 25. From Barton Rodgett. (MG 11 Mar 1746); from Patrick Doran, Annapolis. (MG 30 Sep - 14 Oct 1746).*
Bailey, Margery. From Ann Becham, RI Co Va. (MG 2 Aug 1734)
Bailey, Matthew, 45. From Samuel Morris, nr Baltimore Town. (MG 30 Nov - 19 Dec 1774).
Bailey, Samuel, 30, house joiner, in country two years. From Wm Buckland, Va. (VG & VGR 1 Aug 1771).*
Bailey, Thomas, 27. From Christopher Hytch, nr Bladensburg Md. (MG 6 Aug - 3 Sep 1772).
Bailey, William, shoemaker. From Thos Towson & Thos Stevens, near Baltimore Town. (MG 30 Aug 1753).
Baird, Thomas, weaver. From Archibald Moncraiff, AA Co Md. (MG 28 Jly 1774).
Baker, John, English, short, blacksmith. From Chas Ridgely Jr., BA Co Ironworks Md. (PAG 17 Apr 1760).*
Baker, John, from West of England, 19, tailor. From Robert Pinkney, Annapolis. (MG 7 & 14 Feb 1771).*
Baker, Richard. From John Reed & Nicholas Miller, Baltimore. (VGR 6 Feb 1772).
Baker, Thomas, bricklayer. From Richard Tilghman Earle, QA Co Md. (MG 4 Aug - 8 Sep 1757).
Baker, William, English, 30. From James Plant, CHA Co Md. (MG 5 Jan 1758).*
Baker, William. From Richd Morgan, FR Co Md. (MG 23 Jun - 7 Jly 1768).
Ball, Susanna, came by *Success's Increase* Dec 1773. Runaway from Forceput Va. (VGR 7 Apr 1774).
Banks, Anne. From James Davis, Holston's River, BO Co Va. (VGR 29 Oct 1772).*
Bannel, John, labourer, imported this year From Chas Dorsey, Elk Ridge Iron Works Md. (15 Jly 1756).
Barber, James, English, 25. From Benj Howard, AA Co Md. (MG 20 Jun - 11 Jly 1771).
Barker, Joseph, English, 25. From Richd Crabb, FR Co Md. (MG 11 Aug 1774 - 9 Mar 1775).*
Barker, William, English, 40, 5'8". From Edward Bosman, BA Co Md. (PAG 23 Aug 1770).*

Barnett, Levi, English, 22. From Jeremiah Sheredine, BA Co Ironworks. (PAG 20 Nov 1766 & 18 Jun 1767).

Barns, Hugh, English, 28. From Saml Dorsey Jr., BA Co Md. (MG 18 Feb - 4 Mar 1777).

Barret, Frances, English, 24. From Henry Howard, Northampton Furnace, BA Co Md. (MJ 4 & 11 Jly 1780).

Barret, John, English, 20. From Henry Gassaway, Joppa Md. (MG 4 Jun - 6 Aug 1767).*

Barrington, Mary, Irish, 30. From Thos Miles, FR Co Md. (MG 21 May 1761).

Bartham, George, English, farmer. From Saml Howard nr Annapolis. (MG 7 Mar 1771).

Bartlett, John, English, 43, tinker. From Oliver Hastings, KE Co Md. (PAG 6 Jun 1771).

Bartley, William, Irish, 26. From Walter Beall, FR Co Md. (MG11 Dec 1766 - 1 Jan 1767).

Bate, John, English, 23. From Benj Howard, AA Co Md. (MG 20 Jun - 11 Jly 1771).

Bates, John, English, 27. From Benj Howard, AA Co Md. (MG 20 Jun - 11 Jly 1771).

Bates, Rowland, 23. From Caleb Dorsey, AA Co Md.(MG 10 Jun 1762).

Bath, John, Scot, 5'6", weaver. From Josiah Clapham, FR Co Md. (PAG 16 Oct 1766).

Bathum, George, from West of England. From Saml Howard nr Annapolis. (MG 30 Jly 1772).

Batt, John, 50, 5'8", skindresser. From Valentine Larsch, BA Co Md. (PAG 2 Oct 1760).

Baver, John, 24. From Henry Stevens nr Baltimore Town. (MG 29 Sep 1774).

Beach, Samuel. From Benj Lawrence, AA Co Md. (MG 13 & 20 Jun 1765).

Beacham, George, English, 25. From Rezin Penn, BA Co Md. (MG 11 Oct - 5 Nov 1775).*

Bees, Robert, from Gloucestershire, 22, miner. From James Johnson. FR Co Md (MJ 24 Aug - 7 Sep 1774); from Thos Jacques, FR Co Md (MG 8 Jun - 13 Jly 1775).

Belong, Joseph, from West of England, 35, joiner. From George Steuart, AA Co Md. (MJ 16 Jun - 15 Sep 1774, PAG 22 Jly 1774).

Bener, Charles, 30-40. From Nath Adams, ran from schooner in Pocomoke R. (MG 9 Apr - 14 May 1767).

Benn alias Harwood, John, tailor, born England. From John Ducker, Annapolis. (MG 21 May & 6 Aug 1761).*

Bentley, John,. From John Jevins, Annapolis. (MG 22 Mar 1770).

Best, Thomas, an old man. From John Musgrove, FR Co Md. (MG 9 May 1765).*

Bigerton (Bickerton), George, 16, cooper, imported from Liverpool 6 months ago. From James Frazier, Baltimore. (MJ 5 - 26 Jly 1775).*

Bird, Bartholomew (alias Bertram), 26, middle height, shoemaker. From John Senhouse, AA Co Md. (PAG 6 Mar 1740).*

Birk, John, Irish. From Richd Graham, Dumfries. (MG 26 Apr 1759).

Bisben, Edward, shoemaker, 20. From Enoch Magruder, PG Co Md. (MG 18 & 25 Oct 1764).

Bishop, Joseph, 23, 5'7". From Turbutt Benton Sr., QA Co Md. (PAG 7 Sep 1769).

Blackell, John, English, 26, 6'. From John Footman, BA Co Md. (PAG 18 Oct 1770).

Blagdon, William, from West of England. From Dr. Chas Carroll, Md. (MG 26 Jun - 3 Jly 1751).

Blake, Thomas, 21. From Orlando Griffith, AA Co Md. (5 - 26 Jly 1749).

Blake, William, English, 35, 5'10", shoemaker. From Peter Hunter, BA Co Md. (PAG 7 Jly 1768; MG 26 Jly 1770).*

Blanford, John, 35, from West of England. From Thos Rutland, nr Snowdon's Iron Works AA Co Md. (MG 15 Mar - 12 Apr 1759).

Boardman, James, English, 40. From Benj Wells, BA Co Md. (MG 10 & 17 Jan 1771).

Boatman, Stephen, English, 25, with 3½ yrs to serve. From James Franklin nr Baltimore. (MJ 24 Jun - 21 Oct 1777).

RUNAWAYS

Bond, Elisha, 45, fiddler, from West of England. From Michael Hackett, KE Co Md. (MG 21 Oct - 11 Nov 1747).
Bone, William, 19. From Wm Dimmitt, BA Co Md. (PAG 2 Sep 1742).
Bonner, Thomas, blacksmith. From Saml Galloway, Md. (MG 8 Mar - 24 May 1749).
Booker, John, 31, born Yorkshire, just imported by *Nassau* from Liverpool. From James Duncanson, Fredericksburg Va. (VG 21 Jun 1770, 23 Apr & 13 Aug 1772).
Bools, Robert, English, 28, 5'7". From Patrick Rock, HAR Co Md. (PAG 1 May 1776).
Boot, Daniel, plays drum & flute. From James Riggs, FR Co Md. (MG 26 Apr 1764).
Booth, William, sailor with wooden leg. From Andrew Leitch, Dumfries Va. (VGP 10 Nov 1774).*
Borrow, William, English, 21, 5'8". From Wm Dockery, QA Co Md. (PAG 8 Nov 1759).
Boss, Thomas, English, 40, two years in country. From Richard Croxall, Baltimore Iron Works. (MG 9 & 16 Aug 1753).
Bostock, William, English, 30, 5'4", weaver, imported by *Albion* in Aug 1764. From James Wallace, AA Ironworks Md. (MG 5 Sep - 17 Oct 1765, PAG 12 Sep 1765).
Boswell, Edward, 30, born England, imported felon. Escaped from gaol, CHA Co Md. (MG 16 Jly 1761).
Boswell, Henry, "East India Indian" from West of England, "soldier in last American war", lately (1773) imported. From Benj Nicholson, BA Co Md. (MJ 28 Aug - 25 Sep 1773, 24 Aug - 7 Sep 1774).*
Boswell, Timothy, half brother of Henry Boswell (*q.v.*) "no part Indian", from West of England. From Benj. Nicholson, BA Co Md. (MG 28 Aug - 25 Sep 1773).*
Boswell, Timothy, 30. From Charles Ridgely, AA Co Md. (MG 1 - 16 Jan 1777).*
Bottin, John, 25, 5'8". From Edward Norwood, BA Co Md. (MG 28 Nov 1771 - 9 Jan 1772, PAG 21 Nov 1771).
Boucher, Thomas, from Westchester, England, 30, blacksmith. From Caleb Dorsey, AA Co Md. (MG 6 Oct - 1 Dec 1774).
Bould, John, 44, weaver. From Danl Weedon, James Bryan & Thos Yewell, Kent Is Md. (MG 28 May - 25 Jun 1767).
Bowling, Thomas, Irish, 25, 5'10", arrived 12 months ago. From Reginald Graham, BA Co Md. (PAG 25 Nov 1772).
Bowlls, George, from West of England, 20. From Wm Horn, QA Co Md. (MG 2 Aug 1770 - 17 Jan 1771).
Boyer, Hannah, 23. From Catherine Jennings, Md. (MG 13 Nov 1751); from Danl Wells, Annapolis. (MG 28 May - 28 Sep 1752)..
Boyle, William, English, 28, 5'10", fuller. From Edward Wilmer, CE Co Md. (PAG 31 Jly 1760).
Brabens, James. From Wm Edwards, BA Co Md. (PAG 23 Nov 1769).
Bradbury, Thomas, English. From James Baxter, Ironworks CE Co Md. (PAG 6 Jan 1737).
Bradford, Joseph, Irish, 23, 6'. From Alex Baird, KE Co Md. (PAG 25 May 1754).
Bradshaw, Edward, clerk. From Robert Anson, CE Co Md. (PAG 8 Apr 1756).
Brady, Mary. From Alice Daurs, FR Co Md. (MG 15 - 22 Nov 1764).*
Brett, John, English, 22. From Thos Snowden, PG Co Md. (MG 8 May 1777).*
Brewitt, George, born Nottinghamshire, collarmaker. From Edwd Oursley, BA Co Md. (MG 13 Jan 1757).
Brian, Richard, Irish. From Barnabas Hughes, Baltimore Town. (MG 2-30 Sep 1762).*
Broadbent, John, 22. From George Haile Sr., BA Co Md. (MG 29 Sep - 6 Oct 1763).
Bronon, Patrick, Irish, 18, 5'2". From Joseph Bosley Jr., BA Co Md. (PAG 28 Aug 1766).
Broof (Bruff), John, "convict servant lad." From Jonathan Mullinux. (MG 14 Aug 1755).*
Brooke, Thomas, English, 30, farmer. From Daniel McPherson, nr Portabacco Md. (MG 15 Sep - 13 Oct 1763).

Brookes, John, weaver. From Joseph Johnson, PG Co, Md. (MG 30 Nov - 21 Dec 1748).
Brookes, Thomas, from Essex, England, 29. From Daniel McPherson, CHA Co Md. (MG 2 & 9 Sep 1762.
Brooks, William, English, 30, 5'8". From Jeremiah Sheredine, BA Co Ironworks Md.(PAG 7 Jly 1763).
Broomfield, John, 27, London born, speaks good English. From W Hammond, BA Co Md. (MG 14 - 28 Oct 1746).
Broughton, John, Irish. From Richd Bows & Anthony Holmead, FR Co Md. (MG 9 - 23 Jly 1767).
Brounsnow, John, 20. From Richd Weedon, AA Co Md. (MG 13 Jly 1769).
Brown, James, 35, 5'6". From Richard Graham, BA Co Md. (PAG 21 May 1772).
Brown, John, English, middle height, miller. From Abraham Jarrett, BA Co Md. (PAG 22 Aug 1771).
Brown, John, English, 26, 5'7", used to the sea. From Buckler Bond, HAR Co Md. (PAG 10 Jan 1771; 3 May 1775, MJ 18 Jun - 9 Jly 1774).
Brown, Robert, 23, collar & harness maker, writes well. From Henry Howard, BA Co Md. (MJ 2 - 16 Oct 1776).
Browning, George, shoemaker, born Bristol. From Chris Curtis, PE Co Va. (VG 24 Nov 1774).
Bryan, Elizabeth, 30. From John Thompson Jr., Annapolis. (MG 10 May 1764).
Bryan, Thomas (1770). See Burn.
Buckley, John, Irish, 34, coach maker. From Thos Harvey, BA Co Md. (MG 24 Jun - 1 Jly 1756).*
Bulmore, George, born Yorkshire, 29. From Saml Worthington, BA Co Md. (MG 4-25 Sep 1773).
Bumstead, Harper John, English. From Benj Merryman & John Orrick, BA Co Md. (MG 24 Aug 1775 - 7 Mar 1776).
Burford, Edward. 20. From Thos French, BA Co Md. (MJ 29 Sep - 19 Oct 1778).
Burgess, Charles, from West of England, 25, carpenter. From Wm Reynolds, Annapolis. (MG 7 Mar 1771).
Burk, James, 25, from Dublin, Ireland, broadcloth weaver, has been sailor. From Wm Duvall, FR Co Md. (MJ 25 Nov 1777).
Burk, John, 25, 5'4". From Joseph Osborn of BA Co Md. (PAG 24 Oct 1765).*
Burn, Patrick, Irish, 30. From Saml Norwood, Baltimore Iron Works Md. (MG 11 & 18 Jly 1750)*
Burn alias Bryan, Thomas, Irish, 26, mason. From Thos French, Allegany Mountain. (MG 13 Dec 1770 - 10 Jan 1771).
Burns, Arthur, Irish. From Wm Ellis, CE Co Md. (PAG 30 Apr 1747).
Burnes, John, English, 5'6". From Hercules Kamp, BA Co Md. (PAG 10 Jan 1771).
Burns, Terence, Irish, from Wm Ellis, CE Co Md. (PAG 30 Apr 1747).
Burns, William, English. From Wm Duvall, FR Co Md. (MG 10 Nov 1768 - 5 Jan 1769).
Burny, Edward alias Barnaby, English, 25, ex-soldier. From John Carlyle, Alexandria Va. (MG 16 Aug 1759).
Burritt, Isaac, English, 19. From Caleb Dorsey, Elk Ridge Furnace Md. (MG 27 Sep - 18 Oct 1764).
Burrowes, Frances, born West of England. From John Ducker, Annapolis. (MG 28 Aug - 9 Oct 1760).*
Burroughs, John, 30, farmer, born Leicestershire, imported 1758 by *Trial*. From James McCubbin, Annapolis. (MG 7 Jun - 5 Jly 1759).*
Burrows, John, 33, & his wife. From John Ireland, Carroll's Manor Md. (MG 11 Jun 1761).

RUNAWAYS

Burton, Mary, 36, wearing iron collar. From John Hughes, Patapsco River Md. (MG 2 - 23 May 1754).*
Butler, Edward, alias Donald, Robert, 27, tailor. From Benj Colvard & George Divers, AL Co Va. (VG 16 Jun 1774).*
Butler, Thomas, Irish, 30, plasterer, three years in country. From Chris Lowndes, Bladensburg Md. (MG 14 - 21 Sep 1748, 12 Sep - 3 Oct 1750).*
Butter, William, Irish. From Richd Graham, Dumfries Va. (MG 26 Apr 1759).
Butterell, John, 35. From Simon Vashon, Patapsco Barrens. (MJ 7 & 14 Apr 1778).
Butterwort, James, English, 40, weaver, good scholar. From Thos Beatty. (MJ 16 Oct 1776).
Byers, William, ran with his wife, an indentured servant. From Archibald Moncreiff, AA Co Md. (MG 28 Jly 1774).
Byrne, Charles, Irish, slater & plasterer, 3 yrs to serve. From Patrick McDermott, MO Co Md. (MJ 4 May 1779).

Cadey, Samuel, 30, shoemaker, in country six months. From Edwd Brown Kent Is QA Co Md. (MG 7 Jly 1757).*
Calendar, Philip. From Howard Duvall. (MG 23 Aug - 1 Nov 1770).*
Callaghan, Daniel, Irish. From Thos Lee, Potomac Va. (AWM 26 Jun 1740).
Callahan, William, Irish, 30, 5'6", plasterer. From Andrew Pearce, CE Co Md. (PAG 29 Aug 1765; 4 Sep 1766).
Callis, James, 30. From Caleb Dorsey, Dorsey's Forge AA Co Md. (MG 15 Sep - 6 Oct 1768).
Calvert, Michael, 20, laborer. From David Weedon, James Bryan & Thomas Yewell, Kent Is Md. (MG 28 May - 25 Jun 1767).
Campbell, Charles, from West of England. From Chas Ridgely Jr., BA Co Md. (MG 20 Apr - 14 May 1767).
Campbell, Peter, Irish, 5'4". From Wm Watkins, BA Co Md. (PAG 6 Aug 1752).*
Cane, Margaret, fond of drink and sailors. From Benj. Philpott, CH Co Md. (MG 15 Nov 1764).
Carle, Thomas, Irish, 25. From John Adamson, FR Co Md. (MG 30 Jly - 3 Sep 1761).*
Carman, John, weaver, brother of Richard. From Benj. Young, Hunting Ridge BA Co Md (MG 9 - 30 Aug 1759); from Richard Croxall, Baltimore Ironworks (MG 1 May - 12 Jun 1760).*
Carman, Richard, 40, weaver, born Norfolk, brother of John, imported by *St. George* in Aug 1759. From Benj Young, BA Co Md. (MG 9 - 30 Aug 1759); from Richard Croxall, Baltimore Ironworks Md. (1 May - 12 Jun 1760).*
Carny, Michael, Irish, 25, shoemaker, can write. From Nicholas Worthington near Annapolis. (MG 17 Oct - 7 Nov 1776).
Carr, Henry, English, 6'. From Robert Marcer, CE Co Md. (PAG 10 Nov 1763).
Carr, John, English, 47, 5'10", bricklayer, arrived Jly 1770. From James Franklin, BA Co Ironworks Md. (PAG 26 Jly 1770; 6 Jun 1771).
Car, Matthew, Irish, 30, 5'6", weaver. From John Cromwell, AA Co Md. (1 Jun 1758).
Carr, Michael, 5'7". From Richd Fowler, BA Co Md. (PAG 6 Aug 1765).
Carroll, John, Irish, 30. From Thomas, Samuel & John Snowden, Patuxent Ironworks, PG Co Md. (MG 20 Aug - 1 Oct 1767).*
Carroll, Patrick, Irish, butcher. From Nath Pope, PG Co Md. (MG 27 Dec - 10 Jan 1765, PAG 17 Jan 1765).*
Cartee, Owen, Irish, 20, will make for Philadelphia. From Wm Byus, DO Co Md. (MG 15 & 22 Jun 1748).

1734 - 1788

Carter alias Gasford, Samuel, 23 arrived by *Thornton* Jun 1772. From Rev. Boucher, PG Co Md. (VGR 3 Dec 1772).*
Carter, William, 20. From Edward Osmond, Head of Severn Md. (MG 30 Jun 1768).
Casey, James, 23. From Chris Divers, BA Co Md. (PAG 18 Apr 1748).
Cash, Edmund, English, 33. From near Dr. John Stevenson's copper mines, FR Co Md. (MJ 23 Aug - 13 Sep 1773).
Caswell, William, weaver. From Abraham Ayres, Swan Creek, KE Co Md. (MG 23 Aug 1770).
Catling, James, from London, England, has followed the sea. From John Eason near Frederick Town Md. (MG 9 Aug 1770).*
Cavanach, James, Irish, middle height. From Wm Bennett, BA Co Md. (PAG 15 Jun 1748).
Cavenaugh, John, Irish, 24, 5'4", silk weaver, arrived Summer 1755. From James Breading, CE Co Md. (PAG 12 Feb 1756; 13 May 1756).
Cayton, Anthony, tailor. From Richard Lee. (MG 31 Aug - 19 Oct 1769).
Chaffey, John, English, 5'6". From Nathan Griffith, BA Co Md. (PAG 15 Aug 1771).*
Chambers, Mary, Irish, middle height. From Alex Baird, KE Co Md. (PAG 25 Apr 1754).
Chandler, William, from West of England, 40-45, farmer. From John Walter, BA Co Md. (MG 5 - 19 Jly 1764).*
Chant, Robert. From William Darding & William Corkrill, QA Co Md. (MG 3 Nov 1763).*
Cheek, Edward, English, belonging to Patrick Creagh, Annapolis. From Wm Strachan, master of *Moses & Rebecca* at Benedict Md. (MG 7 Nov - 19 Dec 1750).*
Cherryhome, William, plowman, born Yorkshire. From John Hammond, AA Co Md. (MG 11 - 25 Jly 1750).*
Child, John, English, 30, 5'10", gardener. From Richard Croxall, BA Co Ironworks. (MG 8 Mar - 5 Apr 1764); from James Franklin, BA Co Ironworks Md. (PAG 8 Mar 1764, MG 24 May - 30 Aug 1764).*
Claouss, John Christopher, German, soldier. From John Welsh, BA Co Ironworks Md. (PAG 20 Mar 1766).
Clark, Hugh, Irish, 25, tanner. From Vachel Warfield. (MG 12 Nov 1767).
Clark, John, 38, 5'8", gardener. From Wm Buchanan, BA Co Md. (PAG 20 Jun 1754).
Clark, John, from West of England, 27, blacksmith. From Isaac Harris & Jonathan Pinkney, Annapolis. (MG 8 Nov 1764 - 14 Feb 1765).
Clark, John, 50, 5'9". From Josiah Brown, BA Co Md. (PAG 21 Aug 1766).
Clark, Joseph, English, 25, imported in 1764. From Caleb Dorsey, Elk Ridge Furnace. (MG 27 Sep - 18 Oct 1764, 16 May 1765).*
Clark, Thomas, 40, 5'4", weaver. From James Thomas, KE Co Md. (PAG 26 Mar 1761).
Clark, William. From Renaldo Monk, Ba Co Md. (PAG 11 Jly 1765).
Cleary, Patrick, Irish, 19. From John McNabb, Baltimore. (MG 19 Apr - 10 May 1770).
Clemmisson, Amburst, English, 5'6". From Edwd Bosman, BA Co Md. (PAG 23 Aug 1770).*
Clunis, Thomas (1756). *See* Graham, George.
Coe, Mark, English, 22. From Nicholas Merryman, BA Co Md, lately imported by *Aston Hall*. (MG & MJ 8 & 15 Sep 1774).*
Coe, Richard, from West of England, ran from schooner *Endeavour* in KE Co Md, imported in Feb 1774. From James Braddock, TA Co Md. (MG 1 - 15 Dec 1774, PAG 23 Nov 1774).*
Cole, James, bricklayer. From Richard Lee, Naval Office CH Co Md. (MG 16 Oct 1751).*
Coleman, Samuel, English, 30, baker. From John Chalmers, Annapolis Md. (MG 7 Oct 1747).*
Colen, Philip, 5'5". From Wm Prigg, BA Co Md. (PAG 15 May 1755).

Collens, Robert, English, 5'7". From James Franklin, BA Co Ironworks Md. (PAG 15 Mar 1775).

Collerd, Thomas, 5'7". From Wm Brown & Wm Jones, QA Co Md. (MG 26 Jly - 23 Aug 1770, PAG 26 Jly 1770).*

Collett, William, 21, born Somerset. From Joseph Watkins, Patapsco Furnace Md. (MG 20 & 27 Sep 1759).*

Collier, John, English, 5'6". From Chas Worthington, AA Co Md. (PAG 7 Jly 1773).

Collins, Edmund, 25, 5'8", shoemaker. From John Howard, BA Co Ironworks Md. (PAG 22 Aug 1765).*

Collins, John, 27, pretends to be a doctor. From John Tillotson, QA Co Md. (MG 19 Jun - 17 Jly 1751).*

Collins, John, 23, has West Country dialect. From Caleb Dorsey, Elk Ridge Md. (MG 1 May 1760, 5 & 19 Jun 1760, 16 Apr 1761, 21 Jly & 1 Sep 1763); from Nath Giles, Lancs Co Pa. (PAG 21 Aug & 16 Oct 1760).

Colwell, William, 30, 5'10" schoolmaster. From JohnBosman, TA Co Md. (MG 5 - 19 Apr 1764, PAG 26 Apr 1764).*

Conoway, Michael, Irish. From William Brown, London Town, AA Co Md. (MG 11 & 25 Jun 1767).

Conaway, Michael, Irish. From London Town, AA Co Md. (MG 23 Jun - 29 Sep 1768).

Connell, Alexander, farrier. From Francis King & Henry Hardy, PG Co. (MG 19 Sep 1765).*

Connolly, Dennis, 25. From Michael Coager, RO Co Va.. (VGPu 12 Jun 1778).

Connelly, Lawrence, Irish, 18. From John Dorsey, AA Co Md. (MJ 9 & 18 Dec 1773).

Connerly, Patrick, Irish, 22. From John Trundle & Walter Beall, FR Co Md. (MG 26 Mar - 9 Apr 1767).

Conner, Patrick, 22. From Thomas, Saml & John Snowden, PG Co Md. (MG 20 Aug - 1 Oct 1767).*

Conroy, Michael, Irish, 21-25, shoemaker. From Philip Hall & Isaac Short, Snowden's Ironworks, PG Co Md. (MG 15 Sep - 13 Oct 1774, VGP 21 Sep 1775).

Conwan, Evan, an old Welshman. From Benj Nicholson, BA Co Md. (MJ 28 Aug - 25 Sep 1773).

Cook, Henry, English. From Benj Merryman & John Orrick. (MG 24 Aug 1775 - 7 Mar 1776).

Cook, Miles, English, 30, 5'10". From *Dolphin*, Capt. Craymer, BA Co Md. (MG 11 Aug - 1 Sep 1763, PAG 18 Aug 1763).*

Cook, Stephen, 21. From Wm Bentley, FR Co Md. (MJ 22 Dec 1778 - 5 Jan 1779).*

Cooper, John. From Abraham Clark, PG Co Md. (MG 11 Jun 17670).

Cooper, Thomas, English, 26, 5'3". From Caleb Dorsey, AA Co Ironworks Md. (MG 5 Jun - 7 Aug 1760; PAG 21 Aug 1760).

Cooper, Thomas, of Kent, England, good farmer. From Saml Mansell & Robt Barnes Jr., AA Co Md. (MJ 4 - 18 Oct 1775).

Coot, Samuel, 25, English. From David Gorsuch near Baltimore Town. (MG 16 & 23 Aug 1759, 10 Apr 1760).*

Cosby, Mary, Irish, 20, short. From Timothy Brannin, CE Co Md. (PAG 7 Jun 1750).

Cotney (Courtney), William, born near Bristol, belonging to Anth McCulloch. From Peter Maxwell, Queen's Town Md. (MG 18 Aug - 15 Sep 1757).*

Cottman, Joseph, 20, weaver. From Wm Bosley & John Wilmott Sr., BA Co Md. (MG 15 - 29 Dec 1774).

Courbet, James, English, 19. From Thomas Emory, QA Co Md. (PAG 6 Mar 1760).

Court alias Corrt, James, of Kent, England, 24, lately imported by *Neptune*. From John FA Priggs, PG Co Md. (MG29 Mar - 28 Jun 1764, 21 Jly - 1 Dec 1768).*

Cowden, Susannah, 20. From Wm Randall, BA Co Md. (PAG 11 Jun 1767).*
Cowill, Francis, 40, 5'4". From John Walker, QA Co Md. (PAG 23 May 1771).*
Cowling, William, born West of England, 30, farmer, abt 14 months in America. From
   Richd Croxall, Baltimore Iron Works. (MG 28 Aug - 16 Oct 1755, PAG 21 Aug 1755).*
Cox alias Smith, John, 25. From Caleb Dorsey BA Co Md. (MG 7 - 21 Aug 1766).
Cox, Richard, 45, from West Country. From Saml Blunt, Kent Is QA Co Md. (MG 21 Oct -
   11 Nov 1766).
Cox, Richard, 40, 5'5". From Wm Modesley, QA Co Md. (PAG 9 May 1765).*
Cox, Robert, born Oxfordshire or Northants, just imported by *Apollo*. From Richd Croxall,
   Baltimore Iron Works. (MG 15 Aug - 19 Sep 1754).
Cox, William, 25-30, butcher, from West Country. From Thos Holmes, Annapolis. (MG 26
   Aug - 16 Sep 1746).
Coyl, Owen, Irish, 20, 5'7", jockey, arrived 3 weeks ago. From Wm Webb of BA Co Md.
   (PAG 16 Jly 1773).
Crawley, Jacob, 20, more than 2 years in country. From Henry Stevenson, Baltimore. (MG
   27 Mar 1766).*
Crayton (Craten), James, English, 27, 5'8". From James Wood, BA Co Md. (PAG 21 Aug
   1766).*
Crew, John, 40, born England. From Robt Alexander, FA Co Va. (PC 7 Aug 1767).*
Crosby, James, Irish, 21. From Wm Duvall, AA Co Md. (MG 21 Jly - 8 Sep 1768).*
Cross, Bartholomew, alias Adwell, Richard, 30, English, broke QA Co Jail in Sep 1767.
   From Chris Gardener, AA Co Md. (MG 26 Nov 1767 - 28 Jan 1768).*
Crouch, Richard, 25. From Anne Middleton, Annapolis Md, probably headed towards NC.
   (MG 28 Mar - 9 May 1771, VGR 9 May 1771).*
Crowder (Crowther), Elizabeth, 40, quilter. From Sarah Monro, Annapolis Md. (MG 1 Apr
   - 6 May 1746).*
Culbert, Thomas (1759). *See* Read.
Cullimore, William, from West of England, 35, 5'4", ditcher. From Thomas E Hutchings,
   QA Co Md. (MG 11 & 18 Jly 1765); from John Winterton, KE Co Md, gaoler. (PAG 12
   Dec 1765).*

Dabs, John, English, 23, pretended collier. From Chas Carroll & Co, BA Co Md. (MG 2
   May - 6 Jun 1765).*
Dale, George, English, 22. From Chas Carroll & Co, BA Co Md. (MG 5 - 19 Sep 1754).
Daley, James, Irish, 40, weaver, arrived 20 months ago. From Hugh Coupland, BA Co Md.
   (PAG 9 Jun 1748).
Dane, William, English, 40, blacksmith. From Simon Wickes, KE Co Md. (MG 19 Apr
   1764, PAG 2 Aug 1764).
Danely, Thomas, 36. From Wm Lewis, AA Co Md. (MG 1 Jun 1769).
Danscomb alias Dungan, Patrick, Irish, From Zachariah McCubbin, BA Co Md. (MG 19
   Apr - 7 Jun 1749).
Darbyshire, Jonathan, 35, miller. From Enoch Magruder, PG Co Md. (MG 4 - 25 Oct
   1764).*
Davenant alias Dryton, Samuel, 30, gardener. From Richd Croxall, Patapsco Md. (MG 4
   Aug - 15 Sep 1768).
Davey, Edward, 20. From Robt Weedon, Kent Is QA Co Md. (MG 22 Oct - 9 Nov 1772).
Davie, William of Cornwall, 28. From Saml Middleton, Annapolis. (MG 27 Nov 1765).*
Davidson, Catherine, lately arrived. From George Buchanan, BA Co Md. (PAG 13 Feb
   1750).*
Davis, Edward, English, 5'9", sailor used to the sea. From John Calvert, BA Co Md. (PAG
   18 Jun 1764).

Davis, Edward, imported in 1763 by *Prince William*, ran from *Becky* near Baltimore. From Thos Lawson. (MG 16 & 23 Aug 1764).*

Davis, Edward, English, 30, 5'4", perukemaker. From Joseph Earle, CE Co Md. (PAG 6 Feb 1766).*

Davis, Evan, Welsh, 30, 5'5", arrived in Nov 1768. From Saml Blunt & Jonathan Roberts, QA Co Md. (MG 30 Mar - 18 May 1769, PAG 27 Apr 1769).*

Davis, George, English, 30, bred a baker. From Clement Brooke, Baltimore Ironworks. (MG 8 Sep - 20 Oct 1778).

Davis, John, 25. From George Page, AA Co Md. (MG 19 Sep 1765).

Davis, Mary, middle-aged. From John Catlett, KW Co Va. (VG 25 Feb 1773).

Davis, Sarah, 22. From Paul Rankin, PG Co Md. (MG 27 Apr - 11 May 1758).*

Davis, Thomas, born Wales. From John Dorsey Jr., AA Co Md. (MG 11 Apr - 16 May 1754).

Davis, Thomas, English, 25, 6'0". From John Wilson, QA Co Md. (PAG 8 May 1760).

Davis, Thomas, Irish, 27. From Caleb Dorsey, Elk Ridge Furnace, AA Co Md. (9 - 30 Nov 1769).

Dawson, John, English, 36, 5'5". From Hugh Bryarly, BA Co Md. (PAG 1 Sep 1773).*

Dawson alias Deason, William, English, 30, labourer. From Henry Callister, TA Co Md. (MG 27 Nov - 18 Dec 1755).

Day, Thomas, born Bristol, blacksmith. From Alex Stewart, Geo Freebairn & Michael Depenbough, Baltimore. (MG 15 & 22 Feb 1759).*

Day, William, middle-aged, English, farmer. From Gerard B Causin, Portobacco Md. (MG 21 Nov 1771 - 9 Jan 1772, VGH 6 Feb 1772).*

Deale, Clement. From Edmund Terrill & Clement Reade, CU Co Va. (VG 4 Jun 1772).

Dealy, William, Irish, 5'8". From John Stevenson, BA Co Md. (PAG 15 May 1764).

Dean, Joshua. From London, 40. From Alex Spottswood, Postmaster-General, Jun 1737. (NYG 17 Jly 1738).*

Deason, John (1755). *See* Dawson.

Delany, William, Irish, 45. From David Barclay, BA Co Md. (PAG 21 May 1772).

Demsy, Edward, born Ireland, 26, barber. From Thos Chittam, Bladensburg Md. (MG 27 Jun - 29 Aug 1754).

Dennis, John. From James Dick & Stewart, Newington Ropewalk, Annapolis. (MG 8 Mar 1770).

Dennit, William, English, 27. From Walter Wyle, BA Co Md. (MG 2 - 23 Oct 1766).

Densley, Anthony, English, tall, born West of England. From John Cooper, CE Co Md. (MG & PAG 21 Sep 1758).*

Dey, James, English, 35, labourer. From John Cromwell, AA Co Md. (PAG 1 Jun 1758).

Dickason, Joseph, 18, born Portugal, collier. From Thomas Welsh, AA Co Md. (MG 7 - 21 Jly 1763).*

Dickerson, William, 19. From James Howard, Elk Ridge, AA Co Md. (MG 14 Jun - 5 Jly 1770).

Dilland, James, Irish, lately arrived. From Wm Ellis, CE Co Md. (PAG 2 Oct 1746).

Dobbins, Joseph, 19. From Seth Warfield, Elk Ridge, AA Co Md. (MG 2 - 30 Aug 1770).

Dobinney, Alexander, born Switzerland, speaks French. From Darby Lux & Nich Haile, BA Co Md. (MJ 14 - 28 Jly 1778).

Dobson, Thomas, imported 2 months ago. From Henry Stevenson, Baltimore. (MG 27 Mar 1766).*

Doby, James, 40, 5'8". From Chas Greenbury Griffith, FR Co Md. (PAG 26 May 1768).

Dollason, Robert, Irish. From Thos Davis, near Snowden's Iron Works Md. (MG 5 Sep - 26 Dec 1754).

Dome, William, English. From Robt Roberts, KE Co Md. (PAG 26 Apr 1764).

Donald, Patrick, 22. From Saml Beall Jr., FR Co Md. (MG 27 Aug - 17 Sep 1761).
Donald, Robert (1774). *See* Butler, Edward.
Donaldson, James, ran from *Dolphin* in Patapsco River. From Stewart & Lux, Baltimore. (MG 11 Aug - 1 Sep 1763).*
Donally, Patrick, 22. From Saml Beall, Sheriff of FR Co Md. (MG 18 Jun 1761).*
Donoson, James, English. 26, 5'5". From Capt. Craymer, ship captain, BA Co Md. (PAG 18 Aug 1763).*
Donovan, James, 32, used to the sea, ran from *Johnson*. From John Ashburner. (MG 28 Mar - 25 Apr 1771).*
Dorman alias Holderness, George. Born London, 20. From Saml Love Jr. LO Co Va. (VGPu 25 Jly 1777).*
Dorman, Timothy, 38, seaman. From Joseph Ray, 14 miles above Snowden's Iron Works Md. (MG 24 May - 7 Jun 1759).*
Dorsey, Patrick, 30, belonging to James Richard, Baltimore. From Zachariah McCubbin, BA Co Md. (MG 11 & 18 Jly 1750).*
Dovey, Joseph, English, short, arrived Jun 1758. From Thos Harrison, AA Co Ironworks Md. (PAG 15 May 1760).
Dow, Henry, English, 30, 5'6". From John Footman, BA Co Md. (PAG 18 Oct 1770).
Dowling, Tady, Irish, 24, good ferryman. From James Kelso, Patapsco Ferry, AA Co Md. (MJ 16 Jan 1777).
Driver, William, English, 40. From Caleb Dorsey, AA Co Md. (MG 27 Sep - 18 Oct 1764).
Drury, Thomas, imported this year by the [*Thomas & Sarah*] Capt. Wm. Holmes. From David Gorsuch, Baltimore. (MG 15 & 22 Sep 1757).
Drury, Timothy, 17. From Wm Triplet, KG Co Va. (VG 26 Sep 1771).*
Dryton, Samuel (1768). *See* Davenant.
Dudgen, John, Irish, 24, 5'4", shoemaker. From James Moore, BA Co Md. (PAG 26 Oct 1774).
Dudgen, Joseph, Irish, shoemaker. From James Fisher, HA Co Md. (PAG 26 Oct 1774).
Dufee, Patrick, Irish, 35, imported 8 months ago. From John Baker & Basil Brooke. (MG 23 Jly 1772).
Duffeld, Jacob of Essex, blacksmith, imported by *Douglas* in 1769. From Saml Mummy, BA Co Md. (MG 28 Jun - 12 Jly 1770).*
Duffey, Peter, Irish, lately arrived. From Wm Ellis, CE Co Md. (PAG 2 Oct 1746).
Duncanson, William, 22. From Hugh Wallace & Hugh West, FA Co Va. (MG 2 Dec 1746).
Dungan, Paddy (1749). *See* Danscomb.
Dunn, Daniel, English, 35, 5'7". From John Forwood, BA Co Md. (MG & PAG 18 Oct 1770).*
Dunn, John, Irish, middle height, in this country some time. From Joseph Wood & Adam Vanbebber, CE Co Md. (PAG 11 Oct 1750, MG 14 Nov 1750).
Dunn, Joseph, Irish, 40. From Caleb Dorsey, AA Co Md. (MG 5 Sep 1771).
Dunn, William, Irish, 36. From Joshua Frazier, Annapolis. (MG 11 Jun - 16 Jly 1767).*
Dyer, Thomas, English, 21, 5'6", arrived Aug 1770. From Robt Hinson, KE Co Md.. (PAG 4 Apr 1771).*
Dykes, Moses, English, 20. From John Ireland & Lawrence Robinson, Carroll's Manor Md. (MG 9 Aug 1759, 11 Jun 1761).*

Eagle, Edward, ran from *Beverly* at Port Royal Va. From Wm Dudley, CAR Co Md. (MG 22 & 29 Dec 1763).*
Eating, Jonathan, 26. From Stephen Gill Jr., BA Co Md. (MG 10 Aug 1769).

RUNAWAYS

Edwards alias Redding alias Kay, Elizabeth, 20. From John Davis near Patuxent Iron
Works Md. (MG 20 Apr 1748)
Edwards, William. From Mary Cockey, Kent Is Md. (MG 4 Mar 1756).
Edwin, Francis, 5'5". From Robt Teves, BA Co Md. (PAG 12 Sep 1765 & 6 Nov 1766).*
Elderbeck, George, from West of England, 25, weaver. From Alex Cowan nr Joppa Md.
(MJ 22 Jly - 19 Aug 1777).
Elin (Ealing), Samuel, carpenter & joiner, arrived from London by *Forward* 1738. From
Wm Walker, WE Co Va. (AWM 19 Jly 1739).*
Ellicott, Charles, English, 21, no trade. From Nath Folsom, Bladensburg Md. (MG 9 Nov -
14 Dec 1748).
Elliot, Edward, 30. From Chas Worthington, AA Co Md. (MG 17 - 31 Dec 1772).
Ellis, John, English, 18. From T Worthington, Baltimore Md. (MJ 10 Jly 1776).
Elton (alias Halton), Thomas, short, butcher, has run before. From Thos Rutland, AA Co
Md. (PAG 1 Jun 1769); from Chas Duvall, PG Co Md. (MG 16 Apr - 21 May 1772).*
Emanuel, Ralph, 22, recently arrived in *Justitia*. From Andrew Leitch neard Leedstown Va.
(VG 22 Apr 1775).*
English, Nelly (Mary), 40. From Edwd Breston, BA Co Md. (PAG 10 Nov 1768).*
English, William, former servant to Recuiting Officer at Winchester, ran from *Beverly* in
Va. From Wm Dudley, CAR Co Md. (MG 22 & 29 Dec 1763).*
Entwhistle, Edward, English, weaver. From Jacob Bromwell, Oxford, TA Co Md. (MG 8
Nov - 6 Dec 1753).
Erwin, Francis, Irish, blacksmith. From George Plater, SM Co Md. (MG 8 Mar - 26 Apr
1759).
Etherington, John, English, 20. From Benj Ryan, AA Co Md. (MG 15 Jly 1746).
Evans, John (1754), *See* Flack.
Evans alias Harris, John, tailor. From Basil & John Waring, PG Co Md. (MG 4 Sep - 2 Oct
1766).*
Evans, John, 21, 5'8", shoemaker. From Robt Teves, BA Co Md. (PAG 6 Nov 1766).*
Evans, Lewis, Welsh, 25, tanner & driver. From Thos Williamson, Annapolis. (MG 7 Oct
1747).
Evans, Morris, 36, 5'7". From Nath Scott, QA Co Md. (PAG 5 Apr 1753).*
Evans, Thomas, sailor, in America for 2 years, ran from *William & Anne*. From David
Ross, Bladensburg Md. (MG 12 Aug 1746).*
Evans, Thomas, Welsh, 40. From Wm Horn, Kent Is Md. (MG 30 Oct - 4 Dec 1766).*
Ewdale (Udall), John, 45, carpenter & joiner. From Thos Snowden, near Patuxent Iron
Works Md. (MG 4 Sep - 9 Oct 1751).*
Ewen, John, 22, joiner, arrived 1768. From Wm Buckland, RI Co Va. (VGR 15 Jun 1769,
10 Jan 1771).*
Eyre, John Esq. Lately transported for stealing paper, died 3 days after arrival. (VG 9 Apr
1772).*

Fairbanks, James. From Danl Stephenson, Bladensburg Md. (MG 24 Dec 1760 - 12 Mar
1761).*
Fall, John, 22, painter & glazier. From John Sims, CHA Co Md. (MG 16 Jly - 27 Aug
1752).*
Farrol, Lawrence, Irish, 23. From James Franklin, Baltimore Iron Works Md. (MG 19 Jly -
16 Aug 1759); from Richd Croxall, Baltimore Iron Works Md. (MG 27 Mar - 29 May
1760).
Faulkner, William, born Lincolnshire, 24, tailor. From Wm Lux, BA Co Md. (MG 11 Apr -
16 May, 18 Jly 1754).

Fell, William, English, middle height, wigdresser. From James Dimmitt, BA Co Md. (PAG 2 Aug 1750).*

Ferrell (Farrell), John, English, about 3 years in country. From Chas Hammond or Wm Sellman, AA Co Md. (MJ 18 Mar - 8 Apr 1777).*

Ferrill (Farrell), Francis, school teacher. From John Hammond, AA Co Md. (MG 10 & 19 Jly 1751).*

Fetchman, Anne, English. From Samuel Hart, BA Co Md. (PAG 14 Aug 1746).

Field, Matthew, 30. From Thos Elliott, AA Co Md. (MG 26 Nov - 10 Dec 1772).

Fields, James, 23, 5'8". From Wm Selman, AA Co Md. (PAG 9 Dec 1772).*

Finder, Joseph, English, 30. From James Summers, PG Co Md. (MG 25 Jan - 1 Feb 1753).*

Findley, John, bricklayer, ran from house of Benj Ward, Amelia Va.. From Richd Eppes, CHE Co Va. (MG 5 Sep 1754).

Finn, John, Irish, 20, imported from Dublin 2 months ago. From Mordecai Hammond, BA Co Md. (MG 26 - 30 Sep 1765).

Fish, John, English, 35, shoemaker. From Allen Quinn, Annapolis. (MG 6 Sep - 4 Oct 1759).

Fish, Richard. From John Clarkson, Susquenanna Md. (MG 9 - 30 Aug 1759).

Fisher, Joseph, 40, 5'8". From John Welsh, QA Co Md. (PAG 6 Sep 1759)

Fisher, Laurence, from West of England. From Caleb Dorsey, AA Co Md. (MG 6 Oct - 1 Dec 1774).

Fitch, William, ex soldier. From John Metcalfe, BA Co Md. (MG 26 Apr - 14 Jun 1753).

Fitzgerald, Nell (Eleanor), 30, far gone with child. From Thos Lane, BA Co Md. (MG 6 Oct 1774).*

Flack alias Evans, John, sail maker. From Wm Bicknell, London Town Md. (MG 11 Apr 1754).*

Flanagan, Terence, Irish, 24, middle height. From Benj Tasker, BA Co Ironworks Md. (MG & PAG 27 & 29 May 1746).

Flannakin, Margaret. From Geo Smoot, CHA Co Md. (MG 31 Aug 1769).

Flint, William, from West of England, 22. From Henry Ridgely, FR Co Md. (MG 17 Jun - 7 Jly 1774).

Flood, Samuel, 25, labourer. From Richd Croxall, Md. (MG 4 Aug - 15 Sep 1768).

Floyd, Mary, Irish, imported by *Randolph* in Oct 1766. From Edmund Jennings, Annapolis. (MG 21 Jan - 11 Feb 1768).

Forrester, William, served with Dr. Green in England, imported by *Duke of Cumberland* with Charlotte Hamilton (*q.v.*) & ran away with her. From David Currie, LA Co Va.. (MG 25 Jan 1753).

Foster, George, brickmaker. From Wm Williams Jr., South River Md. (MG 20 Aug 1761).*

Fowler, John, 35, fiddler, brought up to sea, imported from Hull by Capt Cooper. From Thos Dansie, KW Co Va. (MG 26 Jly 1749).

Fowler, John, Irish, 30, 5'10", tanner. From George Scott, AA Co Md.(PAG 7 Dec 1769).*

Fox, John. From George Becraft, AA Co Md. (MG 17 & 24 Jun 1746).*

Franks, Andrew, 26, ropemaker. From Wm Fearson, Williamsburg Va. (VG 15 Aug 1771).

Frazer, Henry, English, 26, 5'8". From Adin Pancoast, FR Co Md. (PAG 14 Jly 1771).*

French, Patrick, Irish, 45. From Alex Wells, nr Baltimore Town. (MG 18 Aug - 1 Sep 1778).

Fry (alias Monger), Joseph, 21. From Chas Carroll, nr Baltimore Town. (MG 10 - 24 Oct 1765).

Fryer, John, 30, 5'7", wheelwright. From Francis Phillips, BA Co Ironworks Md. (MG 1 - 15 Jan 1767, PAG 8 Jan 1767).

RUNAWAYS

Fuller, Thomas, English, 40, with 4 yrs to serve. From Wm Goodwin, BA Co Md. (MJ 22 Jly 1777).*

Gabriel, Solomon, English, 5'3", painter, speaks good Dutch. From Thos Jones, BA Co Md. (MG 12 - 26 Jly 1764, PAG 12 Jly 1764).*

Gafford alias Fields, William, 30, imported by *Patapsco* in 1760, and again transported 1773. From Thos Hawkins, AA Co Md. (MG 10 Aug 1769, MJ 31 Mar 1774).

Gale, George, from West of England, mason. From John Carr, AA Co Md. (MG 1 -22 Sep 1757).

Gale, Joseph (1767). *See* Green.

Gallop, Matthew, English, 30, 5'8", arrived 6 weeks ago. From Alex Stuart, CE Co Md. (PAG 18 Sep 1755).

Gamball, Ralph, 40, ran from *Isabella*. From Smyth & Sadler, KE Co Md. (MG 20 Jly - 10 Aug 1769).

Gardner, John, from West of England. From Thos Rutland, nr Snowden's Ironworks Md. (MG 19 & 26 Sep 1765).

Gardner, John, 24. From Greenbury Griffith, FR Co Md. (MJ 26 Aug - 9 Sep 1773).

Garraughty, John, Irish, 24. From Chas Ridgely Sr., BA Co Md. (MG 25 Sep 1766).

Garret, William. From Thos Rutland, nr Snowden's Ironworks Md. (MG 19 & 26 Sep 1765).

Gasford, Samuel (1772). *See* Carter.

Gaull, George, Scot, 35, schoolteacher. From John McAtee & Henry McPherson. (MG 22 Jun - 20 Jly 1769).

Gaynor, Peter, Irish, 34. From Elam Bailey, nr Baltimore Town. (MJ 25 Feb - 4 Mar 1777).

Gill, Charles, English, 30, 5'6", jockey. From Edward Teal, Rag-Land, BA Co Md. (MG 15 Oct PAG 22 Oct 1761).

Gilliard, William Thomson, English, 30, ex cook to Duke of Northumberland, schoolmaster, speaks French. From Abraham Jarrett, BA Co Md. (MG 12 Nov - 3 Dec 1767).*

Gilson, John, 24. From Robt Ayres, KE Co Md. (MG 24 Oct 1771).

Gingle, Isaac, born West of England, farmer, speaks bad & fast English. From John Metcalfe, Patapsco Md. (MG 21 Sep - 12 Oct 1752, 26 Apr - 14 Jun 1753).

Glover, Henry, blacksmith. From Thos, Saml & John Snowden, PG Co Md. (MG 3 Apr - 22 May 1766).

Goddard, James, English, 28. From Wm Cromwell & John Ebert, BA Co Md. (MJ 2 - 16 Jly 1774).*

Godden, William. From Wm Hall, nr Bladensburg Md. (MG 1 Jly 1762).

Godson, William, brickmaker. From George Scott, AA Co Md. (MJ 28 Jly 1778).

Gold, George, 30, glazier & plumber. From Patrick Creagh, Annapolis. (MG 28 Dec 1748, 14 Jun 1749).

Golding, Peter, English, 45, gardener, imported in 1766. From Philip R Fendall, CHA Co Md.. (MG 21 Jun - 5 Jly 1770).*

Good, Thomas, English, 35, 5'7", miller. From Chas Greenbury Griffith, FR Co Md. (PAG 26 May 1768).

Goodridge, Gilbert, English, arrived Apr 1753. From Edmund Ball, BA Co Md. (PAG 28 Nov 1754).*

Goodwin, Thomas, Irish, 45, middle height. From John Jackson, CE Co Md. (PAG 6 Sep 1744).

Goulden, George, farrier & physician. From James Smith, CHA Co Md. (MG 18 Oct - 1 Nov 1759).

Graham alias Scholar, William, 5'6". From James Christie Jr., BA Co Md. (PAG 29 Jan - 12 Feb 1767).*

Graham, George, alias Clunis, Thomas, Scot, pretends to teach fencing. From John Jordan, Hugh Mitchell & Alex Lothian, CHA Co Md. (MG 29 Jan - 11 Mar 1756).

Graham, George, barber. From John Kinsman, Portobacco Md. (MG 29 Aug - 19 Sep 1754).*

Graigg (Griggs), John, from Kent, England, 30. From Joshua Beall, Bladensburg Md. (MG 29 Sep - 3 Nov 1763). *

Grant, Thomas, from Northants, England, lately imported from Bristol, gentleman's servant. From Richd Croxall, Baltimore Ironworks Md. (MG 25 Aug - 1 Sep 1763).

Gray, William, 19. From Patrick Coutts, Richmond Va. (VG 4 Feb 1773).

Greefes, Henry, Welsh, 40. From Walter Dulany, Md. (MG 24 Aug - 21 Sep 1769).

Green alias Gale, Joseph, 36, farmer, born Wiltshire, arrived by *Justitia* Nov 1766. From Nicholas Flood, Va. (PC 27 Apr 1767).

Green, Peter, English, 42, 5'4". From Samuel Read, FR Co Md. (PAG 12 Apr 1753; letter awaiting him at Annapolis PO MG 29 Apr 1757).

Green, Richard, 50. From Chas Carroll, nr Baltimore Town. (MG 18 Sep 1766).

Green, William, from West of England. From John Hood & Mordecai Selby, AA Co Md. (MG 30 Mar - 11 May 1775).

Greenley, Elizabeth. Executed in Williamsburg for murder of fellow servant. (AWM 16 Dec 1736).

Greenwood, Thomas, English, 23. From Thos Jacques, FR Co Md. (MG 8 Jun - 13 Jly 1775).*

Greeses, Henry, Welsh, 40, 5'6". From Thos Chrisholm, BA Co Md. (PAG 11 Aug 1769).

Griffin, Anne, Welsh, 32. From Edward Osmond, nr Annapolis. (MG 24 Jan & 18 Apr 1765).

Griffin, Edward, 45, short. From Edward Rummer, AA Co Md. (PAG 16 Aug 1744).*

Griffith, John, English, 32. From Elam Bailey, nr Baltimore Town. (MJ 25 Feb - 4 Mar 1777).

Griffith, Philip, 21, tailor. From Tobias Ashmore, KE Co Md. (MG 1 Nov 1770).

Griffiths, John. From Stephen Bryan, Kent Is Md. (MG 4 Aug 1763).

Griffitths, James, born Herefordshire, husbandman, imported by *Trial.*. From Richd Croxall, BA Co Md. (MG 30 Jun - 4 Aug 1757, 11 May - 15 Jun 1758).*

Grimshaw, Edmund, from Lancashire, 21, 5'9", weaver, in country 9 months. From Chas Ridgely., BA Co Md. (MG 30 Apr & 18 Jun - 9 Jly 1767, PAG 13 Aug 1767).

Grimshaw, Job, 40, 5'2", tinker. From John Jones. BA Co Md. (MG 29 Mar - 26 Apr 1764, PAG 8 Apr 1764).

Groves, James, 30. From Anne Pettibone, AA Co Md. (MG 23 Jun - 29 Sep 1768).

Groves, James, English, 40, arrived in *Albion* Aug 1763. From Thos Foster, AA Co Md. (MG 5 Jly - 20 Sep 1764, PAG 15 Aug 1764).

Gummer, Thomas, English, 26, carpenter & sawyer, 5 yrs to serve. From Wm Goodwin, BA Co Md. (MJ 22 Jly 1777).*

Haines, Joseph, 30. From John Legg, Kent Is Md. (MG 19 Nov 1767 - 11 Feb 1768).*

Haines (alias Ainsworth), Robert, English, 22, 5' 7". From Michael Byrne, KE Co Md. (MG 9 - 30 Nov 1769, PAG 9 Nov 1769).

Hales (Hails), George, 22, 5'8", lately arrived. From Tobias Rudisley, BA Co Md. (PAG 7 Aug 1766).

Hall, Edward, from Worcester, England, 40, used to the sea. From Daniel Bowers, nr Baltimore Town. (MG 24 May - 7 Jun 1775).*

Hall alias Attix, George, 18. From John Grant, KE Co Md. (MG 26 Apr - 20 May 1770).

Hall, James alias Potts, John, 20, pretended horse doctor. From Vachel White, South River Md. (MG 19 Sep - 3 Oct 1754).*

Hall, James, 40. From Caleb Dorsey, Elk Ridge Furnace Md. (MG 15 Oct - 17 Dec 1761, 7 & 14 Jan 1762).

Hall, John, Irish. From John Hall, BA Co Md. (PAG 16 Nov 1764).

Hall, William, English, writes well. From Gaither Simpson, AA Co Md. (MG 6 - 20 Sep 1764).*

Hall, William, from West of England, shoemaker, came in Jun 1775 [by *Thornton*]. From John Cockey Owings & Stephen Price. (MG & MJ 13 & 20 Jun 1776).*

Hamilton, Dr. Charles alias Charlotte (1753). Advertised in Chester Co, Pa, pretending to be a man. (MG 25 Jan 1753).

Hamlin, William, from West of England, 25, tall. From Thos Lovering, CE Co Md. (MG & PAG 21 Sep 1758.

Handfield, Thomas, 19. From John Howard, AA Co Md. (PAG 28 Oct 1742.*

Hanway, Thomas, Irish, 30, 5'5". From Wm Parrish, BA Co Md. (PAG 25 Oct 1770).

Harbett, Richard, 21. From Joseph Jacobs, AA Co Md. (MG 7 Aug - 11 Sep 1766).

Hardgraves, Charles. From Edmund Terrill & Clement Reade, CU Co Va. (VG 4 Jun 1772).

Harding, William, English, 30, 5'9". From Richd Jones, BA Co Md. (PAG 13 Jan 1763).

Hardie, John, 60, miller, speaks West Country dialect. From Spencer Ball & Richd Hull, NO Co Va. (MG 11 Jly 1754).

Hardy, John, from Lancashire, 38, 5'9", in country 4 months. From Chas Ridgely, BA Co Ironworks Md. (MG 30 Apr & 18 Jly 1767, PAG 13 Aug 1767).

Hardey, Robert, English, 5'9". From Chas Ridgely Jr., BA Co Ironworks Md. (PAG 10 Aug 1774).

Hardy, Thomas, English, 52. From John Robt Holliday, BA Co Md. (MG 26 Oct - 28 Dec 1775).

Hardy, William, 50, schoolmaster. From Wm Wilmer, KE Co Md. (MG 21 Oct - 11 Nov 1747).

Harford, Patrick, Irish, 21. From John Ridgely, Carrolls Manor Md. (MG 29 Jun - 1 Aug 1748),

Hargrove, Thomas, English, arrived by *Albion* in 1765. From Saml Mansfield, KE Co Md. (MG 25 Aug - 22 Sep 1768).

Harper, Amos, English, 25, farmer. From Henry Howard, BA Co Md. (MJ 4 & 11 Jly 1780).

Harper, Anthony, blacksmith, writes well. From Thos Towson & Thos Stevens nr Baltimore Md. (MG 30 Aug 1753).*

Harper, William, English, 21, 5'4", arrived 9 months ago. From Chas Morgan, KE Co Md. (MG 28 Mar 1771, PAG 4 Jly 1771).

Harris, George. From Wm Darding & Wm Corkrill, QA Co Md. (MG 3 Nov 1763).

Harris, John (1766). *See* Evans.

Harris, John, has run before. From John Wells, BA Co Md. (MJ 18 Jun - 9 Jly & 21 Sep 1774).*

Harris, Robert, English, 25. From James Franklin, nr Baltimore. (MJ 24 Jun - 21 Oct 1777).*

Harris, William, English, shipwright & caulker. From Wm Roberts, Annapolis. (MG 22 May 1766).

Harrison, Robert, 24, lately imported on *Prince Frederick*. From Henry Ridgely, AA Co Md. (MG 20 & 27 Sep 1749).

Harrison, William, 25. From Wm Bosley & John Willmott, BA Co Md. (MG 15-29 Dec 1774).*

Hart, Isaac, 17, Jewish. From Richd Bayne, HAL Co Va. (VGNI 8 Sep 1774).*
Hart, William, Irish, 26, middle height. From Wm Dames, KE Co Md. (PAG 14 Aug MG 19 & 26 Aug 1746).
Harwood (alias Benn), John, English, tailor. From John Ducker, Annapolis. (MG 21 May 1761).
Hateley (Heatley), Ralph, 25. From Daniel Preston, BA Co Md. (MJ 18 Dec 1773 - 20 Jan 1774).*
Hatton alias Jackson, William, born Derbyshire, 25, 5'6", stocking weaver, arrived Jun 1764. From Wm Baxter, CE Co Md. (MG 8 Sep - 13 Oct 1768, PAG 20 Sep 1768); from Francis Phillips, BA Co Md. (MG 8 Sep - 13 Oct 1768, PAG 1 Oct 1767, 15 Sep 1768, 8 Jly 1769).
Hawk, Richard, 13. From George Graham, Dumfries Va. (VGR 23 Jly 1767).
Hawk, William, 5'7". From John Shipley, AA Co Md. (PAG 9 Dec 1772).*
Hawkes, Stephen, English, 27. From Joseph Watkins, AA Co Md. (MG 22 Apr - 30 Sep 1762).
Hawkes, Thomas, English, 30. From John Addison Smith, BA Co Md. (MG 24 & 31 Mar 1763).*
Hawkins, Elizabeth. From Rachel Pottinger, Md. (MG 19 Jly - 23 Aug 1753).*
Hawkins, Stephen, English, 27, 6'0", arrived Jan or Feb 1762. From Joseph Watkins, BA Co Ironworks Md. (PAG 22 Jly & 23 Sep 1762).
Hayne (alias Thist), (John) Michael, German, 32, 5'7", tailor. From R Gresham, KE Co Md. (PAG 6 Jly 1769).
Hays, Daniel, alias Davis, William, from London, 26, cooper. From Daniel McPherson, CHA Co Md. (MG 2 Sep - 11 Nov 1762).
Hays, Michael, 18, 2 months in country. From Richd Thos, John Thos & Shadrick Case, FR Co Md. (MJ 24 Aug 1774).
Hays, Thomas, English, 70. From Richard McCubbin, Annapolis. (MG 6 Sep - 4 Oct 1759).*'
Hayward, Francis, English, 45. From Saml Wickes & Hans Hanson, KE Co Md. (MG 18 Jun - 9 Jly 1767).
Hayward, William, English, 25, shoemaker. From David Gorsuch & John Ensor Jr., nr Baltimore. (MG 18 Apr 1765; PAG 25 Apr 1765).
Haywood, Thomas, speaks good English. From John Pettit, WE Co Va. (MG 21 Jly 1757).
Headen (Heydon), John, blacksmith. From Chas McCarty & Robt Downman, RI Co Va. (VG 5 Aug 1773).*
Heath, James, born Derbyshire, 27. From Robt Wilmot, BA Co Md. (MG 12 Apr 1759).
Hensly, Benjamin, barber in London for 15 yrs. From Henry Callister, TA Co Md. (MG 27 Nov - 18 Dec 1755).
Herbert, Thomas, 30, silversmith. From Wm Alexander, AU Co Va. (VG 18 Feb 1775).*
Herne alias Horne, Pooling, English, 24, 5'8", arrived in Sep 1774 by *Tayloe*. From Alex Henderson Va. (VG 10 Nov 1774, PAG 16 Nov 1774).*
Hewne (or Keirn), Michael, German. From R Gresham, KE Co Md. (MG 29 Jun - 14 Sep 1769).
Hickey, John, 22. From Denton Hammond, Severn R. Md. (MG 2 - 16 Aug 1770).
Hickins, John, 5'8", arrived 6 years ago. From Ephraim Howard, AA Co Md. (PAG 28 Jly 1773).
Hickman, James, English, 22, 5'7", waggoner & plowman. From Alex Walls, BA Co Md. (PAG 7 Jly 1773); from Thos Owings, BA Co Md. (MJ 3 Mar 1774, 10 Apr - 1 May 1776).
Hicks, Elias, 25, shoemaker. From John Jones, BA Co Md. (MG 29 Mar - 26 Apr 1764, PAG 5 Apr 1764).

RUNAWAYS

Higgins, William, English, 36, 5'6", miller. From Edwd Wright, QA Co Md. (PAG 16 Jun 1757).*

Higginson, Joseph, native of London, 21, jobbing blacksmith, in country 4 years. From Saml Daniel, MI Co Va, (VG 8 Apr 1775).*

Highenbottom, William, blacksmith. From Saml Mansell & Robt Barnes, AA Co Md. (MJ 4 - 18 Oct 1775).

Higton, Paul, English, young, ex schoolmaster, talks broad. From John Gorsuch & Job Garretson, Baltimore Md. (MG 4 Jly 1771, VGR 1 Aug 1771).

Hill, Elijah. From Randolph Spicer, FA Co Va. (VGR 15 Apr 1773).*

Hill, John, English, 30. From James Elder, AA Co Md. (MG 2 - 16 Oct 1766); from Thos, Saml & John Snowden, AA Co Md. (MG 20 Aug - 1 Oct 1767, 30 Jun - 11 Aug 1768).*

Hill, John, 26, 5'4", glassmaker, lately arrived. From Matthew Ridley, BA Co Md. (PAG 30 Aug 1770).*

Hill, William, from West of England, blacksmith. From Chas Egleston, DO Co Md. (MJ 27 Nov - 18 Dec 1773).*

Hilyear (Hillier), John, 30, 5'6". From Edwd Norwood, BA Co Md. (PAG 30 Aug 1770, MG 28 Nov 1771 - 9 Jan 1772).

Hinds, David, Irish, 35. From Samuel Love Jr., LO Co Va. (VGPu 25 Jly 1777).*

Hinds, Thomas, English, 23, 5'7", arrived in 1752. From John Love, BA Co Md. (PAG 28 Nov 1754).

Hinton, John, English, 25, gardener, lately imported by *Restoration*. From Ebenezer McClure, BA Co Md. (MG 14 Nov - 19 Dec 1771).*

Hipditch, William, English. From Abraham & Joseph Lewis. LO Co Va. (VGPu 31 Jan 1777).*

Hirley (Hurley), Patrick, Irish. From Benj Welsh, Bush River Furnace Md. (MG 21 May - 8 Oct 1767).*

Hockaday, John, of Devonshire, 40. From Michael Earle, CE Co Md. (MG 17 Apr - 22 May 1766).

Hogan, Dominick, Irish, short, wears iron collar. From Benj Tasker, BA Co Ironworks Md. (MG 5 Jly PAG 11 Jly 1745).

Holder, Edward. English, 40, 6'0", has been transported before. From John Footman, BA Co Md. (PAG 18 Oct 1770).

Holderness, George (1777). *See* Dorman.

Holland, Joseph, English. From Richd Croxall, BA Co Ironworks Md. (MG 9 - 16 Oct 1760, PAG 23 Oct 1760).

Holmes, Joseph, English, 31, middle height, arr. in 1753. From Abednego Botfield, TA Co Md. (PAG 13 Jun 1754)

Holy, George, 23. From Wm Ray Jr., AA Co Md. (MG 31 Jly - 4 Dec 1777).

Hooper, Edward, 24. From Geo Randall, BA Co Md. (MG 21 Dec 1769 - 18 Jan 1770).

Hope, Benjamin, English, 24, in gaol frequently. From D & S Hughes, FR Co Md. (MJ 16-28 Jan 1777).

Hopkins, Hopkin, 25, shoemaker. From Wm Lux of BA Co Md. (PAG 13 Apr 1774).

Horan, Patrick, Irish, 25, 5'6". From George Ewing, CE Co Md. (PAG 9 Feb 1769).

Horne, Pooling - *See* Herne.

Horn, Richard, English, 60, 5'10". From John Knight, QA Co Md. (PAG 24 May 1764).

Houton (Houghton), Edward, English, 26, sawyer, arrived 12 Jun 1743, has run away before. From Jacob Giles, CE Co Md. (PAG 6 Mar 1750).

Ilow (alias Channon), John, from West of England, 20. From Henry Gaither & Henry Griffith, FR Co Md. (MJ 13 Sep - 6 Dec 1775).

Howard, Matthew, English, 35, short, farrier. From John Sherwood, TA Co Md. (PAG 22 Jan 1751).

Howard, Sarah (1752). *See* Knox.

Howland, John, Londoner, 19, schoolmaster. From Sarah Merryman, BA Co Md. (MG 12 Apr 1759).*

Hubbard, James, English, 25, 5'8", sailor. From James Hood, AA Co Md. (PAG 6 Dec 1764).

Hubberd, John, 25, was sailor on man of war. From James Wood, AA Co Md. (MG 18 & 25 Oct 1764).*

Hughes alias Luellin, David, near 40, blacksmith, has worked as free person. From execs of Vincent Askin CHA Co Md. (MG 18 May 1748).

Hughs, John, Irish, 30. From Ephraim Howard, AA Co Md. (MG 11 - 25 Oct 1770).

Hughes, Thomas, 25, 5'5", carpenter. From Caleb Dorsey, AA Co Md. (MG 16 Jun - 8 Sep 1768, 12 Jan - 9 Feb 1769, PAG 19 Jan 1769).

Humphreys, Edward, English. From James Baker, BA Co Md. (PAG 18 Aug 1773).*

Humphreys, Matthew, English, 33, short. From Wm Wrench, QA Co Md. (PAG 12 Apr 1764).

Humphries, John, 20. From Richd Weedon, AA Co Md. (MG 13 Jly 1769).*

Humphries, John, 25. From Geo Backster & Philip Lidick, Baltimore. (MG 24 May - 28 Jun 1770).

Humphreys (alias Knightley), Thomas, 42, tall, blacksmith. From Stephen Bordley, KE Co Md. (PAG 14 May 1760).

Hungerford, Hunter, 26, tall. From Wm McAtee, CHA Co Md. (PAG 8 Jly 1742).

Hunt, James, English, 20. From John Kent, AA Co Md. (MG 16 - 30 Aug 1759).*

Hunt, Robert, 40, ran from *Isabella*. From Smyth & Sadler, KE Co Md. (MG 20 Jly - 10 Aug 1769).

Hunt, William, farmer, 19, escaped from irons. From Caleb Dorsey, AA Co Md. (MG 5 Sep 1771).

Hunter, John, English, 22. From Caroline Orrick, Baltimore. (MG 20 Oct 1763).*

Hurst, Henry. From Thos Robins, OR Co Va. (VGR 4 Aug 1774).*

Hutcheson, William, 26. From the *Dragon*, Capt Robt Johnston, on Little Choptank R. Md. (MG 5 - 26 Oct 1758).*

Hyley, William, from West of England, 40, imported from Liverpool 4 yrs ago. From John F A Priggs, PG Co Md. (MG 21 & 28 Jun 1764).

Igo, Dennis, 27. From Caleb Dorsey, AA Co Md. (MG 19 Mar 1767).

Inch (alias Lee), Ann, 40. From Thos Kirk, FR Co Md. (MG 20 Sep 1770).

Ingram, James (1768). *See* Johnson.

Ingram, Joseph, Irish or English, reportedly now called Wagpels. From Henry Coleman, SP Co Va. (VGP 3 Aug 1775).*

Inman, John, 5'3". From Michael Bateman, QA Co Md. (PAG 28 Apr 1773).

Irwin, Francis, Irish, blacksmith. From Saml Canby, LO Co Va. (VGP 8 Jun 1775).

Irwin, John, English, 22, farmer. From Henry Howard, BA Co Md. (MJ 8 - 22 Jun 1779).

Jackson, Anthony, Yorkshireman, 20, 5'8", arrived in Jly 1770 by *Thornton*. From John Hood, AA Co Md. (MG 13 Sep - 18 Oct 1770, 27 May - 24 Jun 1773, PAG 20 Sep 1770).*

Jackson, Mary, 40, 5'8", born England but speaks as Scot. From Wm Clayton, QA Co Md. (MG 11 May, PAG 15 Jun 1758).

Jacobs, William, from West of England, 30, sailmaker. From Saml Middleton, Annapolis. (MG 29 Nov 1759).

James, John, English, butcher, 5 yrs in country & 2 yrs to serve. From Isaac Perkins, KE Co Md. (MJ 7 Sep 1779, MG 17 Sep - 8 Oct 1779).

James, Joseph, 20, blacksmith. From Ninian Beall, FR Co Md. (MG 10 Oct - 14 Nov 1771).

James, Peter, English, 45. From John Knight, QA Co Md. (PAG 24 May 1764).

James, Thomas, English, 28. From Ely Dorsey, Elk Ridge Md.. (MG 9 - 23 Jly 1761); from Caleb Dorsey (28 May - 25 Jun 1767, 8 Jun - 6 Jly 1769).*

James, Williams, English, 21. From John Carvill Hynson & Richd Hynson, KE Co Md. (MG 27 Jun 1771),

Jarvis, John, English, 25, 5'7", lately arrived. From Peter Butler, BA Co Md. (PAG 19 Jly & 23 Aug 1770).

Jebb, John, English, 30, tall, shoemaker, born Shropshire. From John G Howard, BA Co Md. (MG 23 Jly PAG 6 Aug 1752).*

Jeen, Edward, 40. From Edwd Osmond nr Annapolis. (MG 16 Apr 1761).

Jeffcock, Joseph, 26. From Wm Richardson, QA Co Md. (MG 12 Sep 1765).

Jefferies, William, 30, 5'6", shoemaker. From Jacob Carter, QA Co Md. (MG 10 Jun - 15 Jly 1756, PAG 1 Jly 1756).*

Jefferies, William, 20, shoemaker. From Wm Ridgely & Lancelot Dorsey, AA Co Md. (MG 25 Mar - 15 Apr 1777, 11 Aug - 20 Oct 1778).

Jenkins, Edward, sailor, has been in country before. From Joseph Jacobs, AA Co Md. (MG 7 Aug - 11 Sep 1766).

Jenkins, William, 45. cabinet maker. From Thos Miller, Fredericksburg Va. (VG 2 Jly 1772).*

Jennings, John, English, 5'9", shoemaker. From Benj Kirby, QA Co Md. (PAG 25 Jly 1769).*

Jennings, William, English. From Wm Faris, Annapolis. (MG 8 Aug - 19 Sep 1765).

Jewel, William, 23, 5'6". From Samuel Dorsey Jr., BA Co Ironworks Md. (PAG 20 Sep 1775).*

Johnson, David. From Wm Duvall, AA Co Md. (MG 21 Jly - 8 Sep 1768).*

Johnson, Henry. From Robert Phillips Va 1768 (VN).*

Johnson alias Ingram, James, 18, schoolmaster. From John Clagett, FR Co Md. (MG 14 Jan - 11 Feb 1768).*

Johnson, Reily, 50, shoemaker but passes as doctor. From Wm Young, BA Co Md. (MG 23 & 30 Oct 1766).

Johnson, Robert, English, 20-30, good scholar. From BA Co Md. (MG 15 Jun 1769).*

Johnson, Robert, English, farmer, able to knit, lately arrived by *Thornton*. From James Kelso, AA Co Md. (MG 3 Aug 1775).*

Johnson, Thomas, English, 30, tall. From Alex Lawson, BA Co Ironworks Md. (PAG 20 Apr 1749).

Johnson, William, alias Martin, Thomas, English, 15. From Thos Harvey, BA Co Md. (MG 24 Jun - 1 Jly 1756).

Johnston, John, English, 5'5". From Chas Baker, BA Co Md. (PAG 10 Jan 1771).*

Johnston, John, Irish, 17. From Abraham Wright, BA Co Md. (MJ 20 Feb - 5 Apr 1775).*

Jolly, Matthew, Irish, 25, short. From Benj Tasker, BA Co Md. (MG 27 May - 17 Jun 1746, PAG 11 Jly 1745; 27 May & 29 May 1746).

Jones, Ann, Irish. From Wm Jenkins, BA Co Md. (PAG 10 Oct 1754).*

Jones, David, born Wales, 20, brazier & tinker. From Patrick Creagh, Annapolis. (MG 16 Jly 1752).

Jones, Grace, Welsh, 27, speaks broken Dutch. From David Hook, nr Baltimore. (MJ 5 - 26 Oct 1779).

Jones, Henry, 25. From Caleb Dorsey, AA Co Md. (MG15 Oct - 17 Dec 1761, 7 & 14 Jan 1762).

Jones, Hugh, Irish, 30, 5'5". From George Randell, BA Co Ironworks Md. (PAG 22 Sep 1768).

Jones, James, Welsh. From David & Menoah Singleton, OR Co Va. (VGR 22 Jly 1773).

Jones, John, blacksmith. From Wm Fitzhugh, CA Co Md. (MG 21 Dec 1752).

Jones, John, Irish, 5'10", has been in colonies before. From Wm Jenkins, BA Co Md. (PAG 10 Oct 1754).

Jones, John, 5'7". From Robt Bryerly, BA Co Md. (PAG 15 May 1755).

Jones, John, bricklayer & plasterer, 28. From John Unsworth, Annapolis. (MGG 20 Sep - 20 Dec 1770).

Jones, John, Irish, 18. From John Hood & Joseph Hobbs, AA Co Md. (MG 27 May - 24 Jun 1773).

Jones, John, Welsh, 25, born Liverpool. From Patrick Lockhart, CO Co Va. (VG 26 May 1774).

Jones, Moses, 25, wood collier. From Wm Baxter, Lancashire Iron Works Md. (MG 11 Aug - 15 Sep 1757).

Jones, Richard, 50 or more, was soldier in England., has 22 months to serve. From Benj Rogers, BA Co Md. (MJ 16 Jun - 21 Jly 1778).

Jones, Robert, sailor. From Alex Stewart, Geo Freebairn & Michael Depenbough, Baltimore. (MG 15 Feb - 1 Mar 1759).*

Jones, Samuel, 35. From John Baylis, AA Co Md. (MG 15 Jun - 20 Jly 1748).*

Jones, Thomas, Welsh, 40. From John Collar, Kent Is Md. (MG 14 Jun - 19 Jly 1753).

Jones, Thomas, Welsh, 25, 5'8". From Wm Webb, HAR Co Md. (PAG 7 Aug 1776).

Jones, Thomas, 25. From Wm Ridgely, AA Co Md. (MJ 11 Aug - 17 Nov 1778).

Jones, William, 30, 5'8", weaver. From John Roe, QA Co Md. (PAG 28 Oct 1742).

Jones, William, Welsh, 25, ran from ship with 3 years to serve. From Chas Carroll, BA Co Ironworks Md. (PAG 9 Jun 1743).

Jones, William, Welsh, 5'8". From Joseph Reynolds, FR Co Md. (PAG 14 Apr 1768).

Jones, William, from West of England, 25. From Edwd Burgess, MO Co Md. (MJ 10 - 24 Jun 1777).

Jordan, Jesse, English, 25, shoemaker. From John Hesselius nr Annapolis. (MG 2 Nov - 14 Dec 1769).

Jordan, John, 20. From Vachel Worthington, BA Co Md. (MG 6 Sep 1764).

Jordan, William, 32, 5'5". From Benj Ingram, BA Co Ironworks Md. (PAG 22 Aug 1765)*

Jubb, Joseph, English, 25. From Patrick Lynch, BA Co Md. (MG 13 Jly 1775).

Jupp, William, ran from *Greyhound* in Patapsco R. From D Ross & C Hammond. (MG 23 May 1754)

Kay, Elizabeth (1748). *See* Edwards.

Kay, James, Irish, 23, 5'7". From Wm Webb, HAR Co Md. (PAG 7 Aug 1776).

Keat, John, born in North Country. From Chas Motherby, BA Co Md. (MG 15 Aug 1750).

Kellett, Edward, Irish, 20. From John Kelly, SM Co Md. (MG 30 Nov 1748).

Kelly, John, Irish, 26, can read & write. From Chas Gates, CHA Co Md. (MG 23 Jly - 6 Aug 1767).

Kelly, John, Irish. From John Orme, FR Co Md. (MG 11 & 18 Apr 1771).

Kelly, Michael, Irish, 24, 5'6", arrived a month ago. From James Hutchinson, BA Co Md. (PAG 14 Sep 1769).

Kelly, Thomas, Irish, 26. From James Perry MO Co Md. (VGPu 18 Apr 1777).

Kennedy, Edward, Irish, 5'2". From Wm Coale, BA Co Md. (PAG 19 Apr 1764).

Kern, Michael, German, 5'7", tailor. From Richd Gresham, KE Co Md. (PAG 23 Mar 1769).

Ketch, Tom (1756). *See* Poney, Thomas.

Kettle, John, 25. From Chris Lowndes, Bladensburg Md. (MG 9 - 30 Nov 1752).
Key, Elizabeth (1748). *See* Edwards.
Kibble, Richard, carpenter & joiner, arrived by *Forward* this year. From Wm Walker, WE Co Va. (AWM 19 Jly 1739)
King, Charles, 23, middle height. From John Fuller, BA Co Md. (PAG 26 Jun 1740).*
King, Charles, English, 30, short. From George Brown,BA Co Md. (PAG 11 Jly 1745).
King, John, from West Country. From Edwd Osmond, Carroll's Quarter Md. (MG 16 Apr 1761).*
Kingham, John, English, 27, good scholar. From Alex Wells, BA Co Md. (MG 10 Mar - 7 Apr 1768).*
Kirk, Henry, Irish, 22, middle height, butcher. From Benj Tasker, BA Co Ironworks Md. (PAG 11 Jly 1745, 27 May - 17 Jun 1746)
Kirk, Thomas, transported from London 1765, reportedly kept school in Va, has possible legacy in England. (VCWM 14 May 1788).
Kneller, William, from West of England. From Greenbury Ridgely, AA Co Md. (MG 28 May 1767).
Knight, John, from West of England, 35. From Buckler Bond, HAR Co Md. (MJ 28 Jun - 9 Jly 1774).*
Knowles (Noles), Clement, 26, nailer. From Wm Merritt, AA Co Md. (MJ 7 - 21 Oct 1777).*
Knox alias Howard alias Wilson, Sarah, dancing mistress, born in Yorkshire, fought at Culloden, imported by *Duke of Cumberland* from Whitehaven. From David Currie, LA Co Va. (VG 3 Jly 1752, MG 25 Jan 1753).

Lacy, Hugh, Irish, 50. From Ephraim Howard, AA Co Md. (MG 11 - 25 Oct 1770).
Lacy, Martin, imported by [*Thames*], Capt. Dobbins. From Joshua Dorsey, Patapsco Ferry Md. (MG 19 Sep - 24 Oct 1750).*
Lacey, Thomas, English, 20, 5'6", cobbler. From Philip Liddick, BA Co Md. (MG 24 May - 28 Jun 1770, PAG 7 Oct 1772).
Lake, Thomas, Irish, 26, barber & hairdresser, came last fall. From James Wilson, Hagerstown Md. (MG 7 Apr - 12 May 1774).
Lamb, Joseph. From Thos Hammond, AA Co Md. (MG 10 Dec 1772 - 21 Jan 1773).
Lamberd, James, English, 31, 5'6". From Chas Ridgely Jr., BA Co Ironworks Md. (PAG 10 Aug 1774).
Lamprey, Thomas, 18, 5'10", woolcomber, convicted for attempted rape. From Nathan Farrow, QA Co Md. (PAG 16 Jly 1767, MG 1 Oct 1767).
Landon, John, English, 22, 5'8". From Wm Inman, AA Co Md. (PAG 7 Sep 1769).
Lane, Michael, Irish. From Saml Canby, LO Co Va. (VGP 8 Jun 1775).
Lane, William, 25, 5'9". From Nathan Dorsey, AA Co Md. (PAG 21 Jun 1764, MG 30 Aug - 6 Dec 1764).
Larkin, Patrick, Irish, 23. From Melchizedeck Green, CHA Co Md. (MG 21 May - 25 Jun 1767).
Lavers, William, from West of England, tailor. From Richd Burland, Annapolis. (MG 17 Sep - 19 Nov 1779).
Law, William, English, 50. From Darby Lux & Nicholas Haile, BA Co Md. (MG 14 - 28 Jly 1778).*
Lawrence, John, 19. From Benj Dorsey, FR Co Md. (MG 9 - 23 Aug 1770).*
Lee, Charles, 5'10", watchmaker. From Joseph Osborn, BA Co Md. (PAG 24 Oct 1765).
Legg, Solomon, 45, ran from *Isabella*. From Smyth & Sadler, KE Co Md. (MG 20 Jly - 10 Aug 1769).

Legier, Gabriel John, English, jeweller, speaks French. From Wm Faris, Annapolis. (MG 18 Jun 1761).

Lewed, William, 5'7". From Skelton Standiford, BA Co Md. (PAG 5 Sep 1771).

Lewis, Elizabeth. From John Smith, KE Co Md. (PAG 2 Aug 1764).

Lewis, James, English, 45, nearly 5 years in country. From Thos Smyth, KE Co Md. (MG 30 Sep - 28 Oct 1773).

Lewis, William. From John Wilmot, Annapolis. (MG 29 Aug - 19 Sep 1765).

Lewis, William, English. From James Walker, AA Co Md. (MG 21 Aug - 18 Sep 1766).

Life (alias Roberts), Robert, from West of England. From John Eason, FR Co Md. (MG 9 Aug 1770).

Lightborne, Richard, English, 40, 5'8". From Samuel Massey, QA Co Md. (PAG 16 Jly 1752).*

Lightfoot (alias Linkherd), Thomas, 30. From Richard McCubbin, BA Co Md (MG 23 May 1750).

Linch, Timothy, Irish. From Henry Gassaway, BA Co Md. (MG 4 Jun - 2 Jly 1767).

Lindley, William, English, gardener. From Stephen Steward, West R. Md. (MG 6 - 20 May 1762).*

Lison, John Tom, English, 35. From Benj Howard. AA Co Md. (MG 20 Jun - 11 Jly 1771).

Lloyd (alias Love), Peter, imported in 1751 [by *Thames*], shipwright, given to drink. From Brian Philpot & Thos Ward, Baltimore. (MG 4 - 18 Jun 1752).*

Lloyd, Elizabeth. From Thos Johnson, KE Co Md. (MG 28 Jly 1768).

Lockhart, Thomas, 6'0". From John Almore, BA Co Md. (PAG 17 Aug 1769).*

Logan, William, 23, barber. From Andrew Buchanan, Annapolis. (MG 22 Sep -20 Oct 1757).

Long, John, a youth. From Mary Cockey, Kent Is Md. (MG 4 - 18 Mar 1756).*

Long, Moses, English, tall, talks broad Yorkshire. From Samuel Hart, BA Co Md. (PAG 14 Aug 1746).

Lotan, Richard, from West of England, 40. From Nicholas McCubbin, Annapolis. (MG 26 May 1763).

Lovely, Thomas, English. 6'0". From Andrew Meek, BA Co Md. (PAG 2 Jly 1772).

Low, Joseph, nailer, knows country well & enlisted as soldier, has wife in BA Co Md. From John Harris, AA Co Md. (MG 23 Feb - 23 Mar 1779).

Lucas, George, English, 26, 5'6". From George Lytle, BA Co Md. (PAG 16 May 1771).*

Luellin, David (1748). *See* Hughes.

Lynagh, Thomas, Irish, lately arrived. From Wm Ellis, CE Co Md. (PAG 2 Oct 1746).

Lyon, Robert, Scot, 5'6", fuller. From Jacob Lemmon, BA Co Md. (PAG 9 Jun 1784).*

Mahoney, Michael, Irish, 28, tailor. From George Brichan, CHA Co Md. (MG 15 Oct - 12 Nov 1767).

Mahoney, Thomas, Irish, 20, in country 3 months. From Chas Ridgely & Co, BA Co Md. (MG 20 Aug 1767).

Mallen, John (1755). *See* Marling.

Malone, John, Irish, 20, 5'7". From John Sewell, KE Co Md. (PAG 26 Sep 1765).*

Manly, William, Lancashire man, 25-30, 5'8", sawyer, "most impudent infamous villain." From James Braddock, TA Co Md. (MG 2 Nov - 21 Dec 1775, 9 - 30 May 1776, PAG 8 Nov 1775, 15 May 1776).*

Mansfield, William, born West of England, 21. From John Legg Jr., Kent Is Md. (MG 9 Mar 1759).

Manyfold, Joseph, English. From Saml Norwood, BA Co Md. (MG 22 Apr - 6 May 1773).

Marling alias Mallen, John, born Norfolk, 22, farmer. From John Welsh, Md. (MG 11 Sep - 16 Oct 1755).

Marriott, Joseph, Negro, convicted London. From Benj Welsh, AA Co Md. (MG 27 Jun 1754).*

Marsh, John, 5'5". From John Robert Holliday, BA Co Md. (PAG 16 May 1771, MG 6 - 20 Jun 1771).

Marshman, James, 30-35. From Benj Berry Jr., PG Co Md. (MG 3 Sep 1772).

Martin, Bartholomew, 25. From Wm Allen, BA Co Md. (MG 3 - 17 Dec 1772)

Martin, John, 35-40. From John Smith Prather, Bladensburg Md. (MG 24 May 1759).*

Martin, Thomas (1756). See Johnson, William.

Martin, Thomas, Irish, 25, in country 6 weeks. From John Baker & Basil Brooke. FR Co Md. (MG 23 Jly 1772). See also under Wm Johnson.

Mason, Alexander, 26, shoemaker. From Daniel Weedon, James Bryan & Thos Yewell, QA Co Md. (MG 28 May - 18 Jun 1767).

Masters, Andrew, English, 50. From Henry Howard, BA Co Md. (MJ 15 - 29 Dec 1778).

Matthews, Abraham, born West of England, 40-50. From Thos Rutland, nr Annapolis. (MG 4 - 18 Sep 1755).*

Matthews, John, small. From James Baxter, CE Co Ironworks Md.. (PAG 13 Dec 1739).

McCarty, Lawrence, Irish. From Joshua Dorsey, Patapsco Ferry Md. (MG 19 Sep - 24 Oct 1750).*

Matthews, John, carpenter & joiner. From John Brice, Annapolis. (MG 24 Nov 1763).

Matthews, Thomas, Irish, 23, recently arrived, sailor. From Vachel Worthington, BA Co Md. (MG 6 Sep 1764).

Mattox, Samuel, 16, former Army drummer. From Vernon Hebb, SM Co Md. (MG 5 Jun - 3 Jkly 1766).

Maulding (Moulding), William, English, 26, arrived [by *Thames*] this year. From Orlando Griffith & Jacob Holland, AA Co Md. (MG 28 May - 18 Jun 1752).

Maund alias Philpott, John, 21, imported from London. From Thos James, CHA Co Md. (MG 6 Jun - 1 Aug 1765).

Maycock, William, from West of England, 28, farmer. From John Hood Jr., AA Co Md. (MJ 4 & 11 May 1779).

McBoise, Richard, English, 28. From Patrick Rock, HAR Co Md. (MJ 21 Sep 1774).

McCarty, George, English, 30, lately imported from Bristol by *Restoration*. From Ebenezer Maclure, Baltimore. (MG 14 Nov - 19 Dec 1771).

McClain, Peter, from Philadelphia prison, ran from *Hawk*, BA Co Md. (MG 15 Sep 1757).

McClain, Thomas, 17. From James Mills, SM Co Md. (MG 1 - 29 Mar 1753).

McClue, Catherine, short. From Robert Alison, CE Co Md. (PAG 10 Aug 1749).

McCreary, John, 24, middle height. From Thomas Money, CE Co Md. (PAG 19 Jly 1750).

McCreary, Mary, 47. From Thomas Money, CE Co Md. (PAG 19 Jly 1750).

McDonald, Charles, 30, plasterer. From James Campbell, CHA Co Md. (MG 7 Sep - 5 Oct 1769).

Macdonald, Donald, Irish. From Wm Ellis, CE Co Md. (PAG 2 Oct 1746).

McDonald, John, from West Country, bricklayer. From Wm Chapman, Md. (MG 20 Sep - 1 Nov 1749).

McEvoy, Roger, 5'8". From Humphrey Brooks, BA Co Md. (PAG 14 Jun 1770).

McFee, Duncan, 40, labourer. From Daniel Weedon, James Bryan & Thos Yewell. (MG 28 May - 25 Jun 1767).

McGinley, James. From Thos Periman, AA Co Md. (MJ 24 Aug - 7 Sep 1774).

McKenzie, Patrick, Irish, 20. From Benj Ryan, AA Co Md. (MG 15 Jly 1746).

Mackintosh (Macontosh), Peter, Scot, 28. From John Stansbury, BA Co Md. (MG 1 - 15 Aug 1754).*

Mackman, James, Scot, 20. From Thos Davis, nr Snowden's Iron Works Md. (MG 24 - 31 Jly 1755).

McManus, Henry, 19. From Nathan Harris, AA Co. (MJ 1 - 15 Apr 1777).

McNamara, Michael, Irish, 22, 5'8". From John Sealy, BA Co Md. (PAG 19 Aug 1756).

McVey, Owen, Irish, arrived 20 months ago. From Hugh Coupland, BA Co Md. (PAG 9 Jun 1748).

Meacham, Edward, 40, several years in country, schoolmaster. From John Metcalfe, BA Co Md. (MG 26 Apr - 14 Jun 1753).

Meavis, John, weaver. From John Gaither Sr., AA Co Md. (MG 13 Aug 1772).

Merchant, Sarah (1767). *See* Plint.

Merriott (Meritt), Edward, 45-50, English, joiner. From Wm Brown, London Town Md. (MG 4 Nov 1756, 10 Mar, 7 Apr 1757).*

Milburn, Samuel, from West of England, 27, farmer. From Dr. Chas Carroll, Md. (MG 26 Jun - 3 Jly 1751).

Miles, Robert, 30. From Henry Gassaway, Annapolis. (MG 15 Jly 1762).

Millby alias Willoughby, Robert, born Ireland, weaver, former dragoon. From Lawrence Washington, SM Co Md. (MG 24 Aug - 5 Oct 1748).

Miller, Catherine, Irish. From Joseph Evans, CHA Co Md. (MG 12 Sep - 10 Oct 1771).

Millar, John, Scot, 30, cooper. From Robert Newcom, TA Co Md. (27 Mar 1746).*

Miller, Solomon, from West Country, farmer. From Thos Towson & Thos Stevens, nr Baltimore. (MG 30 Aug 1753).

Millett, George, 17. From Robt Owen & Edwd Penn, FR Co Md. (MG 25 Jly - 1 Aug 1776).

Millner, Thomas, 20, 5'4". From John Howard, BA Co Ironworks Md. (PAG 5 Jly 1764).*

Mitchell, George, plays horn & fife. From Richardson Grason, Wyetown Md. (MG 9 Jun 1774).

Moll, John, born Staffordshire, 30. From John Ridgely, BA Co Md. (MG 11 Apr - 16 May ```1754).*

Monkland, Joseph, miller. From Walter Dulany, Annapolis. (MG 28 Feb, 10 - 17 Apr 1760).

Moone, John, 26. From Zachariah McCubbin, BA Co Md. (MG 11 - 18 Jly 1750).

Moore, John, weaver. From John Row, Bladensburg Md. (MG 30 Aug - 6 Sep 1749).

Morein, John, Irish, 35-40, came in *Tryal*. From John Smith Prather, Bladensburg Md. (MG 24 May - 23 Aug 1759, 6 - 20 Mar 1760).*

Morgan, John, 30, shoemaker & gardener. From Wm Paca, Annapolis. (MG 26 Jun - 9 Oct 1766).

Morris, Evan, 21. From Edwd Gaither, FR Co Md. (MG 10 Jly 1766).

Morris, Hugh, tailor & former soldier, 4 yrs still to serve. From Benedict Calvert, PG Co Md. (MG 15 May - 10 Jly 1777).

Morris, John, 33. From Richd Clement, QA Co Md. (MG 12 - 26 Sep 1765).

Morris, Richard, born near Bristol, shoemaker. From Peter Maxwell, Queen's Town Md. (18 Aug - 5 Sep 1757).

Morris, Thomas, Irish, 35, newly arrived. From Rappahannock Co, BA Co Md.. (PAG 3 Sep 1747).*

Moulding, William, English, 26, imported this year. From Jacob Holland, AA Co Md. (MG 28 May 1752).*

Mullinac (Molineux), Richard, Irish, 45, 5'7", wearing iron collar. From Joshua Owings, BA Co Md. (PAG 16 Feb 1769).*

Murphey, Daniel, Irish, 6'0", sawyer. From Simon Wilmer, KE Co Md. (PAG 25 Jun 1752).*

Murphy, John, born Ireland, 30, joiner. From John Patterson, Alexandria Va. (MG 5 Oct 1758).

Murray, Francis, North Country man, will probably change his name. From Nicholas Dorsey, BA Co Md. (MG 24 Jun - 1 Jly 1746).

Murray, Michael, Irish, 21, 5'8". From Edward Stevenson, FR Co Md. (MG 21 May - 25 Jun 1767, PAG 28 May 1767).

Neale, John, Irish, 28. From Stephen Onion, BA Co Ironworks Md. (MG 31 Mar - 14 Apr 1747, PAG 2 Apr 1747).
Nelson, John, gardener & brickmaker, 30. From Benj Rogers, Baltimore Md. (MG 12 Aug - 24 Sep 1761).
Newcomb, Samuel, 23. From Caleb Dorsey, AA Co Md. (MG 19 & 26 Mar 1767).
Newcomb, William, alias Dodson, John, of Gloucester, England, butcher. From John McDonall, nr Annapolis. (MG 19 & 26 Mar 1767)
Nicholls, Walter, English, 30, 5'7", arrived Mar 1754. From Wm Johnson, BA Co Md. (PAG 26 Nov 1754).*
Nicks, John, English, 25, 6'9", arrived in 1760. From Joseph Watkins, AA Co Ironworks Md. (PAG 22 Jly 1762).*
Norman, Anna Maria, German, middle height. From Wm Williams, BA Co Ironworks Md. (PAG 23 Oct 1746).*
North, Thomas, 30, 5'9", wheelwright. From Francis Phillips, BA Co Ironworks Md. (MG 1 - 15 Jan 1767, PAG 8 Jan 1767).
Norton, John, 26, tailor. From Patrick Grahame, CHA Co Md. (MG 2 - 30 Aug 1770).*
Norton, Patrick, Irish, 24, imported from Dublin 6 weeks ago. From Benj Dorsey, Wm Chew Brown & Valentine Brown, AA Co Md. (MG 10 - 24 Oct 1765).
Nottingham, James, farrier. From John Fendall, Sheriff of CHA Co Md. (MG 27 Jly - 31 Aug 1758).*
Nowland, Lawrence, Irish, 21. From Dennis McLemar, CHA Co Md. (MG 21 May - 25 Jun 1767).
Nunn, Edward, English, 21. From Thos Sappington, AA Co Md. (MG 19 Aug 1773 - 13 Jan 1774).

Oak, William, 22, 5'7", lately arrived, good reaper. From Thos Talbot, BA Co. (MG 28 Jly - 18 Aug 1768, PAG 7 Aug 1766 ?1768).
Oakly, George, 16. From John Cocksey, CHA Co Md. (MG 2 & 9 Aug 1770). *
Orford, Thomas, a lad. From John Fendall, CHA Co Md. (MG 26 Jun - 16 Oct 1760).
Orton, William, English, 29, ex-soldier. From Henry Howard, BA Co Md. (MJ 2 - 16 Oct 1776).
Osburn, Mary, 27. From John Lansdale, nr Annapolis. (MG 5 Jan 1764).*
Osborn, Philip, 25, shoemaker. From Thos Todd, Patapsco R. (MJ 23 Dec 1777 - 6 Jan 1778).
Oulton, John, 25, born in country but bred in London, stabbed John Orrick Md. From Chas Carroll & Co, BA Co Md (MG 7 Jun - 19 Jly 1753, 5 - 19 Sep 1754).
Overington, Thomas, 27, short, tanner. From Samuel Holdruf, AA Co Md. (PAG 14 Jly 1743).
Owen, John, weaver, speaks broad English, in country 2 months. From Chris Lowndes, Bladensburg Md. (MG 23 Oct - 13 Nov 1755)
Owens, Mary, 36, from Shrewsbury. From Wm Simpson, Annapolis. (MG 2 Jly 1767).
O'Bryan, James, Irish, 22. From John Ashford, CE Co Md. (MG 10 - 24 Oct 1750).
O'Brian, James, Irish, 30, 5'10". From John Wallace, KE Co Md. (PAG 26 Sep 1765).
O'Bryan, Lawrence, Irish, 26, imported this summer. From John Dorsey, AA Co Md. (MG 1 - 22 Sep 1757).
O'Hara, Kane, Irish, 22. From Saml Hanson, CHA Co Md. (MG 21 May - 25 Jun 1767).
O'Neil, Cornelius, Irish, 40, imported by *Swale*, Capt John Dickinson. From James Mills, SM Co Md. (MG 1 May - 5 Jun 1760).

Painter, John, English, 30, 5'8". From Jeremiah Sheredine, BA Co Ironworks Md. (PAG 13 Jun 1765).

Pall, John, 5'10". From John Robert Holliday, BA Co Md. (PAG 16 May 1771).

Pane, Stephen, English 24, shoemaker. From Chas Ridgely Sr., BA Co Md. (MG 25 Sep 1766).

Pardon, Catherine. From Constantine Bull, Annapolis. (MG 22 Oct - 4 Nov 1772).*

Parker, Joseph, cooper. From Joshua Hall, BA Co Md. (MJ 21 & 28 Oct 1777).*

Parker, Mary, English, 23. From Wm Thompson, BA Co Md. (PAG 23 Dec 1772).*

Parker, Thomas, West Country man, aged 18. From Orlando Griffith, AA Co Md. (MG 5 Jly 1749, 28 May - 18 Jun 1752).

Parkinson, Benjamin, English, 20, 5'6". From Edwd Norris, BA Co Md. (PAG 17 Aug 1769).

Parks, Richard, English, basketmaker. From John Welsh, BA Co Ironworks Md. (PAG 18 Oct 1770).

Parrott, Jacob, born West of England, 21, footman. From Hugh Jones, CE Co Md. (MG 9 May 1750, 16 - 30 Apr 1752); lately taken up in SM Co Md. From John Tree & Otho Othoson, CE Co Md. (MG 5 Apr 1753).

Parrott, James. From John Tree & Otho Othoson, CE Co Md. (MG 5 - 26 Apr 1753).

Parsons, John, 30, English, short. From V Deaton, AA Co Md. (16 Jun & 3 Nov 1743).*

Partinton, Nancy, 19. From Richd Cooke, SM Co Md. (MG 22 Dec 1763 - 19 Jan 1764).

Passenban, John, 40, 5'8", lately arrived. From Wm Edwards, BA Co Md. (PAG 23 Nov 1769).

Paxman, John, English, 25, weaver, lately imported by *Aston Hall*. From Nicholas Merryman, BA Co Md. (MG & MJ 8 & 15 Sep 1774).

Payton (Paiton), Henry, English, 22, 5'6", sailor. From Jacob Comegys, KE Co Md. (PAG 11 Jun 1765).

Peacock, John, English, shoemaker, skilled printer. From John Hood, AA Co Md. (MG 20 Mar - 11 May 1775, 21 Sep - 12 Oct 1775).

Pearce, Benjamin, English, 30, tall. From Edward Rummey, AA Co Md. (PAG 16 Aug 1744).

Pearce, George, English, 40, arrived Aug 1752. From Wm Jenkins, BA Co Md. (PAG 10 Oct 1754).

Pearce, Robert, ship carpenter, 30, imported by *Falcon* Jly 1755. From Patrick Creagh, Annapolis. (MG 28 Aug - 18 Sep 1755, 15 Jann - 4 Mar 1756).

Pearles, Uriah, 17. Tried for attempted murder on James Peck, Elk Ridge Md but discharged when Peck recovered. (MG 27 Nov, 11 Dec 1755).

Pearson, Thomas, English, 19, 5'6", sawyer. From James Braddock, TA Co Md. (MG 9 May 1776, PAG 15 Jly 1776).

Peather (Pether) alias Pedder, John, English, 27, gardener. From Henry Stevenson nr Baltimore. (MJ 28 May - 9 Jly 1774).*

Peather, Thomas, Yorkshireman, barrister, wife in Baltimore. From Charles Carroll, BA Co Md. (MJ 1 Nov - 15 Dec 1778).*

Pedder, John (1774). *See* Peather.

Pell, John. From John Robert Holliday, BA Co Md. (MG 6 - 20 Jun 1771).

Penick, Joseph, 23, 5'8". From Thos Rutland, AA Co Md. (PAG 1 Jun 1769).

Permit, Samuel, English, 23. From FR Co Md. (MJ 23 Aug - 13 Sep 1775).

Perry, James, 28, 5'6". From Samuel Dorsey Jr., BA Co Ironworks Md. (PAG 1 May 1772).

Perry, William, Irish, 20, tailor. From Edwd Norwood, BA Co Md. (28 Nov 1771).*

Peters, Abraham, English, 24, 5'9". From Buckler Bond, HAR Co Md. (PAG 10 Jan 1771, 3 May 1775).*

Peters, Daniel, 24. From Saml Wickes & Hans Hanson, KE Co Md. (MG 18 Jun - 9 Jly 1767).

Phillips, Thomas, 35. From Caleb Dorsey, BA Co Md. (MG 15 Sep - 6 Oct 1768).*

Philpott, John (1765). *See* Maund.

Picke, Elsa, 30-40, middle height. From Wm Mattingly, BA Co Md. (PAG 30 Oct 1740).

Pickson, John, English, 40, 5'5". From Jeremiah Sheredine, BA Co Ironworks Md. (PAG 7 Jly 1763).

Pierce, Isabella, will pass by name of Bridget Castile. From Thos Lewis, FA Co Va. (MG 21 Jun 1745).

Pinemore, John, 6'0", 22, farmer & tinker, plays fiddle, lately imported from Bristol. From James Croxall, BA Co Md. (MG 25 Aug - 1 Sep 1763), from James Franklin (PAG 8 Mar 1764).

Pinfield, John, 17. From Robt Owen & Edwd Penn, FR Co Md. (MG 25 Jly - 1 Aug 1776).*

Pinkeney, Isaac, 5'8", 35, sailor, served in Navy in last war. From David Gorsuch, BA Co Md. (PAG 17 Oct 1771, MG 31 Oct - 28 Nov 1771).

Pitt, William, 47, 6'0", tallow chandler, arrived 4 weeks ago. From Wm Young Jr., BA Co Md. (PAG 28 Jly 1773).*

Place, John, English. From James Hutchings, QA Co Md. (MG 9 Dec 1762 - 27 Jan 1763).

Platt, John, born Staffordshire, 24, husbandman, imported fall 1752 by *Bideford*. From Dr. Charles Carroll nr Baltimore Iron Works Md. (MG 16 & 23 Nov 1752, 26 Jly - 16 Aug 1753).

Place, John, English. From James Hutchings, QA Co Md. (MG 9 Dec 1762 - 27 Jan 1763).

Plevy, Thomas, English, 30, bricklayer, soldier in Philadelphia in 1763. From Chas Carroll & Co, BA Co Md. (MG 2 May - 6 Jun 1765).

Plint alias Powell alias Merchant, Sarah. From John McDonall nr Annapolis. (MG 19 & 26 Mar 1767).

Poney, Thomas, known as Tom Ketch, having been hangman for AA Co Md. From Thomas John Hammond, nr Annapolis. (MG 10 & 17 Jun 1756).

Ponting, Edward, English, 25, 5'6", shoemaker, from Bristol, arrived Nov 1768. From Jonathan Roberts, QA Co Md. (MG 30 Mar - 18 May 1769, PAG 27 Apr 1769).

Pool, Joseph, English, 35, 5'4", hatter. From Thos Bleamy, BA Co Md. (PAG 30 May 1771).

Poole, Richard, English, 35, 5'4". From Jeremiah Sheredine, BA Co Ironworks Md. (PAG 7 Jly 1763).

Potter, Henry, Irish, 30. From James Cawley, ship captain, BA Co Md. (PAG 9 Aug 1750).

Potts, John (1754). *See* Hall, James.

Powell, Nathaniel, English, 30. From Richard Gresham, KE Co Md. (MG 29 Jun - 14 Sep 1769, PAG 6 Jly 1769); from Roger Colman, QA Co Md. (MG 21 Sep - 16 Nov 1769).

Powell, Sarah (1767). *See* Plint.

Powell, William, 25, shoemaker, from Bristol, England, served in *Rockhall* packet. From Abraham Ayres, KE Co Md. (MG 23 Aug 1770).

Powis (Powes), Samuel, from West of England, 45, tailor & staymaker. From Abraham Jerrett, BA Co Md. (MJ 1 Jun - 9 Aug 1775).*

Pratt, Francis, English, barber, transported before under different name. From John Clement, Baltimore. (MJ 4 Sep - 16 Oct 1773).

Prat, John, 25, 6'0". From Flora Dorsey, BA Co Md. (MG 21 Dec 1769, PAG 28 Dec 1769).*

Pratt, Joseph (1778). *See* Sprout.

Prees, William, 50, 5'6". From John Seale, QA Co Md. (MG 1 - 29 Jun 1769, PAG 1 Jun 1769).

Preston, Thomas, 40-50. From Saml Forwood, BA Co Md. (MG 17 Jun - 8 Jly 1762).*
Prestwood, Richard, English, 40, middle height. From Alex Lawson, BA Co Ironworks Md. (PAG 20 Apr 1749).
Pryce, Edward, English, blacksmith. From Wm Ringgold, nr Chester Town Md. (MG 13 Feb 1755).
Price, Mary. From Robt Reith, Annapolis. (MG 14 & 21 Sep 1769).
Price, Rice (Rees), from West of England. From Robert Roberts, KE Co Md. (MG 19 Apr 1764, PAG 26 Apr 1764).
Price, Thomas, English, 30, 5'10", tailor. From Larkin Randall, BA Co Md. (MG 8 Nov 1770 - 17 Jan 1771, PAG 8 Nov 1770).
Price, William, carpenter. From Caleb Dorsey, Elk Ridge Iron Works Md. (MG 15 & 22 Jly 1756).*
Priest, Henry, born West of England, shoemaker. From Peter Maxwell, Queen's Town Md. (MG 18 Aug - 15 Sep 1757).
Pritchard, Jacob, from West of England, 25, "great rogue." From Alex Wells, BA Co Md. (MG 17 Sep - 12 Nov 1767, 10 Mar - 7 Apr 1768).
Pritchard, John. From Stephen Bryan, QA Co Md. (MG 4 Aug 1763).
Pritchard, Thomas, 30. From Richd Scott, AA Co Md. (MJ 8 Aug 1780).
Pugh, Hugh, (alias Hawkins, Henry), 19, lately imported by *Trial*. From John Orrick, Baltimore Town. (MG 28 Jun - 5 Jly 1759, 27 Mar 1760).
Pugh, Simon, English, 28, 5'5", ran from *Dolphin* in Patapsco R. From Stewart & Lux, Baltimore. (PAG 8 Aug 1763, MG 11 Aug - 1 Sep 1763).*
Purchase, Richard, English, 30, 5'5", arrived Nov 1763 by *Betsy*. From Thos Harrison, AA Co Md. (PAG 12 Sep 1765).
Purvis (Pervis), Anne. From John Brown, PG Co Md. (MG 14 Aug 1755).
Putcherd, William, shoemaker. From Henry Howard & R Coxall, Carroll's Manor AA Co Md. (MG 29 Sep - 6 Oct 1757).
Pyner, Thomas, joiner. From Thos Nickolls Jr., FR Co Md. (MG 29 Aug 1754).*

Quick, Robert, English, 40, 5'6". From Thos Boyer, KE Co Md. (PAG 26 Sep 1765).

Rain, James, from West of England, 35, mason. From Caleb Dorsey, AA Co Md. (MG 16 Jun - 26 Sep 1754).
Rainbird, Joseph, English, cabinet maker & joiner. From Richard Lee, Naval Office, CHA Co Md. (MG 16 Oct 1751, 27 Aug - 30 Nov 1752).*
Rancome, Thomas, 30, ditcher & well digger. From Richd Barnes, RI Co Va. (MG 24 Mar 1747).
Randall, Thomas, English, ran with new spade & much money. From Chas Foreman. KE Co Md. (MG 20 Jun - 18 Jly 1771).
Raner, John, 27, former soldier, ran from Copper Works, FR Co Md. From James Perry & John Bond, FR Co Md. (MG 31 Oct - 5 Dec 1754).
Rankin, Thomas, born Cheshire, 30. From Thos Rutherford, FRV Co Va. (MG 15 Sep 1747).
Raven, Thomas, English, 27, blacksmith. From Walter Beall, FR Co Md. (MG 11 Dec 1766 - 1 Jan 1767).*
Raw, Thomas, English, 26, tall. From Jonathan Chapman, BA Co Ironworks Md. (PAG 30 Jly 1747); from Nathan Chapman, ST Co Ironworks Va. (PAG 16 Apr 1748).*
Rawl, David, West Country man, 30, shoemaker. From Thos King, Annapolis. (MG 2 & 9 Sep 1746, 7 Oct 1747).
Rawson, Daniel, Irish, 28, served on man of war. From Wm Brown, AA Co Md. (MG 27 Sep - 11 Oct 1764).

Reed, James, English, 29, former sailor, in country before. From Walter Beall, FR Co Md. (MG 11 Dec 1766 - 1 Jan 1767).
Reed, John, English, 30, blacksmith. From Thos Owen & Kennedy Farrel. (MG 12 - 26 Jly 1745).
Read, John, English, 24, 5'8". From Edwd Bosman, BA Co Md. (PAG 20 Jly 1769); from James Franklin, BA Co Ironworks Md. (PAG 4 Jly 1771).
Reed, John, 33, tailor. From James Scott, BA Co Md. (MJ 18 & 25 Sep 1773).
Read alias Culbert, Thomas, jeweller & ring engraver. From John Inch, Annapolis. (MG 7 - 21 Jun 1759).
Ready, Thomas, 23. From John Forrest Davis, FR Co Md. (MG 9 & 16 Apr 1772).*
Redding, Elizabeth (1748). *See* Edwards.
Reese, John, Welsh. From Chas Griffith Jr., AA Co Md. (MG 9 & 16 Oct 1760).*
Reeves, William, 27, 5'5", lately arrived. From Thos Treves, BA Co Md. (PAG 19 Jly 1770).
Reynolds, James, Irish, 26, 5'8". From John Bull, BA Co Md. (MG & PAG 12 Apr 1770).
Rhodes, John, born Hampshire, 25, imported by *Dragon*. From Thos Griffin, nr Baltimore Iron Works Md. (MG 5 - 26 Oct, 21 Dec 1758).*
Rhoads, Richard, 26, 5'6", bricklayer. From Thos Jones, BA Co Md. (PAG 12 Jly 1764).
Rice, James, 20. From Patrick Lynch, Patapsco Neck Md. (MG 13 Jly 1775).
Rice, John, 2 months in country. From John Stevenson, BA Co Md. (MG 15 - 27 Oct 1774).*
Richard, Francis, English, 45, 6'0", blacksmith. From James Macklen, KE Co Md. (PAG 7 Jly 1763).*
Richards, Anthony, 30. Ran with Susanna, wife of Robt Grier, Dumfries Va, in Oct 1769. (VGR 14 Dec 1769)*
Richards, Stephen, from Cornwall, 28, 5'6". From James Johnson, FR Co Md. (24 Aug - 7 Sep 1774); from Denton Jacques, FR Co Md. (MG 16 Jly - 29 Aug 1776, PAG 24 Jly 1776).
Richards, William, 40. From Aquila Brown, QA Co Md. (MG 12 Apr - 10 May 1764).
Richardson, John, born Yorkshire, wheelwright & waggon maker, imported by *Lux* in 1755. From Joseph Watkins Md. (MG 26 May - 9 Jun 1757).
Richardson, John, English, 35-40. From Benj Berry Jr., PG Co Md. (MG 3 Sep 1772).*
Rickaby , Thomas, 26, middle height. From Chas Green, BA Co Md. (PAG 14 Jly 1743).
Ricketts, John, 27, sailor. From John Williams, AA Co Md. (MG 23 Nov - 7 Dec 1752).*
Rider, Mary, imported Oct 1748. From Dr. Chas Carroll, Annapolis. (MG 19 Apr 1749).*
Riley, James, Irish, 30. From Richd Owings, BA Co Md. (MG 6 Aug - 15 Oct 1772).
Reily, John, Irish, 35, 5'9". From Bernard Preston Jr., BA Co Md. (MG & PAG 12 Apr 1770).
Robbins, Sarah, English, 25, 5'2". From Henry Williams, FR Co Md. (PAG 14 Jly 1773).
Roberts, Evans, English, 33, 5'0". From Joseph Chavier, QA Co Md. (PAG 6 Jun 1765, 27 Mar 1766).
Roberts, Hugh, born Shropshire, farmer & maltster, imported by *St. George*. From Capt. Jas Dobbins of sd ship. (MG 6 & 13 Apr 1747).*
Roberts, John. From Nathaniel Marsh of Chester Town Md. (MG 13 Feb 1755).
Roberts, John, English, 21. From Saml Wade Magruder & Benedict Craiger, FR Co Md. (MG 20 Jly 1769).
Roberts, John, hostler, 5½ yrs in country. From Joshua Dorsey Jr., AA Co Md. (MJ 6 & 13 Nov 1773).*
Roberts, William, Welsh, 26, 5'9". From Thos Harrison, AA Co Ironworks Md. (PAG 18 Jun 1767).
Roberts, William, English, 44, blacksmith. From John Gorsuch & Job Garretson, Baltimore. (MG 4 Jly 1771).

Robertson, John, 14, 4'0", talkative & literate. From John Robert Holliday, BA Co Ironworks Md. (MG 8 Aug 1771 - 9 Apr 1772, PAG 15 Aug 1771).

Robertson, Lawrence, Irish, 16. From John Dorsey, AA Co Md. (MG 25 Jun - 30 Jly 1772).

Robinson, Thomas, English, 30, tall. From Daniel Pocock, BA Co Md. (PAG 6 Aug 1752).*

Rodd, John, gardener. From James McCubbin, Annapolis. (MG 5 Jan 1758).

Roe, James, 35, tailor. From Colin Ferguson, KE Co Md. (PAG 4 Apr 1766).

Roger, Thomas, English, 30, 5'10". From James Franklin, BA Co Ironworks Md. (PAG 15 Mar 1775).

Rogers, Abraham, English, 30, 5'8". From James Reppeth, QA Co Md. (PAG 20 Apr 1758).

Rogers, Sarah, English, short, breeches maker. From Hugh Poulk, QA Co Md. (PAG 2 Jan & 10 Jly 1766).

Rogers, Thomas, English, 25, 5'8". From James Bleake, KE Co Md. (MG 6 Oct 1757, PAG 13 Oct 1757).

Rogers, Thomas, 28, tailor. From Cornelius Garretson, Baltimore. (MJ 17 - 31 Mar 1778).

Rose (Ross), Edward, 30. From James Moore, BA Co Md. (MG 17 Aug 1748).*

Ross, John, 5'4". From Wm Brown, QA Co Md. (PAG 26 Jly - 23 Aug 1770),

Ross, Peter, Irish, blacksmith. From Cornelius Howard, nr Annapolis. (MG 20 Mar - 29 May 1751).

Rowlands, Richard, 23. From John Collier, Kent Is Md. (MG 17 & 24 Mar 1757).

Rowling, Thomas, 25. From Seth Warfield, AA Co Md. (MG 8 & 15 Sep 1757).

Rowls, Francis, from West of England, shoemaker. From Spencer Ball, NO Co Va. (MG 11 Jly 1754).

Rudge, William, 27, recently imported by *Restoration*. From Ebenezer McClure, Baltimore. (MG 14 Nov - 19 Dec 1771).*

Ryan, Richard, Irish, 18. From Benj Dorsey, Wm Chew Brown & Val Brown, AA Co Md. (MG 10 - 24 Oct 1765).

Sabrie, Samuel, sawyer, writes well. From David Rose, Bladensburg Md. (MG 13 Feb 1751).

Saitee (Saltee), Benjamin, miller. From David Wolstenholme, Windmill, Annapolis. (MG 18 Sep - 4 Dec 1760).

Sale, Simon, 21. From Caleb Dorsey, AA Co Md. (MG 9 - 30 Nov 1769).

Sales, Mortimer, Irish, fiddler, lately imported from Bristol. From Richd Croxall, BA Co Md. (MG 25 Aug - 1 Sep 1763).

Salter, Samuel, short. From Alex Lawson, BA Co Ironworks Md.(PAG 3 Apr 1746). Steward of Nottingham Ironworks, BA Co. (MG 20 Apr 1757).*

Samples, James, hempdresser, in country two months. From Chris Lowndes, Bladensburg Md. (MG 23 Oct - 13 Nov 1755).

Sandels, John, from Shropshire, 28, has run before. From Michael Earle, CE Co Md. (MG 17 Apr - 22 May 1766, PAG 17 Apr 1766).

Sanders, John, 25. From Chas Ridgely Sr., BA Co Md. (MG 3 - 24 Jly 1766).

Sanders, William, 22. From Josias Clapham, FA Co Va. (MG 20 Jun 1747).

Sanders, William, tailor, speaks broken English. From Chas Griffith, nr Annapolis. (MG 14 Sep 1758).

Sanguine, Thomas, born West of England, blacksmith. From Jacob Bromwell, TA Co Md. (MG 8 Nov - 6 Dec 1753).

Sarten, James, born West of England, plowman. From Richd Croxall,Carroll's Manor Md. (MG 29 Sep - 6 Oct 1757).

Savage, Bartholomew, born Ireland, carpenter. From David Ross, Bladensburg Md. (MG 27 - 10 Sep Aug 1761).*

Sawyer, Charles, English, 21, 5'7", brickmaker. From Thos Price, AA Co Md. (PAG 20 Apr 1774).*

Saxon, George, English, 32. From Wm Roberts, Annapolis. (MG 29 Nov 1759).*

Sayer, Anne, pregnant. From James Bleake & Ann Milton, KE Co Md. (MG 6 Oct 1757).

Scholar, William (1767). *See* Graham.

Scott, Thomas, English, 30-40, served in Navy. From Francis Dawes, BA Co Md. (MJ 19 Jun 1776).*

Scowfield, William, English, 22. From Benj Nicholason, BA Co Md. (MG 25 Sep 1773, 4 Jun - 9 Jly 1774, 30 Nov - 19 Dec 1774).

Sears, George, 19, brought up as jockey. From Joshua Dorsey, AA Co (MG 12 Jun - 31 Jly 1760).

Searson, Samuel, 29, 5'9", wheelwright. From Francis Phillips, BA Co Ironworks Md. (MG 1 - 15 Jan 1767, PAG 18 Jan 1767).

Sergentson (Sergeason), John, Yorkshireman, brought up as jockey. From Hugh Thomas. (MG 18 Apr - 25 Jly 1750).

Sexton, Thomas, 25. From Seborn Tucker, AA Co Md. (MG 23 Jun 1774).

Seymour, George, English, 50, 6'0". From Joseph Watkins, AA Co Md. (MG 22 Apr - 30 Sep 1762, PAG 22 Jly & 23 Sep 1762).

Shaddock, Charles, 26, tall. From Samuel Hanson, CHA Co Md. (PAG 8 Jly 1742).

Shaw, Timothy, Irish, 35, 5'5", arrived a month ago. From Daniel Hughes, FR Co Ironworks Md. (PAG 3 Aug 1774).

Sheffield, Isaac, plasterer & painter. From Wm Hammersley, SM Co Md. (MG 11 Sep 1755).*

Sheldon, John, English, 30, 6'0", nailer. From John Forwood, BA Co Md. (PAG 6 Jan 1773).*

Shepard, John, English, 30, 5'10". From Thos Eliot, BA Co Md. (PAG 17 Oct 1765).

Sheppard, William, shoemaker. From Joseph Duvall, PG Co Md. (MG 24 Oct 1771, 27 Jun - 14 Nov 1776).*

Shields alias Wilson, John, Scot, 30, 5'8". From John Dorsey, AA Co Md. (MG 30 Sep 1770 - 21 Feb 1771, PAG 13 Sep 1770).

Shooter, Thomas. From Benj Duvall, Md. (MG 21 & 28 Jun 1753).

Shortoe, John, English, 22, farmer. From Henry Howard, BA Co Md. (MJ 8 - 22 Jun 1779).

Shotton, Benjamin, 5'8", shoemaker, has run twice before. From Thos Smyth, KE Co Md. (PAG 22 Jly 1756).

Shovel, John. From John Musgrove, FR Co Md. (MG 9 May 1765).

Shunk, John, 23. From Joshua Cockey, BA Co Md. (MG 28 May - 18 Jun 1761).

Sidall, John, born Lancashire, farmer, imported in Capt [Francis] Lowndes' ship. From Robt Chesley, SM Co Md. (MG 27 Apr - 4 May 1758).

Silcocke, Jacob, English, 21, 5'7", collar & harness maker, speaks broken Dutch, plays violin. From Jacob Myers, BA Co Md. (MG 10 - 24 Jan 1771, PAG 14 Mar 1771).

Simmins, Edward, shoemaker. From Wm Iiams, AA Co Md. (MG 5 & 12 Jly 1770).*

Simmons, John, English, 18. From Alex Stenhouse, BA Co Md. (MG 23 Apr - 21 May 1761).

Simmons, Thomas, English, 27. From John Ensor Jr. of BA Co Md. (MG 18 Apr 1765, PAG 25 Apr 1765).*

Simmons, Vincent, 28, shoemaker. From Thos King, Annapolis. (MG 24 Aug - 9 Nov 1748).*

Simmons, William, English, barber. From Wm Duvall, AA Co Md. (MG 8 Sep - 10 Nov 1768, 10 Nov 1768 - 5 Jan 1769).*

Simms (alias Smith), John, 30. From John Howard, AA Co Md. (PAG 28 Oct 1742).

Syms, John. From John Smyth, Kent Is Md. (MG 7 - 21 Sep 1758).

Singewood, James, English, 30, middle height, arrived this year. From Benj Tasker, BA Co Ironworks Md. (MG 1 May - 12 Jun 1760, PAG 15 May 1760).

Smart, James, 5'6", arrived 6 months ago. From Thos Johnson, BA Co Md. (PAG 20 Jan 1767).

Smart, William, English, 22, waggoner. From William Ditto of BA Co Md. (PAG 22 Aug 1771).

Smith, John. From Patrick Creagh, Annapolis. (MG 4 - 25 Apr 1754).

Smith, John, Scot. From Pleasance Goodwin, nr Soldier's Delight, BA Co Md. (MG 17 Aug 1758).

Smith, John. From Michael Bence, FR Co Md. (MG 15 - 29 Sep 1761).

Smith, John (1766). *See* Cox.

Smith, John, son of Joseph Smith (*q.v.*), 25, gypsy. From Thos, Saml & John Snowden, AA Co Md. (MG 17 Sep - 8 Oct 1767, 30 Jun - 11 Aug 1768, 3 Aug - 14 Dec 1769).*

Smith, John Adam, 30, gardener. From Chas Carroll, BA Co Md. (MG 6 & 13 May 1773).

Smith, Joseph, gypsy, old man. From Thos, Saml & John Snowden, AA Co Md. (MG 17 Sep - 8 Oct 1767).

Smith, Lawrence, Irish, 30. From Joseph Smith, BA Co Md. (MG 26 Jly - 16 Aug 1759).

Smith, Richard, English, 20, 5'6". From Ephraim Howard, AA Co Md. (MG 29 Mar - 5 Apr 1764, PAG 9 Aug 1764).

Smith, Thomas, English, 35. From Thos Rutland, nr Snowden's Iron Works AA Co Md. (MG 15 Mar - 12 Apr 1759).

Smith, Thomas, Welsh. From Nathan Lane nr Annapolis. (MG 3 Feb - 10 Mar 1763).

Smith, William., Irish, 20. From John Dorsey, AA Co Md. (PAG 2 Jly 1761).

Smith, William, English, 30, 6'0". From Joshua Owings, BA Co Md. (PAG 16 Feb 1769).

Smith, William, gypsy, 40. From Thos, John & Saml Snowden, AA Co Md. (MG 17 Sep - 8 Oct 1767).

Snailum, Richard, born Lancashire, 32. From Caleb Dorsey, AA Co Md. (MG 7 Oct - 11 Nov 1756).

Snale, Samuel, labourer, imported this year by [*Lux*]. From Caleb Dorsey, Elk Ridge Iron Works Md. (MG 15 & 22 Jly 1756).

Snow, William, 40. From Caleb Dorsey, AA Co Md. (MG 19 & 26 Mar 1767, 11 May - 15 Jun 1769).

Soden, Benjamin, English, 27. From Chas Beatty, John Hanson & James Johnson, FR Co Md. (MJ 1 - 15 Sep 1778).

Soles, Joseph, farmer. From John Campbell, Annapolis. (MG 28 Feb 1760).

Soulsby, John, Scot, arrived Jun 1769. From James Walker, AA Co Md. (PAG 27 Jly 1769).

Sparks, William, English, 40, butcher. From Isaac Ashley, KE Co Md. (PAG 23 Jly 1747).

Spencer, John, Scot, 40, carpenter & joiner, 4½ yrs to serve. From Henry Ridgely, AA Co Md. (MG & MJ 5 Jun - 17 Jly 1777).

Spencer, Joseph, English, 30. From James Baxter, CE Co Ironworks Md. (PAG 13 Dec 1739).

Springate, William, born in Wales, bred in Bristol, 5'4", gardener. From Daniel Chamier, BA Co Md. (MG & PAG 4 Jly 1771).

Springer, William, 23, gardener. From Job Garretson, BA Co Ironworks Md. (PAG 13 Jly 1775).

Sprout, Joseph, 22, 5'9". From Joseph Nicholson Jr., KE Co Md. (PAG 18 Dec 1766).

Sprout alias Pratt, Joseph, English, good groom. From Henry Howard, BA Co Md. (MJ 25 Aug - 8 Sep 1778).

Stafford, Nathaniel, 27. From Thos Gassaway, AA Co Md. (MG 1 & 8 Aug 1765).*

Stafford, Thomas, Irish, 21, tall. From Henry Owens, AA Co Md. (PAG 24 Sep 1767).

Stamp, Roger, from West Country, 40. From Ebenezer Perkins, KE Co Md. (MG 21 Oct - 11 Nov 1747)

Stanfield, James, 21, broadcloth weaver. From Nicholas Slade, Baltimore. (MJ 2 & 9 Jan 1775).

Stanton, William. From Wm Harvey, BA Co Md. (PAG 11 Jly 1765).

Stapleton, Thomas, 25. From Stephen Compton, CHA Co Md. (MG 10 May - 7 Jun 1770).*

Statten, Thomas, English, 21. From Chas Walker, BA Co Md. (MJ 31 Mar 1774).

Stead, Samuel. From Brice T B Worthington, Annapolis. (MG 11 - 25 Jly 1750).

Steel, James, 18. From Richd Weedon, AA Co Md. (MG 13 Jly 1769).

Sterling, William, Irish, 28. Fro m John Francis & Clement Trigg, PG Co Md. (MG11 Jun - 9 Jly 1767).

Stevens, Charles, 45. From John Brown, Elk Ridge Md. (MG 7 Apr 1757).

Stephens, Richard, English, tall, horse-cutter. From Wm Ware, CE Co Md. (PAG 8 Jly 1756).*

Stevens, Richard, Prussian born,. From John Ducker, AA Co Md. (MG 20 Dec 1762 - 5 May 1763, PAG 27 Jan 1763).

Stevens, Thomas, 25. From Thos Sollers, BA Co Md. (MG 2 Jun - 14 Jly 1768).

Stewart, John. From Robt Killisson, Md. (MG 27 Jun - 24 Oct 1754).*

Steuart, Stephen, 30, lately arrived by *Aston Hall*. From John Hood, AA Co Md. (MG 18 Aug - 1 Sep 1774).

Stickwood, Jonathan, born Cambridgeshire, 21, 5'8". From Wm Goodwin, BA Co Md. (MG 14 Sep - 2 Nov 1769, PAG 14 Sep 1769).

Stilling, John. From Thos Rutland nr Annapolis. (MG 4 Sep - 23 Oct 1766, 12 Jly - 9 Aug 1770).

Stone, Godfrey, Dutch, 35, 6'0". From Charles Ridgely Jr., BA Co Ironworks Md. (MG 8 Aug 1765, PAG 26 Sep 1765).

Stratland, Thomas, English, 26, 4 yrs to serve. From Wm Simpson, AA Co Md. (MG 8 & 15 Jly 1777).

Stringer, Thomas, 25, 5'6". From John Addison Smith, BA Co Md. (MG 24 & 31 Mar 1763; from Francis Phillips, BA Co Md. (MG 8 Sep - 13 Oct 1768, PAG 14 Sep 1768).

Strong, John. From Zachariah McCubbin, BA Co Md. (MG 23 May 1750).*

Strong, John, English, 35, shoemaker & ex-soldier. From James Gittings, BA Co Md. (MJ 25 Nov - 9 Dec 1777).*

Strong, Peter, born Ireland, carpenter. From Alex Stewart, Baltimore Md. (MG 15 Feb - 1 Mar 1759).*

Suffolk, Richard, 25. From Saml & John Snowden, AA Co Md. (MG 22 Jun - 17 Aug 1775).*

Sullivan, Daniel, sailor or weaver, lately arrived. From Joseph Wood & Adam Vanbebber, CE Co Md. (MG 14 Nov 1750); apprehended in CE Co Md for killing Donald McKennie.(MG 10 Apr 1751).

Swift, Jeremiah, born Braintree, Essex, 23, well educated. From John Hatherley of Elk Ridge Md. whose sons he killed. (MG 20 Mar 1751); to be executed. (MG 24 Apr 1751).*

Sydenham, John Swain, 27, from West Country, shoemaker. From Benedict Calvert, Annapolis. (MG 19 Jly - 9 Aug 1753).

Sylvester, Richard, from West of England, 28, farmer. From Elisha Warfield, AA Co Md. (MJ 10 May 1775).*

Symonds, William, 25, 5'5", barber, lately arrived. From Wm Russell, BA Co Md. (PAG 30 Aug 1770).*

Syms - *See* Simms.

Talbot, Henry, from West of England, smith. From Isaac Harris & Jonathan Pinkney, Annapolis. (MG 7 Jly, 16 Aug - 6 Sep 1764).

Talbot, James, English, 30. From John Bosley, BA Co Md. (MG 12 Apr 1759).

Tandy, John Merry, English, 30, wheelwright. From Wm Collings, KE Co Md. (MG 29 Mar - 5 Apr 1770).

Tasker, Margaret, English, 18, imported by *Betsy* Nov 1763. From Joseph Watkins, AA Co Md. (MG 19 Jan 1764).

Taylor, John, from Worcestershire, 22. From Thos Jacques, FR Co Md. (MG 8 Jun - 13 Jly 1775).

Teen or Tern, Edward, 40. From Edwd Osmond, Carroll's Quarter nr Annapolis Md. (MG 11 Apr 1761).

Tew, Charles, English, 25, 5'8". From Wm Kensey, KE Co Md. (PAG 17 Jly 1760).

Thomas, Henry, 37, 5'10". From Thos Cockey, BA Co Md. (PAG 10 Oct 1761).

Thomas, John, 25. From Chris Carnan, Baltimore Md. (MG 10 Jly - 14 Aug 1760).*

Thomas, John, 32, imported from London. From Thos James, CHA Co Md. (MG 6 Jun - 1 Aug 1765).*

Thomas, John, English, 20. From Mordecai Hammond, BA Co Md. (MG 26 Sep - 3 Oct 1765).*

Thomas, John, 23, farmer. From Thos Johnson Jr., FR Co Md. (MG 2 Mar - 11 May 1769).

Thomas, John, Welsh, 25. From Caleb Owings, BA Co Md. (MG 16 & 23 Mar 1775, 24 Feb - 3 Mar 1778).*

Thomson, Charles, 45. From James Trapnell, nr Baltimore. (MJ 2 - 16 May 1780).

Thompson, Edward, from Shropshire, 29, 6'0", lately arrived. From Andrew & Henry W Pearce, CE Co Md. (PAG 29 Aug 1765, 17 Apr 1766; MG 17 Apr - 22 May 1766).

Thomson, Lawrence, Irish, imported by *Tryal* Sep 1768. From Geo Wilson Sr., PG Co Md. (MG 12 Sep - 10 Oct 1771).

Thompson, William, 30, tall, confectioner. From Abraham Jarrett, BA Co Md. (PAG 12 Nov 1767).

Till, John, 40. From Caleb Owings, BA Co Md. (MJ 16 - 30 Nov 1779).*

Tink, John, 22. From Henry Griffith Jr., AA Co Md. (MG 11 - 25 Jun 1772).

Tinsley, John, born West of England. From Thos Rutland, AA Co Md. (MG 15 Mar - 12 Apr 1759, 12 Jly - 6 Sep 1759).

Tipping, Thomas, Welsh, 40, 5'7", arrived in Jly 1770 by *Thornton*. From Benj Dorsey, FR Co Md. (MG 9 - 23 Aug 1770, PAG 20 Sep 1770).*

Tizerd, Elizabeth, born West of England, arrived in *Falcon* in Jly 1755. From Thos Parker, Annapolis. (MG 28 Aug - 18 Sep 1755).

Todd, John. From John Dorsey, AA Co Md. (MG 17 Sep - 29 Oct 1761).

Tongue, John, English. From John Coppage, QA Co Md. (MG 29 Mar - 19 Apr 1764).

Tonge, Robert, 30. From Eliz Donaldson, SM Co Md. (MG 11 - 25 May 1748).

Toole, David, Irish, 24, 5'4". From John Robert Holliday. BA Co Md. (MG 8 Aug 1771 - 9 Apr 1772, 16 & 23 Oct 1773, PAG 15 Aug 1771, 10 Aug 1774).

Tool, Thomas. From John Jevins, Annapolis. (MG 22 Mar 1770).

Townsend, Miles (1776). *See* Wilson, James.

Townsing, William, 20, 5'6". From James Walker, AA Co Ironworks Md. (PAG 27 Jly 1769).

Trend, John, 28, weaver. From Edwd Osmond, AA Co Md. (MG 19 Nov - 17 Dec 1767).

Trewick, Nicholas, 40, short, miner. From Robt Cooke, SM Co Md. (PAG 16 May 1745).

Tricked (Tricket), Edward, watchmaker. From Chris Prunck, FR Co Md. (MG 25 Aug 1768).*

Trimble, Cornelius (Trembley, Corney), Irish, coach harness maker. From Chas Ridgely & Co., BA Co Md. (MG 15 Nov - 20 Dec 1764).*

Trow, John, English, carpenter. From Richd Henderson, Bladensburg Md. (MG 13 & 20 Jun 1754).*

Truelock, Giles, English, 40. From Benoni Price, PG Co Md. (MG 3 Jun 1762).*

Tucker, Anthony, born West of England, weaver. From John Mayne, QA Co Md. (MG 16 Sep - 7 Oct 1756).

Tucker, George. From Francis King & Henry Hardy, PG Co Md. (MG 19 Sep 1765).*

Tummer, John, from Norfolk, 22, plowman. From Wm Lux, BA Co Md. (MG 26 Apr - 24 May 1764, PAG 3 May 1764).

Turner, George, soap boiler & tallow chandler, 50. From Andrew Steiger, Baltimore. (MG 20 Aug 1761).*

Turner, John, from West of England, 35. From John Berryman, KE Co Md. (MG 27 Aug - 3 Sep 1769).*

Turner, William, ran from *Isabella*. From Smyth & Sadler, KE Co Md. (MG 20 Jly - 10 Aug 1769).

Tyler, Edward, from West of England, 17. From George Risteau, BA Co Md. (MG 7 & 14 May 1767).

Tynan, Thomas. From Richd Bows & Anthony Holmead, FR Co Md. (MG 9 - 23 Jly 1767).

Udell, John, Irish. From John Hammond & Robt Langford, AA Co Md. (MG 10 Jly 1751).

Unrick, Rosannah, Dutch, 30, leatherdresser. From Daniel Rees, BA Co Md. (MJ 30 Dec 1773 - 20 Jan 1774).

Unthank, Daniel, 20, 5'8". From Aquila Price, BA Co Md. (MG 12 & 19 Nov 1772, PAG 11 Nov 1772).*

Van De Huvile, Jan Jonas, from Rotterdam, 40, physician. From Thos Willcox, PG Co Md. (MG 6 Dec 1764).

Vainwright - *See* Wainwright.

Vernal, George, English, 25, farmer. From Henry Howard, BA Co Md. (MG 15 - 29 Dec 1778).

Voice, William, Welsh, 5'10", 45, plasterer. From Thos Chrisholm, BA Co Md. (MG 24 Aug - 28 Sep 1769, PAG 31 Aug 1769).

Vyans, Margaret, born Ireland. From Henry Weedon, Kent Is Md. (MG 14 Jun - 19 Jly 1753).

Wagpels, Joseph (1775). *See* Ingram.

Wainwright (Vainwright), John, from West of England, 15. From Saml Osburn, QA Co Md. (MG 25 Jun 1761).

Wainwright, William (1769). *See* Williamson.

Wakefield, John, English, husbandman, 35-40, imported by *Bideford* this fall. From Widow Buchanan, nr Baltimore Iron Works Md. (MG 16 & 23 Nov 1752).

Waldron (Walden), William, 27.5'5". From Thos Johnson, BA Co Md. (PAG 20 Jan 1757).*

Walker, John, 40, 5'9". From James Harrison, CE Co Md. (PAG 27 May 1756).*

Walker, Robert, English, 44, 5'10". From *Dolphin*, Baltimore Md. (MG 11 Aug - 1 Sep 1763, PAG 18 Aug 1763).

Walton, Thomas, Yorkshireman, 5'8", 28. From Edwd Stevenson, FR Co Md. (MG 21 May - 25 Jun 1767, PAG 28 May 1767).

Warburton (Worberton), William, English, wheelwright. From Richd Gresham, KE Co Md. (MG & PAG 31 Jly 1766).

Ward, Francis, English,, 5'6". From Joseph Reynolds, FR Co Md. (PAG 14 Jly 1768).

Ward, John, from West Country, 27. From Charles Carroll & Co Md. (MG 6 May - 3 Jun 1756).

Ward, John, from West Country, bricklayer or mason, 50. From Daniel Surrell, QA Co Md. (MG 26 Jun - 10 Jly 1760).

Ward, Joseph. From Abraham Woodward & Gilbert Yealdhall, AA Co Md. (MG 30 Aug 1772).*

Ward, William, 22, 5'8". From James Brooks, FR Co Md. (MG 14 May 1772, PAG 21 May 1772).*

Ware, John, English, 23. From John Hamill, CHA Co Md. (MG 11 Sep 1760).

Waring, William. From Thos Rutland, AA Co Md. (MG 19 & 26 Sep 1765).

Warner, Thomas, 5'9", gardener. From John Wilmot, BA Co Md. (MG 8 Jly - 12 Aug 1756, PAG 15 Jly 1756).*

Warriker, William, English, 25, 5'3", arrived in Jly 1770. From John Hood, AA Co. Md. (MG 13 Sep - 18 Oct 1770, PAG 10 Sep 1770).*

Watkins, Samuel, born West of England, gardener, 22. From Chas Carroll, Annapolis. (MG 29 Nov 1759).

Watkinson, Francis, from Derbyshire, 27. From Richd Croxall, BA Co Md. (MG 5 - 19 Sep 1754, 6 May - 3 Jun 1756).

Watson, Hugh, Tinker. From Nathan Rigbie, BA Co Md. (PAG 3 May 1739).

Watson, Isabella, 25, imported by *Neptune* in 1764. From John F A Priggs, PG Co Md. (MG 21 & 28 Jun 1764, 21 Jly - 1 Dec 1768).*

Watson, Thomas, English, 25, 5'8". From Chas Ridgely Jr., BA Co Ironworks Md. (MG 8 Aug 1765, PAG 26 Sep 1765).*

Watts, Henry, 26, butcher. From Saml Middleton, Annapolis. (MG 22 Nov 1749).

Watts, Samuel, 30. From Joseph Jacobs, BA Co Md. (MG 4 & 11 May 1769).

Watts, William, a youth. From Charles Cockey, Kent Is Md. (MG 4 - 18 Mar 1756).

Wbaland (*sic*), Timothy, Irish, lately arrived. From Wm Ellis, CE Co Md. (PAG 2 Oct 1746).

Weakly, Samuel, 15, with 5 yrs to serve. From Wm Ridgely & Lancelot Dorsey, AA Co Md. (MJ 25 Mar - 15 Apr 1777).

Weaver, Thomas, butcher. From Wm Collings, KE Co Md. (MG 29 Mar - 5 Apr 1770).

Webb, Samuel, English, 5'0". From Wm Slade, BA Co Md. (PAG 13 Oct 1763).

Webber, William, 50. From Eliz Payne, Baltimore. (MJ 30 Jun 1778).

Welch, Thomas, English, tall. From James Baxter, CE Co Ironworks Md. (PAG 30 Aug 1739).

Weldon, William, Irish, joiner. From Stephen Steward. (MG 6 - 27 May 1773).*

Wells, Edmund, 18, served in Navy. From Thos Sappington, AA Co Md. (MG 4 Jly 1776).

Wells, Jeremiah, born Sussex, farmer. From R Jones, NO Co Va. (MG 21 Sep 1748).*

Welsh, Richard, English, 27, imported from Dublin 6 weeks ago. From Benj Dorsey, Wm Chew Brown & Valentine Brown, AA Co Md. (MG 10 - 24 Oct 1765).

West, James, 15, imported from London. From Thos James, CHA Co Md. (MG 6 Jun - 1 Aug 1765).*

Westall, George, English, 24. From Joseph McCubbin, nr Snowden's Iron Works Md. (MG 12 Jly - 6 Sep 1759).

Wetheridge, Isaac, English, 30, short, shoemaker. From John Senhouse, AA Co Md. (PAG 16 Jun 1743).

Whealan, Edward, short. From George Ashman Jr., BA Co Md. (PAG 10 Jly 1760).

Wheatley, Thomas, 27, 5'8". From Aquila Price, BA Co Md. (MG 12 Nov - 24 Dec 1772, PAG 11 Nov 1772).

White, Christopher, Irish, 30, 6'0". From Thos Beach, AA Co Md. (PAG 24 Sep 1767).*

White, John, lately imported by *Hawk*, Capt Wm Few. From Jacob Giles, BA Co Md. (MG 15 - 29 Sep 1757.

301

White, John, Irish, 23. From Vachel Worthington, BA Co Md. (MG 6 Sep 1764).*
White, William, From Richd Brook & Edwd Owen, FR Co Md. (MG 2 - 16 Oct 1766).*
White, William, ran from PG Co Md Jail after imprisonment for killing Benedict Wood. (MG 27 Nov - 4 Dec 1766).
Whitefield, Daniel, short. From Wm Edwards, BA Co Md. (PAG 23 Nov 1769).
Whitmore, Joseph, farmer, 30, speaks West Country dialect. From Walter Dulany, Annapolis. (MG 10 - 24 Jun 1756).
Whitton, John, 24, lately imported. From Chas Ridgely, BA Co Md. (MG 5 - 19 Apr 1764, 5 Mar 1767).
Wilcocks, John, English, 21, 6'0". From Edwd Stevenson, FR Co Md. (PAG 21 May - 25 Jun 1767); from Daniel Hughes, FR Co. Ironworks Md. (PAG 5 Oct 1774).
Wilcox, Robert, 5'10". From Wm Bennett, BA Co Md. (PAG 15 May 1755).
Wild, Abraham, from Manchester, England, weaver. From Amos Garrett, BA Co Md. (MG 29 Oct - 19 Nov 1767).
Wilding, Henry, 24. From Robt Rechs, nr Baltimore. (MJ 22 Jly - 19 Aug 1777).*
Wilkins, John, English. From Flora Dorsey, AA Co Md. (MG 29 Nov 1764).
Wilkinson, George, tailor. From Michael Bence, FR Co Md. (MG 15 - 29 Sep 1763).*
Wilks, James, English, 22, 5'5". From Patrick Rock, HAR Co Md. (MJ 21 Sep 1774, PAG 1 May 1776).
Wilks, Thomas, 40, brickmaker. From Patrick Creagh, Md. (PAG 30 Dec 1742).*
Williams, Benjamin, West Country man, tailor. From Richd Tilghman Earle, QA Co. (MG 14 Aug - 11 Sep 1760).
Williams, Edward, English, 37, cooper, arrived 4 weeks ago. From Wm Young Jr., BA Co Md. (PAG 28 Jly & 25 Aug 1773).*
Williams alias Willoughby, Elizabeth, 25, pretty tall woman (Laura 46). From Richd Barnes, RI Co Va. (MG 24 Mar 1747).
Williams, George, 5'7", transported before. From Wm McCubbin Jr., AA Co Md. (PAG 17 Sep 1767).*
Williams, Henry, shoemaker, took his tools. From Robt Couden, Annapolis. (MG 13 Feb 1751).
Williams, Henry, from North Wales. From Wm Chipley. (MG 24 Nov 1774).
Williams, James. From James Fendall, CHA Co Md. (MG 26 Jun - 16 Oct 1760).
Williams, Jane, ran with Wm Duncanson (*q.v.*). From Hugh West, FA Co Va. (MG 2 Dec 1746).
Williams, Jared (Jarratt), English, 30, with 3½ yrs to serve. From Henry Howard, BA Co Md. (MJ 25 Mar - 15 Apr 1777)
Williams, John, Welsh, tinker. From Hugh Conn, PG Co Md. (PAG 27 Jun 1745).
Williams, John, born Herefordshire, farmer, 30. From Chas Carroll & Co, BA Co Md. (MG 7 Jun - 19 Jly 1753).
Williams, John, English, 38. From Robt Roberts, KE Co Md. (PAG 3 Nov 1763).*
Williams, John, sailmaker. From Wm Gartrell, FR Co Md. (MG 10 & 17 May 1764).*
Williams, John, English, 30, tailor. From Elisha Warfield, AA Co Md. (MJ 10 - 31 May 1775*
Williams, Margaret, Welsh, short, arrived 16 Jan 1744. From Hugh Conn, PG Co Md. (PAG 22 Jun 1745).
Williams, Richard, born Herefordshire, hatter. From Nath Waters, Annapolis. (MG 2 - 30 Nov 1758).*
Williams, Robert, English, 45, 5'6". From Joshua Owings, BA Co Md. (PAG 16 Feb 1769).
Williams, Thomas, 22. From Joseph Jacobs, AA Co Md. (MG 9 - 30 May 1771).
Williams, Thomas, 32, English, ex-soldier. From Wm Goodwin, BA Co Md. (MJ 18 Mar - 8 Apr 1777, 22 Jly 1777).*

Williams, William, 30, 5'6". From Thos Harrison, AA Co Ironworks Md. (PAG 27 Jly 1769).*

Williamson, William, English, cabinet maker, three years in country. From John Gody, CHA Co Md. (MG 5 & 12 Oct 1758).*

Williamson alias Wainwright, William. From PG Co Md. (MG 23 Nov - 21 Dec 1769).

Willis, Thomas, 30. From Walter Dulany, Annapolis. (MG 2 Aug 1770).

Willoughby, Elizabeth (1747). See Williams.

Willoughby, Elizabeth, English. From John Drummond, CE Co Md. (MG 10 & 17 Oct 1750).

Willoughby, Robert (1748). See Millby.

Wilson, Ann, from Lancashire, 45, 5'2". From James Braddock, TA Co Md. (MG 2 Nov - 21 Dec 1775, PAG 8 Nov 1775).*

Wilson, James alias Townsend, Miles, 25, mason, in country 3 yrs. From Thos Sappington, AA Co Md. (MG 4 Jly 1776).

Wilson, John, Irish, 27, 6'0", soldier in England & at Carthagena, speaks plain English. From Stephen Onion, BA Co Ironworks Md. (PAG 20 Jun 1745, MG 31 Mar - 14 Apr 1747).

Wilson, John (1771). See Shields.

Wilson, Sarah (1752). See Knox.

Winey (Viney), Thomas, lately imported from Kent by *Litchfield*. From Wm Fitzhugh, WE Co Va. (MG 23 Aug 1749).*

Winter, John, house painter, hired to man in Va. From John Fendall, CHA Co Md. (MG 26 Jun - 7 Aug 1760).

Wittengem, David, 25. From Joshua Dorsey, AA Co Md. (MG 18 Aug - 1 Sep 1757).

Wood, Robert, born Gloucestershire, 25, wheelwright & carpenter. From Nicholas Minskie, Annapolis. (MG 17 Sep - 1 Oct 1761).

Wood, Samuel, from London. From Robt Morris, TA Co Md. (MG 6 - 20 Sep 1745).*

Wood, Thomas, born Lincolnshire, 42, farmer. From John Carnan Md. (MG 26 Jly - 9 Aug 1759, 30 Oct 1760).

Wood, Thomas, 25. From Emory Sudler, KE Co Md. (MG 14 Feb 1771).

Woodcock, Thomas, English, 30. From Chas Carroll & Richd Croxall, Baltimore Iron Works Md. (MG 6 May - 3 Jun 1756, 27 Mar - 29 May 1760).

Woolridge, Stephen, Cornishman, 23, farmer, recently imported from Bristol. From Jacques & Johnson. (MG 15 Apr 1773).

Worgar, John, 35. From Stephen Stewart, AA Co Md. (MG 8 Aug - 14 Nov 1771).

Worley, William, 24. From Ely Dorsey, AA Co Md. (MG 9 - 23 Jly 1761).

Wright, Benjamin, English, 47, blacksmith. From James Howard, AA Co Md. (MJ 23 Sep - 17 Nov 1778).

Wright, John, shoemaker. From John Hammond, AA Co Md. (MG 11 - 25 Jly 1750).

Wright, John. From Patrick Creagh, Annapolis. (MG 4 - 25 Apr 1754).

Wright, John, English, 25. From James Walker, AA Co Md. (MG 21 Aug - 18 Sep 1766).*

Wright, Joseph, English, 40, short. From John Howard, AA Co Md. (PAG 15 May 1760).

Wright, Martin, Irish, 40. From John Carlyle, Alexandria Va. (MG 16 Aug 1759).*

Wright, Samuel, 38, millwright. From Wm Whetcroft, AA Co Md. (MG 10 Jly - 13 Nov 1777).*

Yorath, David, born Wales, mason, 33. From David Wolstenholme, Annapolis. (MG 23 Sep - 4 Nov 1756).

Young, Richard, speaks West Country dialect. From Daniel Pocock, BA Co Md. (MG 21 Apr - 5 May 1757).

SOME CASE STUDIES

Roger Ekirch, in *Bound for America: The Transportation of British Convicts to the Colonies, 1718-1775* (Oxford: Clarendon Press, 1987) discussed the practice of transporting felons. He pointed out the alarm felt by Maryland colonists over the arrival of these convicts, who, it was feared, would bring gaol fever and other pestilence and other vicious habits (Ekirch:135, 137).

Convicts were employed for their various skills. Many of them were purchased to work in the ironworks (Ekirch:144-145). Ekirch attempted to trace 145 convicts named in Kent County records, but was only able to identify five of them. None were well to do. He also attempted to trace 395 additional males imported into Kent and Queen Annes Counties but only eight could be identified. (Ekirch:180-181).

Research by Bob Barnes has shown that many early inhabitants of Baltimore County started life in Maryland as detainees "at His Majesty's Pleasure." Sentenced to death for what were often very minor crimes, convicted felons were allowed to choose the option of transporting, and once they had served their time, many established themselves, acquired land by patent, purchase, or lease, and settled down to raise families. Their descendants may well feel proud that they overcame any blot on their record, and went on to become respectable citizens.

Of the 19 case studies presented here, all were married, 14 are recorded as having had children, and some are known to have descendants living today. All but six of them possessed land, although many of them started by taking out leases on My Lady's Manor or Gunpowder Manor. Perhaps many of those who were tenants of Lord Baltimore or of Thomas Brerewood hesitated to support the revolutionary movement for fear of losing their leases. Seven were known to be Non-Jurors, and four probably died or moved away long before the Revolution began. On the other hand Jonathan Ady served in a military company and two of Robert Constable's sons took the Oath while one served in the militia.

Most of the individuals were farmers but David Benfield was a physician, and Renaldo Monk and William Jessop were connected with iron-making.

BIOGRAPHICAL SKETCHES

JONATHAN ADY. Born about 1719, sentenced in 1737 in Middlesex, England, to be hanged for theft but reprieved and transported by the *Pretty Patsy* to Maryland to serve. his 14 years' sentence (CBEB). He settled in Baltimore Co., and on 4 April 1743 married Rebecca York, daughter of James and Rachel York (BCF). On 15 November 1743, Thomas Brerewood leased to Ady 60 acres of My Lady's Manor, the lease to run for the lifetimes of Jonathan, aged 24, his wife Rebecca, aged 17, and their daughter. Rachel, aged 14 days. (BALR TB#C:433). On 3 December 1745 he mortgaged this land to John Ridgely (BALR TB#D:407). On 10 October 1746 Thomas Brerewood leased 11 lots (originally leased to Nicholas Seaver) in Charlottetown to Ady, the leases to run for the lifetimes of Ady, aged about 27, his wife Rebecca, aged about 22, and son William, aged about four. (BALR TB#E:352). During the Revolutionary War Jonathan served as a private in Capt. Robert Harris's Co. of the Flying Camp (BCF). In 1781, then of Harford Co., William, son of the emigrant Jonathan Ady, married with four children, was convicted of the murder of Vincent Richardson in 1779 while both were in drink. (PPGC 477). He and others petitioned for a pardon which was evidently granted for in 1783 he was living in Gunpowder Upper and Lower Hundreds, owning 102 acres, part of Bond's Pleasant Hills (BCF).

Jonathan Ady was the father of (BCF): Rachel, born December [but more likely October] 1743, who married Nathan Yearly; William, born 23 August 1745; Elizabeth, born 23 August 1747; Ralph, born 14 December 1749; Jonathan, born 23 January 1752; Margaret, born 16 August 1754; Hannah, born 1 September 1756; Sarah, born 23 October 1758; James, born 23 December 1760; Rebecca, born 22 February 1762; and Joshua, born 10 April 1767.

THOMAS ASKERON was sentenced to death for highway robbery in Yorkshire, England, at the Summer Sessions of 1744; was reprieved in the following year and was bonded to be transported for 14 years in May 1745. (CBEB:22). He was in Baltimore County by 18 October 1755 when he purchased 132¾ acres, part of White Oak Bottom, from Thomas Matthew (BALR BB#I:463). The index to Baltimore County Debt Books shows that between 1757 and 1771 Askeron owned tracts called Westphalia, Haywood, New Castle, and Griffith's Neighbor. In 1762 he purchased 170 acres, part of Westphalia, from Nicholas Ruxton Gay (BALR B#K:382). He was listed as a taxable in Delaware Hundred in 1763 (IBCP:7). As Thomas "Ashram" he was listed in Sheriff Aquila Hall's Assessment Ledger, c. 1762-1765 (IBCP:17). Thomas "Askren" signed the petition for removing the County seat to Baltimore Town in 1768 (IBCP:39). In 1770 Solomon Stocksdale sold Thomas Askeron 109 acres called Griffith's Neighbors. (BALR AL#A:641).

On 22 June 1771 Thomas Askeron, with the consent of his wife Martha, sold to Harry Dorsey Gough parts of the following tracts: 13 acres called Haywood, patented to Askeron on 1 April 1761; 80 acres called New Castle, patented on 21 January 1763; 170 acres Westphalia, and 109 acres Griffin's Neighborhood. Askeron was able to sign his name (BALR AL#C:488). He does not appear in BARP or the 1783 AL.

DAVID BENFIELD of Oxford, England, practitioner of physic and surgery, was transported to Maryland in 1771. He died in Harford Co. before May 1779. In 1772 he wrote to his former jailer in Oxford and this letter was published in the *Maryland Historical Magazine* (MHM 37:196). In 1778 he took the Oath of Fidelity and Allegiance to the State of Maryland (HARP).

In 1779 David Benfield died leaving a will dated 24 January, proved 17 May 1779. He left his plantation to his wife Hannah Benfield. He named his mother Mary Benfield; his father-in-law Thomas Elliott; his sister-in-law Mary Benfield, wife of William Benfield, living at great Barrington, near Burford in Oxfordshire; and his nephew David Benfield, son of [the said] William and Mary. Trustees were: Robert Amoss Esq., Aquila Thompson, gent., Christopher Dawson, John Adams, Henry Fawcet, John Brown (late of Oxford), John Wayne, Samuel Day, Sarah Woodman, and William Wood. Executors were to be his wife Hannah Benfield, Robert Amos, and Aquila Thompson. The will was witnessed by George Hughes Worsley, Solomon Brown, and John Brown (HAWB AJ#2:31). On 17 May 1779 estate papers [possibly an inventory] were filed by executors Hannah Benfield and Robert Amos. There was no distribution, and an administration account filed in 1780 stated there were no kindred (Harf. Co. Estate File 155, in *Heirs and Legatees of Harford County*, by Henry C. Peden).

CHARLES BOSSOM of Oxford, England, was sentenced to transportation in 1763 and was shipped to Maryland. In about 1772 he was married and had two children. He lived near his countryman Dr. David Benfield on My Lady's Manor in Baltimore Co. (MHM 37:196). In 1773 he appeared in the tax list of North Hundred where he is shown as living with Joseph Whitehead. (1773 TL, p. 45). In 1778 Bossom was a Non-Juror to the Oath of Allegiance. In 1782 he was involved in the evaluation of confiscated proprietary reserve lands in Baltimore County (BARP). In the next year he was in North Hundred, owning 68 acres called

CASE STUDIES

Bossom's Plot where his household consisted of one white male and six white inhabitants (1783 TL). The 1798 Particular Assessment List of North Hundred shows that he owned 143 acres called Bossom's Spot where improvements included a hewed log dwelling house, one story, 20' x 16', and a log barn, 24' x 20' (George Horvath. *Particular Assessment Lists, 1798, Baltimore and Carroll Counties*. Westminster: Family Line Publications).

ROBERT CONSTABLE was sentenced at Middlesex, England, in February, was transported to Maryland in March 1729 by the *Patapsco Merchant*, and is listed in a Landing Certificate in December 1729 (CBEB). A Robert Constable patented 145 acres in Anne Arundel Co. Constable's Range on 25 March 1745 (MPL PT#1:218).

A Robert Constable married Judith Cook on 7 June 1736 in St. Paul's Parish, Baltimore Co. (BAPA 1:33). He was dead by 4 January 1755 when his estate was inventoried by James Cary and John Ensor, Jr., and valued at £55.4.6. John and Robert Constable signed as next of kin. Frances Constable was the administratrix. (MINV 60:151, 154). He left a widow Frances and children (BCF; BARP): John (who took the Oath of Fidelity in 1778); Robert; and probably Thomas (took the Oath of Fidelity in 1778 and was an ensign in the Baltimore Town Battalion in May 1781).

Thomas Constable, of Baltimore Co., carpenter, one of the sons of Robert Constable, deceased, deposed on 23 October 1785 that his father kept a family Bible in which he entered the names and ages of his children, including: Robert (brother of the deponent), who was born on 14 June 1737. The Bible has been lost or misplaced (BACT 4:79).

RICHARD CULVERWELL was sentenced at the Somerset Quarter Sessions for 14 years, in October 1758, and was transported in May 1759 (CBEB). An advertisement in 1771 stated he was from Cheddar, Somerset, and shipped to Maryland in May 1759 on the *Atlas*, from Bristol. He was urged to apply to Capt. John McKerdy of the *Royal Charlotte* (MG 6 June 1771). In 1774 he was on the Taxation List for Baltimore West Hundred. (IBCP:90). In 1778 he was a Non-juror (BARP). Between 1784 and 1787 he paid for a pew in St. Paul's Parish (BAPA: 1:147). The 1796 Baltimore City Directory showed he was a constable.

The following may have been children of Richard Culverwell: Stephen, married Miss Griffith in October 1801 by Rev. Roberts (BA 30 Oct 1801); Martha, married in March 1802 William Jordan by Mr. McCombs (BFG 19 March 1802); and Elizabeth, married in November 1808 Henry Peck, by Rev. Roberts (BFG 10 Nov 1808).

DANIEL CURTIS may be the Daniel Curtis alias. Richardson who was sentenced to be transported as a convict from Middlesex Sessions in September or October 1750 (CBEB).

A Daniel Curtis married Rachel Pearce on 5 November 1758 (BATHa:2) and died in August 1794. In 1760 he was in the List of Baptists in the Congregation of John Davis who contributed to the sufferers from the Boston Fire (Calendar of Maryland State Papers: The Black Books, Document 1007). [If Daniel Curtis became a Baptist it might explain why no births were recorded in St. Thomas Parish after the birth of his daughter Hannah]. In 1763 Curtis was a taxable in Back River Upper Hundred (IBCP:5), and in 1768 signed a petition favoring the removal of the county seat from Joppa to Baltimore Town (IBCP:27).

Curtis was appointed overseer of roads in 1775, his territory to run from "Armstrong's to Monkton Mill, and from Daniel Shaw's to the main road leading to the chappel [possibly St. James' Chapel, My Lady's Manor] and from the road above Bacon's smith shop that leads to

Coxes Ford on the great Falls of the Gunpowder and from thence until it intersects the main road from Wheeler's Mill to Charles Gorsuch's." He was continued as overseer of roads from 1776 to 1777 (BAOR:81, 83).

On 13 Jan 1777 Daniel Curtis gave testimony concerning John Ross, saying that Ross "drank [made a toast] confusion to Lord Howe" (CMSP Red Books Part 2, document 866). Two weeks later Constantin O'Donnell deposed that he heard both John Ross and Daniel Curtis drink "confusion to Lord Howe and Lord Dunmore in Baltimore jail." (Ibid., document 899). In 1778 Curtis did not take the Oath of Allegiance, possibly out of fear of losing his rented land on My Lady's Manor. In 1782 he was one of the "Petitioners of My Lady's Manor," (CMSP Red Books, Part 3, document 1258).

Daniel Curtis was living as late as 1783 in Mine Run Hundred where he owned 128 acres of Armstrong's Lot. His household consisted of two white males and four white inhabitants (BATL 1783). The diary of Rev. John Coleman recorded the death of Daniel Curtis at about 1 p.m..on 3 August 1794 (BAJA:50).

Daniel and Rachel were the parents of (BATHb:53; SCBC:63): Joseph, born 7 August 1757 or 1759; Hannah, born 15 June 1761; and William, married . . . Sheppard and lived in the 10th District of Baltimore Co.)

JASPER GODBY, son of Jasper Godby of London, was sentenced in London in 1747 and transported to Maryland early in the following year by the *St. George*: he was registered in March 1748 in Kent Co. records. On 25 May 1755 he married Ann Bosell (SJSG, 212). On 20 September 1756 he wrote to his father and mother in London telling them he was then living with his former master Chyhewik in Baltimore Co., asking them not to think ill of him for not coming home but making no mention of his marriage. He expressed the wish that God would have taken his brother Edward and sent love to the wife of his brother William. (NGSQ Vol. 65 No. 4, p. 267).

GEORGE HATCHER, son of Thomas Hatcher of St. Margaret, Westminster, by his second wife Catherine, was brought up by a parish nurse after the death of his father in 1722. He was apprenticed to a blacksmith in 1732 but served only half his term and soon fell into bad ways. He was arrested in 1738 for robbery, convicted, and sent to Virginia for seven years by the *Dorsetshire*. There he was sold as a blackmith to James Jones, an undertaker and builder of King George Co. and was "a noted good worker." On Jones's death in 1744 he was sold on to Charles Ewell who removed to Prince William Co.

After advertisements had been placed inviting claims to the estate in Cheriton, Hampshire, England, of Thomas Hatcher who died in 1732, several people came forward to testify that the felon George Hatcher was his grandson. The descent, according to depositions made in London in 1745, was as follows:

Thomas Hatcher Sr. was twice married. By his first wife he had a son Thomas [above], and a daughter Elizabeth who died in about 1720 and daughters Catherine and Susanna. The said Catherine Hatcher married William Avenell and brought suit with her husband in 1743 against John Hickman of Hitchen Stoke, Hampshire, claiming the Cheriton estate. Thomas Hatcher Jr. had children George Hatcher [above] who was named "Doctor" and went to the West Indies and a daughter who went from place to place. (PRO: C11/154/2, 448/8, 1588/26, C12/322/11, NQSQ Vol 61, p. 201-203).

CASE STUDIES

The suit in Chancery was decided in 1746 in favour of the plaintiffs but without any further mention of George Hatcher.

WILLIAM ISGRIG of London was sentenced in April 1740 and transported to serve his seven year term by the *Essex* (CBEB), arriving in Maryland in May 1740. On 20 July 1749 he posted bond for John Jones and in 1750 Isgrig witnessed the will of Richard Rutter. On 1 May 1755 William Isgrig testified he was well acquainted with Renaldo Monk, and knew Monk was indisposed because he broke two ribs (MDTP 36:152). On 16 December 1757 he posted bond for the administration of Richard Rutter's estate; William Nicholson and William Lux were securities (MDTP 36:441). On 6 November 1758 he filed an administration account of Rutter's estate. The inventory was valued at £96.11.5, and after all debts were paid, there was a balance of £33.6.5 (MDAD 42:230). On 23 October 1759 he filed another account of the estate showing a balance due of £5.10.6 (MDAD 44:5). Yet another inventory of the estate was filed on 14 November 1759 showing it to be worth £6.17.6 (MDTP 37:310); and a final inentory submitted on 10 September 1761 showed a balance due of £6.0.5 (MDAD 46:438; MDTP 38:219). In 1765 as executor of Richard Rutter, William Isgrig was summoned to court for a balance of £6.0.5 due from June 1762. [Evidently Isgrig had not distributed it among the heirs] (BAMI 1765:50). In 1768 he was again summoned to court to render an account of the balance on Rutter's estate of £5.0.6. A notation indicates that the case was struck off (BAMI 1768-1769:unpaged).

On 17 March 1761 William Isgrig conveyed land to Daniel Isgrig BALR AL#H:26-).In 1763 W[illiam] Isgrigg, Sr. in 1763 was listed as a taxable in Soldier's Delight Hundred (IBCP), and on 20 March 1764 William Isgrig and John Jones advertised for runaways (MG). On 31 October 1765 William Isgrig was security for Elisha Hall and his wife Mary as administratrix of the estate of John Forty (MDTP 41:220). On 10 June 1766 William Isgrig, Sr. mortgaged land to John Ridgely (BALR B#P:93). On 17 January 1767 he witnessed the will of William Harvey (BAWB 3:188) and in 1768 he signed the petition favoring Baltimore Town as the County Seat (ARMD 61:523). On 17 May 1771 he leased 135 acres, part of Eli O'Carroll, from Charles Carroll of Duddington. The lease was to run for the lifetimes of William, and his sons Michael Nicholson and Daniel Isgrig (BALR AL#H:249) The consideration was 816 lbs tobacco to be paid yearly on 1 Dec. William agreed to erect a grist mill, to plant 135 apple trees within five years, and not to use more wood than he, his wife, children, and two servants (three if his children could not work the land) could use.

In 1773 William Isgrig appeared on the tax list of Delaware Hundred and was the only taxable in the household, so his oldest son must have left home, and his second son had not yet reached the age of 16 (IBCP). In 1778 William Isgrig refused to take the Oath of Fidelity to the State of Maryland but William Isgrig, Jr. swore the Oath before the Hon. Jesse Dorsey (BARP). In 1780 William Isgrig assigned land to [his son] Daniel for the use of Methodist preachers (BALR WG#F:249); and in February 1781 conveyed to the same the residue of the lease made in 1771.

In 1783 William Isgrig is listed in the Tax List for Gunpowder Upper Hundred; he owned no land but his household consisted of four white males, and seven whites (1783 AL). On 18 July 1800 he witnessed the will of Aaron Packer (BAWB 7:14).

ABRAHAM JARRETT of Baltimore County may be the Abraham Jarrett or Jarrow from Essex, England, who was transported in August 1721 by the ship *Owner's Goodwill,* and listed in a landing certificate dated Maryland, July 1722. (CBEB). He was in Baltimore Co. by 1732 when he purchased 100 acres of Mary's Delight from Edmund Hays, Jr. On 9

November 1733 Francis Freeman conveyed 50 acres (one-half of the tract) to Abraham Jarrett, cordwainer (shoemaker). (BALR HWS#M:4).

The Tax List for 1737 shows Abraham Jarrett as head of a household in Upper Hundred North of Gunpowder (IBCW:16) and in March 1741 he, his wife Eleanor, and Francis Freeman conveyed 50 acres of Rachel's Delight to Patrick Vance. On 1 September 1741 he purchased 150 acres on the south side of Gunpowder River. In 1750 he is listed in the Baltimore Co. Debt Book as owning 100 acres called Mary's Delight and 76 acres called Hopewell (BCF:360).

He died in Baltimore Co. leaving a will dated 2 August 1747 and proved 13 Dec. 1757, naming his wife Eleanor and children Abraham and Mary. Administration bond was posted on 9 January 1758 by Eleanor Bussey with William Grafton and Michael Collins as sureties. His estate was inventoried and valued at £480.6.4 by James Scott and James Preston. The inventory was signed by . . . Pickett and John Buttery as creditors and by Abraham Jarrett and Mary Bussey as kin. Eleanor Jarrett, the administratrix [*sic*] filed the inventory on 1 January 1759, (MINV 66:135). The relict Eleanor later married Michael McGuire and they took out administration on the estate on 3 July 1759 and 31 March 1759. Abraham and Eleanor Jarrett were the parents of at least two children: Abraham; and Mary, who married Jesse Bussey; and possibly others not named in the will.

WILLIAM JESSOP, progenitor of the Baltimore Co. family, may well be the William Jessup of Suffolk who was sentenced to hang for stealing a gelding but reprieved on condition of transportation in Lent 1738. He was shipped in June 1738. (CBEB).

William Jessop and Margaret Walker were married on 25 June 1748 in St. Paul's Parish, Baltimore. Co. (BAPA); he described himself as a collier and became a manager of the Baltimore Company. In October 1755, William Jessop at the Baltimore Iron Works, had a letter waiting for him at the Annapolis Post office (MG 25 Oct 1755); and in April 1757, as a collier at the Baltimore Iron Works, reported a runaway Irish servant (MG 7 April 1757). On 11 June 1756 John Floyd, Thomas Floyd, and Thomas's wife Rachel conveyed 50 acres, part of Brother's Expectation, to William Jessop; Henry Maynard and his wife Zepporah acknowledging receipt of full satisfaction for Zepporah's right of dower (BALR BB#I:570). On 26 February 1776 William Jessop directed property to be conveyed after his decease to his children William, Nicholas, Abraham, Charles, and Esther (BACT 3:199, 200, 201, 2020, 203). William Jessop Sr. and his son Nicholas were Non-Jurors to the Oath of Fidelity in 1778, but signed the Oath in 1781 (BARP).

Jessup died leaving a will dated March 1781, proved 23 Oct. 1781, naming wife Margaret, who was to have his plantation and personal estate for life; sons Nicholas and Abraham, who were to have the plantation at the death of his wife). The children Elizabeth Teal, William, Nicholas, Charles and Abraham Jessop, and Esther Ford were to divide personal estate at death of his wife and the sons William and Nicholas were to be executors. Nathan Owings, Robert Hudson and Isaac Henry were witnesses (BAWB 3:438, which states the widow claimed her thirds). William and Nicholas Jessop posted the administration bond on 3 November 1781, with George Teal and John Howard Ford as sureties (BAAB 5:99). On 6 August 1782 William Jessup and Nicholas Jessup advertised they would settle the estate (MJBA 6 Aug 1782). Margaret Jessop, widow, on 24 September 1783, conveyed property to her daughter Action Jessop (BACT 3:386). An account of their father's estate was submitted for administration on 18 April 1792 by William and Nicholas Jessup. (BAAD 11:39).

CASE STUDIES

William and Margaret (Walker) Jessop were the parents of: Elizabeth, born 17 September 1750, died 12 September 1814 in Tennessee, married George Teal in 1770; William, born 28 July 1755; Nicholas, born 5 July 1757; Charles, born 6 November 1759; Esther, born 21 May 1762, died 11 May 1803, married John Howard Ford; and Abraham, born 18 March 1766.

PETER MASON was sentenced in Middlesex in February and transported to Maryland in April 1741 by the *Speedwell* or *Mediterranean*. (CBEB). A Peter Mason and Mary Davis were married. in St. John's Parish on 6 October 1744 (SJSG:191). On 29 June 1762 Peter Mason was one of many debtors listed in the inventory of Col. Charles Christie of BA Co. (MINV 78:98-132), while on 3 August 1774 he was listed as a "desperate debtor" in the inventory of Col. William Young of BA Co. (MINV 120:1-13).

In 1778 Peter Mason Sr. and Peter Mason Jr., then living in Mine Run Hundred, were non-Jurors to the Oath of Allegiance. (BARP). In 1790 Peter Mason was living in Harford Co., with two free white females (1790 CE:79). He must have died or moved away soon thereafter and he does not appear in any Harford Co. probate records. Peter Mason was the father of at least one son: Peter, born about 1757.

RENALDO MONK was born in about 1702, giving his age as 52 in 1754 (Henry Peden, *More Maryland Deponents* (FLP), citing BA. Co. Land Commissions, 1:40), and died in BA Co. in 1769. He came into Maryland as a convict and died a man of considerable property.

In 1742 Rinaldo Monk of Wiltshire was sentenced to 14 years transportation and shipped to Maryland where he was landed in November of that year. (CBEB:559). By 1747 he was living in Prince George's Co., (near the Patuxent Iron Works), when he advertised for a runaway mulatto (MG 11 Aug 1747). On 6 July 1748, living near Mr. Snowden's Iron works at Patuxent, he reported a runaway servant from the Baltimore Iron Works (MG 6 July 1748). He moved to BA Co. by July 1755 when he surveyed 125 acres called Cook's Adventure Resurveyed. In July 1758 he surveyed 20 a. Monk's Discovery (GSV 1:42).

He married some time before 28 July 1755, Rachel, executrix of Edward Riston (BCF:453), and died in BA Co. leaving a will dated 20 Sep 1768, proved 14 Aug 1769. To sons Renaldo and William he left one shilling each; to his daughter Sarah Carreck £30 and £20 respectively; and to his daughter Mary 125 acres of Cook's Adventure Resurveyed, 26 or 27 acres, part of Angel's Fortune, 20 acres called Monk's Discovery, and the residue of his personal estate. Henry Reaston and daughter Mary were to be co-executors. Richard Gott, Anthony Gott and John Adam Beard were witnesses. (BAWB 3:123). An administration bond on his estate was posted on 14 Aug. 1769 by Henry Reaston with Richard and Anthony Gott as sureties (BAAB 2:239). George Risteau and William Randall on 2 June 1770 appraised the personal property of "Ronaldo Munk" at a value of £182.15.7. Mary Munk and Sarah Carrick signed as next of kin while Henry Reaston, executor, filed the inventory on 19 Dec 1770 (MINV 104:360), having compiled a list of debts owing to the estate totalling £63.4.11. (MINV 105:93). Reaston took out administration on 10 December 1770, 9 July 1771, and 13 Feb 1775 (BAAD 6:225, 253, and 7:110).

Renaldo and Rachel Monk were the parents of: Renaldo; William; Sarah, married . . . Carreck; and Mary [Mary, daughter of Rinaldo Monk "late of the City of London in that part of Great Britain called England, by Rachel his wife "] married William Jacob on 19 July 1772 at Ranger's Forest (BAPA 1:37-38).

EDWARD MORTIMER was sentenced at Quarter Sessions in Bradford, Yorkshire, England, in January 1725, transported by the *Supply*, and certified as having landed in Maryland in 1726. (CBEB). Edward Lee, alias Edward Mortimer, ran away from Gorsuch's Point on Patapsco river, from Dr. Charles Carroll of Annapolis. Carroll said Lee would pretend to have a discharge from Gideon Howard, (with whom he lived), or perhaps a pass from Benjamin Howard, one of the justices of AA Co. The runaway was described as "being true Newgate breed" (MG 19 July 1734).

On 25 November 1742 Edward Mortimer leased two parcels of My Lady's Manor, 33½ acres, and 76¾ acres, for the lifetimes of himself, age 39, his wife Eleanor, aged 39, and Hester Bray, aged 18 (BALR TB#C:206). Edward Mortimore, living in the Fork of Gunpowder in BA Co., reported a runaway servant man, Thomas King (MG 26 July 1745).

CHARLES MOTHERBY of Middlesex was sentenced in May 1723, transported in July 1723 by the *Alexander*, and certified as having been landed in Annapolis in September 1723 (CBEB). He was born in about 1696, since he gave his age as about 86 in a deposition made on 29 June 1782 (BACT 3:301).

In August 1750 Motherby advertised for the return of a runaway servant, John Keat. In that year he owned 250 acres called Mount Organ and 50 acres called Motherby's Adventure (BADB). He had patented 50 acres called Adventure on 13 June 1734 (MPL EI#3:288).

On 14 May 1735 Rebecca Newman, widow of John Newman, conveyed part of Mount Organ to Charles Motherby on condition that he take care of her for life (BALR HWS#M:219). He did better than that, he married her on 14 December 1736 (BCF). Rebecca was his first wife. He married secondly before 20 May 1742 Priscilla, executrix of John Simpson; and thirdly, before 5 August 1747 Ann . . . . (BCF). This last marriage did not fare well for on 25 September 1755 Motherby recorded in BALR TR#E:--- that his wife Ann had eloped. In August 1749 he was summoned by the Vestry of St. Thomas' Parish for unlawful cohabitation with Ann Strang and in August 1750 was indicted by the Grand Jury on the same charge. (See Reamy and Reamy's *St. Thomas Parish Registers* for further details).

In 1778 Motherby took the Oath of Fidelity before the Hon. Edward Cockey (BARP). A series of depositions made on 31 January 1785 in Baltimore Co. Chattel Records reveals some interesting facts about his later life.

Edward Talbott, age not given, affirmed that William King had given in [reported] six negroes and that Charles Motherby had given in 115 acres called Bring Me Home (BACT 4:173).

Susannah Baxter, age 75, deposed that in October 1774 she had heard Charles Motherby say he had given all his negroes to his daughter Elizabeth, wife of William King (BACT 4:173).

Joseph Hammond, age 47, deposed that Charles Motherby had given his negroes to his daughter Elizabeth King, and that Motherby himself had been sent into this country as a transport for seven years (BACT 4:174).

Charles and Ann Motherby were the parents of: John, born 5 August 1747; and Elizabeth, born 23 May 1749, married by January 1785 William King.

312

CASE STUDIES

WHARTON RUTLESS was transported from the City of London in May 1736 by the *Patapsco Merchant* to Maryland. (CBEB). He was in BA Co. in January 1746 when he advertised that his wife Hannah had left him for a man named Peter Hines; Rutlis said he would no longer honor her debts (MG 31 Jan 1746).

A survey of BA Co. Land Records from 1659-1757 fails to show Rutless buying or selling any land, or witnessing any deeds. He may have died or moved away.

WILLIAM SEABROOK (See Richard S. Wheeler, *Seabrooks of Maryland and Pennsylvania*. MGSB 34 (2) 137-154). Son of Jonas and Deborah (Spelworth) Seabrook, he was baptized on 3 May 1713 [possibly at St. James Clerkenwell, London]. "William Seabrook, of St. Ann's Parish, Aldersgate, was indicted for feloniously stealing a Hat, value 5s, the property of Thomas Painter, the 25th of August last" (Proceedings at the Old Bailey from 28 August to 1 September 1730) and sentenced to be transported. He was duly embarked in the ship *Forward*, George Buckeridge, master, sailing from London in November 1730 and being landed at Potomac in January 1731. He went to Maryland and by January 1738 had married Jemima, daughter of Capt. Richard Gist. His descendants are traced in the Wheeler article referenced above.

On 26 March 1742 Christopher Gist and his wife Sarah conveyed 100 acres called Pleasant Green to his [Christopher's] sister Jemima Seabrooke, and her husband, William Seabrooke (BALR TB#A:132). By 1750 Seabrooke owned 100 acres called Taylor's Farm and 50 acres called London. In 1761 he conveyed Taylor's Farm to Peter Gosnell, and stated that the tract had formerly been laid out for Thomas Taylor (BCF).

William Seabrook was the father of (BCF): James, born 4 October 1738; Agnes, born 18 March 1742/3; George, born 25 February 1747; and Elizabeth, born 29 December 1749.

JOHN SHEWBRIDGE was convicted in Middlesex in January 1726 for stealing several pairs of stockings to the value of 4s.10d. from a London shopkeeper. He was transported to Maryland in February 1726 on board the *Supply* and certified in May 1726 as having been landed in Annapolis. (CBEB). (William Shewbridge, *The Shewbridge Family of Harper's Ferry*. (Baltimore: 1960), pp. 2-3).

In November 1742 Shewbridge leased part of My Lady's Manor for the lifetimes of his children Elizabeth, aged 7, Mary, aged 5, and John, aged 2 (BCF). As a planter of BA Co. in March 1743 he was sued by N. Ruxton Gay (BACP TB#TD:163). On 16 January 1745 he mortgaged to Charles Ridgely the 70 acres he leased from Thomas Brerewood (BALR TB#D:417. Either he or his son John was listed on a 1783 tax list of Berkeley co. [West] Virginia (William Shewbridge:4).

John Shewbridge married Mary Norris on 28 September 1732 (BCF) and was the father of (BCF): Charles, born about May 1733; Eliza, born 2 June 1733; Mary, born 30 January 1735; Isabella, born 4 November 1737; John, born 26 June 1739; Frances, born 12 September 1741; and Susannah, born 28 March 1743.

CATHERINE TYRWHITT. In March 1726 Catherine Territt or Tirrit of Gravesend, Kent, was tried at the Assizes in Rochester, Kent. She was charged with stealing jewelry including gold rings and a silver chain, was found guilty and sentenced to be transported for seven years (Letter to Robert Barnes from Peter Wilson Coldham, 9 January 1997). She was transported in June 1726 by the *Loyal Margaret*, and registered as having been landed in Maryland in December 1726. (CBEB).

Catherine Territt or Tyrwhitt may be one of the few Maryland convicts who could boast a Royal Descent and a coat of arms. Her claim to royal antecedents is set out in *Plantagenet Ancestry of Seventeenth Century Colonists,* by David Faris (Baltimore: Genealogical Publishing Co., Inc., 1996), p. 276; *The Royal Descents of 500 Immigrants to the American Colonies or the United States Who Were Themselves Notable or Left Descendants Notable in American History,* by Gary Boyd Roberts (Baltimore: Genealogical Publishing Co., Inc., 1993), p. 340; and "Tyrwhitt of Stainfield," *Burke's Extinct and Dormant Baronetage.* (Repr.: Baltimore: Genealogical Publishing Co., Inc.), pp. 539-540.

ARMS of Tyrwhitt: Gules, three tyrwhitts, or lapwings, Or (C:540)

1. Sir PHILIP TYRWHITT, son of Sir Philip and Anne, and a descendant of King Edward I of England, died about 1688. He married. Penelope, daughter of Sir Erasmus de la Fontaine, Kt., of Kirby Bellers, Lincolnshire. Burke states that Sir Philip and his wife had twelve children, but only one son and one daughter reached maturity. However, there was probably another son, name unknown. Sir Philip was the father of: Sir John; another son; and a daughter who married Sir Edward Southcot.

2. Sir JOHN TYRWHITT, son of Sir Philip and Penelope, died in November 1741. He married twice and had issue, but the male line of his descendants died out with his son, Sir JOHN de la Fountain Tyrwhitt, Bart.

3.. . . TYRWHITT, son of Sir Philip, married a Miss Gilbert. His family has been reconstructed by the depositions given below, found in Baltimore Co. Chattel Records. He and his wife had one daughter: Catherine.

4. CATHERINE TYRWHITT, daughter of (3), and niece of Sir John (2), married Joseph Yates of BA Co.

Joseph Yates, a widower whose wife Susanna died in May 1735, married on 15 September 1735 Catherine Territt [transcribers have read her name as Herritt, but the following depositions recorded on 5 April 1773 identify her; it is not known why statements made in 1744 failed to be recorded officially for 29 years] (HAGE:47).

Marshall Lemmon deposed in 1744 that he knew the family of Turwhitts als. Turretts in Lincolnshire. He knew that John Turwhitt had a younger brother [name not given] and his only child was Catherine Turwhitt, since Yate. The deponent was at school with her in Lincolnshire and has seen and been acquainted with her since her coming to America (BACT 3). The deponent went on to say that the younger brother married against his father's consent a young woman named Gilbert, sister of Joshua and George Gilbert of London. One brother was a barber, the other a merchant or shopkeeper, and the deponent was present when the said Catherine was owned by Sir John Tyrwhitt to be the only child of his brother. Catherine was frequently taken by her father in a coach to visit her uncle (BACT 3). The deponent knew Catherine to be the woman who married Joseph Yates in BA Co., and George Gilbert Yates was the only child of that marriage (BACT 3). The deposition was taken at the request of Rowland Sheppard. (BACT 3:12-13).

CASE STUDIES

Ann Shea deposed on 10 November 1744 to the same facts narrated by Marshall Lemmon and referred to the uncle as Sir John Tyrwhitt, Bart. She stated that she had had letters from the Gilberts of London. (BACT 3:13).

John Osborn deposed on 21 August 1772 that Rowland Sheppard bought Catherine Tyrwhitt's time. She had come into Maryland over 40 years earlier and married Joseph Yates by whom she had a son George Gilbert Yates, now living in BA Co. (BACT 3:14).

Elizabeth Gundrey deposed on 14 Aug 1772 that she was present when Catherine Yeates, wife of Joseph Yeates, then living on a plantation belonging to John Atkinson in Bush River Neck, was brought to bed in or about the year 1738, and bore a son named George Gilbert Yates (BACT 3:15). Joseph and Catherine were the parents of: George Gilbert Yeates.

On 24 August 1772 George Gilbert Yeats and Ishmael Morris entered into an agreement. Morris promised to use his utmost endeavors to procure an estate now depending in England said to belong to the said George Gilbert Yeates. Yeates, in turn, promised to pay Morris ½ of whatever estate, monies, etc., that might be recovered. Each bound himself to the other for £50,000 (BACT 3:16). Yeates, aged 34, now intending to go to Great Britain, gave power of attorney to Ishmael Morris stating that Sir John Tyrrett d ied in 1728. [He actually died later]. [His niece] Catherine left the Kingdom of England on board the vessel commanded by Capt. Weston [Wheaton] in 1736. She married Joseph Yeates and had one son, the said George Gilbert Yeates. Shortly thereafter Joseph Yeates died intestate. Catherine died intestate in about 1746, leaving George Gilbert Yeates as an orphan aged eight (BACT 3:170).

Unfortunately, George Gilbert Yates seems to have disappeared from the Maryland scene after this. Did he return to England? Was he successful in claiming a share of the Tyrwhitt or Gilbert estates? Perhaps additional research will reveal the answers.

JOSEPH WINKS or WINCKS of London, possibly son of Roger and Jane Winks, who was baptised on 13 August 1721 at St. Mary's, Whitechapel, Stepney, Middlesex, was sentenced to transportation to the colonies in January and was transported in February 1742 by the *Industry* to Maryland (CBEB). There is no proof that the Joseph who came to Maryland was the Joseph who was baptized in 1721, but there is a strong possibility that the two men were the same.

A Joseph Winks is listed as head of household in Mine Run Hundred in the 1773 Tax List of BA Co. (IBCP:74), and as Joseph Winks Sr., he was living in 1778 when he was a non-juror to the Oath of Allegiance (BARP:196). He may have been the father of: Joseph Wink Jr., born about 1740; and possibly of Jacob Wink, born in 1755; a private in Capt. Keeports' German Regiment, in service in 1776 (BARP:296).

INDEXES

An asterisk beside an entry indicates that the name appears more than once on that page

Index of Persons

317

Index of Persons

Index of Persons

Index of Persons

Index of Persons

Index of Persons

Index of Persons

Index of Persons

Index of Persons

Index of Persons

Index of Persons

Billings, John 184,248
Billingsley, Charles
   108
   Francis 32
   Jane 81
Billis, John 247
Bills, William 147,153
Bilson, Benjamin 190
   William 134
Bilth, James 241
Bince, William 232
Bine, Mary 98
   Stephen 210
Bingham, Benjamin 44
   Elizabeth 229
   Joseph 62
Bingley, John 188
Binks, Jacob 4
Binn, Mary 235
Binnell, Alice 59
Binney, James 80
Binnifield, John 203
Binns, Mary 262
Binstead, Thomas 47
Binsted, John 141
   Mary 153
Birch, Anne 36,209
   Edward 193
   Esther 158
   John 5,122,187
   Joseph 8,103
   Mary 83,177
   Moses 168
   Richard 44,240
   William 80,85
Birchman, William 85
Bird, Anthony 232
   Bartholomew 83,267
   Bertram 83,267
   Charles 92
   Eleanor 168
   Francis 32
   George 69,83
   John 79,179,206,
      211,216,244*,247,
      252,259
   Joseph 41
   Lydia 105
   Matthew 147
   Samuel 219
   Susanna 151

Bird, Thomas 32,97,
   189,201,216,241
   William 101,238
   William Reynolds
      189
Birdworth, Mary 133
Birk, Eleanor 172
   John 267
   Peter 220
   Richard 101
Birkenshaw, Joyce 30
   Nicholas 30
Birkett, Samuel 123
Birks, John 236
Birt, Robert 142
Bisbee, James 131
Bisben, Edward 267
Bishop, Elizabeth 32
   Gamaliel 47
   George 260
   Giles 178
   Henry 256
   John 78,230
   Joseph 267
   Lucas 200
   Martha 52
   Mary 1,256
   Roger 245
   Thomas 21
   William 64,97,131
Bisse, Mary 100
Bisset, Alexander 143
   Robert 216
Bissett, James 134
   Mary 17
Bissick, John 100,103*
Biswell, Mary 129
Bivon, Joseph 58
Blachford, Thomas 192
   William 192
Black, Andrew 262
   Ann 173
   Barbara 57
   Eleanor 262
   Henry 197
   Joseph 116
   Robert 59,173
   William: 2,3*,4*,5*
Black Bess 1
Black George 232
Black Jack 92,141

Black Jenny 17
Black Moll 161
Blackband, Elizabeth
   136
Blackborn, Herbert 88
Blackbourn, Elizabeth
   109
   James 70
   John 87,130
   Margaret 49
Blackburn, Benjamin
   236
   Catherine 143
   John 192
   Thomas 242
   William 190
Blackell, John 267
Blackerby, Ann 65
Blackett, Joshua 85
Blackford, Thomas 261
   William 238
Blackgrove, John 233
Blackhead, William 63
Blackhood, John 113
Blacklock, Martha 15
Blackman, Robert 27
   William 240
Blackmore, Edmond
   262
   James 72,166
   Robert 239
   Thomas 93
   William 240
Blacksby, Edward 9
Blackstone, John 7,123
   Zebulon Thrift 151
Blackwell, Charles 94
   Deborah 228
   Elizabeth 142
   Henry 8,10,78
   Sarah 5
   William 156
Blackwood, Hamilton
   135
Blades, Henry 119
Blagdon, William 267
Blair, Margaret 41
   Mary 181,257
Blake, Ann 197
   Charles 151
   Daniel 117

327

Index of Persons

Index of Persons

Index of Persons

Index of Persons

331

Index of Persons

Brindley, Jonathan 4
Brinkinshire, Richard 150
Brinkley, James 150
Brinklow, John 176
Brinsford, Thomas 239
Brinton, Benjamin 32
Brisk, John 14
  William 17
Bristol, John 233
Bristow, John 89
  Margaret 40
  Susannah 77
  William 15
Britchford, John 35
Briton, John 203
Britt, John 84
Brittain, Ann 33
  James 161
  John 23
  Thomas 127
Britton, John 19
  Nicholas 265
  Samuel 186,195
Broad, James 210
  Mary 76
  Robert 246
Broadas, Joseph 246
Broadbent, John 268
  Richard 254
Broadbridge, Elizabeth 210
Broadfield, William 252
Broadhead, Caleb 201
  Thomas 164
Broadstreet, John 26
Broadway, Edward 116
  John 94
  Robert 20
Broadwood, James 230
Brocas, Thomas 64
Brock, Mary 224
  Samuel 32
Brocker, John 174
Brockington, Philip 103
Brocklebank, Jonathan 153
Brocklehurst, William 173

Brockley, Catherine 101
  Thomas 135
Brockman, John 121
Brockwell, James 85
  Thomas 175
Broderick, Joseph 189
Brogden, Ann 95
Brome, Elizabeth 136
Bromfield, James 159
  Robert 5
Bromidge, James 219
Bromley, Catherine 62
  Edward 78
  John 58
  Margaret 78
Brompton, Richard 16
Bromwell, Jacob 276,295
Bromwich, Samuel 174
Bronkee. Abraham 145
Bronon, Patrick 268
Broof, John 268
Brook, Richard 302
  William 1
Brooke, Basil 275,288
  Clement 274
  Roger 265
  Thomas 268
Brooken, Joseph 43
Brooker, Edward 141
  Jane 159
  John 35
  Penelope 100
  Richard 226
  Robert 57
  Susanna 232
Brookes, Agnes 173
  Badger 223
  Edward 134
  George 232
  Jane 142
  John 269
  Josiah 43
  Mary 51
  Richard 177,223
  Samuel 84
  Susanna 232
  Thomas 99,269
  William 134
Brookfield, Joseph 220

Brooking, Samuel 138
Brookman, James 49
Brooks, Ann 122
  Catherine 117
  Edward 79
  Elizabeth 35
  Francis 85
  Humphrey 288
  James 40,182,301
  Jane 37
  John 48,98
  Mary 168
  Matthew 46,94
  Robert 36
  Samuel 25
  Sarah 186
  Thomas 132,143, 150,172,204
  William 29,218,269
Brooksby, Samuel 171
Broom, James 103
  John 33,35
  Mary 165
Broomfield, John 269
  Thomas 252
Broomhall, Mary 99
  Sarah 46
Broster, Susan 38
Broughton, Elizabeth 158
  Eunice 50
  John 269
  Samuel 70
  Thomas 105,158
  William 112
Brounsnow, John 269
Brown, Alice 118
  Andrew 246
  Ann 69,145,155, 230*,246
  Aquila 294
  Bartholomew 220
  Catherine 1,109,145
  Charles 46,130,203
  Christian 104,148
  Daniel 210
  Edward 101,204, 231,270
  Eleanor 191
  Elizabeth 13,28,44, 60,109,131,145,

Index of Persons

Index of Persons

Index of Persons

Index of Persons

Index of Persons

Index of Persons

Index of Persons

Caustin, Paul 212
Cavanach, James 271
Cave, Felix 142
  George 58
  John 212
  Patrick 110
  Richard 204
  Thomas 212
Cavenagh, Hannah 221
  Honor 103
  Thomas 230
Cavenaugh, John 271
Cavendish, Margaret
  135
Cawdell, John 88
  Mary 105
Cawkin, Alice 84
Cawley, James 292
  John 209
Cawthorne, Charles 8
Cay, Elizabeth 156
Caydor, Edward 14
Cayley, William 206
Cayton, Anthony 271
  William 241
Ceaton, John 195
Chad, William 98
Chadwick, Elizabeth
  38
  Hannah 57
  John 116
Chaff, Patrick. 197
Chaffey, James 171
  John 271
Chalkley, Ann 163
  John 54
  Thomas 261
Challoner, George 107
Chalmer, Alexander 55
Chalmers, John 271
  Margaret 158
Chamberlain, Ann 91
  George 81
  Mary 177
  Philip 218
  Richard 3
  Samuel 232
  William 161
Chamberlaine,
  Elizabeth.55
  Richard 115

Chambers, Ann 96
  John 128
  John 181
  Margaret 155
  Mary 116,170,171,
  271
  Stephen 33
  Thomas 62,90,99
  William 258
Chameron, Mary
  Catherine 241
Chamier, David 297
Chamneys, John 79
Champaigne, Nicholas
  27
Chandler, Elizabeth 30
  Hester 118
  John 162
  Joseph 52,236
  Mary 17,66
  William 210,271
Chaney, Richard 5
  Samuel 3
Channam, William 211
Channell, Edmund 91
Channon, John 282
Chant, Robert 271
Chantler, Nathaniel
  210
Chapbell, Charles 1
Chapel, Alice 191
Chaple, Henry 63
Chaplin, Catherine 104
  Thomas 70
  William 196
Chaplow, James 125
Chapman, Anne 7
  Charles 135
  Henry 85
  Jacob 104,136
  James 209
  John 17,21,119,136
  Jonathan 293
  Joseph 197,216,220
  Margaret 5
  Mary 85
  Peter 109
  Richard 216,235
  Samuel 248
  Stephen 259,262

Chapman, Thomas
  22,28,143,186,231
  William 92,130,143,
  177,242,288
Chapp, Thomas 76
Chappel, Grace 93
  William 180
Chappell, Benjamin
  178
  Mary 103
Chapperlin, Mary 233
Chapple, Elizabeth 214
  Joseph 75
Charbilies, Maria
  Louisa 193
Charles, John 251
Charleton, Elizabeth 70
  Thomas 25
Charlock, Nicholas 72
Charlton, Jane 165
  John 98
  Josiah 31
Charman, Isabel 10
Charter, John 209
Chasemore, Joseph 144
Chassereau, Pearce
  John Anthony 193
Chatham, Ann 246
Chattell, Thomas 208
Chattenau, Anthony
  228
Chatterley, Charles 216
Chauncer, Henry 45
Chavier, Joseph 294
Chavin, Elizabeth
  165,166
Cheek, Edward 271
  George 98
Cheeke, William 147
Cheeseman, Richard
  118
  Robert 23
  William 79
Chelew, Nicholas
  61,72
Cheney, Charles 41
  Elizabeth 54
  John 52
  William 247
Cheriton, Elizabeth 159

339

Index of Persons

Index of Persons

Clarke, Leonard 157
Margaret 71,148
Mary 47,94,114,116,
120,146
Philip 206
Phillis 223
Richard 42,214,258
Robert 188
Samuel 81
Sarah 172,177,262
Susanna 5
Thomas 9,127,152,
193,253
William 27,71,114,
123,137,146,193,
207,220,225,258
Clarkin, John 17
Clarkson, John 277
Richard 247
Claron, Thomas 30
Clavier, William 261
Claxton. Ann 214
George. 197
John 26,85
William 130
Clay, Anne 22
Elizabeth 90,170
Granger 132
John 155
Joseph 65,257
Samuel 7
William 211
Claymore, Margaret 67
Clayton, Ann 105
James 233
John 136,153,233
Joseph 225
Samuel 138
Sara 88
Susannah 197
Thomas 122,194
William 99,105,259,
283
Clean, William 189
Cleary, Patrick 271
Cleaver, Charles 108
Edward 164
Robert 115
Cleford, Thomas 128
Clefts, Philip 97
Cleghorn, Robert 224

Cleham, Elizabeth 146
Clement, John 292
Richard 289
Robert 8
Clements, Ann 174
Edward 256
Elizabeth 118,171
James 199
John 163
Jonas 1
Margaret 101
Mark 240
Richard 212
Samuel Felix 239
Thomas 196
Clemmenshaw, Eliz.
225
Thomas 225
Clemmisson, Amburst
271
Clemson, William 74
Clendon, Charles 143
Clendon, Susan 41
Clerk, Isaac 24
Samuel 11
Clerke, James 115
Margaret 12
Stephen 6
Cleveland, John 245
Clever, James 60
William 90
Cleverly, John 180
Cleverton, Ann 153
Clewes, Mary 168
Clewley, Joseph 248
Clews, Richard 224
Cliff, Matthew 26
Clifford, Ann 189,203
Edward 209
John 34
William. 197
Clift, Thomas 261
Clifton, Thomas 169
William 262
Clifts, Mathew 26
Clinch, Elizabeth 220
William 173
Clinton, John 140
Susan 41
Valentine 22
Clisby, William 201

Clitheroe, John 50
Cloathier, William 103
Clodd, Robert 199
Cloden, Garrett 147
Clogg, Robert 93
William 93
Cloore, Agnes 77
Close, Richard 10
Clough, John 105
Clowds, Millicent 11
Clowes, Elizabeth 123
Clubb, Alexander 229
Cluff, Hannah 31
Clunis, Thomas
271,279
Clutterbuck, Joseph 41
Cly, Henry 216
Clymer, Margaret 67
Coade, Robert Fowler
96
Coager, Michael 272
Coal, Mary 32
Coale, Joseph 92
William 285
Coaly, John 216
Coant, John 199
Coars, Isaac 101
Coates, Benjamin
154,155
George 89
John 84,94,131,184
Mary 13
Coats, James 128
Cobane, Joseph 181
Rachael 181
Cobb, Daniel 57
Samuel 113
Cobbey, Walter 39
Cobble, Priscilla 154
Cobbs, Richard 94
Cobert, John 178
Cobey, Sarah 177
Cobham, James 228
Cobitch, William 39
Coblin, William 228
Cobridge, John 81
Cock, Ann 35
Eleanor 220
John 138
Richard 61,180

341

Index of Persons

Index of Persons

Index of Persons

Index of Persons

Index of Persons

Index of Persons

Index of Persons

Index of Persons

Index of Persons

350

Index of Persons

351

Index of Persons

Index of Persons

Index of Persons

Index of Persons

Index of Persons

Emtage, John 110
Endersby, Thomas 136
Endsor, Edward 154
England, Elizabeth
 164,172
 John 27,83
English, Christian 178
 Elizabeth 156
 George 26
 James 73
 Mary 189,276
 Nelly 276
 Rebecca 38
 William 176,276
Ennis, Richard 16
Enoch, William 204
Ens, Thomas 39
Ensor, Abraham
 217*,218
 John 265,281,296,
 307
Entwhistle, Edward
 276
Enwood, John 246
 Mary 111
Eoy, Thomas 90
Eppes, Richard 277
Eppingstall, John 258
Erick, Hans 177
Erith, Jeffery 163
Erkeen, Thomas 188
Erle, Richard 54
Erouselle, Philip 211
Errington, John
 184,189
Erskine, Thomas 221
Erwin, Esther 168
 Francis 276
Esbury, James 238
 Thomas 63
Esling, Samuel 35
Essex, Richard 236
 William 141
Esthers, Sarah 126
Etheridge, Sarah 244
 Thomas 15
Etherington, John 276
 Terence 225
 William 91
Etteridge, Thomas 183

Eusden, Mary 76
 William 76
Eustead, William 125
Eustice, Thomas 254
Evans, Alice 48
 Ann 69,94
 Benjamin 204
 Catherine 111,234
 Charles 244
 Edward 52,60,129,
 132,223,227
 Elias 237
 Elizabeth 37,57,204,
 209,241
 Evan 213
 Evey or Evan
 104,105
 Francis 46
 George 229
 Henry 45,248
 James 3,85,145,228
 Jane 116
 Job 20
 John 35,118,140,
 155,177,186,190,
 191,193,211,240,
 276*,277
 Joseph 121,289
 Lewis 276
 Mary 82,89,91,95,
 131
 Mary Jane 190
 Morris 184,276
 Patrick 6
 Philip 183
 Richard 17,38,89,
 252
 Robert 62,178
 Samuel 115,232,239
 Sarah 121
 Simon 71
 Susannah 207
 Thomas 106,
 172,262,276*
 Timothy 123
 William 6,106,124,
 180,237,239,244,
 253
 Winifred 28
Evatt, Henry 42
 Mary 113

Eve, John 156
Everard, John 41
Everee, John 199
Everett, James.
 108,191,258
 John 3,41,51,191
 Joseph 247,251
 Robert 47
 William 171
Everill, Andrew 119
Everin, Richard 39
Everitt, Andrew 119
Evershett, Thomas 55
Everton, John 252
Every, John 241
 Mary 241
 Robert 259
Eves, Jane 101
 John 165
 Joseph 54
 Richard 110
 William 133
Evett, Elizabeth 83
Evins, Henry 213
Ewdale, John 276
Ewell, Charles 308
Ewen, John 105,201,
 276
 William 67
Ewens, John 52
 William 241
Ewer, Thomas 63
Ewers, Martha 104
Ewin, John 169
Ewing, George 282
 Samuel 97
Exall, Susannah 230
Exelby, John 84
 Mary 116
Exell, Ann 146
Extell, Emanuel 91
Eyes, John 188
Eyles, Martha 190
 Mary 124
Eylmore, Symon 6
Eyre, James 79
 John Esq. 227,276
 Thomas 34
Eyres, Joseph 34
 Robert 76

Index of Persons

Index of Persons

Index of Persons

Index of Persons

Index of Persons

362

Index of Persons

Gaffney, Ann 81
  Henry 81
  Michael 264
  Patrick 105
Gafford, William 278
Gaffy, Mary 255
Gag, Margaret 68
Gage, John 48
Gahagan, Farrant 164
  John 244
Gailks, Mary 67
Gainer, Magdalene 27
  Sarah 142
  Thomas 234
Gaines, John 31
Gainsley, Jane 84
Gaither, Edward 289
  Henry 282
  John 289
Galaspy, George 255
Gale, Christopher 187
  Dorothy 121
  George 278
  Jane 55
  John 23,100,127
  Joseph 278,279
  Richard 1
  Robert 216
  Thomas 55
Galin, James 208
Gall, Samuel 185
Gallagher, Charles 225
Gallant, Ambrose 100
Galleof, Ann 91
Gallop, Matthew 278
Galloway, James 108
  John 103
  Peter 3,5*
  Samuel 268
Gallway, Thomas 82
Galpin, William 223
Gamball, Ralph 278
Gambell, James 126
  John 12
  William 6
Gamble, Thomas 120
Gammon, Richard 188
Gandy, Elizabeth 26
Gane, John 34,35
Ganey, James 118

Gannon, John 222
  Michael 222
Garbitt, William 62
Garbutt, Richard 234
Gard, Christopher 232
Gardener, Charles 273
  Rachel 3
  Sarah 120
Gardiner, Elizabeth
  197
  James 13
  Jane 193
  John 209,222
  Luke 207
  Mark 234
  Philis 192
  Sarah 212
  Susannah 207
  Thomas 105
  William 156
Gardner, Elizabeth
  71,110,111
  Francis 67
  George 253
  Henry 35
  John 210,278*
  Margaret 64
  Mary 119
  Richard 133
  Samuel 112
  Thomas 150
Gargle, Elizabeth 225
Garland, Edward 67
Garland, Elizabeth 67
  Joseph, 131
  Sarah 164
Garle, Christopher 46
Garment, William 163
Garne, Thomas 239
Garner, Elizabeth 150
  Leda 261
Garnes, Lewis 246
Garnett, John 69,242
  Margaret 57
  Mary 69
  Richard 83
Garnon, Judith 176
Garnons, William 216
Garrard, Robert 130
Garraughty, John 278

Garraway, Jeremiah 17
Garrell, William 38
Garretson, Cornelius
  295
  Job 282,294,297
Garrett, Amos 302
  Bartholomew 244
  Elizabeth 157
  Gilbert 193
  John 137
  Joseph 42,259
  Martha 139
  Mary 22,256
  Philip 186
  Richard 251
  Thomas 3
  Valentine 53
  William 51,278
Garrick, Arthur 131
Garrison, Elizabeth
  258
Garrway, John 139
Garth, James 248
Garton, William 206
Gartrall & Roberts
  257*,260
Gartrell, William 302
Garvey, Mary 143
Gascoine, Sarah 25
Gascoyne, Elizabeth
  214
  Richard 40
  Sarah 158
  William 123
Gascy, John 15
Gasford, Samuel
  230,271
  Samuel 271,278
Gaskin, John 2,3,5
Gasking, John 180
  Richard 180
Gason, William 169
Gassaway, Henry
  267,287,289
  Thomas 297
Gasson, Edmund 49
  Henry 67
Gate, Stephen 129
Gaten, William 14
Gater, Alexander 166

Index of Persons

Index of Persons

Index of Persons

Index of Persons

Index of Persons

Index of Persons

Index of Persons

Index of Persons

371

Index of Persons

Index of Persons

Index of Persons

Index of Persons

Hermitage, George 141
 Mary 21
 Thomas 26
Hermond, William 59
Herne, John 180
 Mary 222
 Pooling 251,281
 Thomas 130
Herod, George 187
Heroe, Rebecca 104
Heron, Henry 163
 John 186
Herring, Catherine 109
 Elizabeth 230
 Henry 241
 James 27
 John 63
 Mary 208
 Michael 25
Herringshaw, Ruth 45
Herrington, Roger 227
Herryman, John 128
Hersey, Martha 174
Hesketh, William 128
Heskett, William 128
Hesselius, John 285
Hesseltine, Gustavus 5
Hetherington, John 87
 Walter 27
Heweston, Anne 51
Hewet, Ann 166
Hewett, Edward 67
Hewitt, Ann 71
 Christopher 77
 Elizabeth 4
 John 197
 Joseph 77
 Lewis 43
 Rachell 35
 Robert 8
 Thomas 95,166
Hewne, Michael 281
Hewood, Joseph 34
Hewson, Edward 12
 John 17
 Mary 2
 Thomas 8
Heydon, John 281
 Michael 201
 William 124
Heywood, John 204

Hiats, John 138
Hibbard, Samuel 68
Hibberd, William 249
Hibbins, Nicholas 71
Hickes, Richard 49
Hickey, Cicily 171
 David 205
 Jane 159
 John 281
Hickins, John 281
Hickman, Benjamin 51
 Brogden 95
 Elizabeth 19,47
 James 281
 John 75,78,165,308
 Richard 166
 Sarah 51
 Seymour 259
 Smith 258
 Stephen 148
 William 69
Hicks, Abraham 257
 Ann 81,88,234
 Elias 281
 Elizabeth 237
 George 259
 Henry 32
 James 18
 John 134
 Rebecca 214
 Silvia 214
 Thomas 28,35
 William 70,240
Hickson, Ann 91
 Benjamin 168
 Mathew 215
Hide, Elizabeth 244
 Henry 45
 John 259
 Joseph 24,28
 William 244
Higby, Mary 117
Higday, Thomas 8
Higginbottom, Richard 32
 Thomas 249
Higgins, Ann 228
 Edward 9
 Elizabeth 45
 Hannah 141
 John 14,184

Higgins, Joseph 207
 Mary 8,40
 Matthew 156
 Susanna 74
 William 157,255,282
Higginson, Charles 83
 Eleanor, 71
 John 99
 Joseph 6,216,282
Higgonson, Wm. 158
Higgs, George 89
 James 53
 John 219
 Mary 99
 Susanna 139
 William 211
Higham, Elizabeth 190
 Farwell 152
Highby, Samuel 264
Highenbottom, William 282
Highfield, Jane 66
Highmore, Richard 121
Highton, William 48
Higton, Paul 282
Hilkes, John 134
Hill, Ann 189
 Benjamin 71
 Edward 122
 Elijah 228,282
 Elizabeth 53,107,228
 George 190
 Henry 81,121
 James 121,136
 Jane 223
 John 2,34,46,147,
  183,192,197,199,
  214.231.282*
 Joseph 147
 Luke 28
 Mary 22,113,124,
  243,262
 Richard 76,187
 Robert 33,154,248
 Samuel 87
 Sarah 215
 Shadrack 127,260
 Thomas 14,15,34,54,
  92,116,203,233
 William 211,243,
  266,282

375

Index of Persons

Index of Persons

Index of Persons

Index of Persons

Index of Persons

Hyatt, Elizabeth 246
  Peter 4*
  Sarah 99
  William 255
Hyde, Elizabeth 110
  Richard 51
  Sarah 182
  Thomas 154
Hyder, Stephen 210
Hyland, Michael 216
Hyley, William 283
Hymes, Michael 213
Hynes, John Martin
  197
Hynson, John Carvill
  284
  Richard 284
Hytch, Christopher 266
Hyth, John 101

Ibbert, Charles 225
Igo, Dennis 283
Iiams, William 296
Iliffe, Margaret 183
Illingworth, Israel 19
  Jonathan 30
Ilsen, William 171
Imbey, Mary 108
Imer, Richard 184
Imeson, John 209
Impey, Alice 137
  Thomas 87
Incell, William 171
Inch, Ann 213,283
  John 213,294
  Thomas 71
Ineon, Richard 69
Ingersole, Ann 89
Ingham, Anne 19
Inglebird, William 74
Inglesby, Mary 95
Inglesent, Martha 264
Ingleton, Christopher
  44
Inglish, Sarah 107
Ingman, Grace 36
Ingmire, Robert 149
Ingoll, John 153
Ingram, Augustus 51
  Barbara 19

Ingram, Benjamin 285
  Elizabeth 170,243
  Grace 36
  Jacob 191
  James 74,195,284
  John 170,207
  Joseph 230,283
  Mary 10,162,225
  Mordecai 127
  Richard 3,75
  Robert 52
  Stephen 72
  William 20*,51
Inkley, William 257
Inks, John 193
  William 193
Inman, John 283
  Millicent 126
  William 286
Innes, George 193
  Solomon 89
Innis, Ann 242
  David 163
  James 190
  Walter 131
Inns, John 209
Inon, Henry 18
Insell, Elizabeth 150
Ireland, Anne 7
  Edward 228
  Elizabeth 212
  John 269,275
  Mary 54
  Richard 178
  Thomas 143
  William 77,213
Ireman, James 54
Irish Nell 104
Irish Pegg 46
Irish, Richard 65
Iron, Aaron 161
Ironmonger, Robt. 255
Irons, William 145
Irving, John 85
Irwin, Francis 283
  John 283
  Susanna 116
Irwing, John 14
Isaac, John 239
  Lazarus 207

Isaacs, James 242
  Lyon 228
  Mary 78
  Rachael 88
  Solomon 89,160,184
  Tobias 101
  William 7
Isaacson , Susan 28
  William 7,48
Isdell, William 250
Isedale, Isabella 168
Isgrig, Daniel 309*
  William 87,309*
Israel, John 256,258
  Sabate 143
Isted, Edward 113
Iverson, Peter 226
Ivery, Bryan 116
Ives, Edward 87
  Joanna 33
  William 42
Iveson, William 217
Izack, Samuel 171
Izard, Abraham 154
  Ann 133

Jack above Ground 176
Jack, James 210
Jack, Jane 50
Jackson, Ann 105
  Anthony 215,283
  Bryan 122
  Dorothy 150
  Edward 68
  Eleanor 23
  Elizabeth 46,85,88,
   95*,172
  George 165,175
  Isaac 190
  James 22,58,145,
   168,209,222,225
  Jane 58
  John 17,32,81,103,
   120,178,231,278
  Joseph 128
  Margaret 21
  Mary 18,91,162,189,
   195,226,283
  Richard 209
  Robert 94,105,216

Index of Persons

Index of Persons

Index of Persons

Index of Persons

Index of Persons

Index of Persons

Index of Persons

Index of Persons

389

Index of Persons

Index of Persons

Index of Persons

Index of Persons

393

Index of Persons

Index of Persons

Index of Persons

Index of Persons

Index of Persons

Index of Persons

Index of Persons

Index of Persons

Index of Persons

Index of Persons

404

Index of Persons

Index of Persons

Index of Persons

Index of Persons

Index of Persons

Index of Persons

Index of Persons

Index of Persons

413

Index of Persons

414

Index of Persons

415

Index of Persons

Index of Persons

Index of Persons

Index of Persons

419

Index of Persons

Index of Persons

Index of Persons

Index of Persons

Shadwell, John
178,184
Shaen, William 168
Shaftoe, Edward 47
Shakerly, Sampson 19
Shakespear, Samuel
211
William 193
Shale, Sarah 43
Shales, Daniel 179
John 30
Shamble, Elizabeth
Mary 96
Shambler, John 98
Shand, Philip 29
Shanks, Elizabeth 10
John 59
Shann, William 38
Shaplin, William 24,29
Sharborn, John 188
Shard, Emanuel 37
Sharkey, Lewis 254
Sharlow, Elizabeth 22
Sharp, Eleanor 190
Elizabeth 164
Mary 55
Robert 50
Thomas 90,232
William 28,76
Sharpcliff, Thomas 57
Sharpe, Christopher
121
Elias 29
Elizabeth 95
Frances 56
John 52
Robert 219
Sharpells, Henry 64
Sharper, William. 28
Sharpless, Catherine
117
John 87,234
Sharpley, James 262
Sharplift, Thomas 57
Sharwell, John 202
Shaw, Alice 50
Ann 76
Charles 255
Daniel 218,307
Dorothy 60
Elizabeth 78

Shaw, George 34
James 105
Jane 171
John 2,77,229
Mary 111,115,140
Robert 47
Samuel 25,230
Thomas 125,130
Timothy 296
Walter 190
William 11,26,69,86
Shay, Gervase 135
Jarvis 135
Shays, Mary 100
Shea, Ann 315
Sheaf, William 120
Shean, James 243
Joseph 97
Shearing, Mary 238
Shearman, Elizabeth
186
Shears, Isaac 263
Leonard 235
Mary 44,169
Thomas 256
Sheen, Mary 51
William 249
Sheene, George 209
Sheerman, William 149
Sheers, John 77
Sheffield, Isaac
142,296
John 49
Joseph 171
Thomas 137
Sheirs, Richard 243
Sheldon, John 296
Mary 237
Thomas 202
Sheldrick, Elizabeth 54
Shelley, John 260
Philip 169
Susannah 214
Shelock, James 156
Shelton, Edward 143
Elizabeth 156
Hannah 172
Henry 51
James 169
John 259
Jonah 160

Shelton, Walter 14
Shepard, John 296
William 17
Shepheard, John 162
Shepherd, Ann 129
Charles 240
Conrad 246
Dorothy 143
Elizabeth 31,43,51
John 67
Margaret 30
Martha 63
Mary 144
Philip 51
Richard 63
Samuel 45
Sara 52
Thomas 22,25,189
William 124,203,231
Sheppard, Charles 140
Hannah 69
Mary 73
Robert 249
Rowland 314,315
William 209,252,296
Sheppeard, Mary 12
Shepperd, Philip 238
Sherborne, Sarah 11
Sheredine, Jeremiah
267,269,291,292
Sherer, John 180
Sheridan, John 181
Sheriff, Matthew 72
Sherlock, John 76
Ralph 128
Silvia 36
Simon 35
William 130
Sherman, Rachael 172
Susannah 197
Sherrar, William 234
Sherrard, Bernard 208
Francis 54
George 219
John 145
Thomas 119
Sherratt, Nathaniel 135
Sherridan, Catherine
152
Sherrington, William
54

423

Index of Persons

Index of Persons

Index of Persons

Index of Persons

427

Index of Persons

Index of Persons

429

Index of Persons

430

Index of Persons

Index of Persons

Index of Persons

Index of Persons

Index of Persons

Index of Persons

436

Index of Persons

Index of Persons

Index of Persons

Index of Persons

Index of Persons

Weldon, Robert
  William 231
  William 301
Welham, James 247
Wellam, Robert 130
Welland, Richard 202
Wellard, Thomas 112
Wellbrand, Mary 255
Welbred, Mary 255
Welldon, George 209
Weller, John 90
  Sarah 238
  William 15
Welling, Elizabeth 90
  John 90
  Richard 137
  Thomas 152
Wellins, John 188
Wells, Alexander
  277,286,293
  Ann 7,50,86,151
  Benjamin 267
  Catherine 160
  Daniel 83,268
  Edmund 301
  Edward 82,259
  Elizabeth 11
  Elizabeth Mary 96
  Granby Thomas 225
  James 97
  Jeremiah 95,234,301
  John 42,82,117,174,
  280
  Joseph 35,79,86,126
  Joshua 192
  Mariah 27
  Mary 87
  Paul William 205
  Samuel 83
  Sarah 9,17
  Thomas 67,73,238
  Valentine 141
  William 96,118,156,
  247
Wellthresher, Joseph
  115
Wellum, Jane 17
Welman, Matthew 68
Welsh, Ann 115
  Benjamin 282,288
  Edward 48

Welsh, Eleanor 82
  George 70
  John 78,115,139,
  271,277,287,291
  Joseph 93
  Mary 101
  Richard 301
  Samuel 207
  Thomas 111,117,274
Wenden, James 196
Went, Elizabeth 166
  James 85
Wentland, Ann 55
Wentworth, Eliz. 247
West, Ann 227
  Benjamin 57
  Henry 244
  Hugh 275,302
  James 185,258,301
  Jarvis 66
  John 5,34,146,164,
  174,182,192,202,
  231,248
  Joseph 113
  Joshua 134
  Luke 233
  Mary 79
  Matthew 162
  Richard 147
  Roger 118
  Sarah 76,172
  Stephen 4
  Thomas 33,79,206
  William 34,50,225
Westall, George 301
Westbrook, William
  227
Westcoate, Peter 225
Westcote, Thomas 152
Westell, Patience 42
Westfield, Richard 110
Westhall, Henry 261
Westlake, Joseph 1
Westley, Samuel 175
Westmore, Elizabeth
  48
Weston, George
  148,161
  John 117,153
  Margaret 190
  Mary. 148

Weston, Thomas 256
  William 255
Westwood, William
  199
Wetherall, Jane 177
  Thomas 177
  William 7
Wetherell, Francis 22
  George 20
  James 20
  John 158
Wetherford, Thomas
  125
Wetheridge, Isaac 301
Wetherill, William 11
Wettie, Thomas 124
Weyman, Michael 42
Whale, Charles 28,33
  William 70
Whalebone, Duke 76
  John 19
Whaley, William 143
Whalock, James 123
Whalon, Pevice 230
Wharley, John 86
Wharton, Benjamin 21
  Cuthbert 11
  James 183
  John 57
  Katherine 44
  Sarah 78
  Susannah 55
  Thomas 229
  William 217,221
Whatman, William 89
Whealan, Edward 301
Wheatfield, George
  182
Wheatherhead, Joseph
  68
Wheatland, Mary 177
Wheatley, Elizabeth
  113
  George 255
  Henry 38
  Hester 39
  John 63,105
  Mary 157,217
  Thomas 301
  William 52,92
Wheaton, John 31

442

Index of Persons

443

Index of Persons

Index of Persons

Index of Persons

Index of Persons

Index of Ships

Index of Ships

CPSIA information can be obtained at www.ICGtesting.com
Printed in the USA
LVOW101625190613

339339LV00017B/761/P